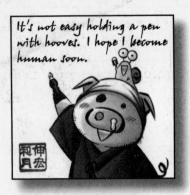

It's not easy holding a pen with hooves. I hope I become human soon.

Two summers ago, I was invited as a guest to an anime convention called Anime Expo. I wasn't too thrilled about it at first, but the people who I went with were so funny that I found myself laughing for 10 days straight. It turned out to be a very valuable experience. I've tried to keep the enjoyment of "laughter" in mind while drawing this series. It might be hard to make you laugh out loud, but it would make me really happy if I could at least make you chuckle.

—Nobuhiro Watsuki

Nobuhiro Watsuki earned international accolades for his first major manga series, **Rurouni Kenshin**, about a wandering swordsman in Meiji Era Japan. Serialized in Japan's WEEKLY SHONEN JUMP from 1994 to 1999, **Rurouni Kenshin** quickly became a worldwide sensation, inspiring a spin-off short story ("Yahiko no Sakabatô"), an animated TV show and a series of novels. Watsuki's latest hit, **Buso Renkin**, began publication in WEEKLY SHONEN JUMP in June 2003.

BUSO RENKIN
VOL. 1
The SHONEN JUMP ADVANCED
Manga Edition

STORY AND ART BY
NOBUHIRO WATSUKI

Translation and English Adaptation/Mayumi Kobayashi
Touch-up Art & Lettering/James Gaubatz
Design/Yukiko Whitley
Editors/Michelle Pangilinan & Urian Brown

Managing Editor/Frances E. Wall
Editorial Director/Elizabeth Kawasaki
VP & Editor in Chief/Yumi Hoashi
Sr. Director of Acquisitions/Rika Inouye
Sr. VP of Marketing/Liza Coppola
Exec. VP of Sales & Marketing/John Easum
Publisher/Hyoe Narita

BUSOU RENKIN © 2003 by Nobuhiro Watsuki. All rights reserved.
First published in Japan in 2003 by SHUEISHA Inc., Tokyo.
English translation rights in the United States of America and
Canada arranged by SHUEISHA Inc. The stories, characters and incidents
mentioned in this publication are entirely fictional.

Printed in the U.S.A.

Published by VIZ Media, LLC
P.O. Box 77010
San Francisco, CA 94107

SHONEN JUMP ADVANCED Manga Edition
10 9 8 7 6 5 4 3 2
First printing, August 2006
Second printing, August 2006

THE WORLD'S MOST
CUTTING-EDGE MANGA

SHONEN JUMP ADVANCED

www.shonenjump.com

www.viz.com

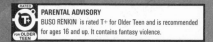

SHONEN JUMP ADVANCED MANGA EDITION

Buso Renkin™

ブソウレンキン

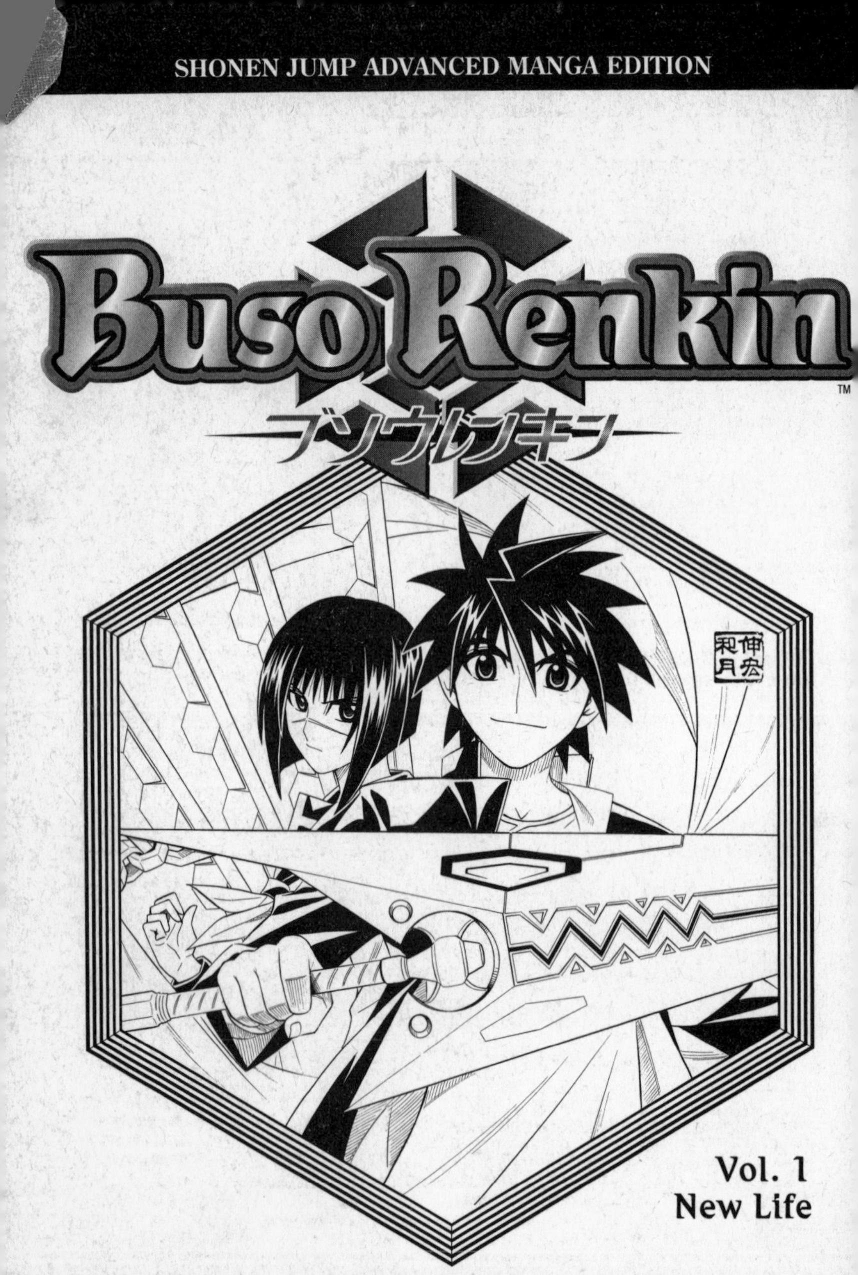

Vol. 1
New Life

STORY & ART BY
NOBUHIRO WATSUKI

BUSO RENKIN
Volume 1: New Life

CONTENTS

CHAPTER 1: NEW LIFE

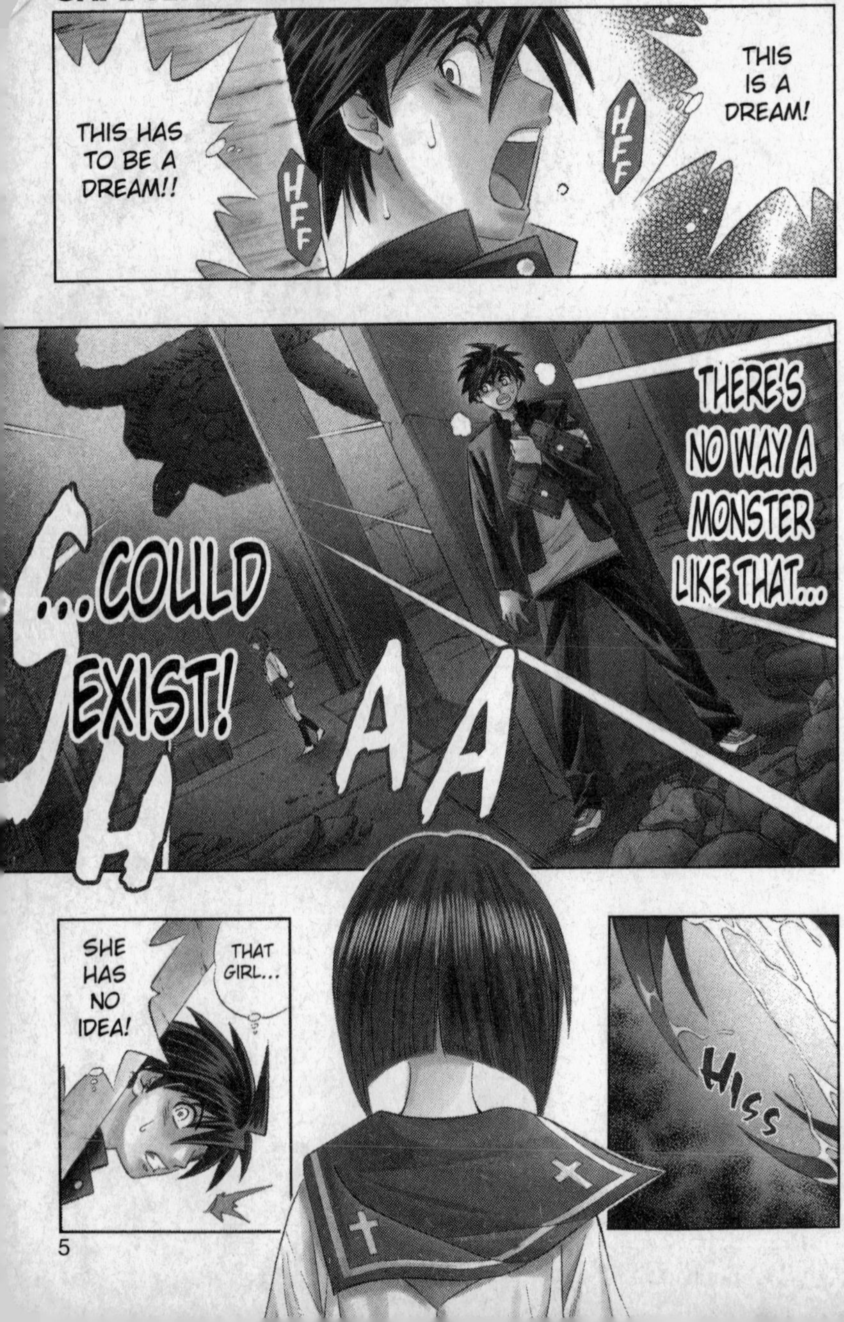
THIS IS A DREAM!
HFF
THIS HAS TO BE A DREAM!!
HFF
THERE'S NO WAY A MONSTER LIKE THAT...
...COULD EXIST!
AAAH
HISS
THAT GIRL...
SHE HAS NO IDEA!

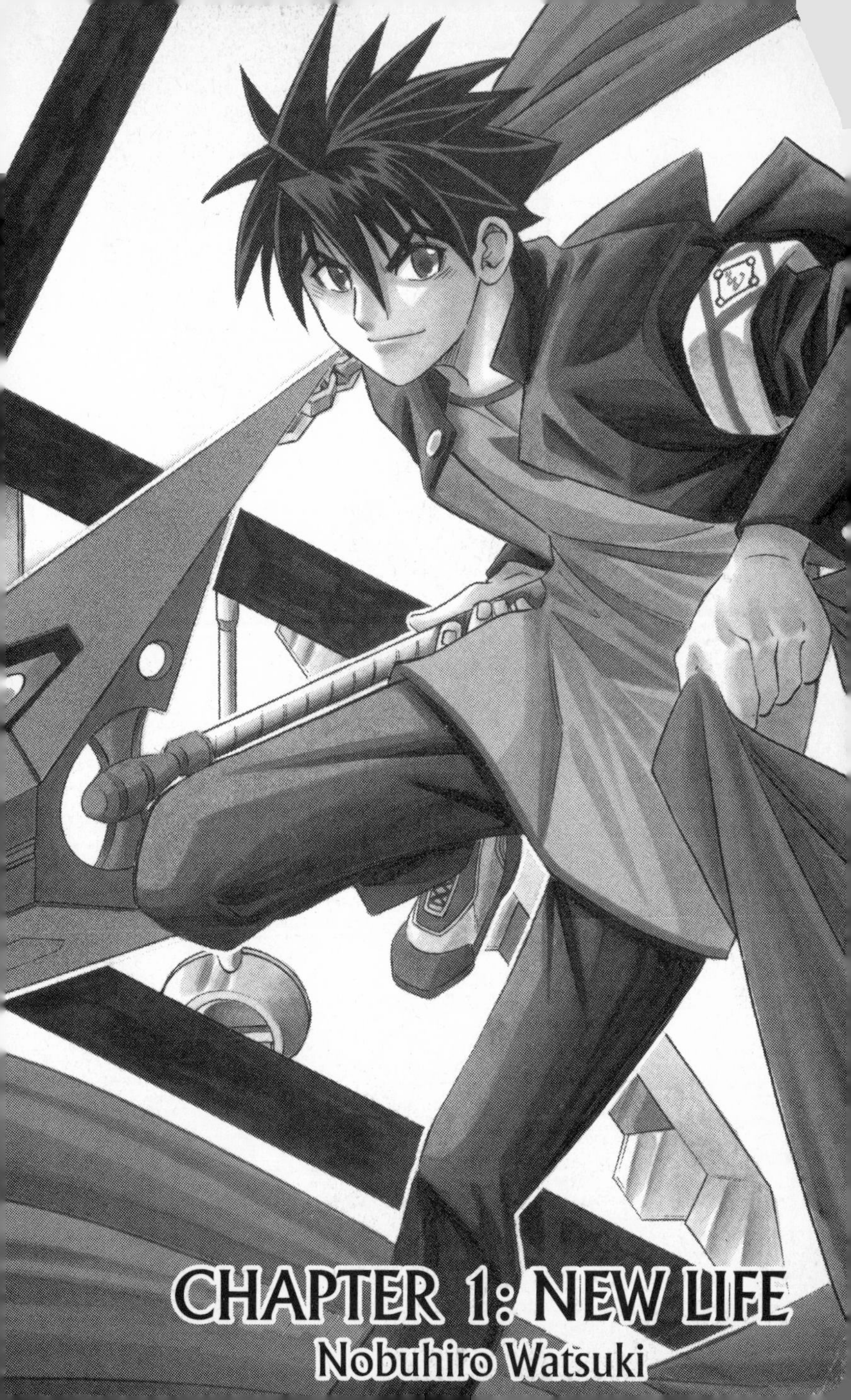

CHAPTER 1: NEW LIFE

Nobuhiro Watsuki

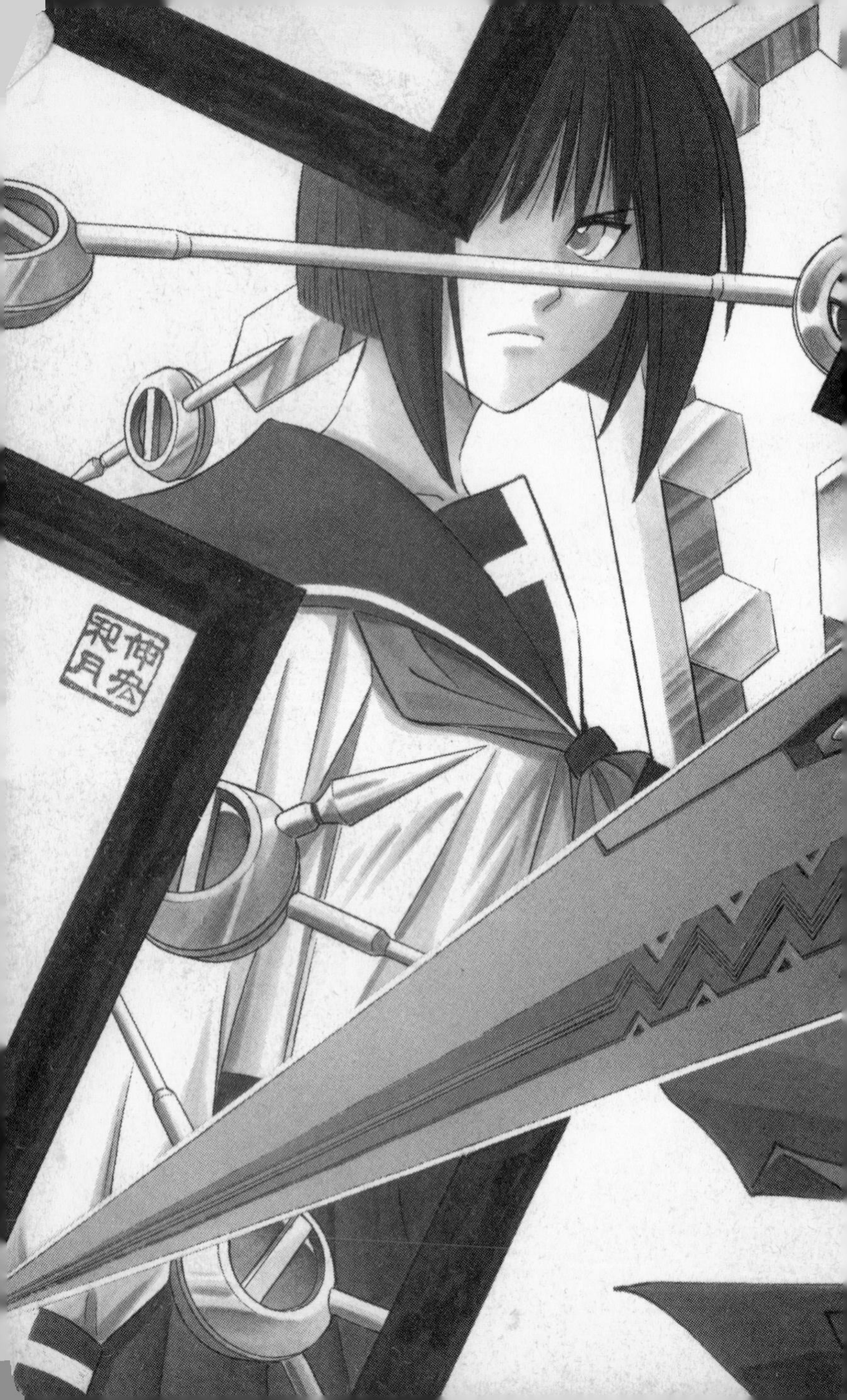
伸宏和月

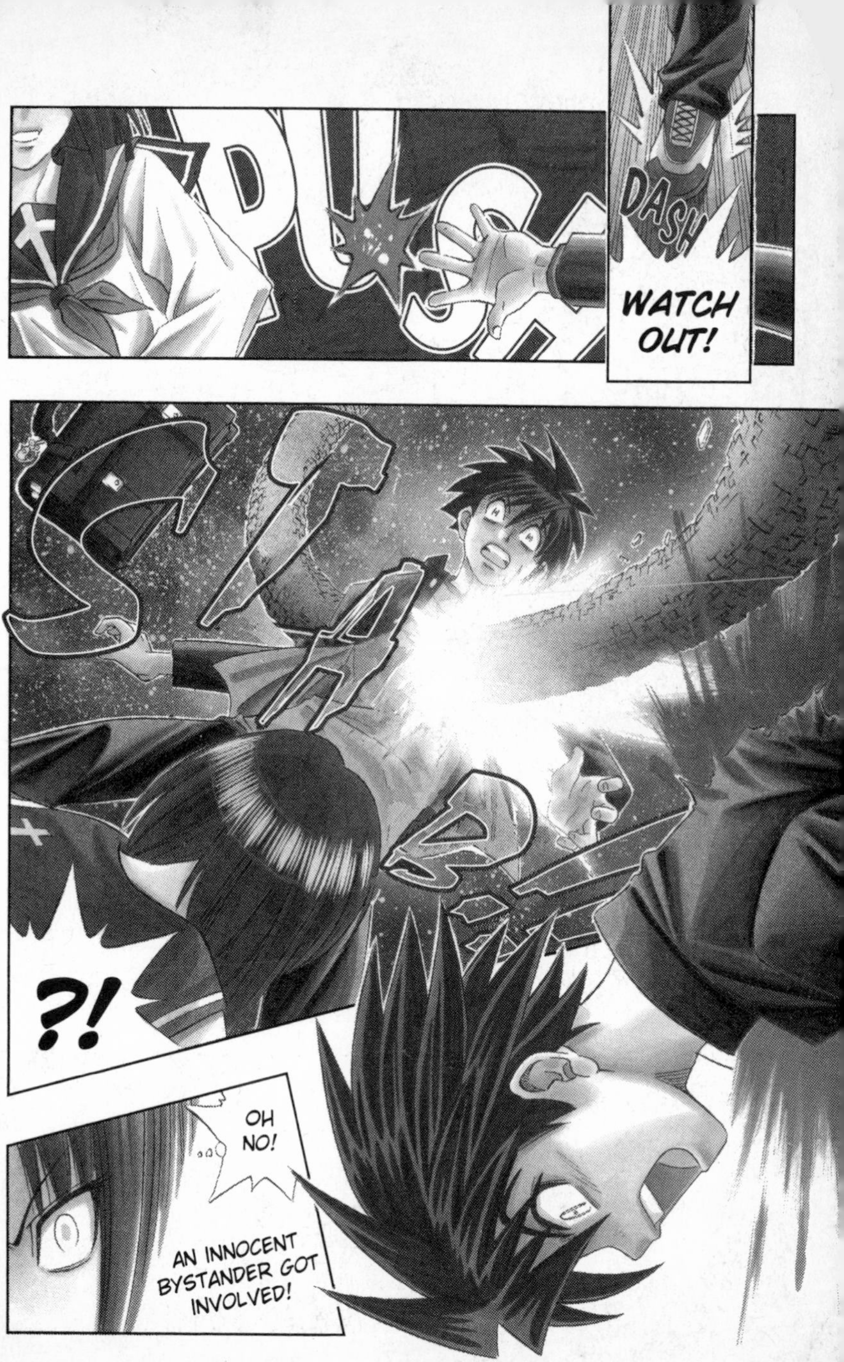
DASH
WATCH OUT!
?!
OH NO!
AN INNOCENT BYSTANDER GOT INVOLVED!

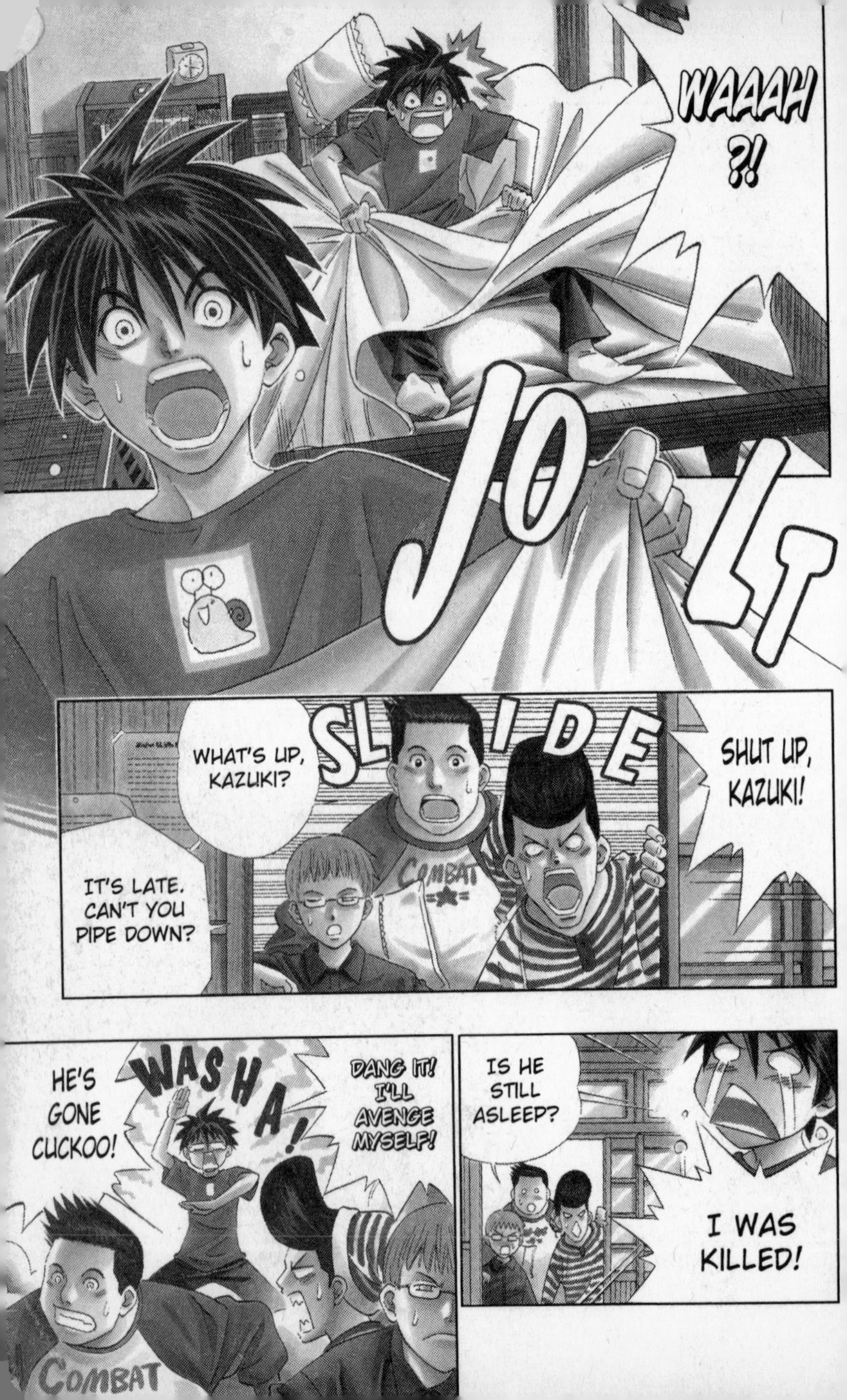
WAAAH ?!
JOLT
SHUT UP, KAZUKI!
SLIDE
WHAT'S UP, KAZUKI?
IT'S LATE. CAN'T YOU PIPE DOWN?
IS HE STILL ASLEEP?
I WAS KILLED!
DANG IT! I'LL AVENGE MYSELF!
WASHA!
HE'S GONE CUCKOO!

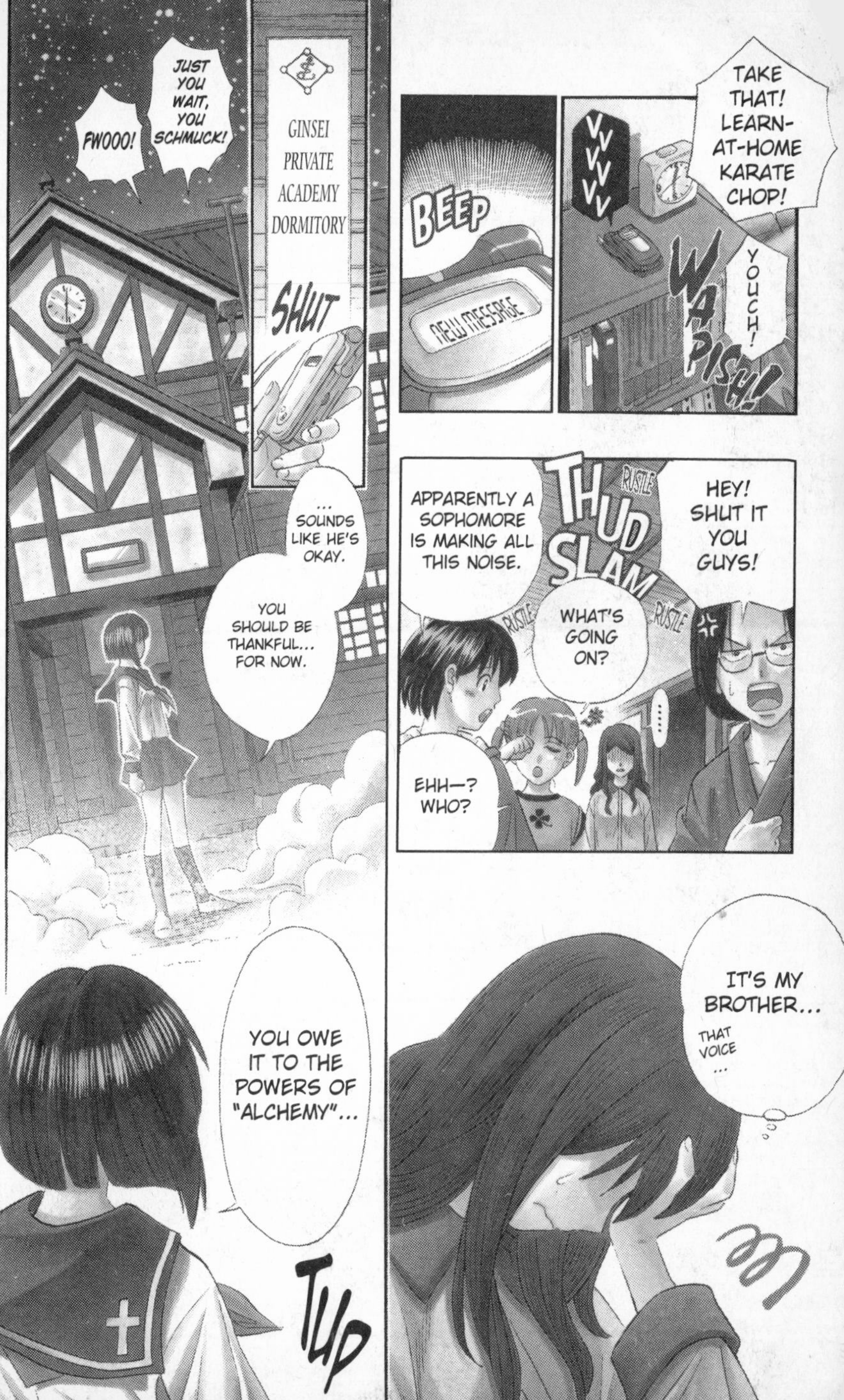
TAKE THAT! LEARN-AT-HOME KARATE CHOP!
VVVVVV
YOUCH!
WAPISH!
BEEP
NEW MESSAGE
HEY! SHUT IT YOU GUYS!
RUSTLE
THUD SLAM
APPARENTLY A SOPHOMORE IS MAKING ALL THIS NOISE.
RUSTLE
WHAT'S GOING ON?
RUSTLE
......
EHH—? WHO?
JUST YOU WAIT, YOU SCHMUCK!
FWOOO!
GINSEI PRIVATE ACADEMY DORMITORY
SHUT
... SOUNDS LIKE HE'S OKAY.
YOU SHOULD BE THANKFUL... FOR NOW.
IT'S MY BROTHER...
THAT VOICE ...
YOU OWE IT TO THE POWERS OF "ALCHEMY"...
TUP

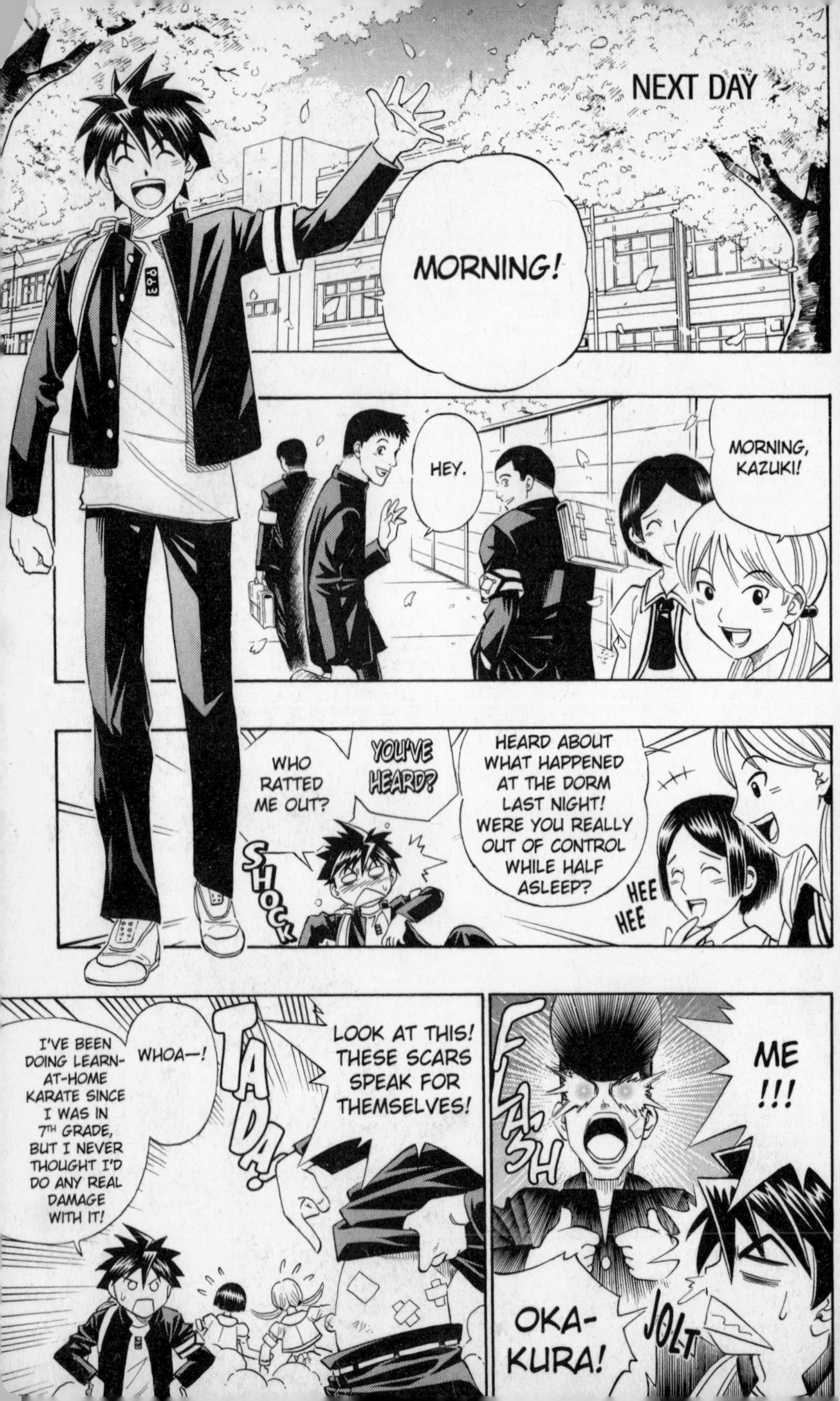
NEXT DAY
MORNING!
MORNING, KAZUKI!
HEY.
HEARD ABOUT WHAT HAPPENED AT THE DORM LAST NIGHT! WERE YOU REALLY OUT OF CONTROL WHILE HALF ASLEEP?
HEE HEE
YOU'VE HEARD?
WHO RATTED ME OUT?
SHOCK
ME !!!
FLASH
OKA-KURA!
JOLT
LOOK AT THIS! THESE SCARS SPEAK FOR THEMSELVES!
TADA!
WHOA—!
I'VE BEEN DOING LEARN-AT-HOME KARATE SINCE I WAS IN 7TH GRADE, BUT I NEVER THOUGHT I'D DO ANY REAL DAMAGE WITH IT!

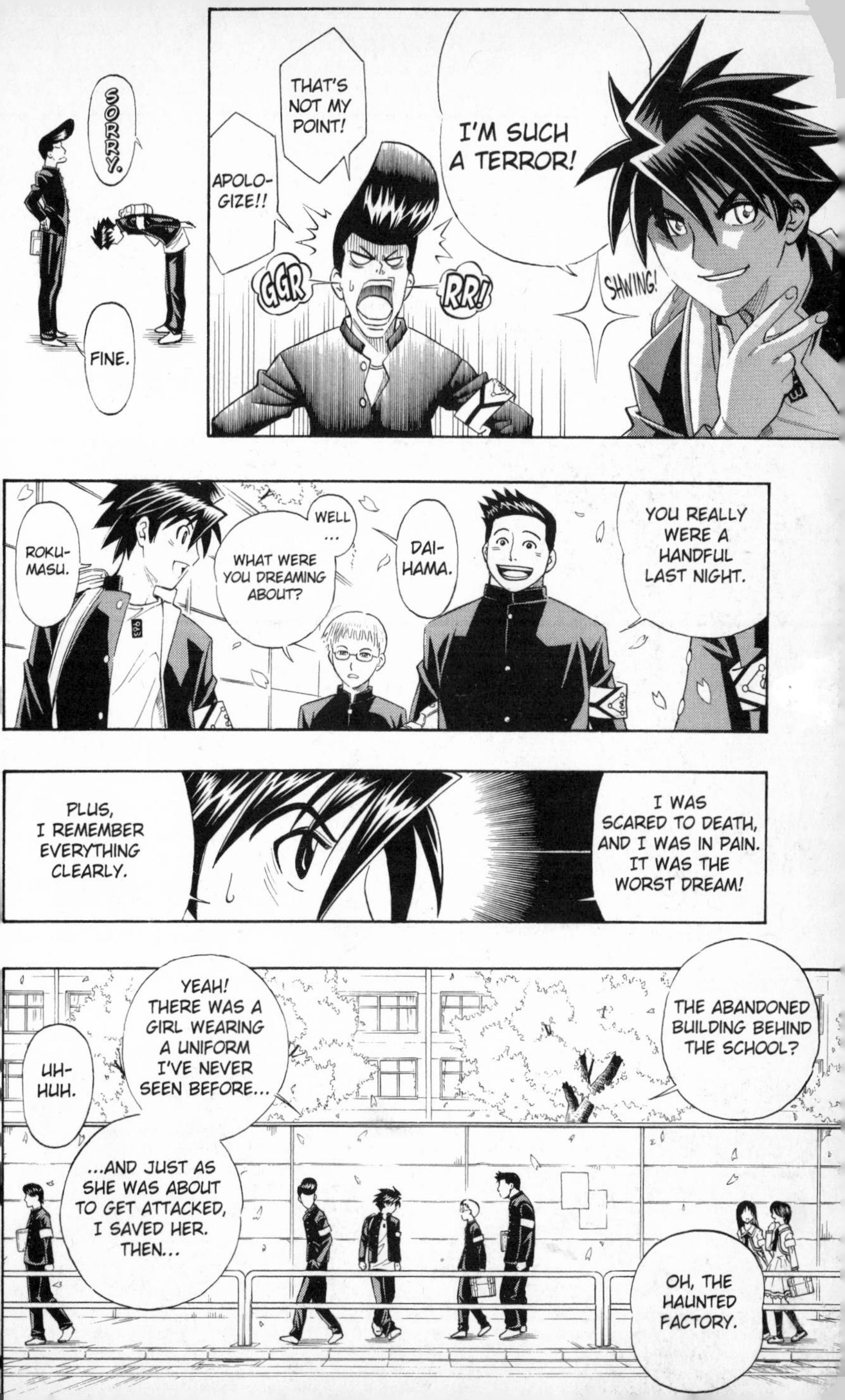

I'M SUCH A TERROR!
SHWING!
THAT'S NOT MY POINT!
APOLOGIZE!!
GGR
RR!
SORRY.
FINE.
YOU REALLY WERE A HANDFUL LAST NIGHT.
DAI-HAMA.
WELL ...
WHAT WERE YOU DREAMING ABOUT?
ROKU-MASU.
I WAS SCARED TO DEATH, AND I WAS IN PAIN. IT WAS THE WORST DREAM!
PLUS, I REMEMBER EVERYTHING CLEARLY.
THE ABANDONED BUILDING BEHIND THE SCHOOL?
YEAH! THERE WAS A GIRL WEARING A UNIFORM I'VE NEVER SEEN BEFORE...
UH-HUH.
...AND JUST AS SHE WAS ABOUT TO GET ATTACKED, I SAVED HER. THEN...
OH, THE HAUNTED FACTORY.

READ THIS WAY

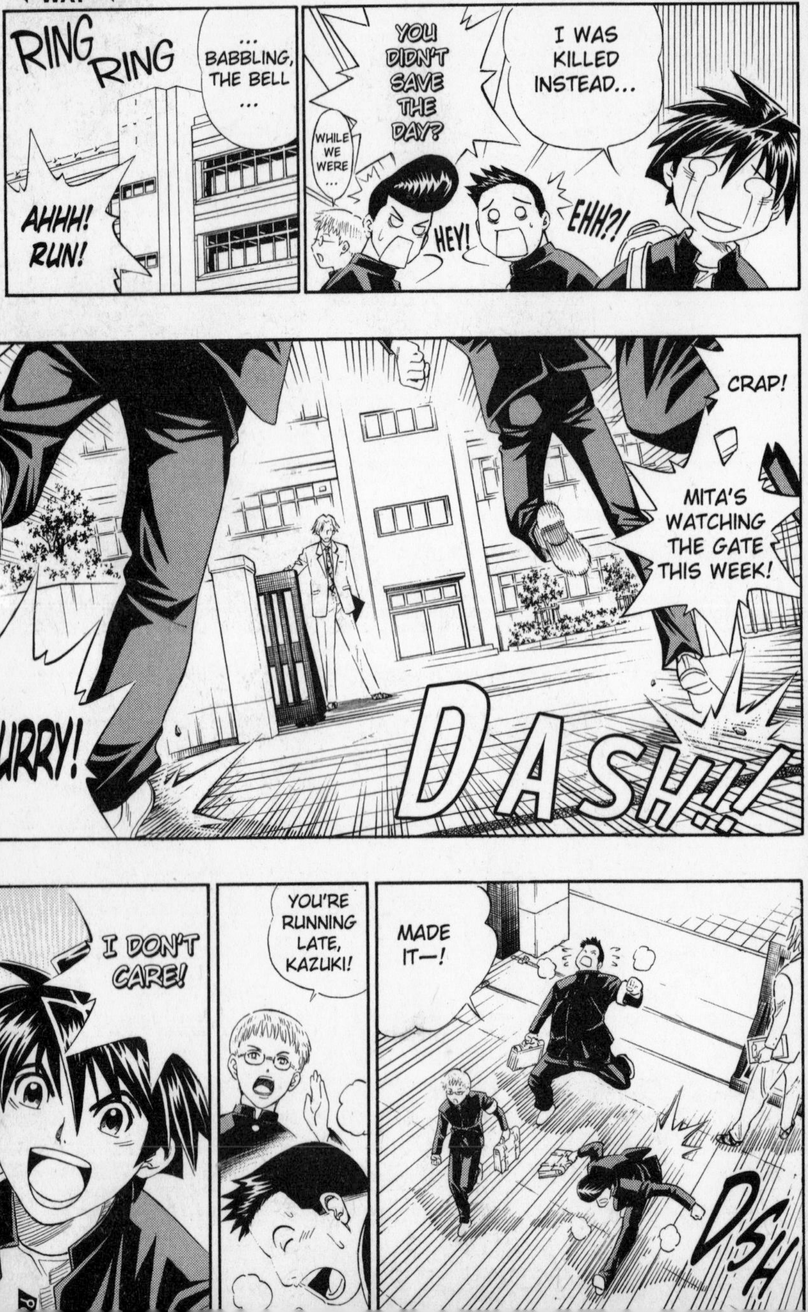
I WAS KILLED INSTEAD...
EHH?!
YOU DIDN'T SAVE THE DAY?
HEY!
WHILE WE WERE ...
... BABBLING, THE BELL ...
RING RING
AHHH! RUN!
CRAP!
MITA'S WATCHING THE GATE THIS WEEK!
DASH!!
HURRY!
MADE IT—!
DSH
YOU'RE RUNNING LATE, KAZUKI!
I DON'T CARE!

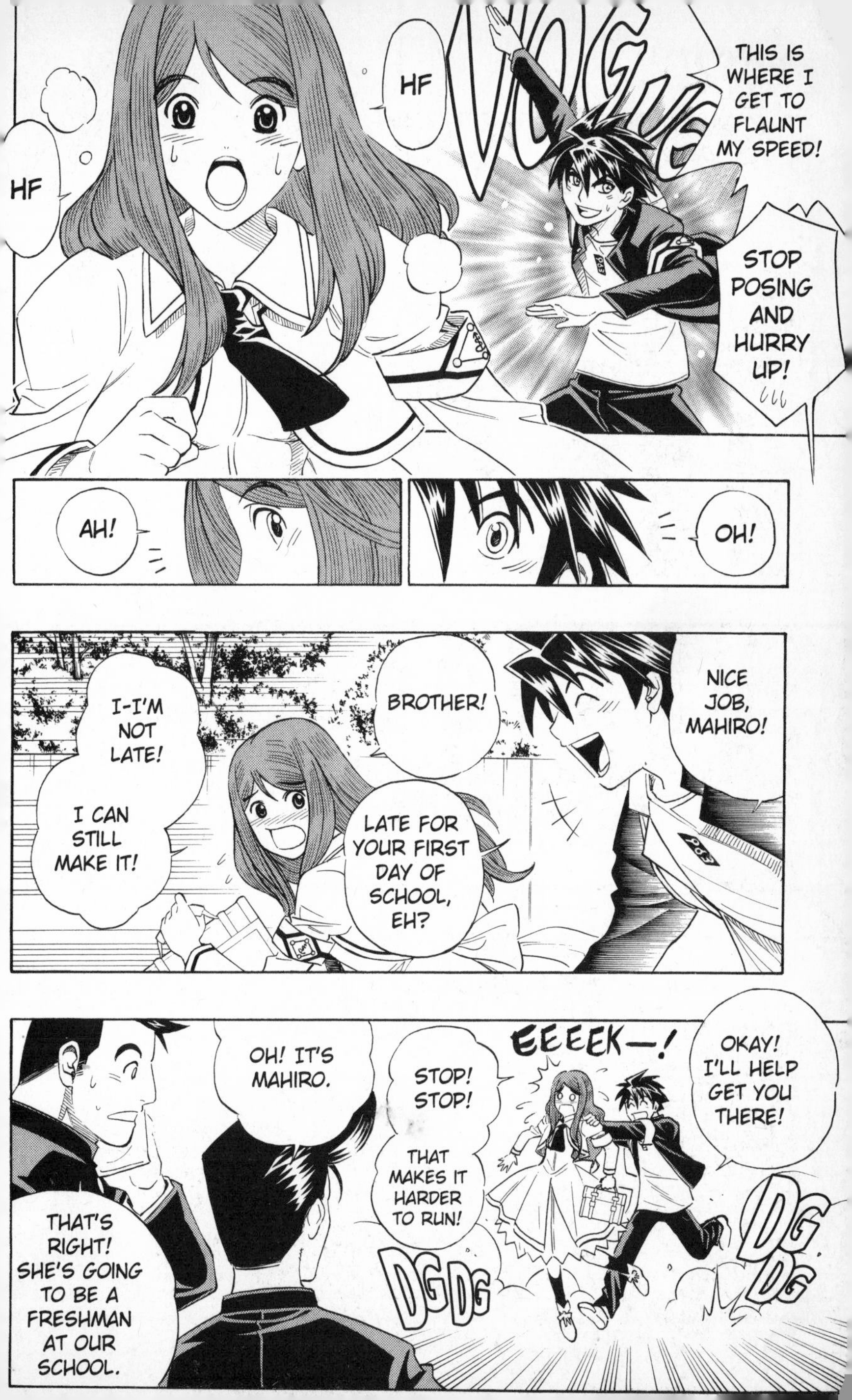
THIS IS WHERE I GET TO FLAUNT MY SPEED!
STOP POSING AND HURRY UP!
HF
HF
OH!
AH!
NICE JOB, MAHIRO!
BROTHER!
LATE FOR YOUR FIRST DAY OF SCHOOL, EH?
I-I'M NOT LATE!
I CAN STILL MAKE IT!
OKAY! I'LL HELP GET YOU THERE!
EEEEK—!
STOP! STOP!
THAT MAKES IT HARDER TO RUN!
DG DG
DG DG
OH! IT'S MAHIRO.
THAT'S RIGHT! SHE'S GOING TO BE A FRESHMAN AT OUR SCHOOL.

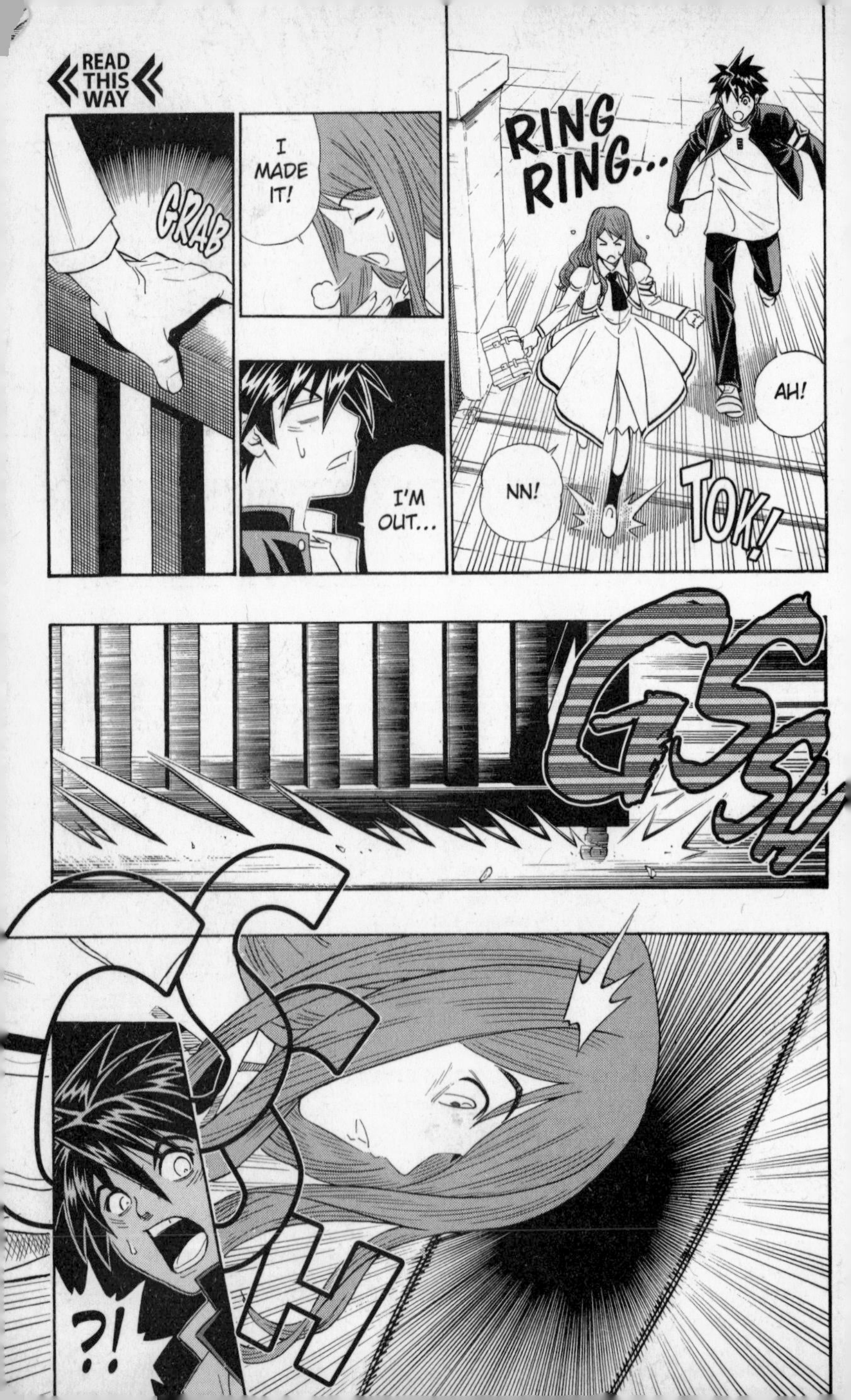
READ THIS WAY
RING RING...
AH!
NN!
TOK!
I MADE IT!
I'M OUT...
GRAB
?!

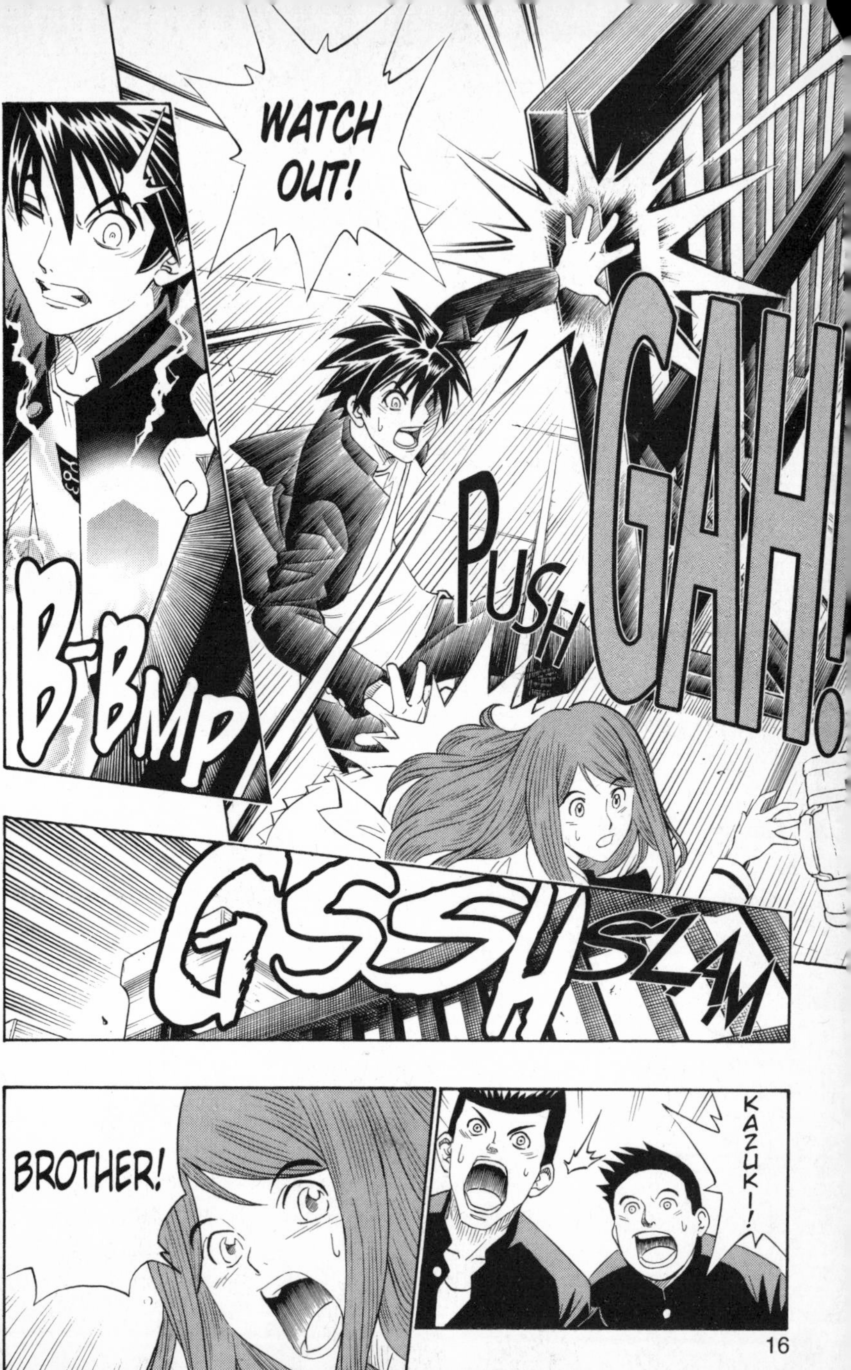
WATCH OUT!
GAH!!
PUSH
B-BMP
GSSH
SLAM
KAZUKI!
BROTHER!

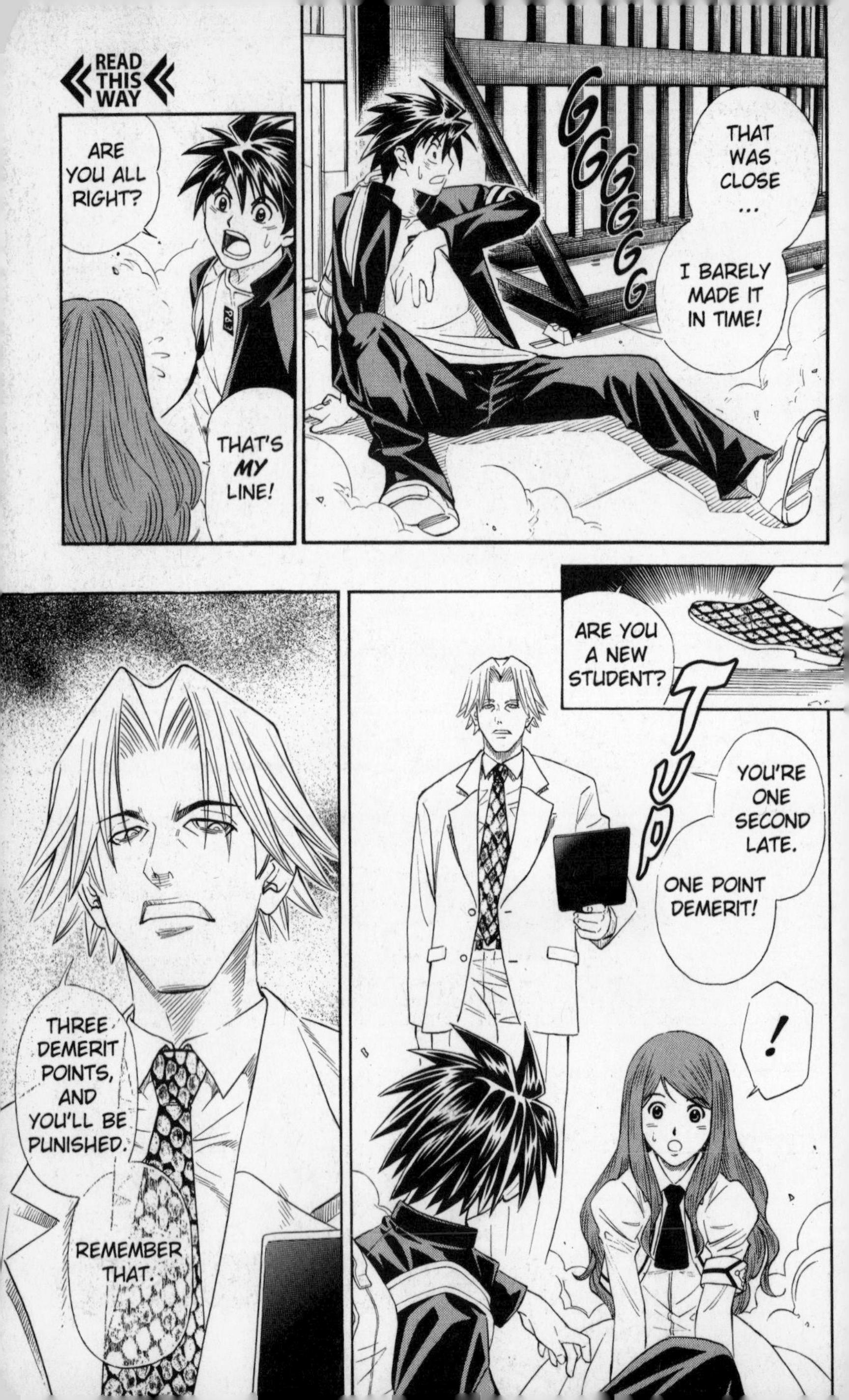
READ THIS WAY
GGGGGG
THAT WAS CLOSE...
I BARELY MADE IT IN TIME!
ARE YOU ALL RIGHT?
THAT'S *MY* LINE!
ARE YOU A NEW STUDENT?
TUP
YOU'RE ONE SECOND LATE.
ONE POINT DEMERIT!
!
THREE DEMERIT POINTS, AND YOU'LL BE PUNISHED.
REMEMBER THAT.

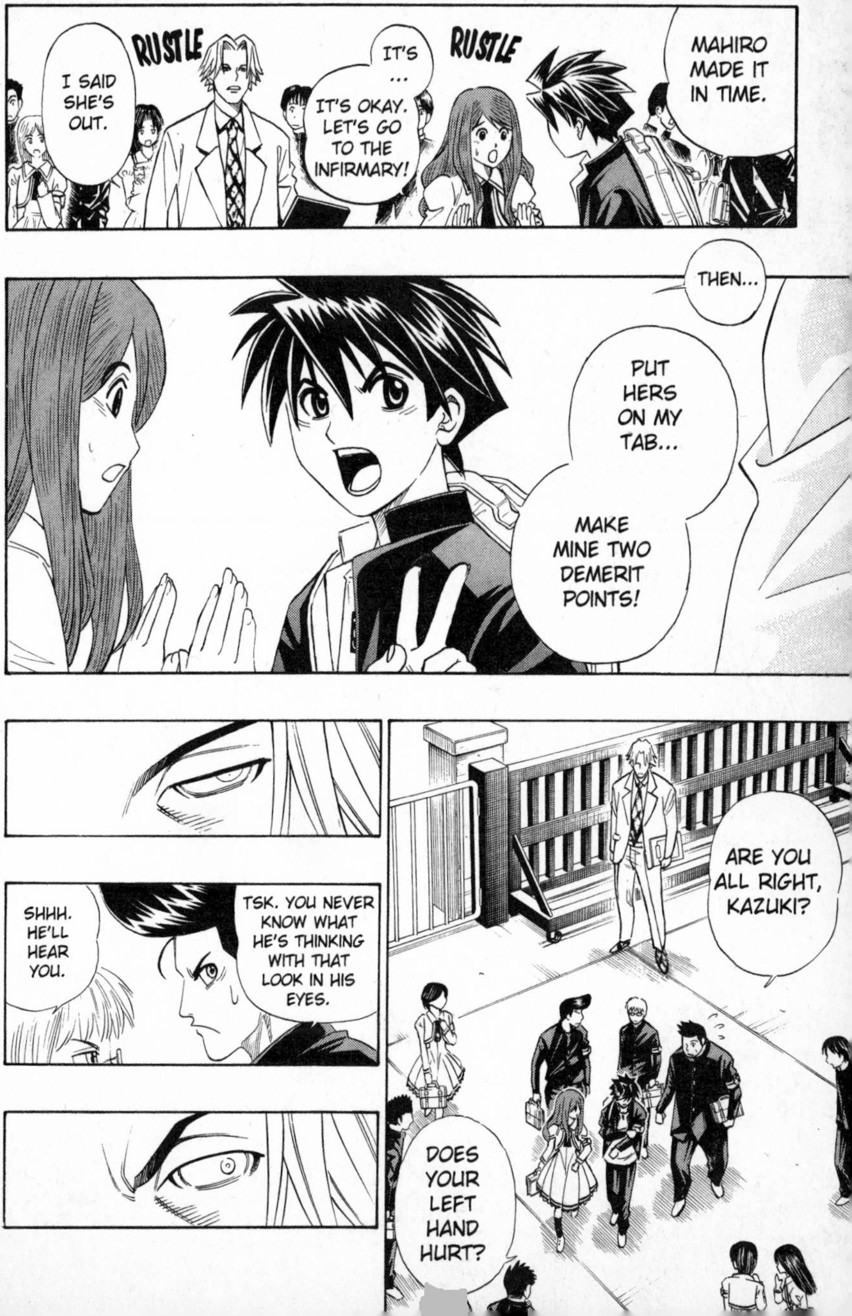
MAHIRO MADE IT IN TIME.
RUSTLE
IT'S ...
IT'S OKAY. LET'S GO TO THE INFIRMARY!
RUSTLE
I SAID SHE'S OUT.
THEN...
PUT HERS ON MY TAB...
MAKE MINE TWO DEMERIT POINTS!
ARE YOU ALL RIGHT, KAZUKI?
DOES YOUR LEFT HAND HURT?
TSK. YOU NEVER KNOW WHAT HE'S THINKING WITH THAT LOOK IN HIS EYES.
SHHH. HE'LL HEAR YOU.

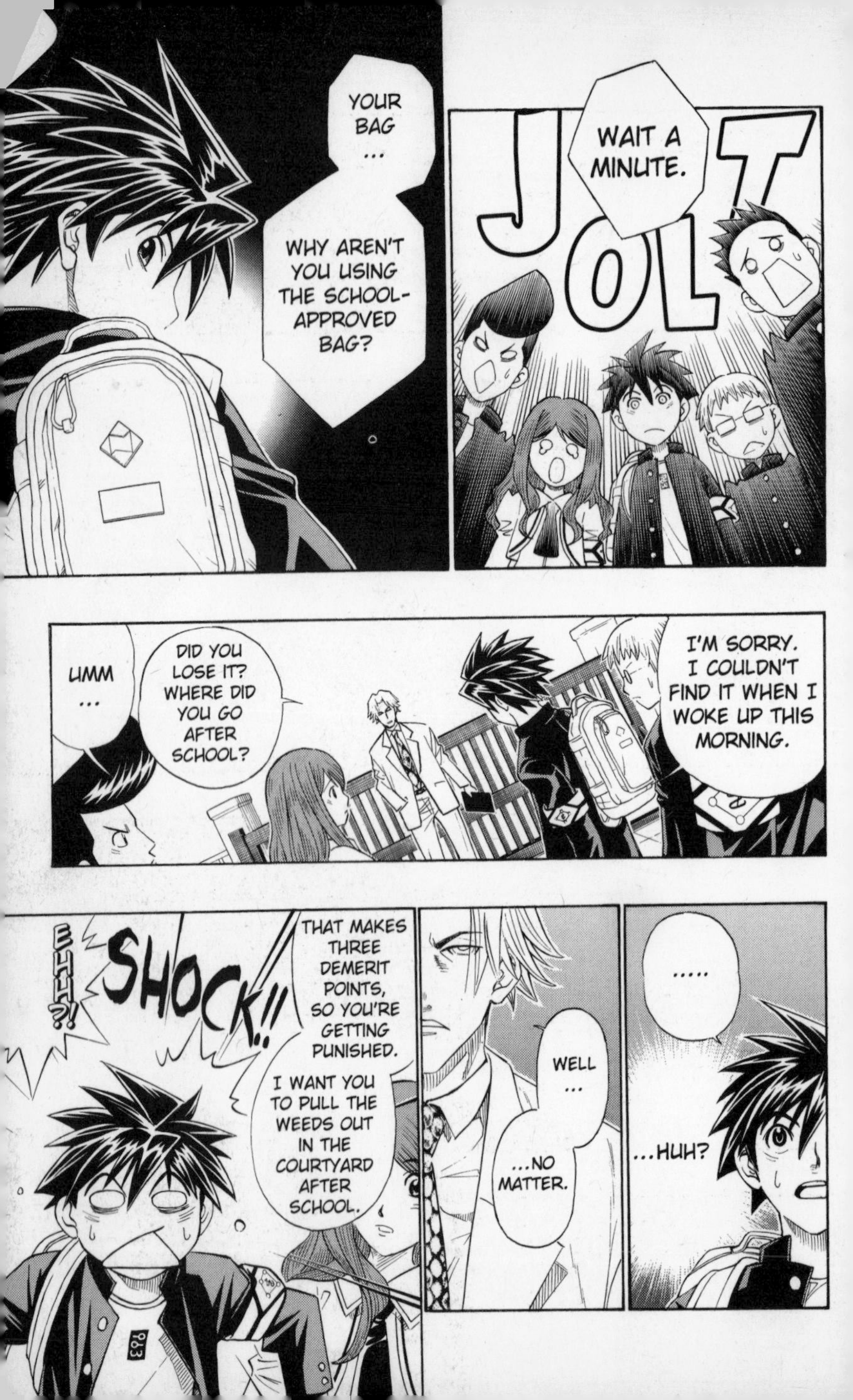
JOLT
WAIT A MINUTE.
YOUR BAG ...
WHY AREN'T YOU USING THE SCHOOL-APPROVED BAG?
I'M SORRY. I COULDN'T FIND IT WHEN I WOKE UP THIS MORNING.
DID YOU LOSE IT? WHERE DID YOU GO AFTER SCHOOL?
UMM ...
.....
...HUH?
WELL ...
...NO MATTER.
THAT MAKES THREE DEMERIT POINTS, SO YOU'RE GETTING PUNISHED.
I WANT YOU TO PULL THE WEEDS OUT IN THE COURTYARD AFTER SCHOOL.
SHOCK!!
EHHH?!

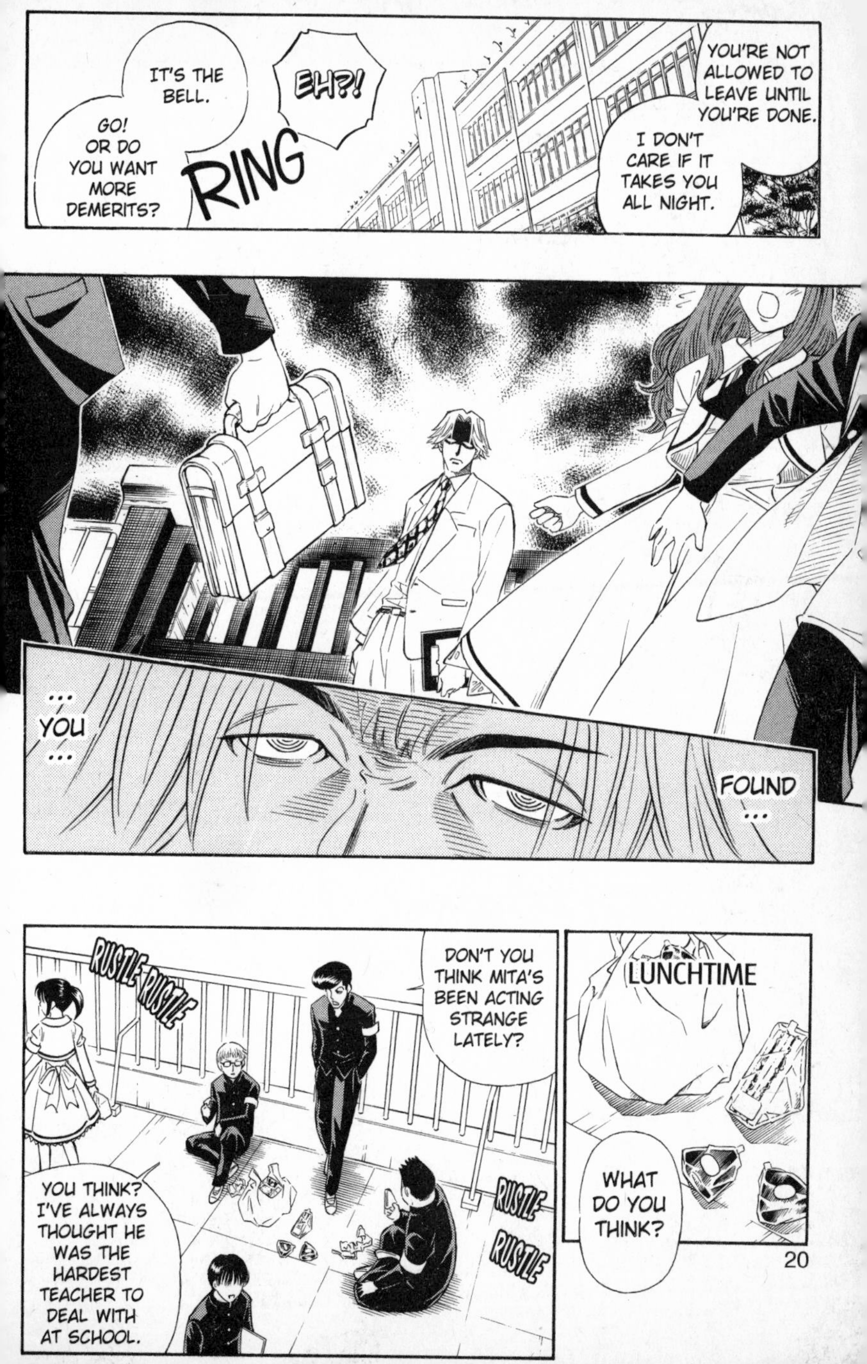
YOU'RE NOT ALLOWED TO LEAVE UNTIL YOU'RE DONE.
I DON'T CARE IF IT TAKES YOU ALL NIGHT.
EH?!
RING
IT'S THE BELL.
GO! OR DO YOU WANT MORE DEMERITS?
FOUND ...
... YOU ...
LUNCHTIME
WHAT DO YOU THINK?
DON'T YOU THINK MITA'S BEEN ACTING STRANGE LATELY?
RUSTLE RUSTLE
RUSTLE RUSTLE
YOU THINK? I'VE ALWAYS THOUGHT HE WAS THE HARDEST TEACHER TO DEAL WITH AT SCHOOL.

READ THIS WAY

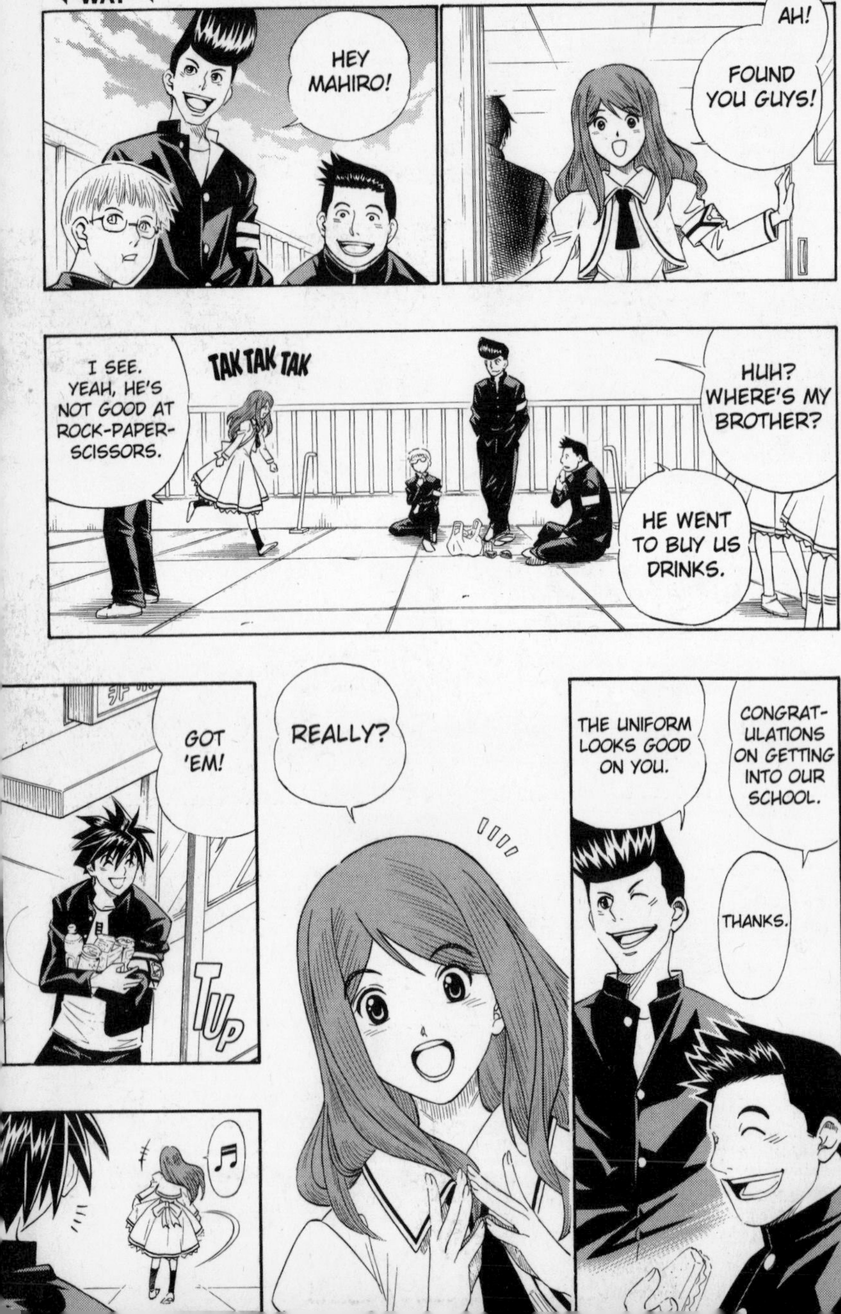
AH!
FOUND YOU GUYS!
HEY MAHIRO!
HUH? WHERE'S MY BROTHER?
HE WENT TO BUY US DRINKS.
TAK TAK TAK
I SEE. YEAH, HE'S NOT GOOD AT ROCK-PAPER-SCISSORS.
CONGRAT-ULATIONS ON GETTING INTO OUR SCHOOL.
THE UNIFORM LOOKS GOOD ON YOU.
THANKS.
REALLY?
GOT 'EM!
TUP
♪

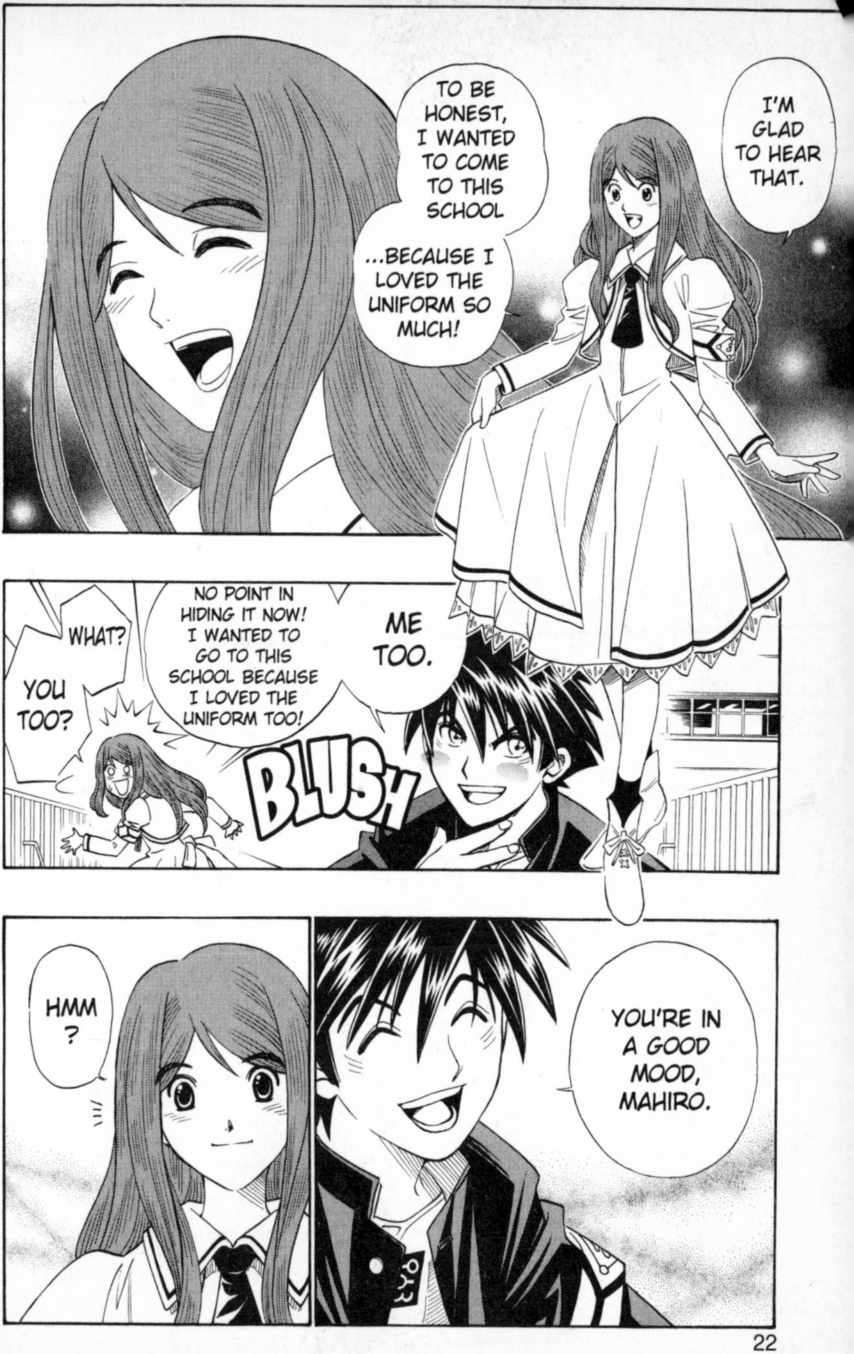
I'M GLAD TO HEAR THAT.
TO BE HONEST, I WANTED TO COME TO THIS SCHOOL
...BECAUSE I LOVED THE UNIFORM SO MUCH!
ME TOO.
NO POINT IN HIDING IT NOW! I WANTED TO GO TO THIS SCHOOL BECAUSE I LOVED THE UNIFORM TOO!
BLUSH
WHAT?
YOU TOO?
YOU'RE IN A GOOD MOOD, MAHIRO.
HMM ?

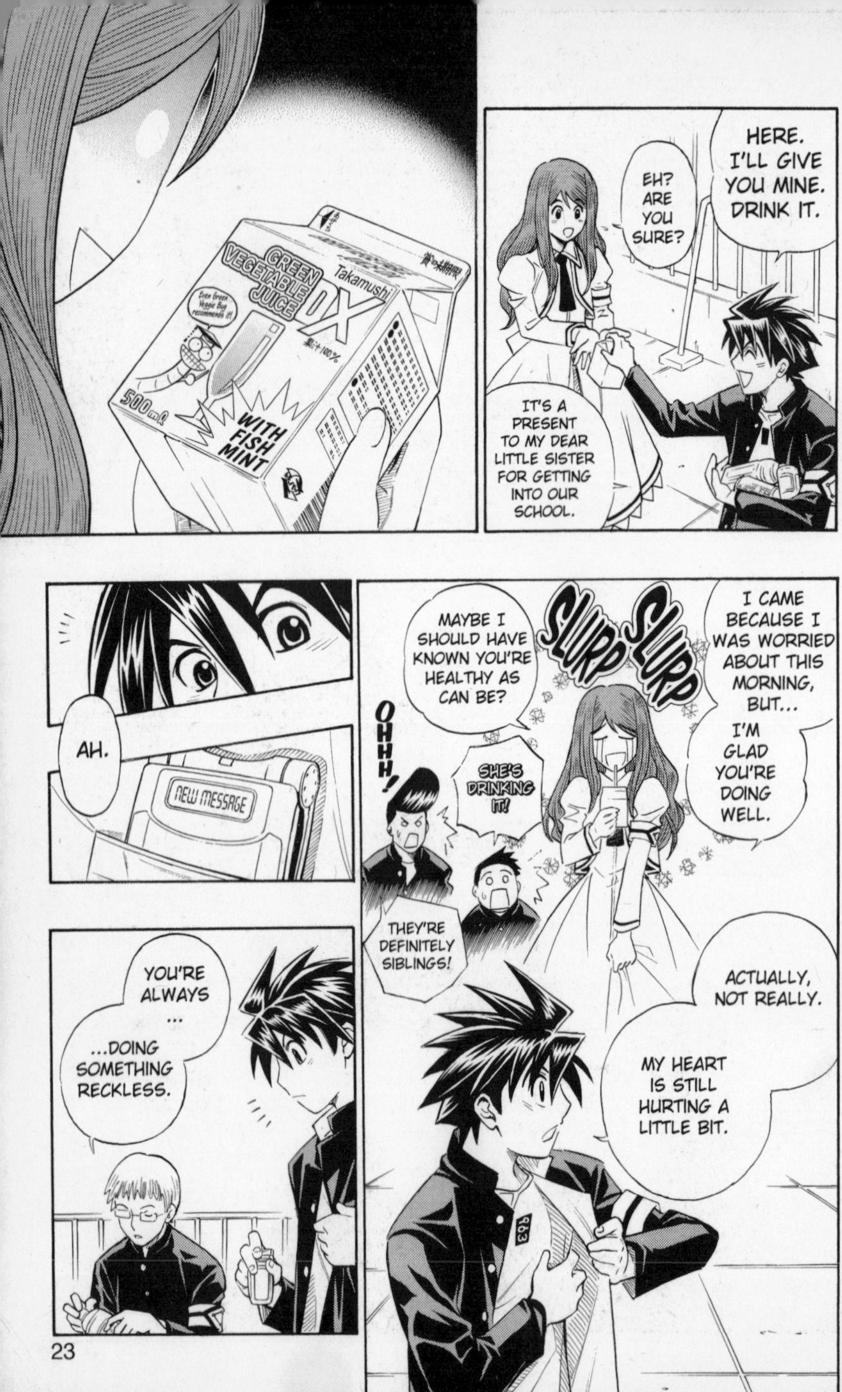
HERE. I'LL GIVE YOU MINE. DRINK IT.
EH? ARE YOU SURE?
IT'S A PRESENT TO MY DEAR LITTLE SISTER FOR GETTING INTO OUR SCHOOL.
GREEN VEGETABLE JUICE
Takamushi
DX
果汁100%
Even Green Veggie Bug recommends it!
500ml
WITH FISH MINT
I CAME BECAUSE I WAS WORRIED ABOUT THIS MORNING, BUT...
I'M GLAD YOU'RE DOING WELL.
SLURP SLURP
MAYBE I SHOULD HAVE KNOWN YOU'RE HEALTHY AS CAN BE?
OHHH!
SHE'S DRINKING IT!
THEY'RE DEFINITELY SIBLINGS!
AH.
NEW MESSAGE
ACTUALLY, NOT REALLY.
MY HEART IS STILL HURTING A LITTLE BIT.
YOU'RE ALWAYS ...
...DOING SOMETHING RECKLESS.

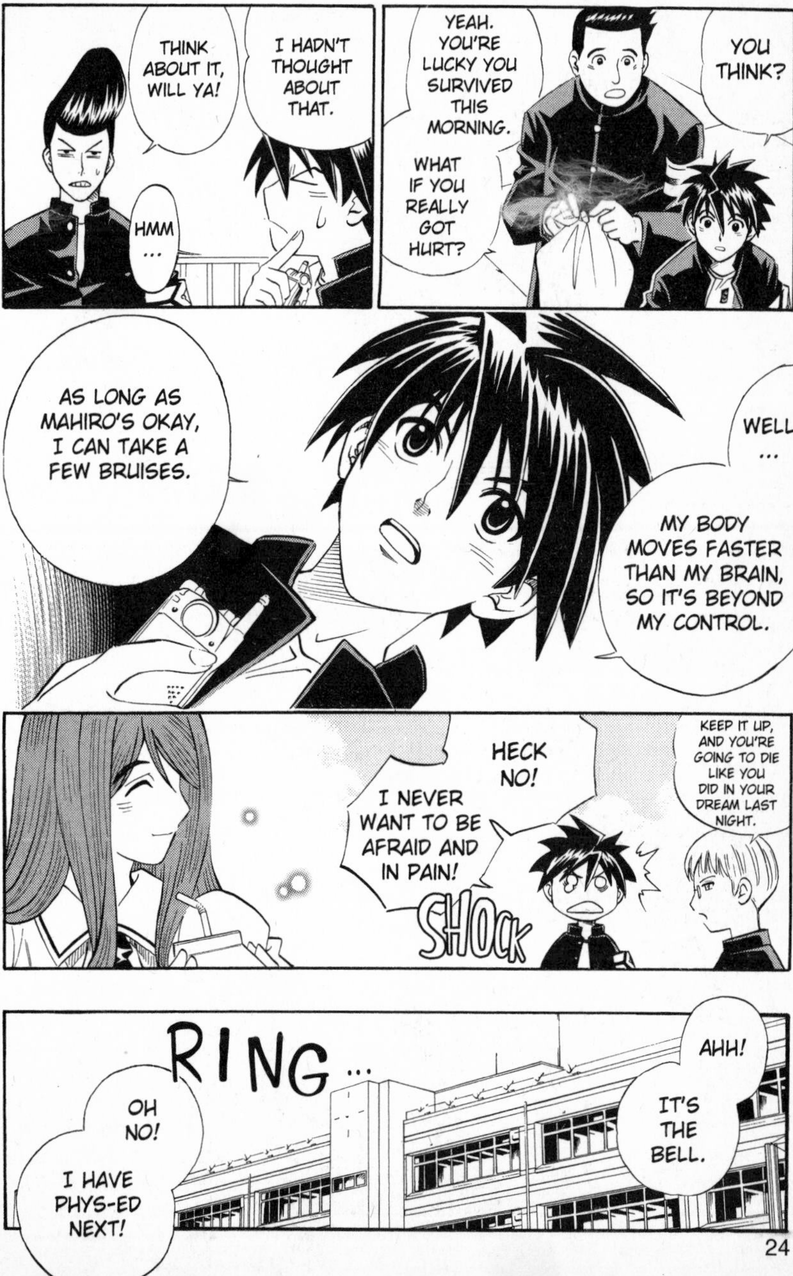

YOU THINK?
YEAH. YOU'RE LUCKY YOU SURVIVED THIS MORNING.
WHAT IF YOU REALLY GOT HURT?
I HADN'T THOUGHT ABOUT THAT.
THINK ABOUT IT, WILL YA!
HMM ...
WELL ...
MY BODY MOVES FASTER THAN MY BRAIN, SO IT'S BEYOND MY CONTROL.
AS LONG AS MAHIRO'S OKAY, I CAN TAKE A FEW BRUISES.
KEEP IT UP, AND YOU'RE GOING TO DIE LIKE YOU DID IN YOUR DREAM LAST NIGHT.
HECK NO!
I NEVER WANT TO BE AFRAID AND IN PAIN!
SHOCK
AHH!
IT'S THE BELL.
RING...
OH NO!
I HAVE PHYS-ED NEXT!

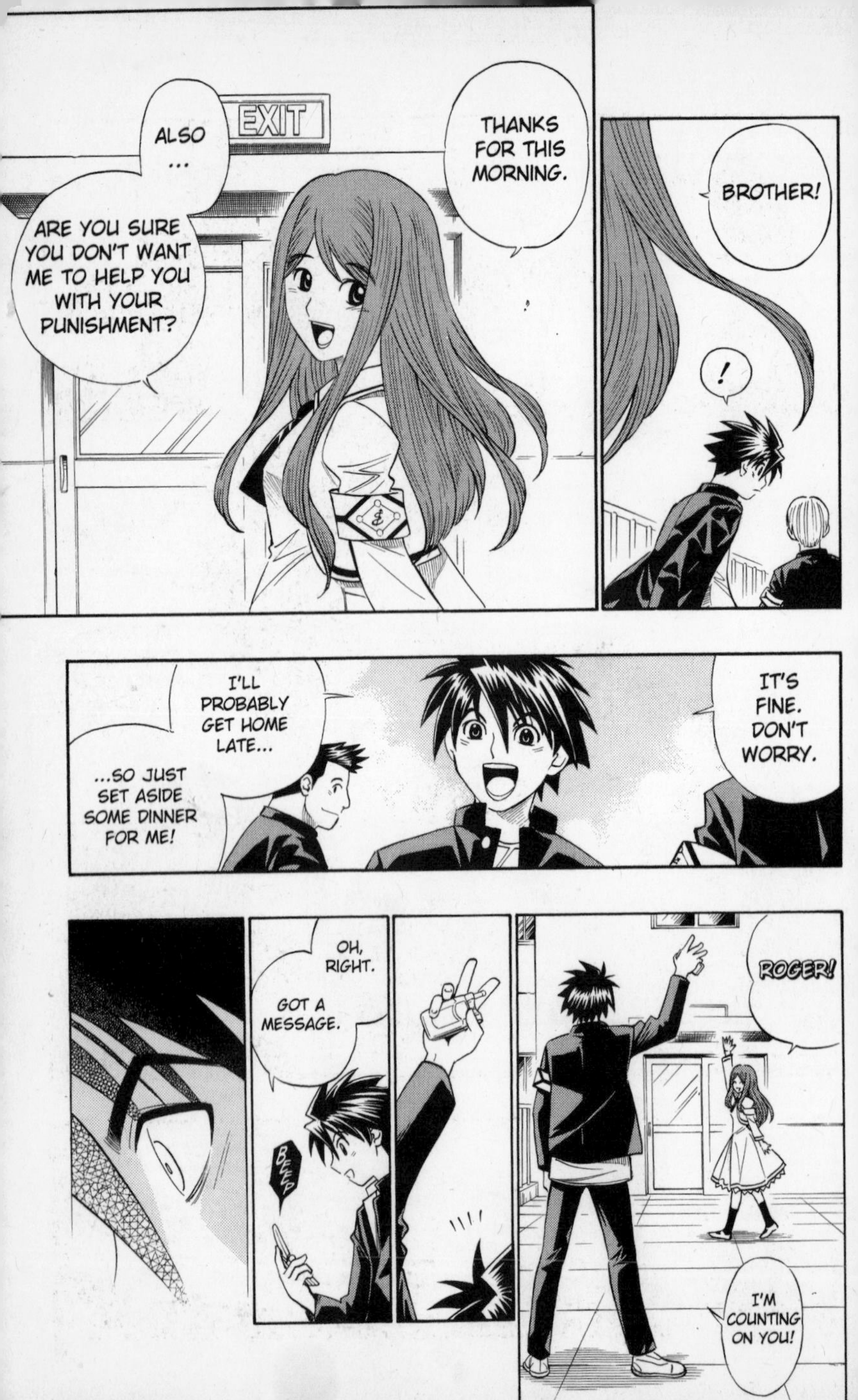
BROTHER!
!
THANKS FOR THIS MORNING.
ALSO ...
ARE YOU SURE YOU DON'T WANT ME TO HELP YOU WITH YOUR PUNISHMENT?
IT'S FINE. DON'T WORRY.
I'LL PROBABLY GET HOME LATE...
...SO JUST SET ASIDE SOME DINNER FOR ME!
ROGER!
I'M COUNTING ON YOU!
OH, RIGHT.
GOT A MESSAGE.
BEEP

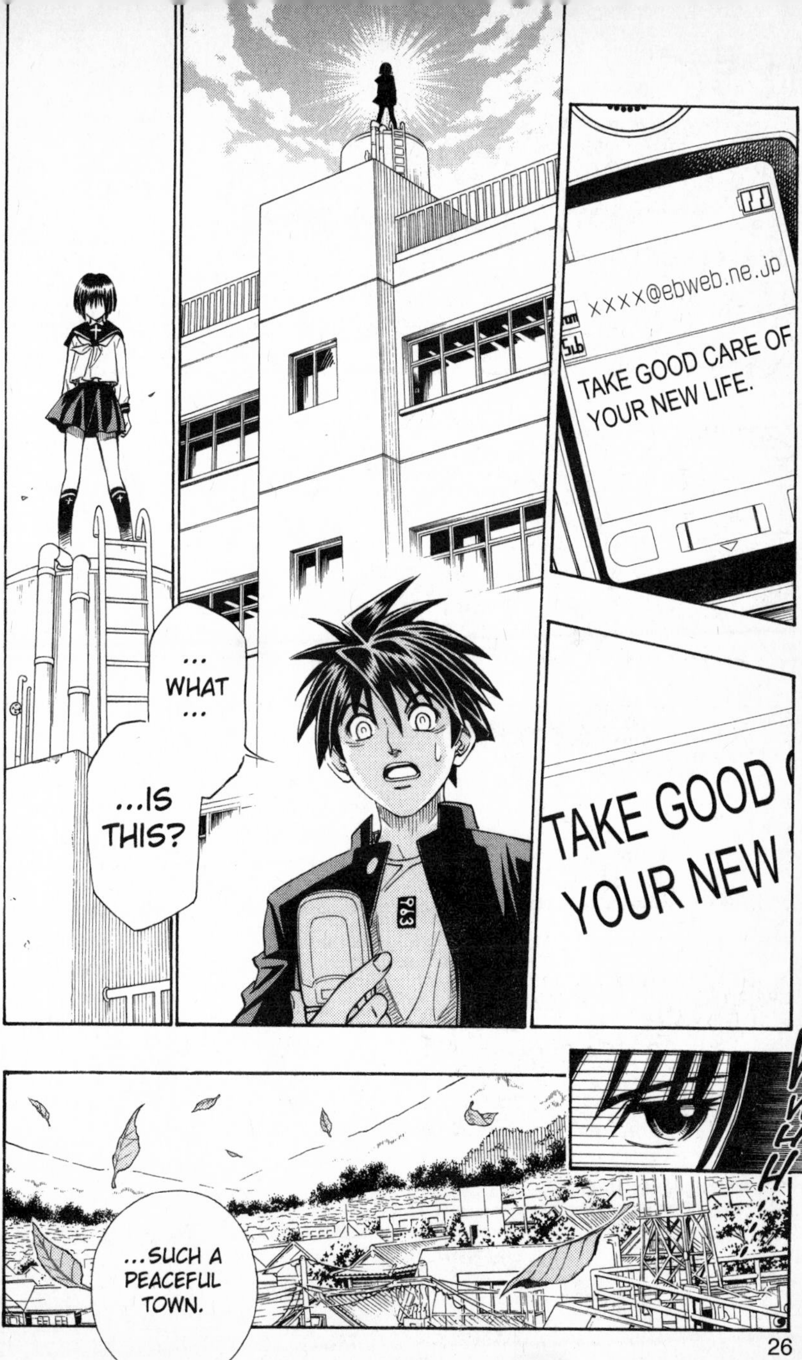
xxxx@ebweb.ne.jp
TAKE GOOD CARE OF YOUR NEW LIFE.
TAKE GOOD
YOUR NEW
... WHAT ...
...IS THIS?
...SUCH A PEACEFUL TOWN.

READ THIS WAY

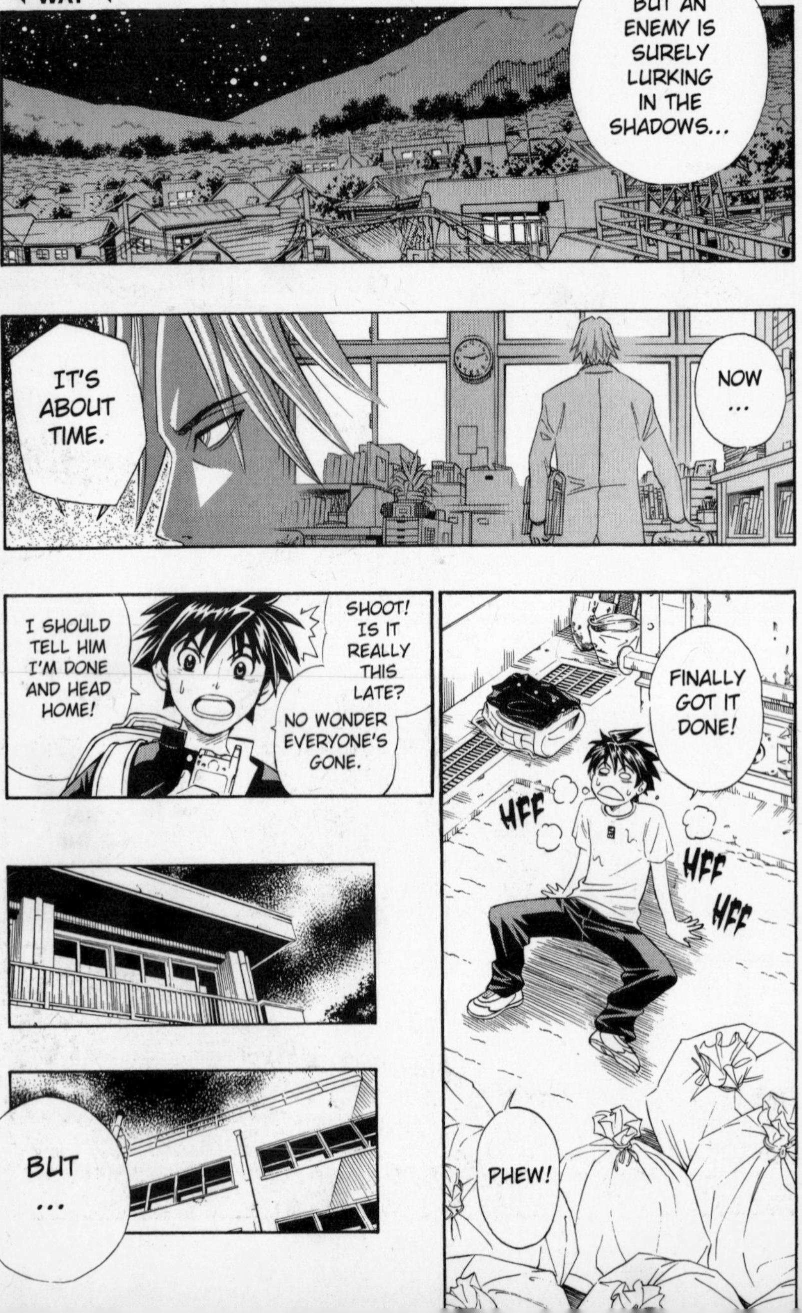
BUT AN ENEMY IS SURELY LURKING IN THE SHADOWS...
NOW ...
IT'S ABOUT TIME.
FINALLY GOT IT DONE!
HFF
HFF
HFF
PHEW!
SHOOT! IS IT REALLY THIS LATE?
NO WONDER EVERYONE'S GONE.
I SHOULD TELL HIM I'M DONE AND HEAD HOME!
BUT ...

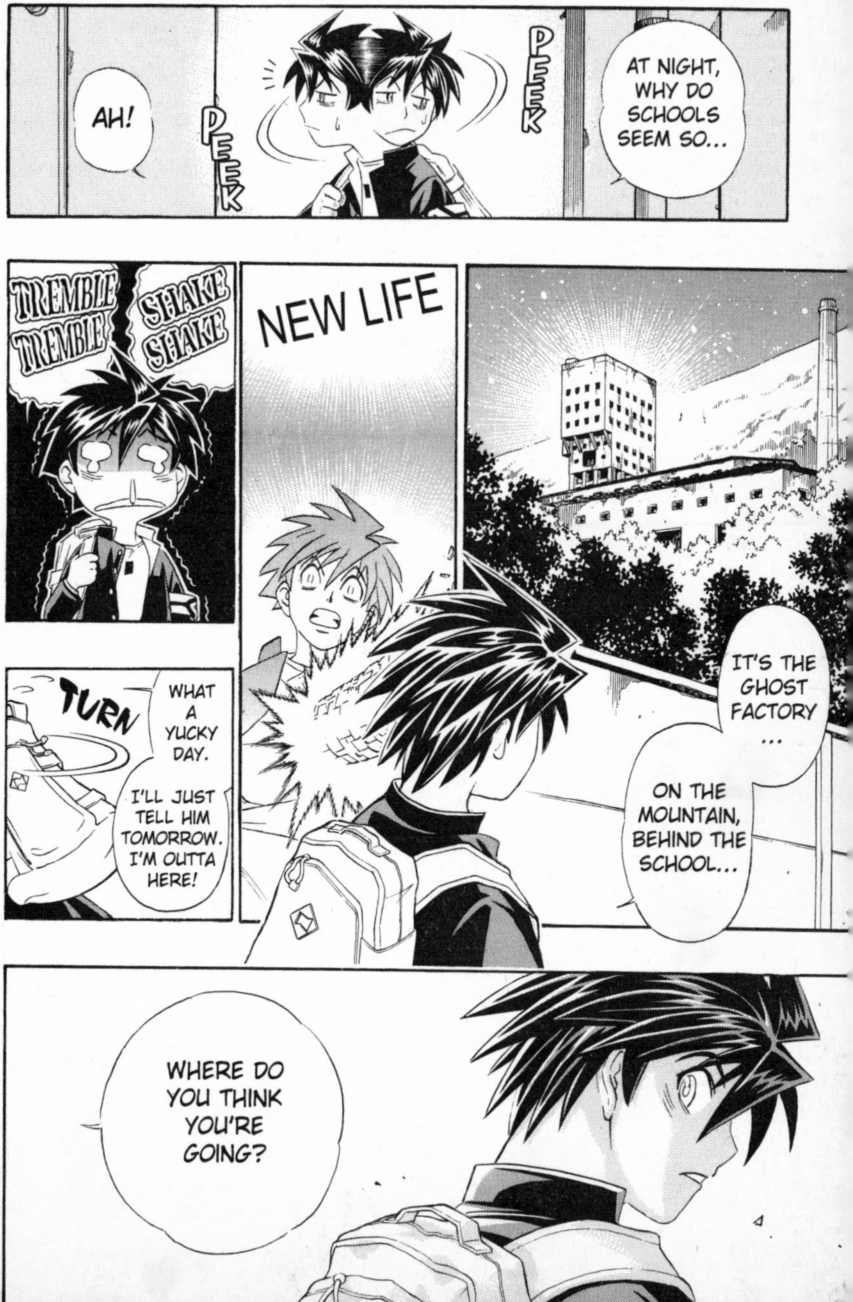
AT NIGHT, WHY DO SCHOOLS SEEM SO...
PEEK
PEEK
AH!
IT'S THE GHOST FACTORY...
ON THE MOUNTAIN, BEHIND THE SCHOOL...
NEW LIFE
SHAKE SHAKE
TREMBLE TREMBLE
TURN
WHAT A YUCKY DAY.
I'LL JUST TELL HIM TOMORROW. I'M OUTTA HERE!
WHERE DO YOU THINK YOU'RE GOING?

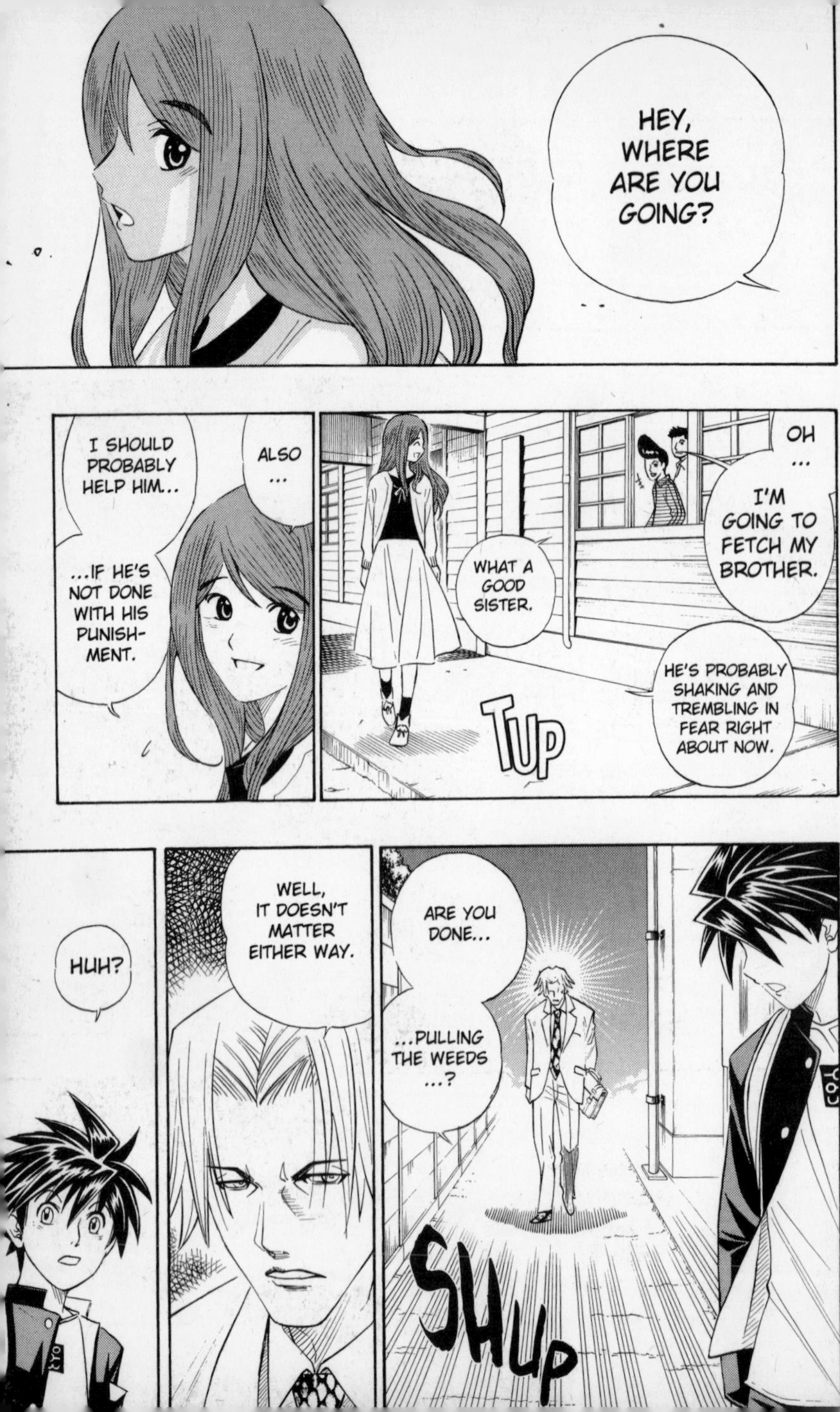
HEY, WHERE ARE YOU GOING?
OH ... I'M GOING TO FETCH MY BROTHER.
WHAT A GOOD SISTER.
HE'S PROBABLY SHAKING AND TREMBLING IN FEAR RIGHT ABOUT NOW.
TUP
ALSO ...
I SHOULD PROBABLY HELP HIM...
...IF HE'S NOT DONE WITH HIS PUNISH-MENT.
ARE YOU DONE...
...PULLING THE WEEDS ...?
SHUP
WELL, IT DOESN'T MATTER EITHER WAY.
HUH?

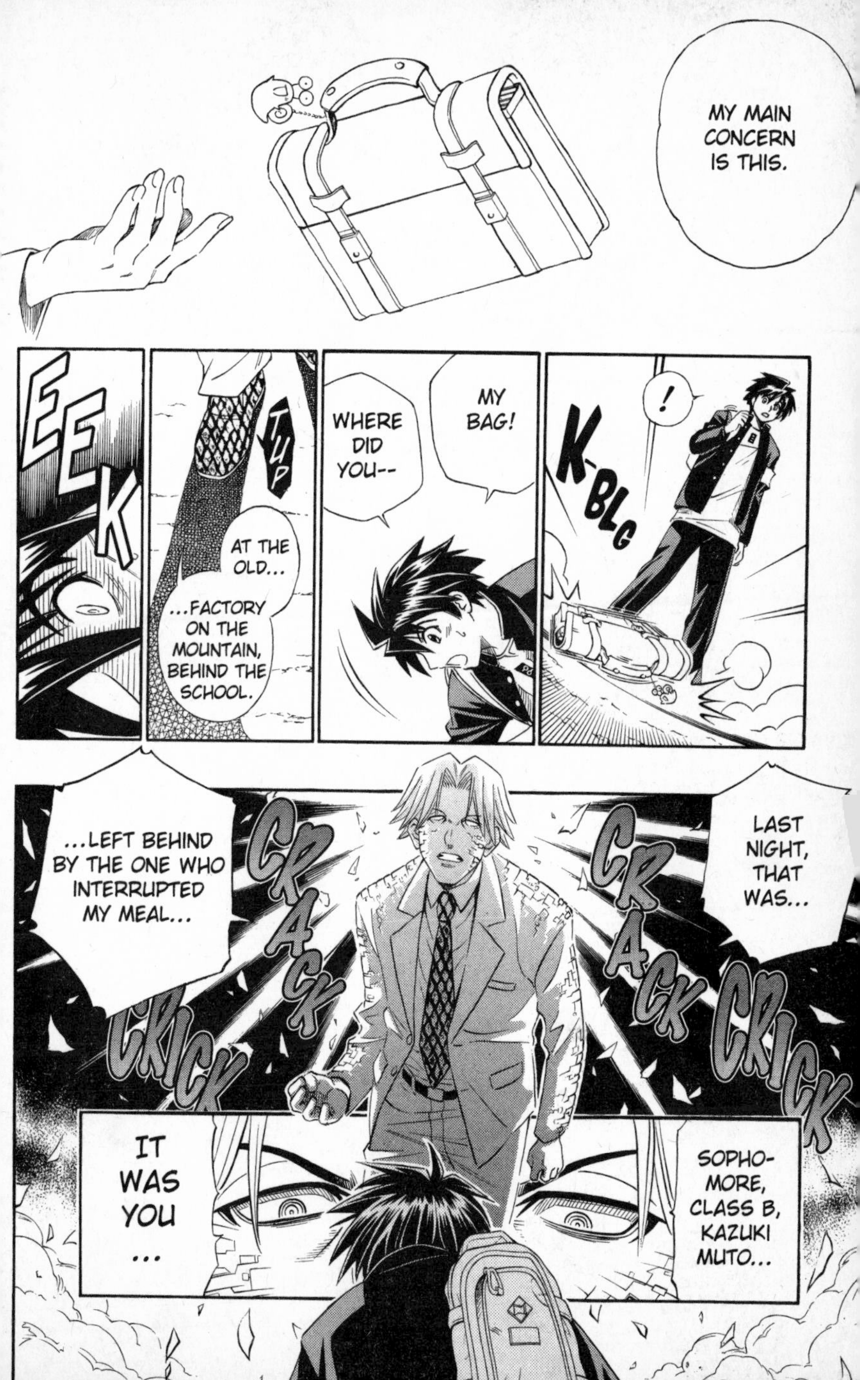
MY MAIN CONCERN IS THIS.
!
K-BLG
MY BAG!
WHERE DID YOU--
TUP
AT THE OLD...
...FACTORY ON THE MOUNTAIN, BEHIND THE SCHOOL.
EEK
LAST NIGHT, THAT WAS...
CRACK
CRICK
CRACK
...LEFT BEHIND BY THE ONE WHO INTERRUPTED MY MEAL...
CRICK
SOPHO-MORE, CLASS B, KAZUKI MUTO...
IT WAS YOU ...

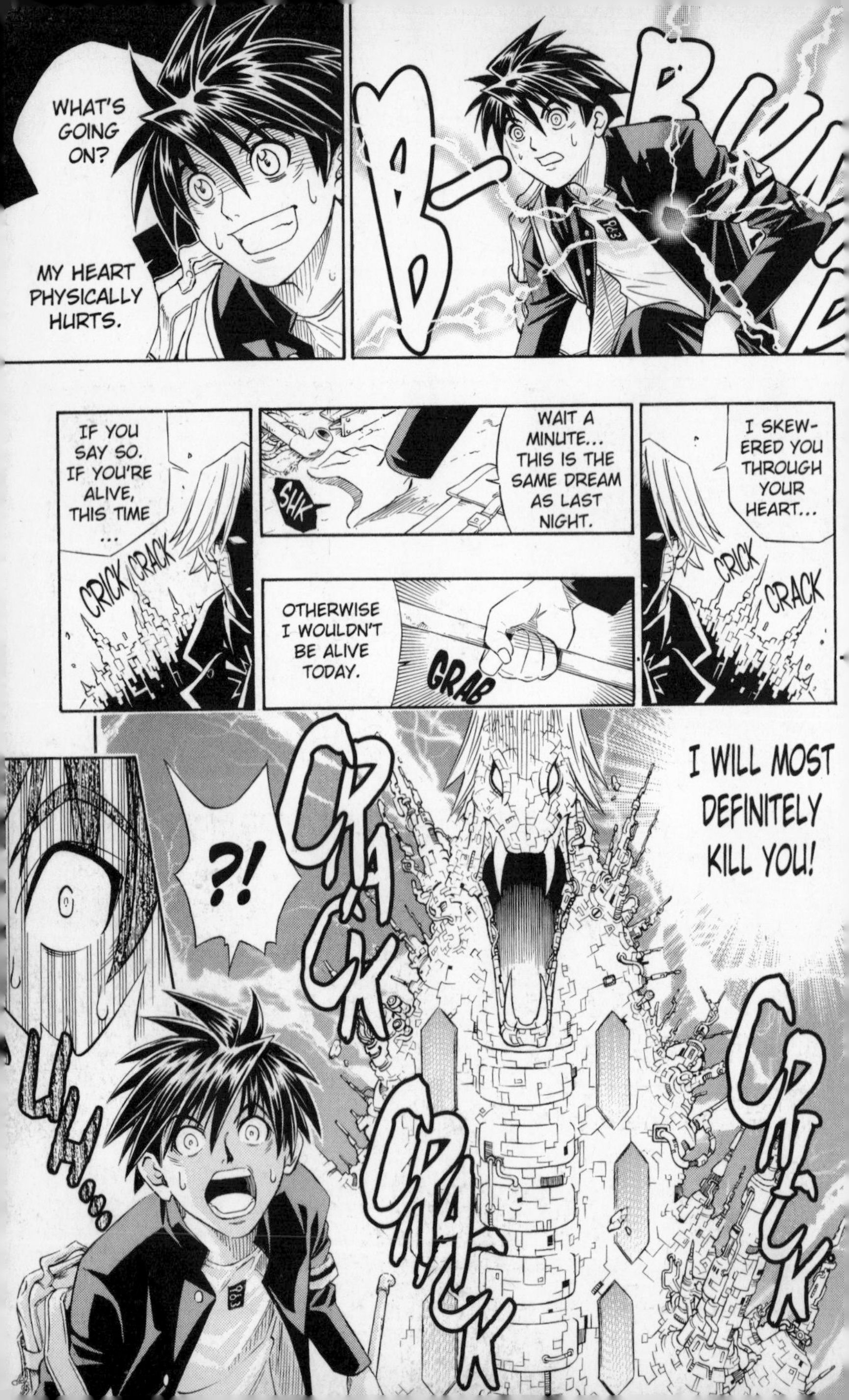
B-
WHAT'S GOING ON?
MY HEART PHYSICALLY HURTS.
I SKEWERED YOU THROUGH YOUR HEART...
CRICK
CRACK
WAIT A MINUTE... THIS IS THE SAME DREAM AS LAST NIGHT.
SHK
OTHERWISE I WOULDN'T BE ALIVE TODAY.
GRAB
IF YOU SAY SO. IF YOU'RE ALIVE, THIS TIME ...
CRICK CRACK
I WILL MOST DEFINITELY KILL YOU!
CRACK
CRACK
CRACK
?!
UH...

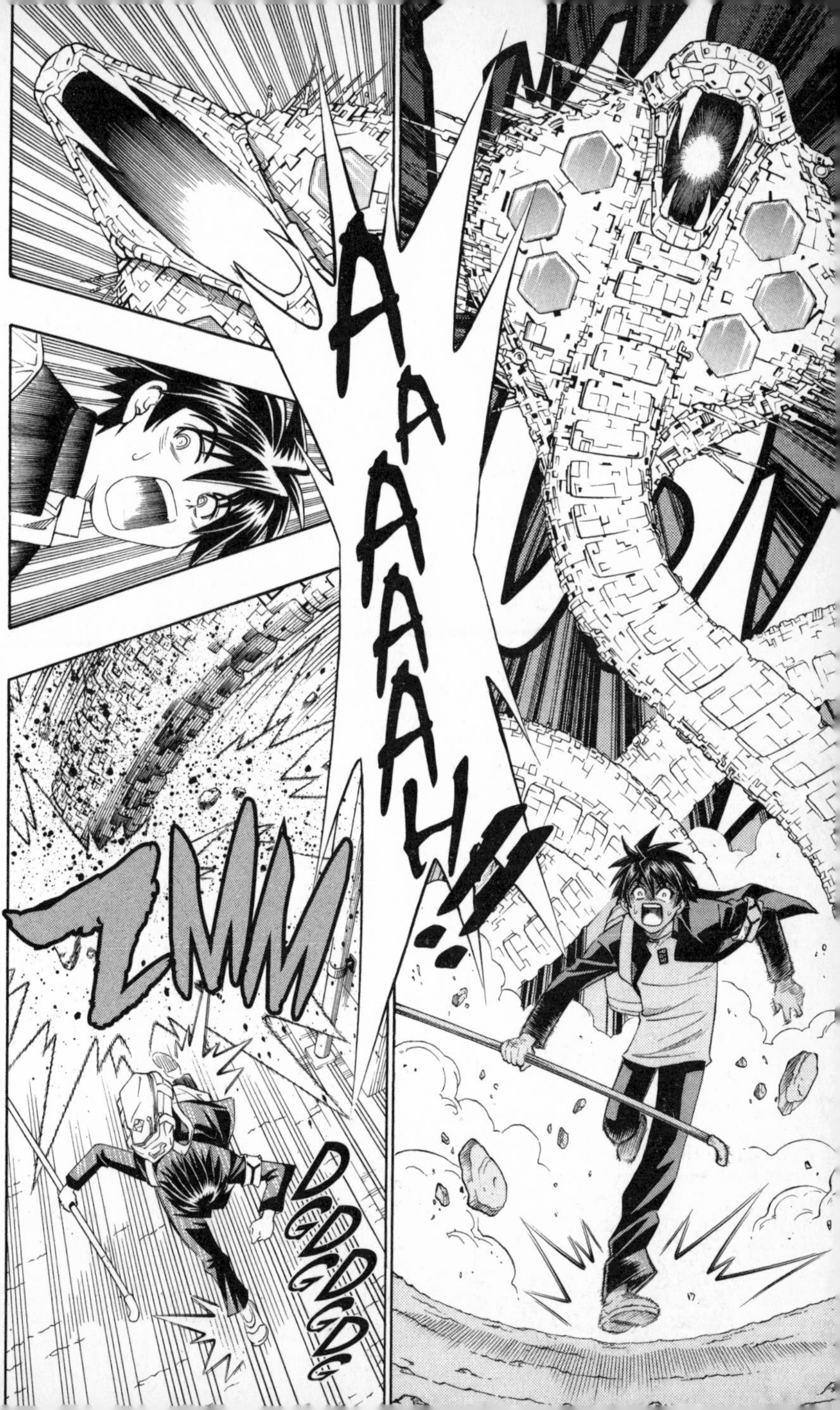
AAAAAH!!
ZMMM
DGDGDGDG

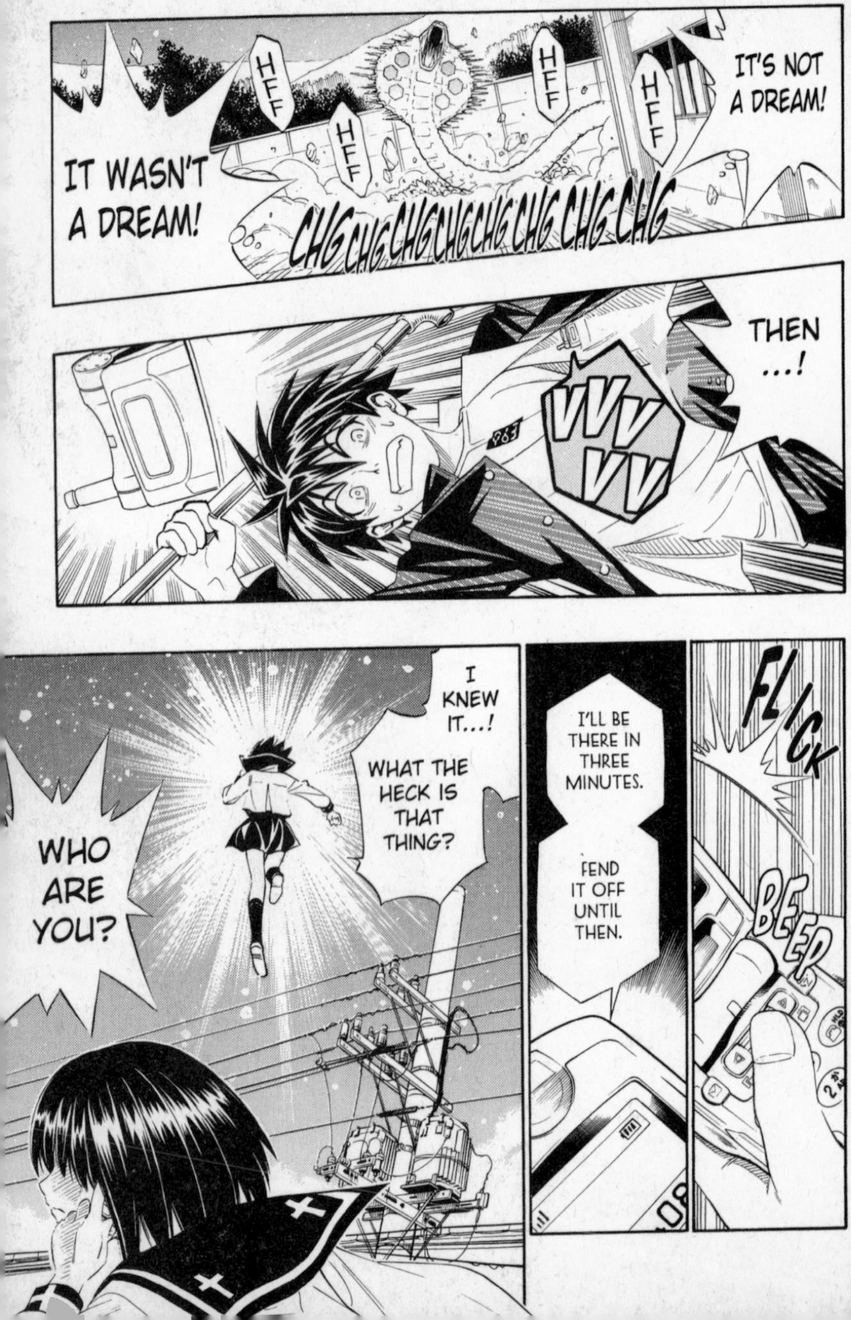
IT'S NOT A DREAM!
HFF
HFF
HFF
HFF
CHG CHG CHG CHG CHG CHG CHG CHG
IT WASN'T A DREAM!
THEN ...!
VVV VV
FLICK
BEEP
I'LL BE THERE IN THREE MINUTES.
FEND IT OFF UNTIL THEN.
I KNEW IT...!
WHAT THE HECK IS THAT THING?
WHO ARE YOU?

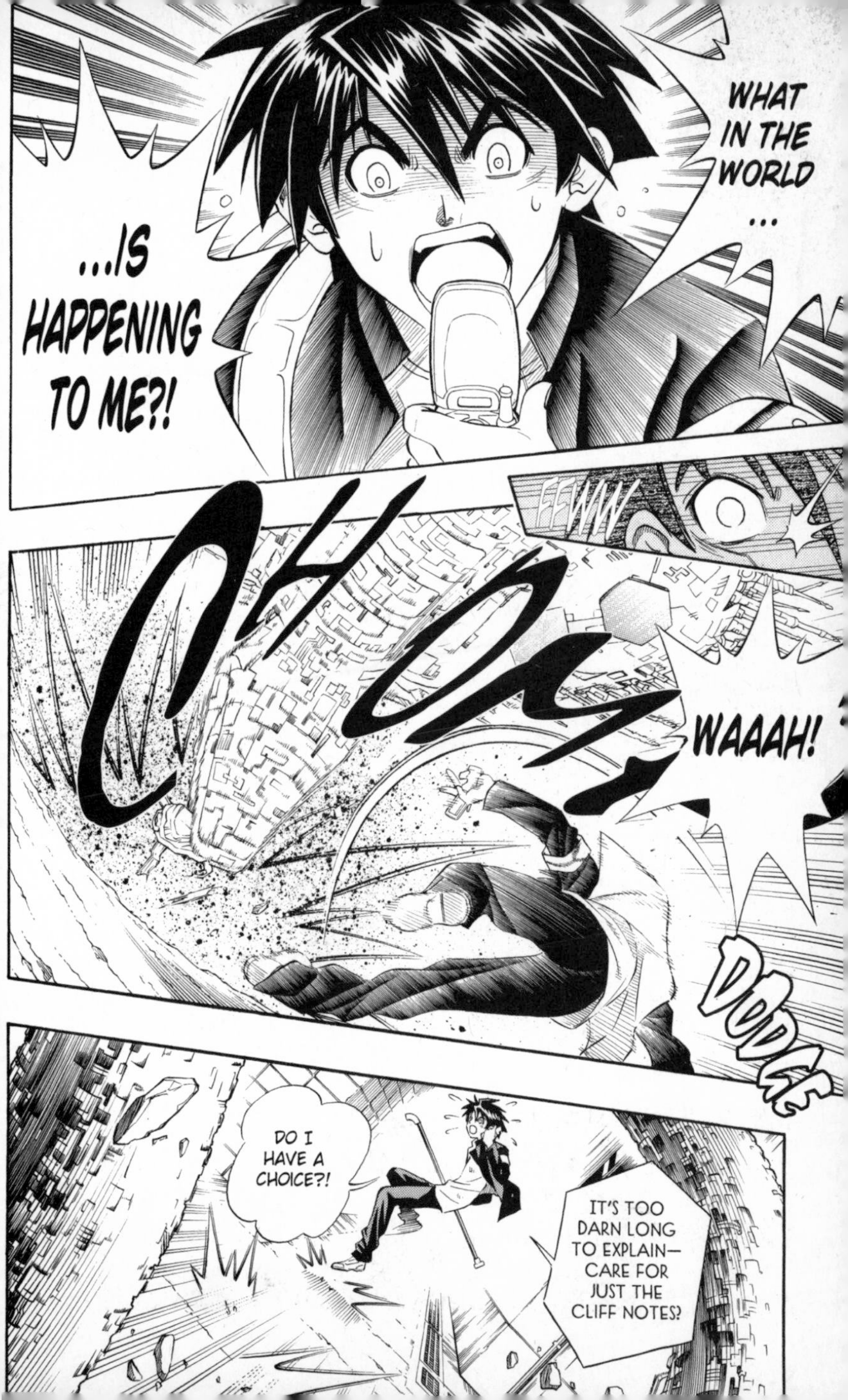
WHAT IN THE WORLD...
...IS HAPPENING TO ME?!
FFWW
WAAAH!
DODGE
IT'S TOO DARN LONG TO EXPLAIN—CARE FOR JUST THE CLIFF NOTES?
DO I HAVE A CHOICE?!

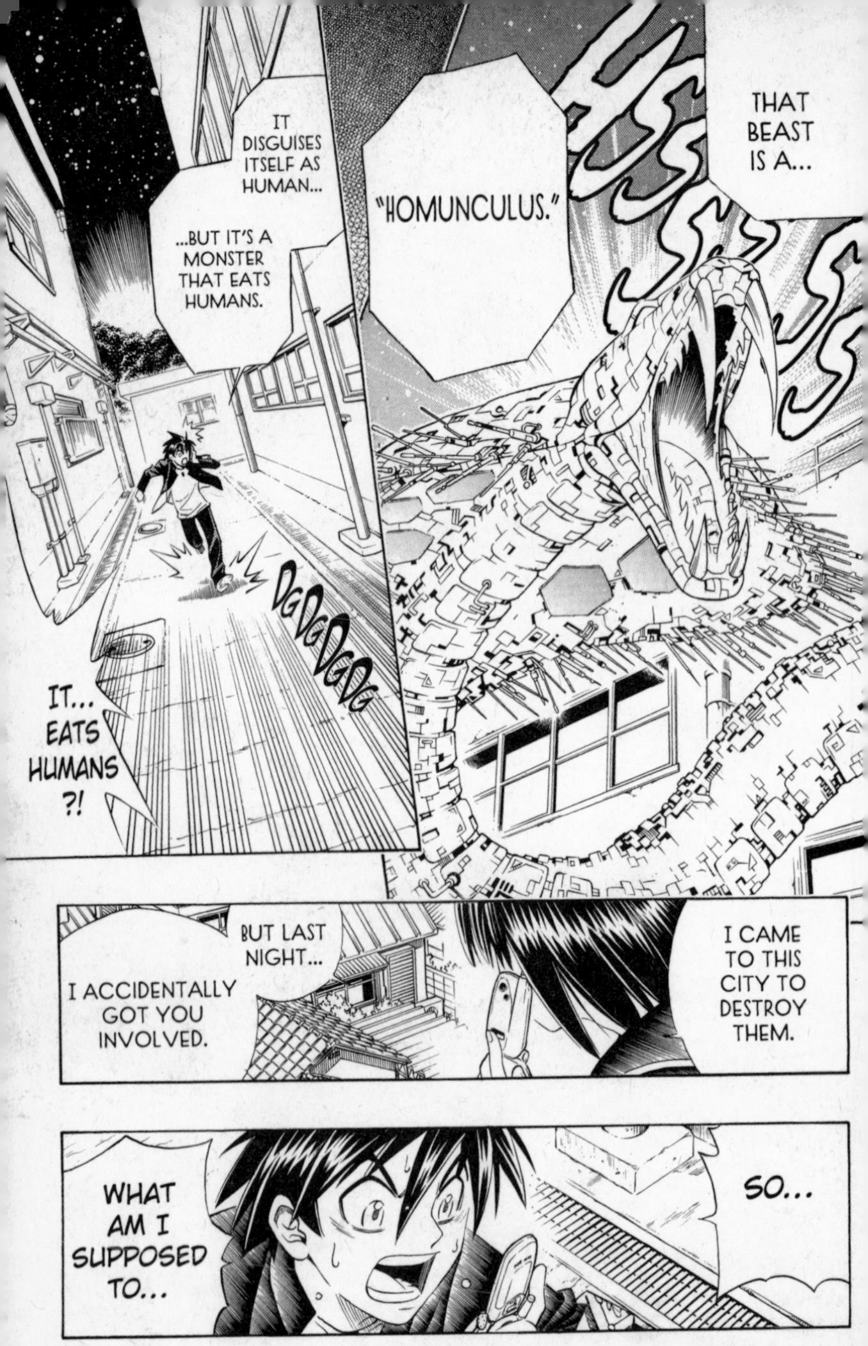
THAT BEAST IS A...
"HOMUNCULUS."
IT DISGUISES ITSELF AS HUMAN...
...BUT IT'S A MONSTER THAT EATS HUMANS.
DGDGDGDG
IT... EATS HUMANS?!
I CAME TO THIS CITY TO DESTROY THEM.
BUT LAST NIGHT...
I ACCIDENTALLY GOT YOU INVOLVED.
SO...
WHAT AM I SUPPOSED TO...

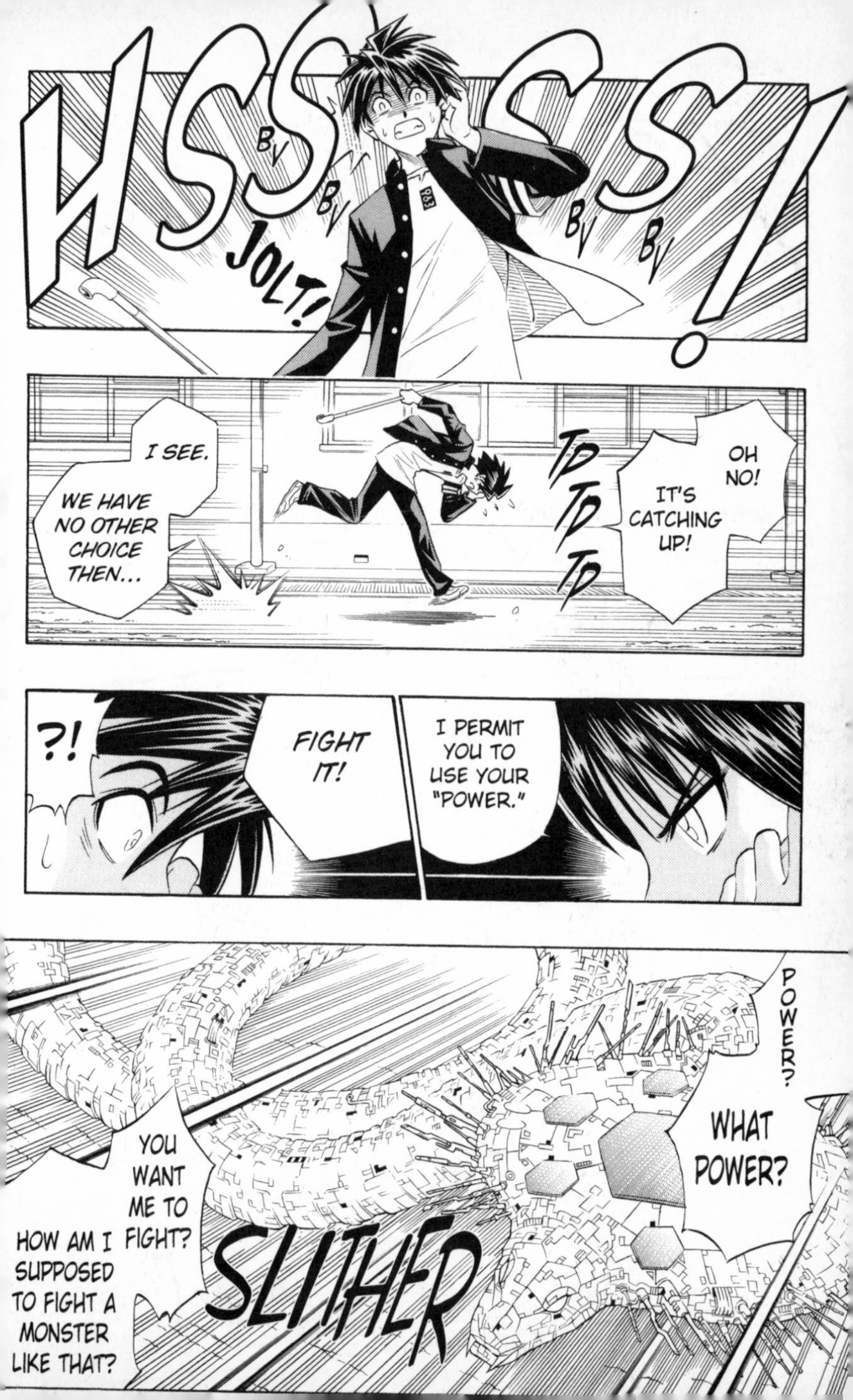
HSSSSS!
BV BV
JOLT!
BV BV
OH NO!
IT'S CATCHING UP!
TP TP TP
I SEE.
WE HAVE NO OTHER CHOICE THEN...
I PERMIT YOU TO USE YOUR "POWER."
FIGHT IT!
?!
POWER?
WHAT POWER?
YOU WANT ME TO FIGHT?
SLITHER
HOW AM I SUPPOSED TO FIGHT A MONSTER LIKE THAT?

READ THIS WAY

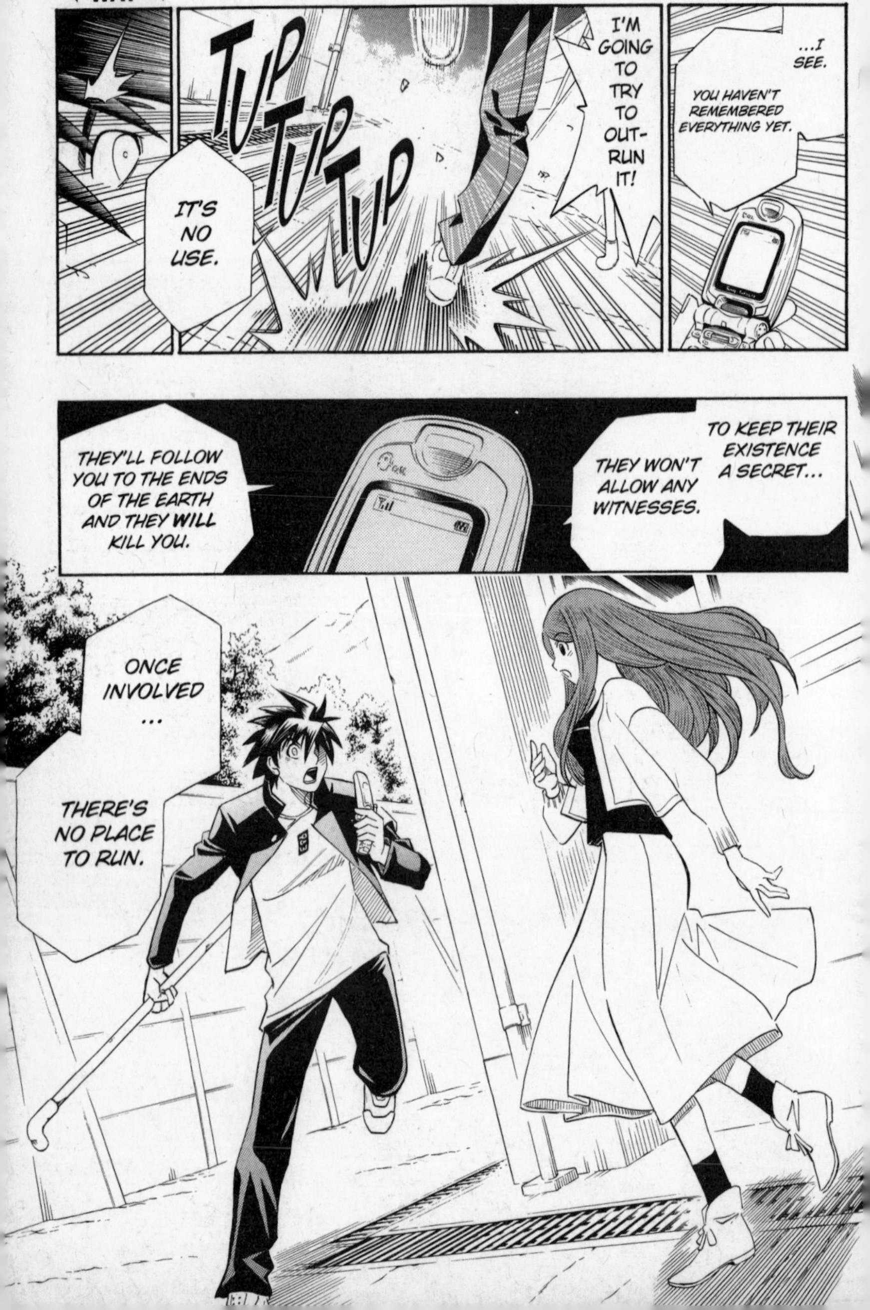

...I SEE.
YOU HAVEN'T REMEMBERED EVERYTHING YET.
I'M GOING TO TRY TO OUT-RUN IT!
TUP TUP TUP TUP
IT'S NO USE.
TO KEEP THEIR EXISTENCE A SECRET...
THEY WON'T ALLOW ANY WITNESSES.
THEY'LL FOLLOW YOU TO THE ENDS OF THE EARTH AND THEY WILL KILL YOU.
ONCE INVOLVED ...
THERE'S NO PLACE TO RUN.

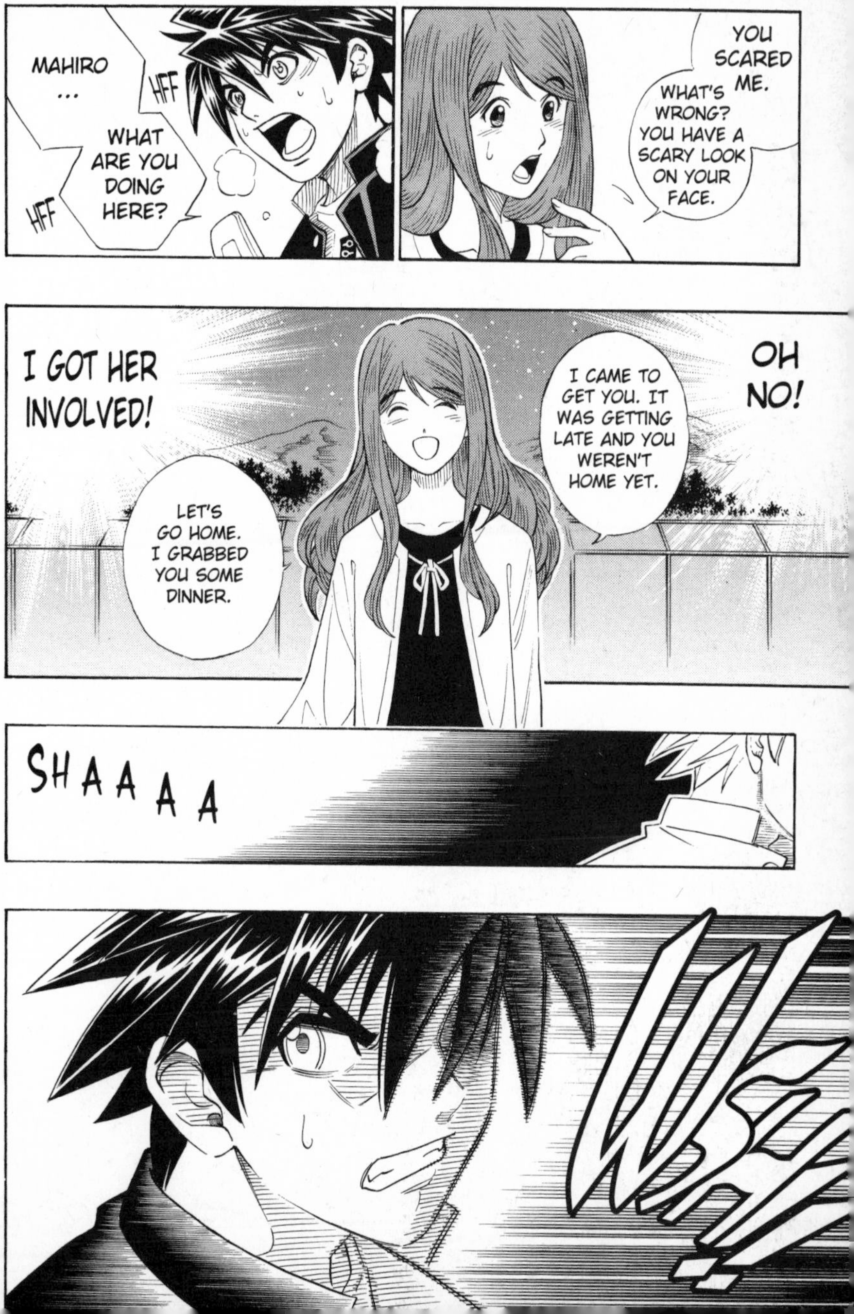
YOU SCARED ME.
WHAT'S WRONG? YOU HAVE A SCARY LOOK ON YOUR FACE.
MAHIRO ...
HFF
WHAT ARE YOU DOING HERE?
HFF
OH NO!
I CAME TO GET YOU. IT WAS GETTING LATE AND YOU WEREN'T HOME YET.
LET'S GO HOME. I GRABBED YOU SOME DINNER.
I GOT HER INVOLVED!
SHAAAAA

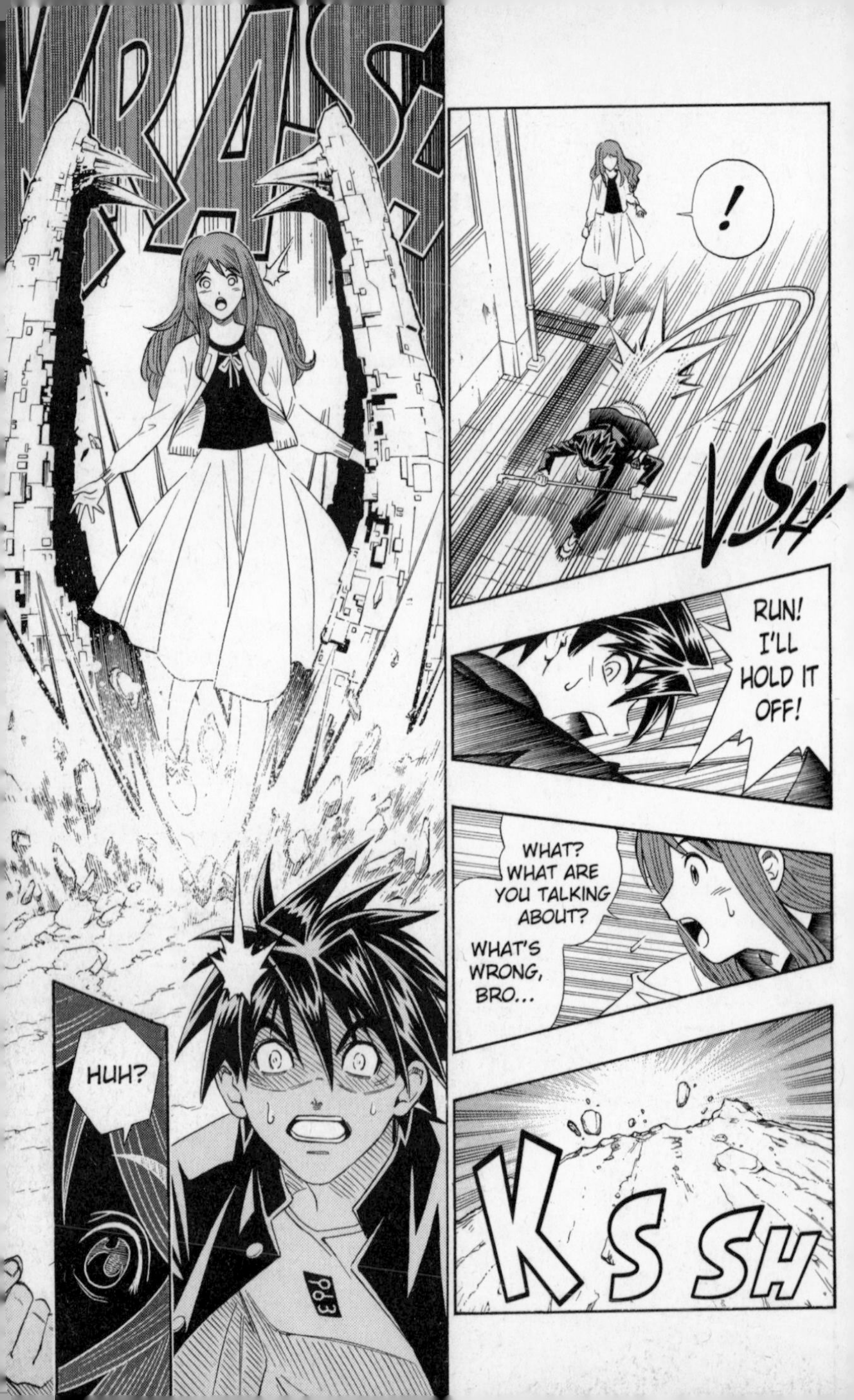
!
V.S.H
RUN! I'LL HOLD IT OFF!
WHAT? WHAT ARE YOU TALKING ABOUT?
WHAT'S WRONG, BRO...
KSSH
VRASH
HUH?

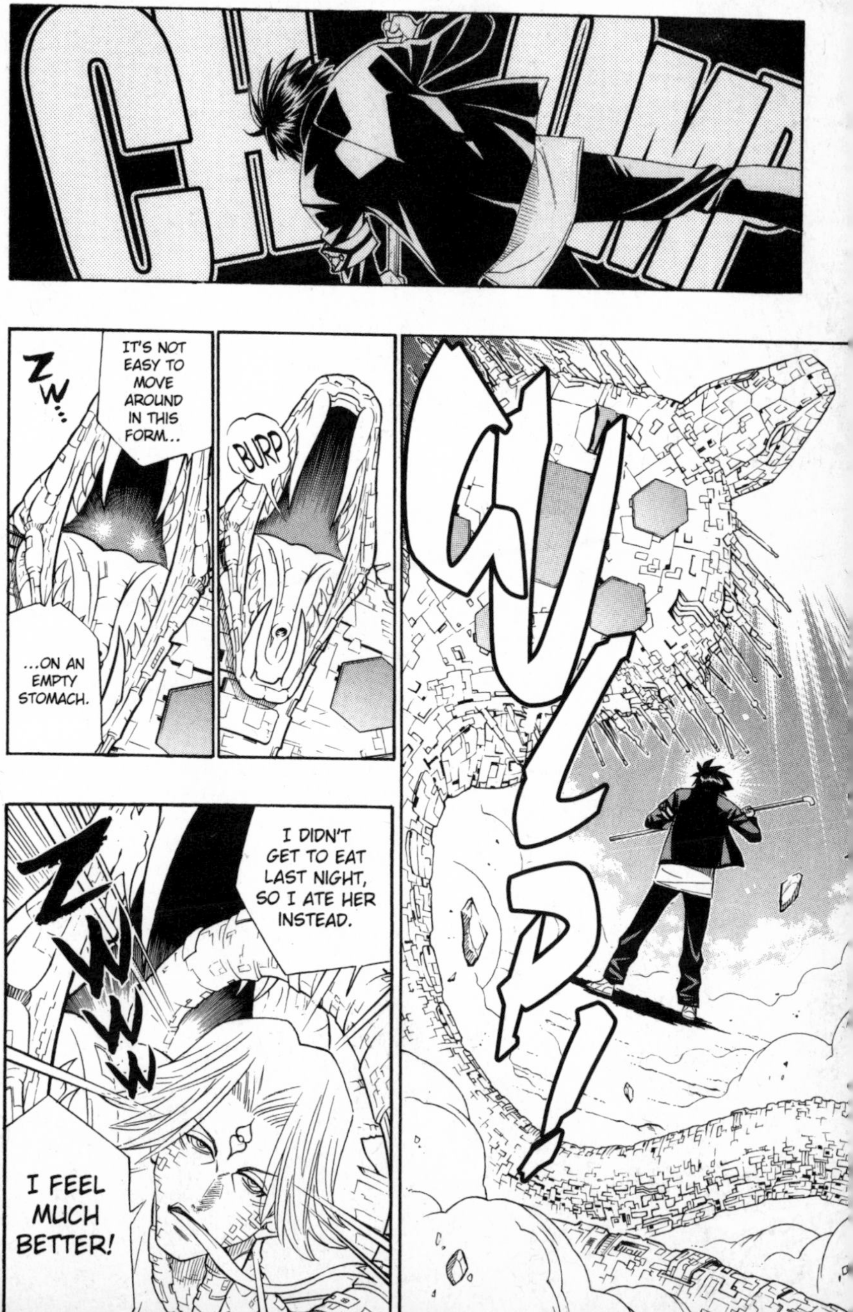
GULP!
BURP
ZW...
IT'S NOT EASY TO MOVE AROUND IN THIS FORM...
...ON AN EMPTY STOMACH.
I DIDN'T GET TO EAT LAST NIGHT, SO I ATE HER INSTEAD.
ZWWWW
I FEEL MUCH BETTER!

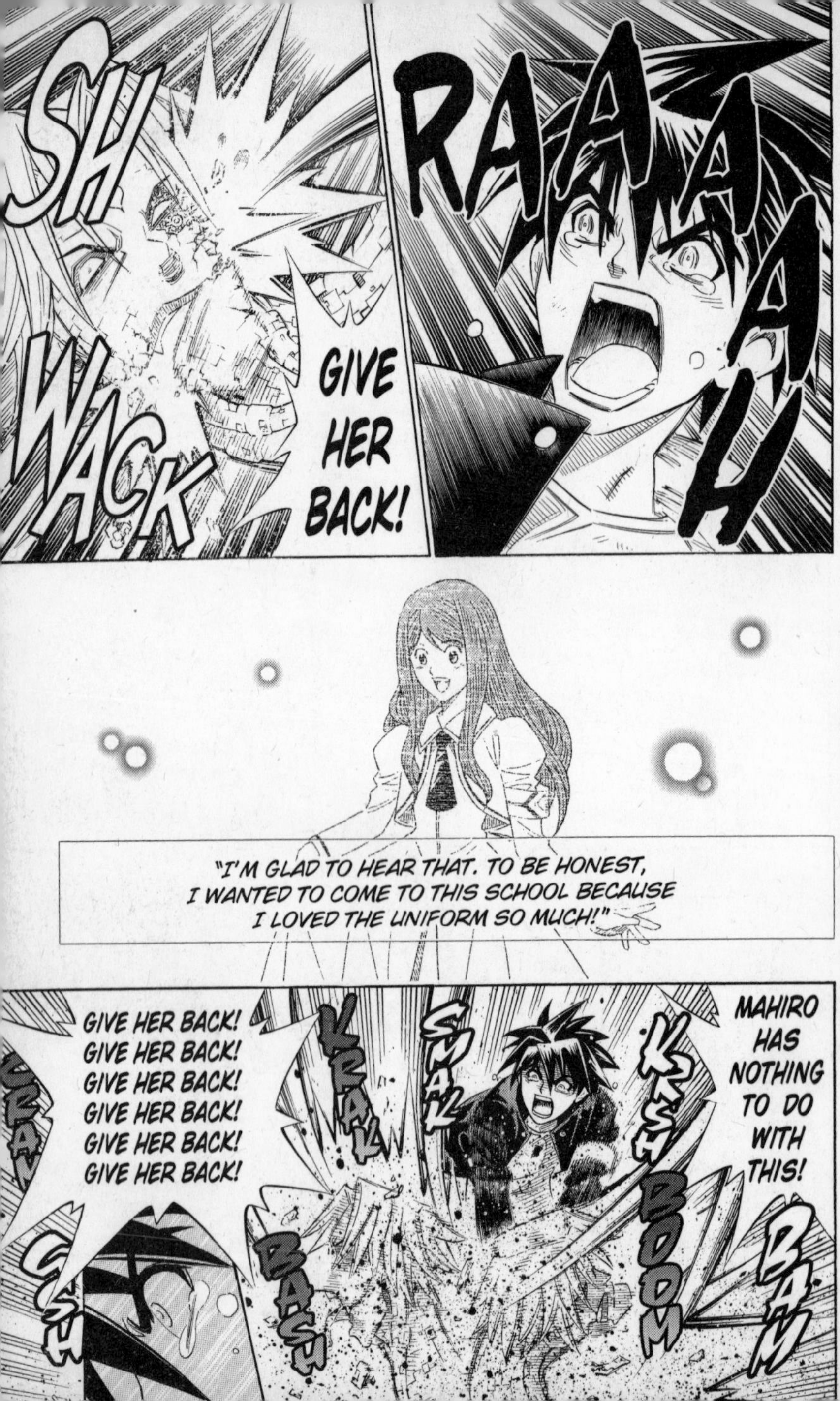
RAAAAAAH
SHWACK
GIVE HER BACK!
"I'M GLAD TO HEAR THAT. TO BE HONEST, I WANTED TO COME TO THIS SCHOOL BECAUSE I LOVED THE UNIFORM SO MUCH!"
MAHIRO HAS NOTHING TO DO WITH THIS!
BAM
KRSH
BOOM
SMAK
KRAK
BASH
GIVE HER BACK!
GIVE HER BACK!
GIVE HER BACK!
GIVE HER BACK!
GIVE HER BACK!
GIVE HER BACK!

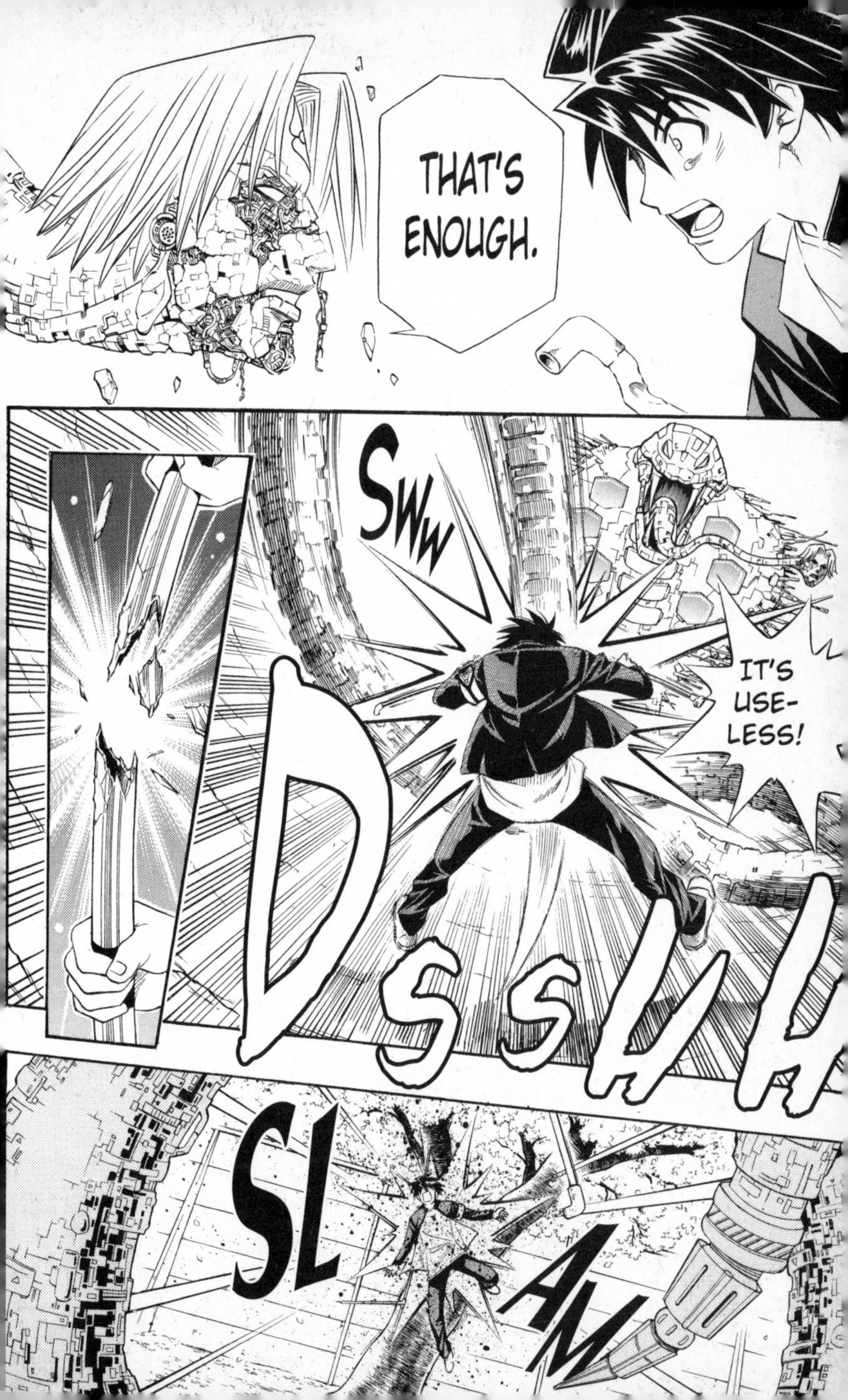
THAT'S ENOUGH.
SWW
IT'S USE-LESS!
DSSHH
SLAM

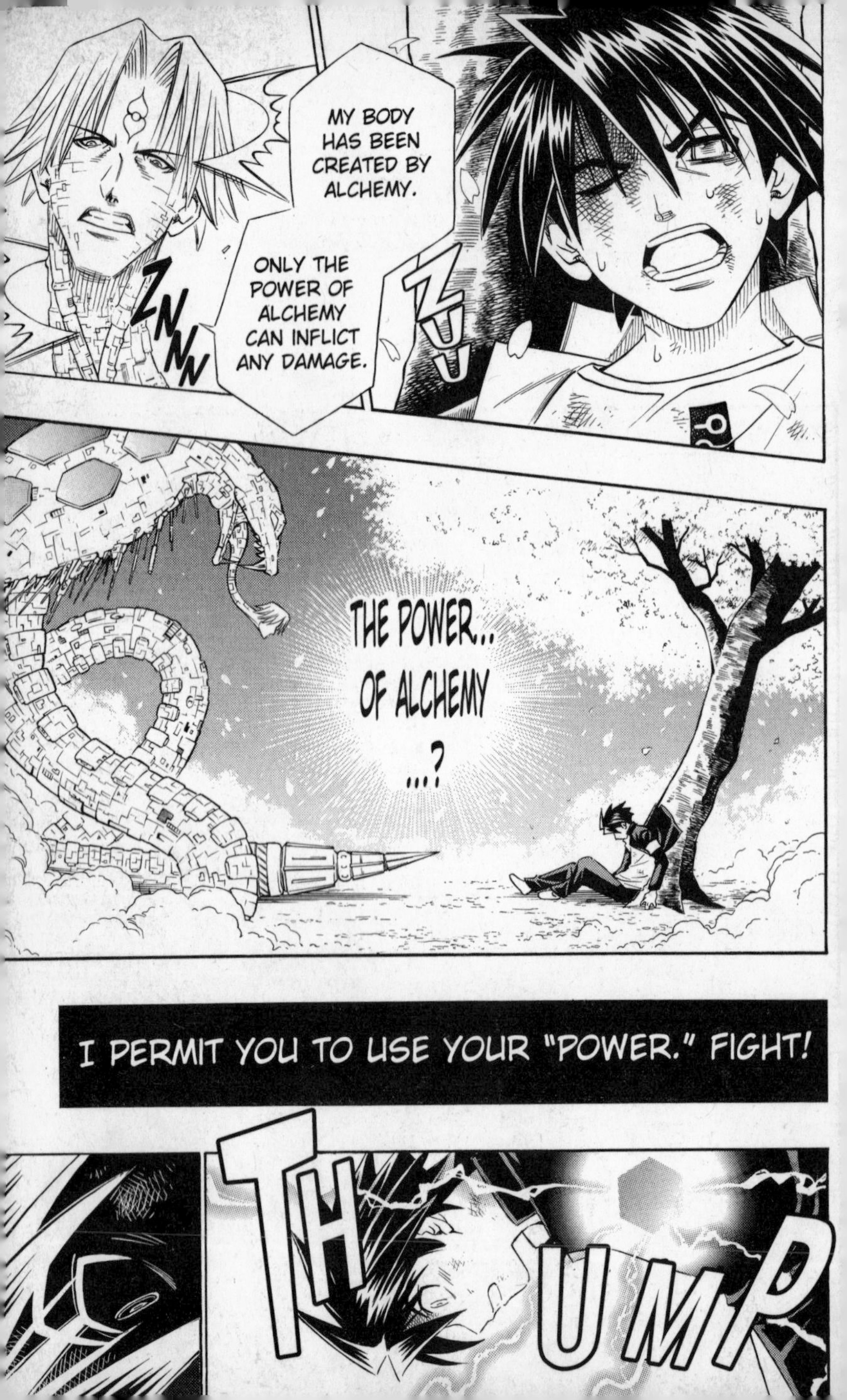
ZUU
MY BODY HAS BEEN CREATED BY ALCHEMY.
ONLY THE POWER OF ALCHEMY CAN INFLICT ANY DAMAGE.
ZNNN
THE POWER... OF ALCHEMY ...?
I PERMIT YOU TO USE YOUR "POWER." FIGHT!
THUMP

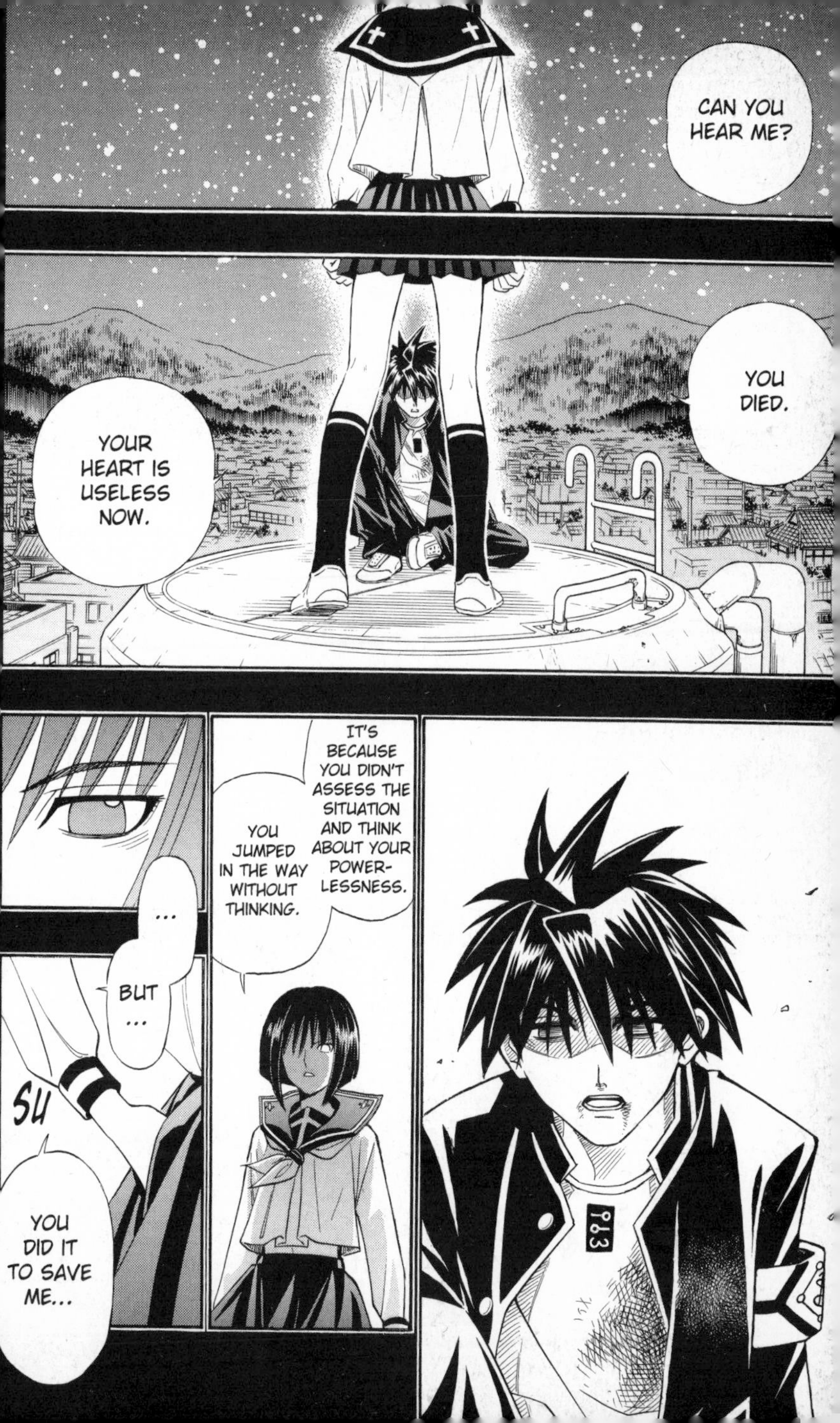
CAN YOU HEAR ME?
YOU DIED.
YOUR HEART IS USELESS NOW.
IT'S BECAUSE YOU DIDN'T ASSESS THE SITUATION AND THINK ABOUT YOUR POWER-LESSNESS.
YOU JUMPED IN THE WAY WITHOUT THINKING.
...
BUT ...
SU
YOU DID IT TO SAVE ME...

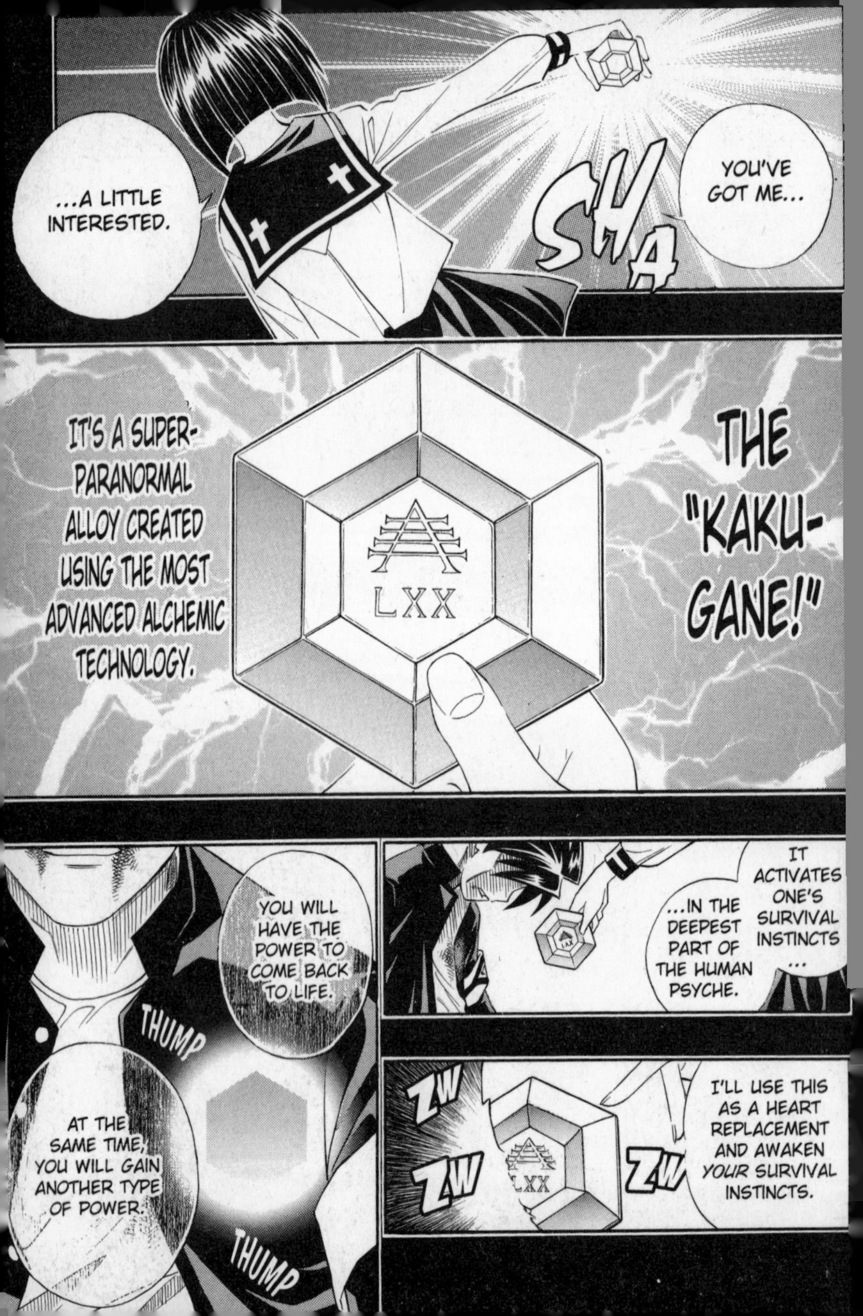
YOU'VE GOT ME...
SHA
...A LITTLE INTERESTED.
THE "KAKU-GANE!"
IT'S A SUPER-PARANORMAL ALLOY CREATED USING THE MOST ADVANCED ALCHEMIC TECHNOLOGY.
LXX
IT ACTIVATES ONE'S SURVIVAL INSTINCTS...
...IN THE DEEPEST PART OF THE HUMAN PSYCHE.
I'LL USE THIS AS A HEART REPLACEMENT AND AWAKEN *YOUR* SURVIVAL INSTINCTS.
ZW
ZW
ZW
LXX
YOU WILL HAVE THE POWER TO COME BACK TO LIFE.
THUMP
AT THE SAME TIME, YOU WILL GAIN ANOTHER TYPE OF POWER.
THUMP

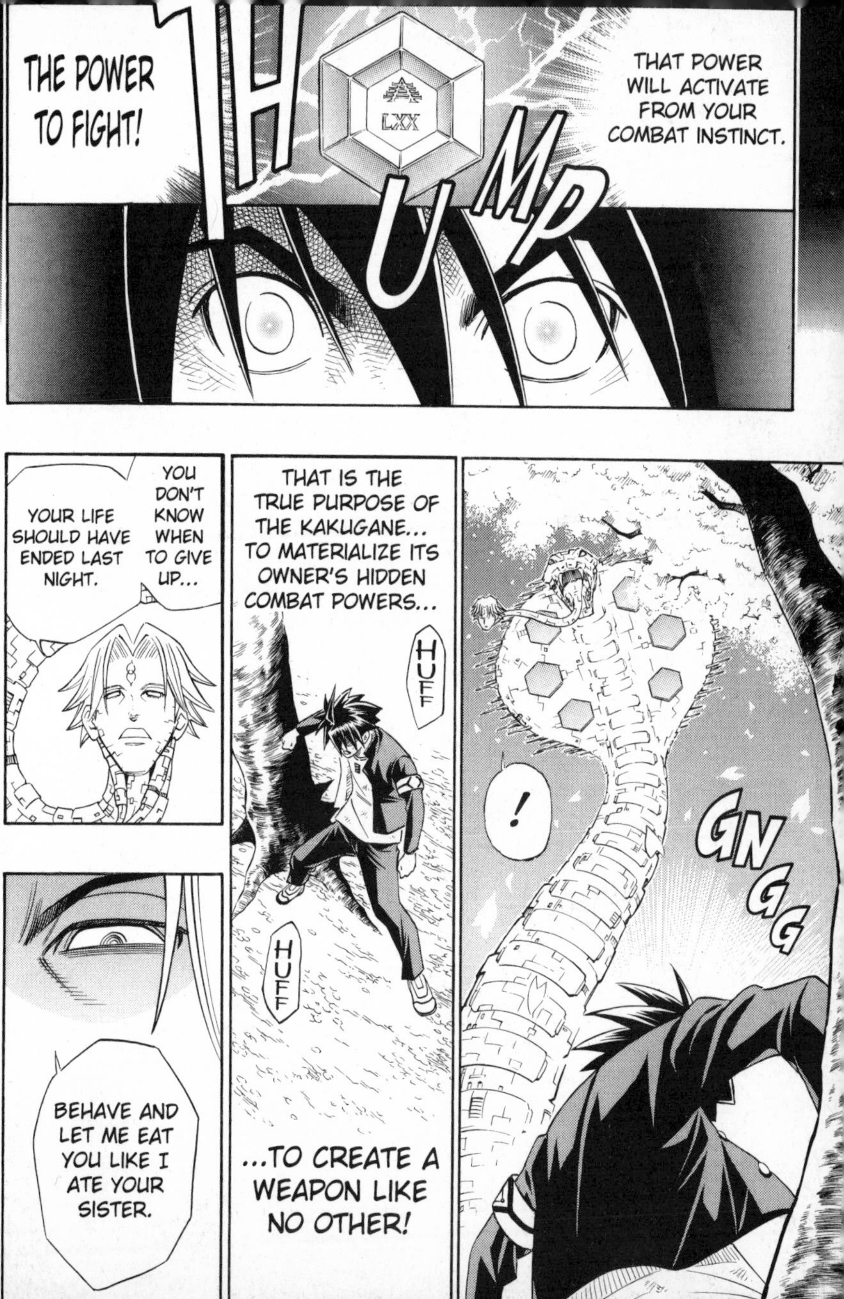
THAT POWER WILL ACTIVATE FROM YOUR COMBAT INSTINCT.
HUMP
THE POWER TO FIGHT!
!
GNGG
THAT IS THE TRUE PURPOSE OF THE KAKUGANE... TO MATERIALIZE ITS OWNER'S HIDDEN COMBAT POWERS...
HUFF
HUFF
...TO CREATE A WEAPON LIKE NO OTHER!
YOU DON'T KNOW WHEN TO GIVE UP...
YOUR LIFE SHOULD HAVE ENDED LAST NIGHT.
BEHAVE AND LET ME EAT YOU LIKE I ATE YOUR SISTER.

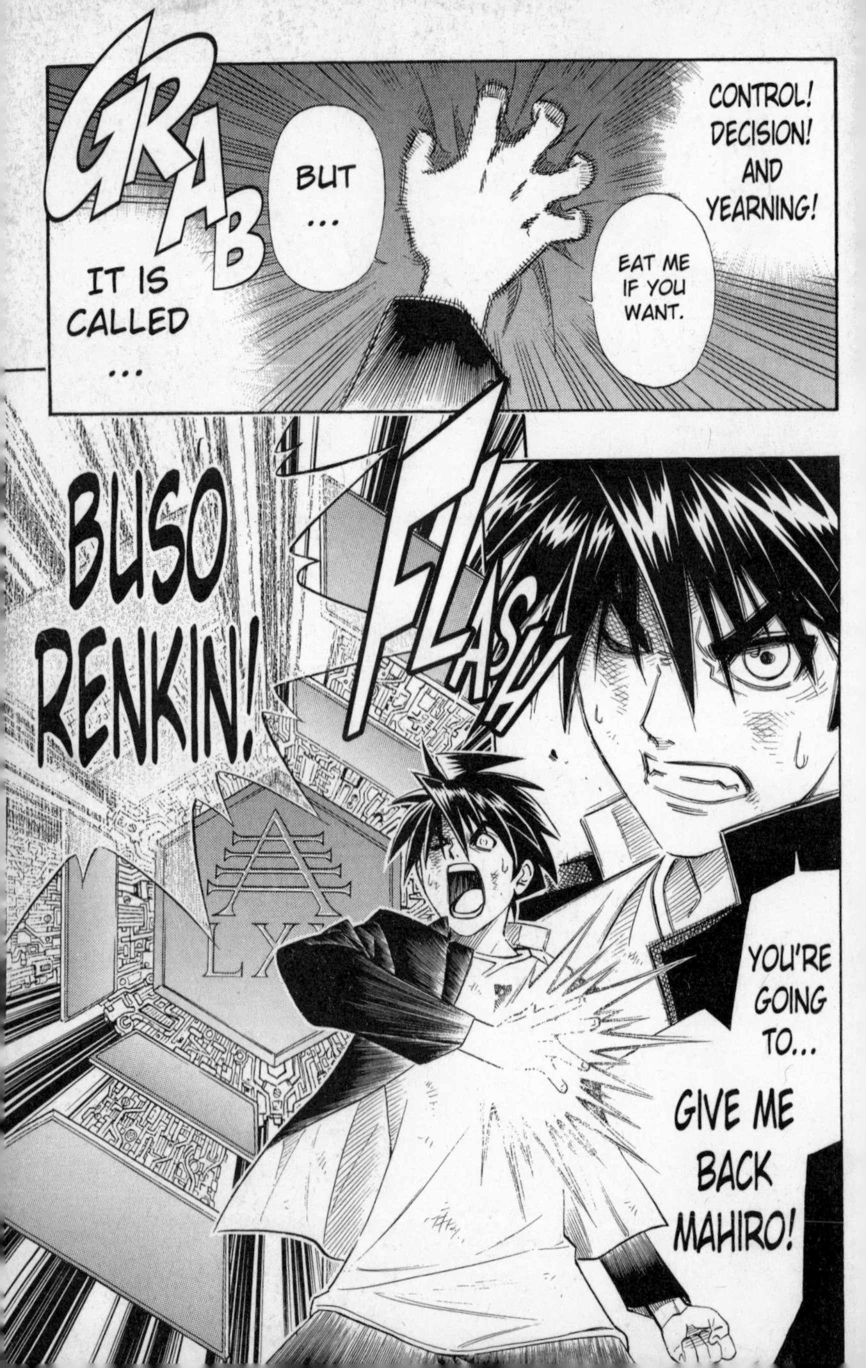
CONTROL! DECISION! AND YEARNING!
EAT ME IF YOU WANT.
BUT ...
GRAB
IT IS CALLED ...
FLASH
BUSO RENKIN!
YOU'RE GOING TO...
GIVE ME BACK MAHIRO!

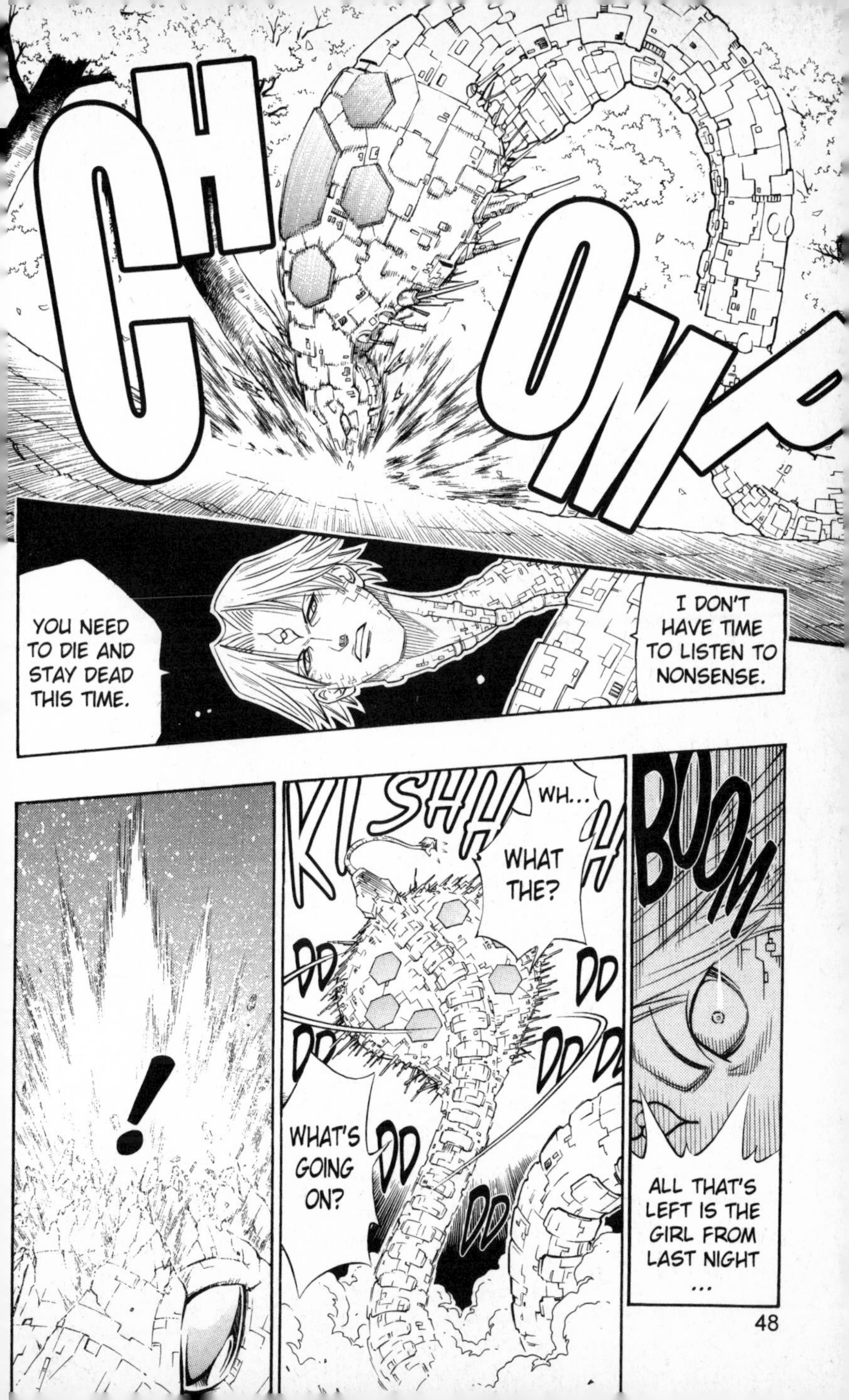
CHOMP
I DON'T HAVE TIME TO LISTEN TO NONSENSE.
YOU NEED TO DIE AND STAY DEAD THIS TIME.
BOOM
ALL THAT'S LEFT IS THE GIRL FROM LAST NIGHT ...
KISHHH
WH...
WHAT THE?
DD DD DD DD DD DD DD DD
WHAT'S GOING ON?
!

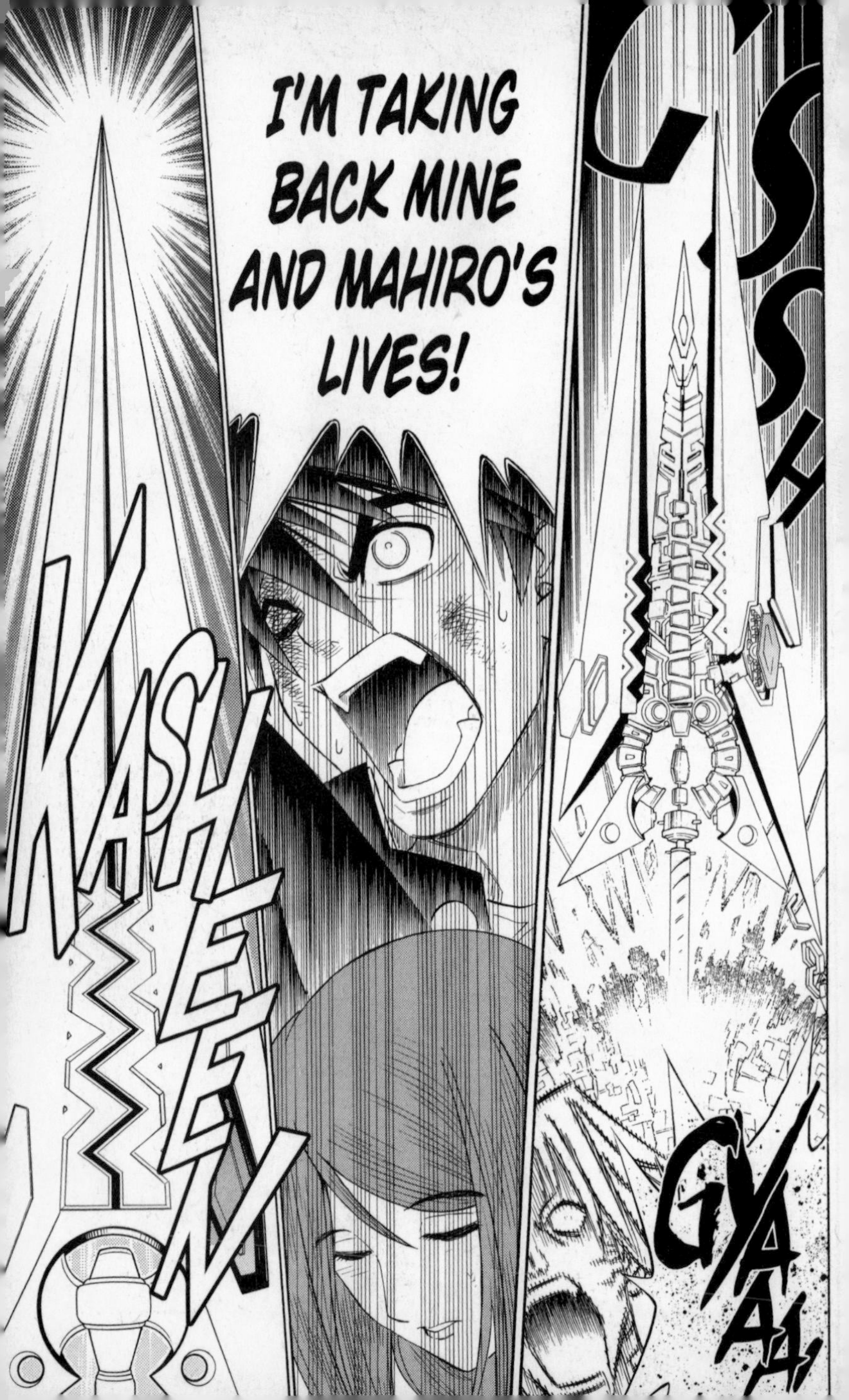
GISH
GYAAA
I'M TAKING BACK MINE AND MAHIRO'S LIVES!
KASHEEN

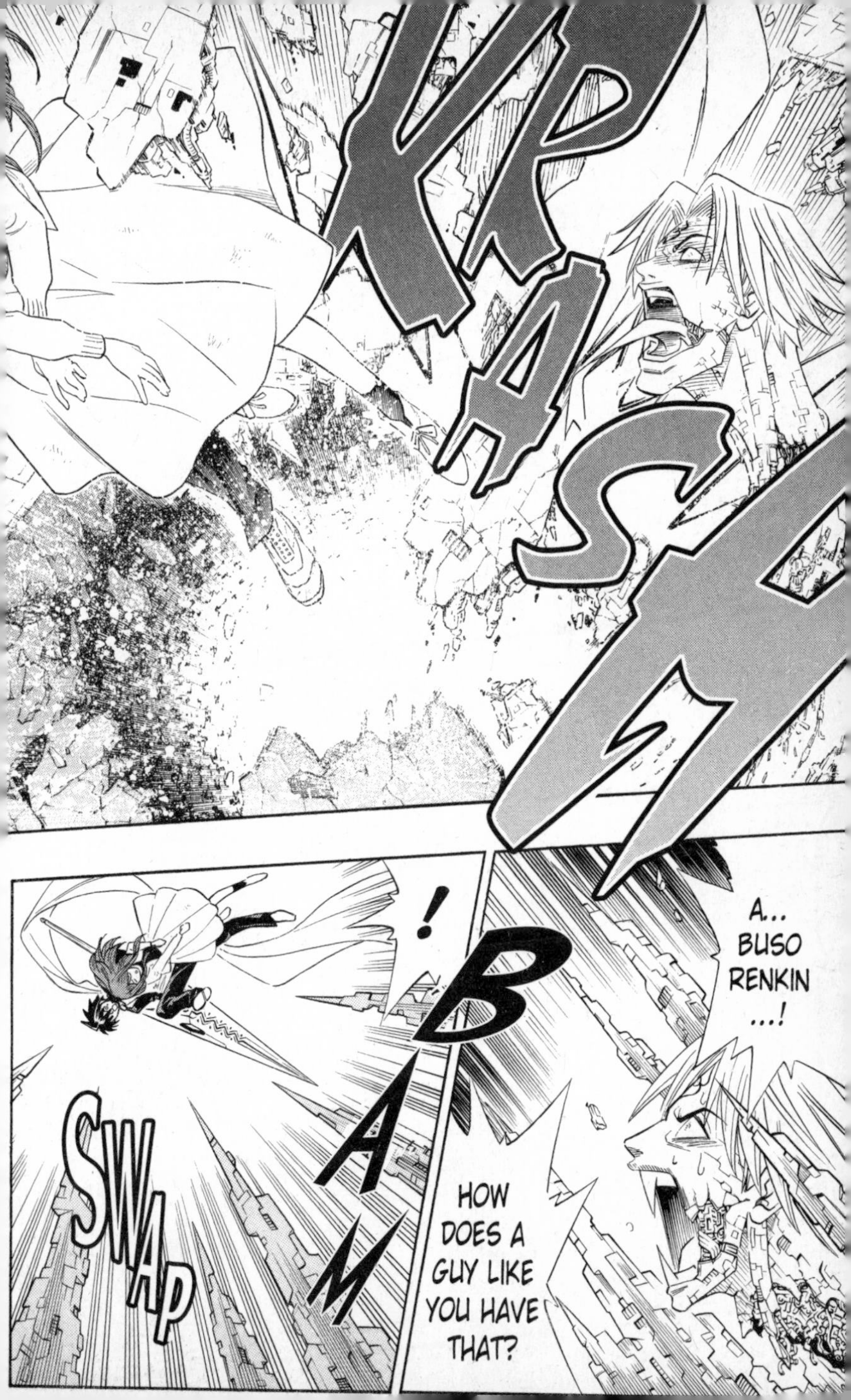
KRASH
A... BUSO RENKIN ...!
HOW DOES A GUY LIKE YOU HAVE THAT?
BAAM
!
SWAP

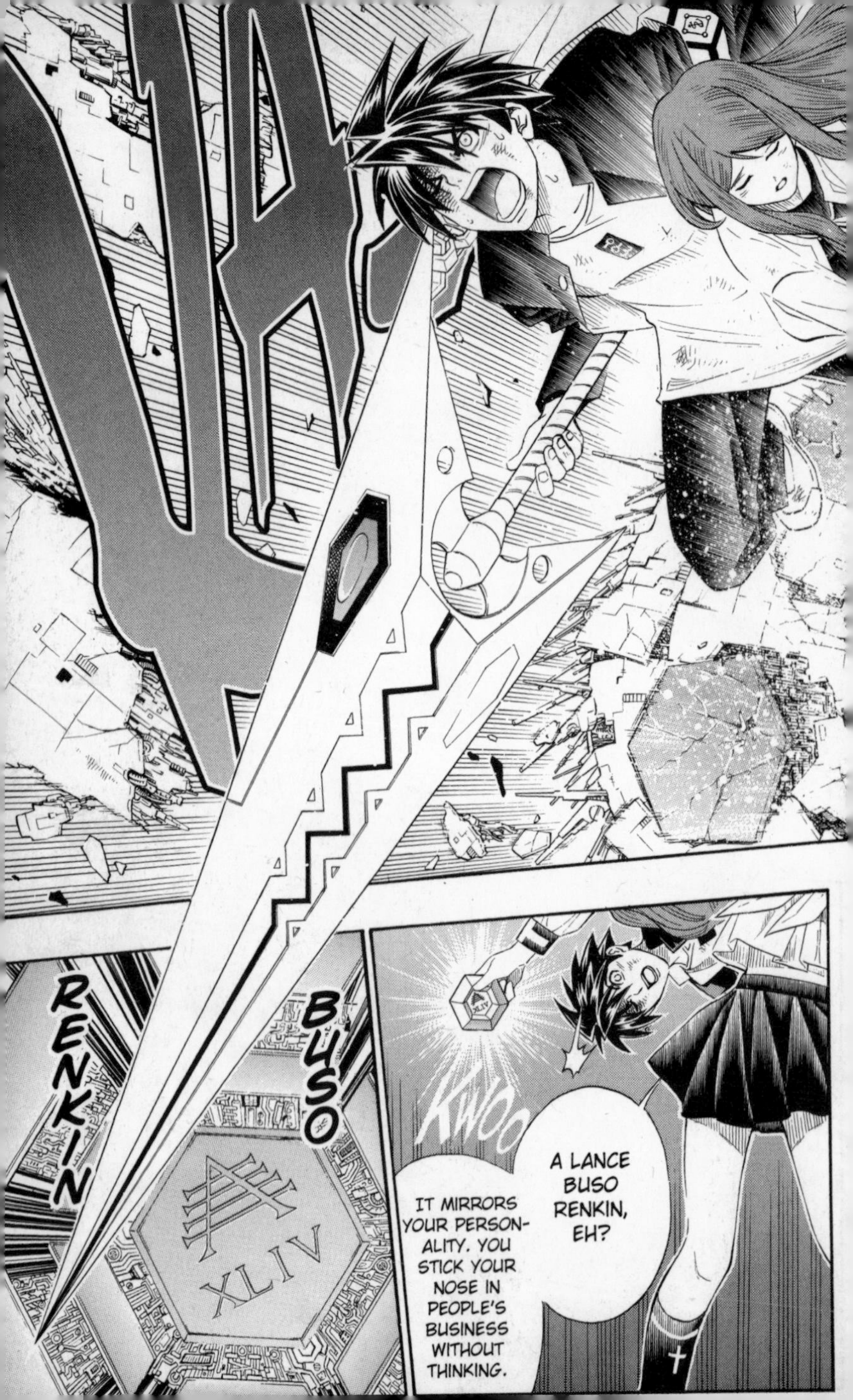
BUSO
RENKIN
KWOO
A LANCE BUSO RENKIN, EH?
IT MIRRORS YOUR PERSON-ALITY. YOU STICK YOUR NOSE IN PEOPLE'S BUSINESS WITHOUT THINKING.
XLIV

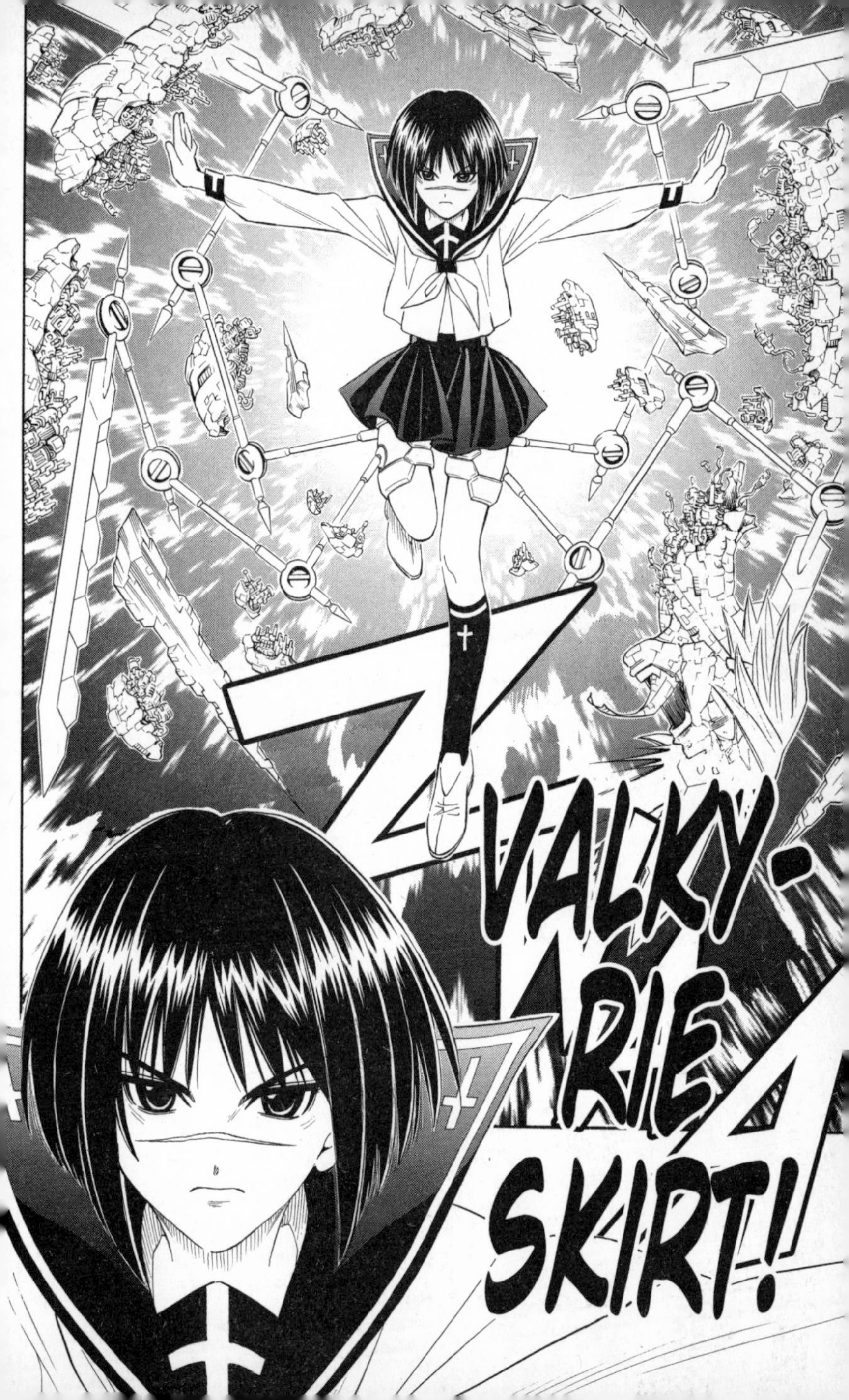
VALKY-RIE SKIRT!

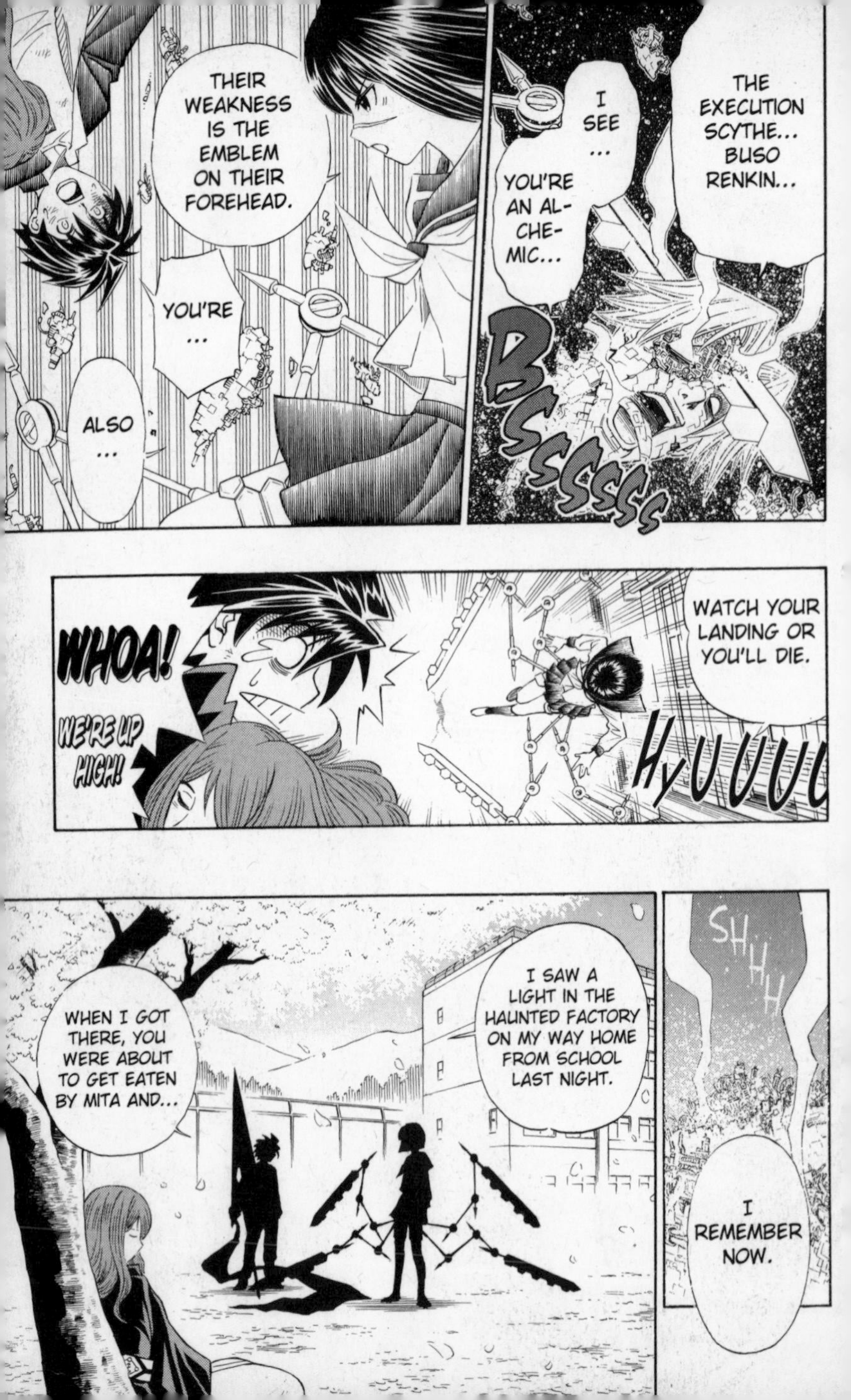
THE EXECUTION SCYTHE... BUSO RENKIN...
I SEE ...
YOU'RE AN AL-CHE-MIC...
BSSSSSS
THEIR WEAKNESS IS THE EMBLEM ON THEIR FOREHEAD.
YOU'RE ...
ALSO ...
WATCH YOUR LANDING OR YOU'LL DIE.
HYUUUU
WHOA!
WE'RE UP HIGH!
SHHH
I REMEMBER NOW.
I SAW A LIGHT IN THE HAUNTED FACTORY ON MY WAY HOME FROM SCHOOL LAST NIGHT.
WHEN I GOT THERE, YOU WERE ABOUT TO GET EATEN BY MITA AND...

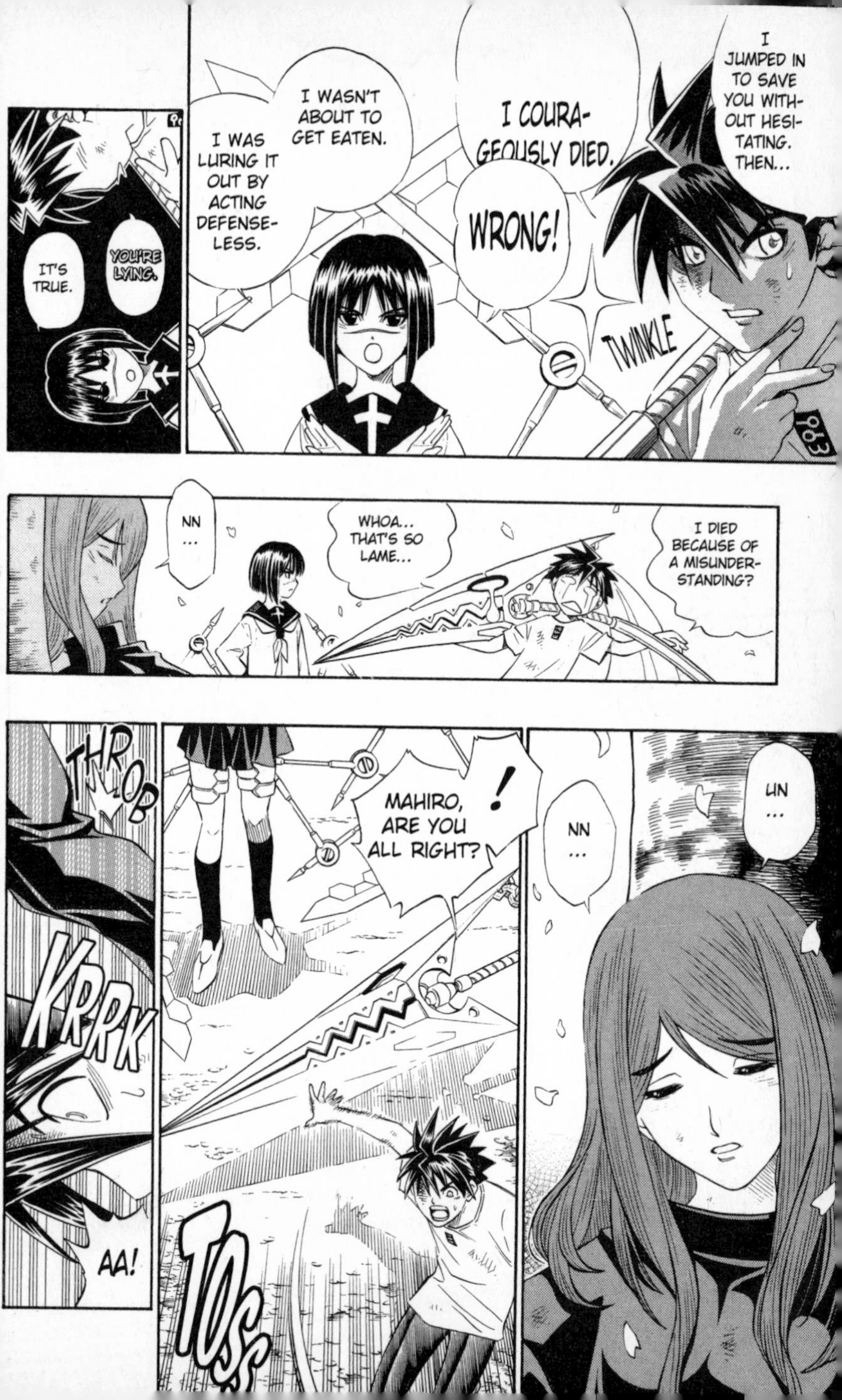

I JUMPED IN TO SAVE YOU WITH-OUT HESI-TATING. THEN...
I COURA-GEOUSLY DIED.
WRONG!
TWINKLE
I WASN'T ABOUT TO GET EATEN.
I WAS LURING IT OUT BY ACTING DEFENSE-LESS.
YOU'RE LYING.
IT'S TRUE.
I DIED BECAUSE OF A MISUNDER-STANDING?
WHOA... THAT'S SO LAME...
NN ...
UN ...
NN ...
!
MAHIRO, ARE YOU ALL RIGHT?
TOSS
THROB
KRRK
AA!

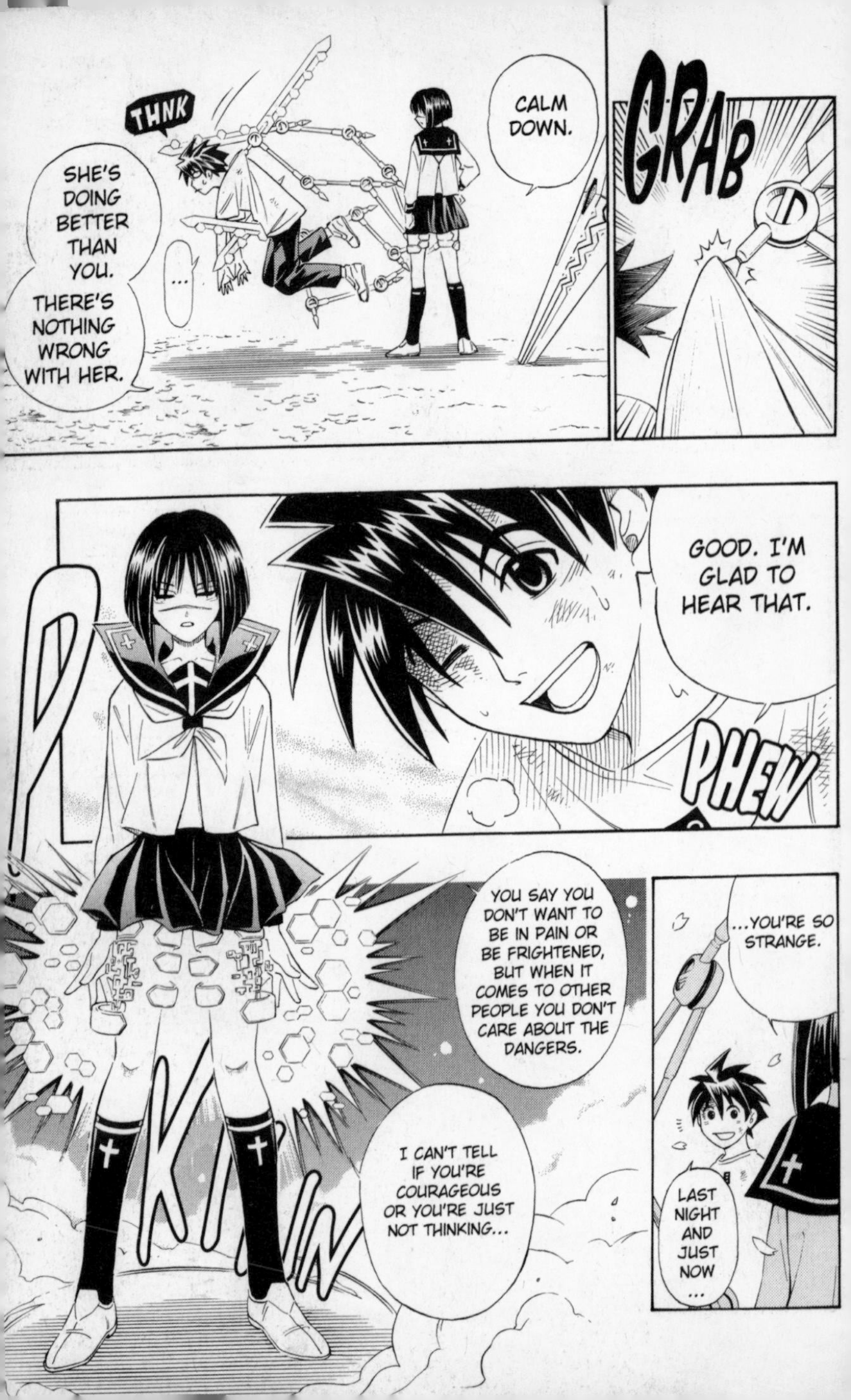
GRAB
CALM DOWN.
THNK
SHE'S DOING BETTER THAN YOU.
THERE'S NOTHING WRONG WITH HER.
...
GOOD. I'M GLAD TO HEAR THAT.
PHEW
...YOU'RE SO STRANGE.
LAST NIGHT AND JUST NOW...
YOU SAY YOU DON'T WANT TO BE IN PAIN OR BE FRIGHTENED, BUT WHEN IT COMES TO OTHER PEOPLE YOU DON'T CARE ABOUT THE DANGERS.
I CAN'T TELL IF YOU'RE COURAGEOUS OR YOU'RE JUST NOT THINKING...

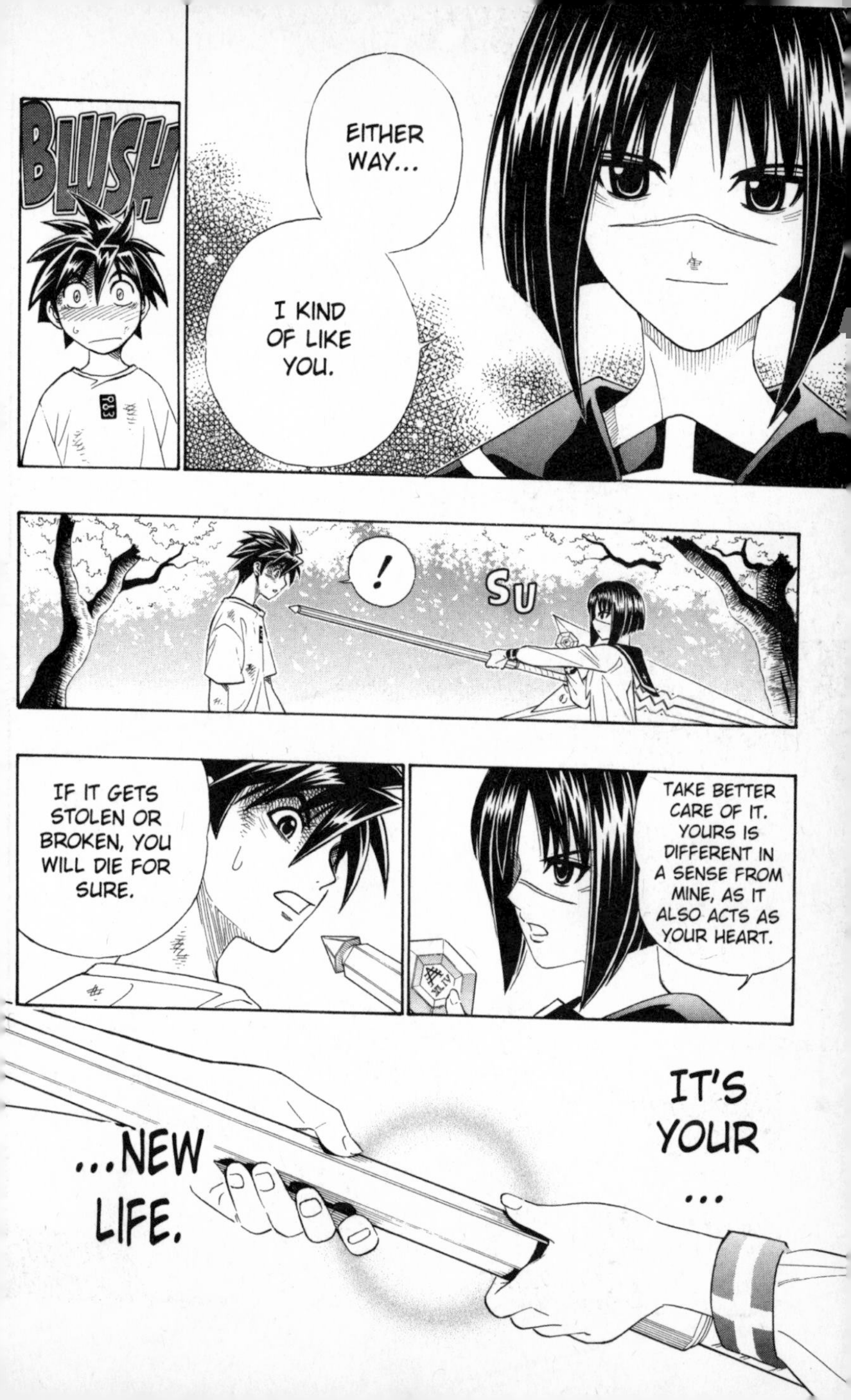

EITHER WAY...
I KIND OF LIKE YOU.
BLUSH
SU
!
TAKE BETTER CARE OF IT. YOURS IS DIFFERENT IN A SENSE FROM MINE, AS IT ALSO ACTS AS YOUR HEART.
IF IT GETS STOLEN OR BROKEN, YOU WILL DIE FOR SURE.
IT'S YOUR ...
...NEW LIFE.

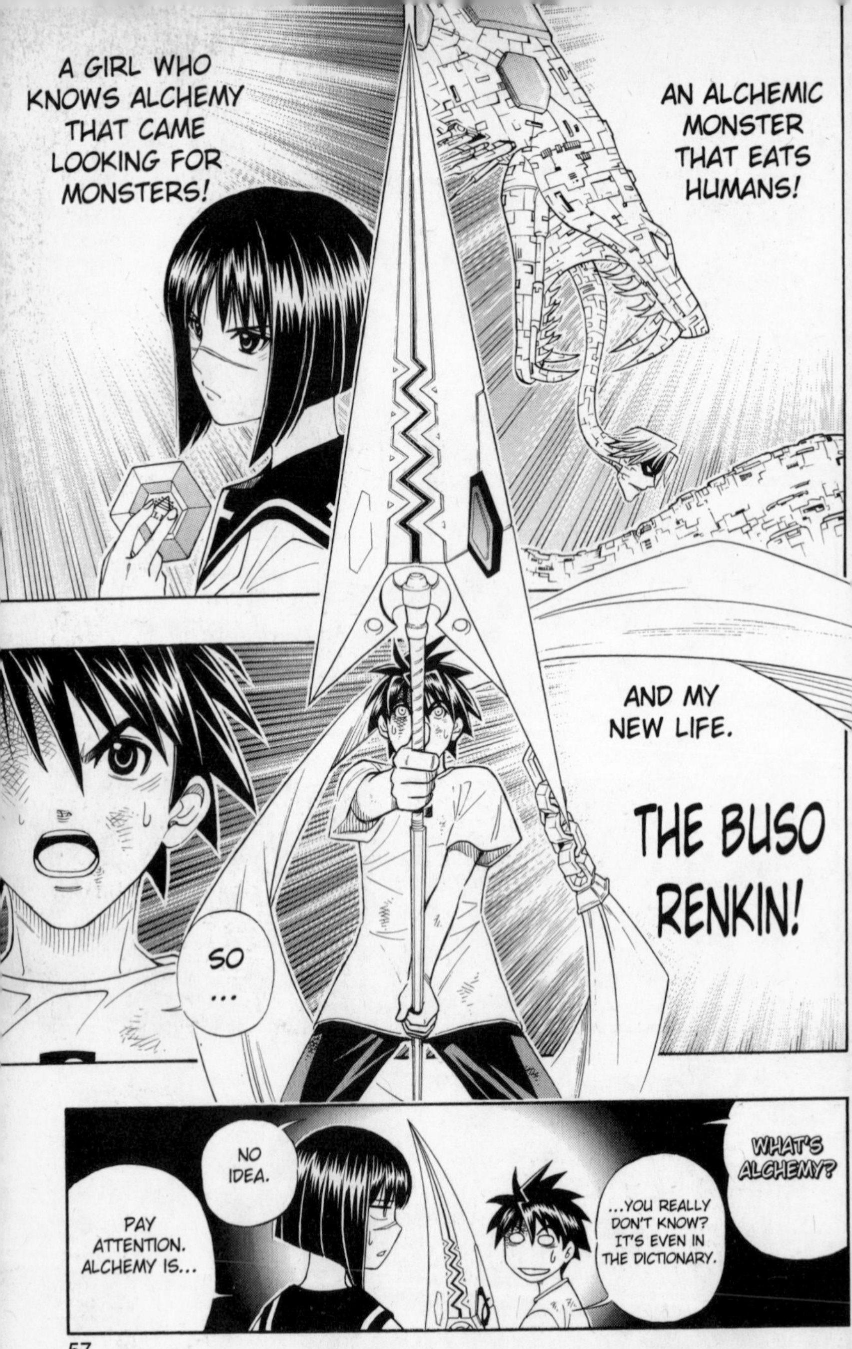
AN ALCHEMIC MONSTER THAT EATS HUMANS!
A GIRL WHO KNOWS ALCHEMY THAT CAME LOOKING FOR MONSTERS!
AND MY NEW LIFE.
THE BUSO RENKIN!
SO ...
WHAT'S ALCHEMY?
...YOU REALLY DON'T KNOW? IT'S EVEN IN THE DICTIONARY.
NO IDEA.
PAY ATTENTION. ALCHEMY IS...

Character File No. 1

Kazuki Muto

- Height: 170 cm; Weight: 59kg
- Born: December 1st; Sagittarius; Blood type: O; 16 years old
- Favorites: Curry rice, green veggie juice, golden yellow color, older women
- Dislikes: Shitake mushrooms, math
- Hobby: Reading manga
- Things he is good at: A lot of things ("No point in hiding it now! I'm a Master of XYZ!")
- Affiliation: Private Ginsei Academy 2nd Year High School Student (Classroom B) E Dorm resident

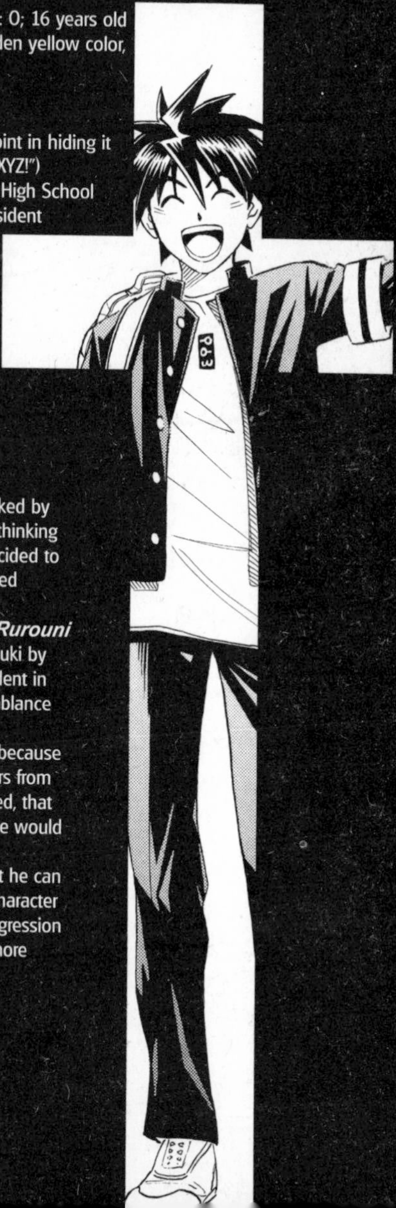

Author's Notes

- He is a character who will grow and be liked by people. It was difficult to draw him while thinking of him as the main character. Instead I decided to go back and use all the characters I enjoyed drawing as his base.
- For some reason Misao Harumachi from ***Rurouni Kenshin*** stood out. I conceptualized Kazuki by imaging Misao as a male high school student in the present. (You can still see some resemblance in his bangs.)
- The reason he's a bit of a space cadet is because I was thinking about mainstream characters from various recent Shonen manga. I also figured, that between a space cadet and a joker, people would prefer the space cadet more.
- He doesn't like pain and being scared, but he can act tough in order to protect others. This character makes me feel like I want to draw the progression of how he grows stronger and becomes more caring while at times feeling hesitant.

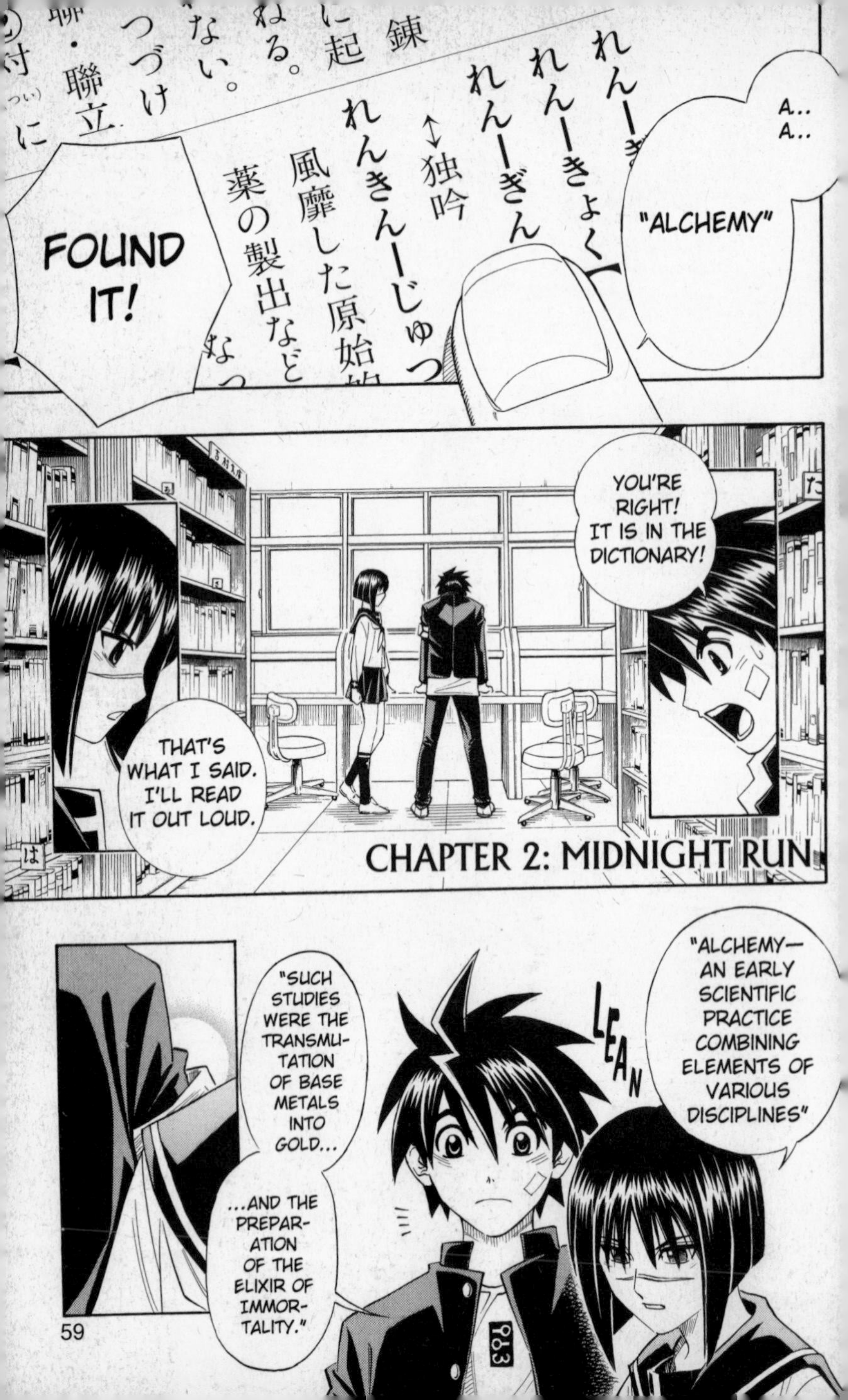
A... A...
"ALCHEMY"
FOUND IT!
YOU'RE RIGHT! IT IS IN THE DICTIONARY!
THAT'S WHAT I SAID. I'LL READ IT OUT LOUD.
CHAPTER 2: MIDNIGHT RUN
"ALCHEMY—AN EARLY SCIENTIFIC PRACTICE COMBINING ELEMENTS OF VARIOUS DISCIPLINES"
LEAN
"SUCH STUDIES WERE THE TRANSMUTATION OF BASE METALS INTO GOLD...
...AND THE PREPARATION OF THE ELIXIR OF IMMORTALITY."

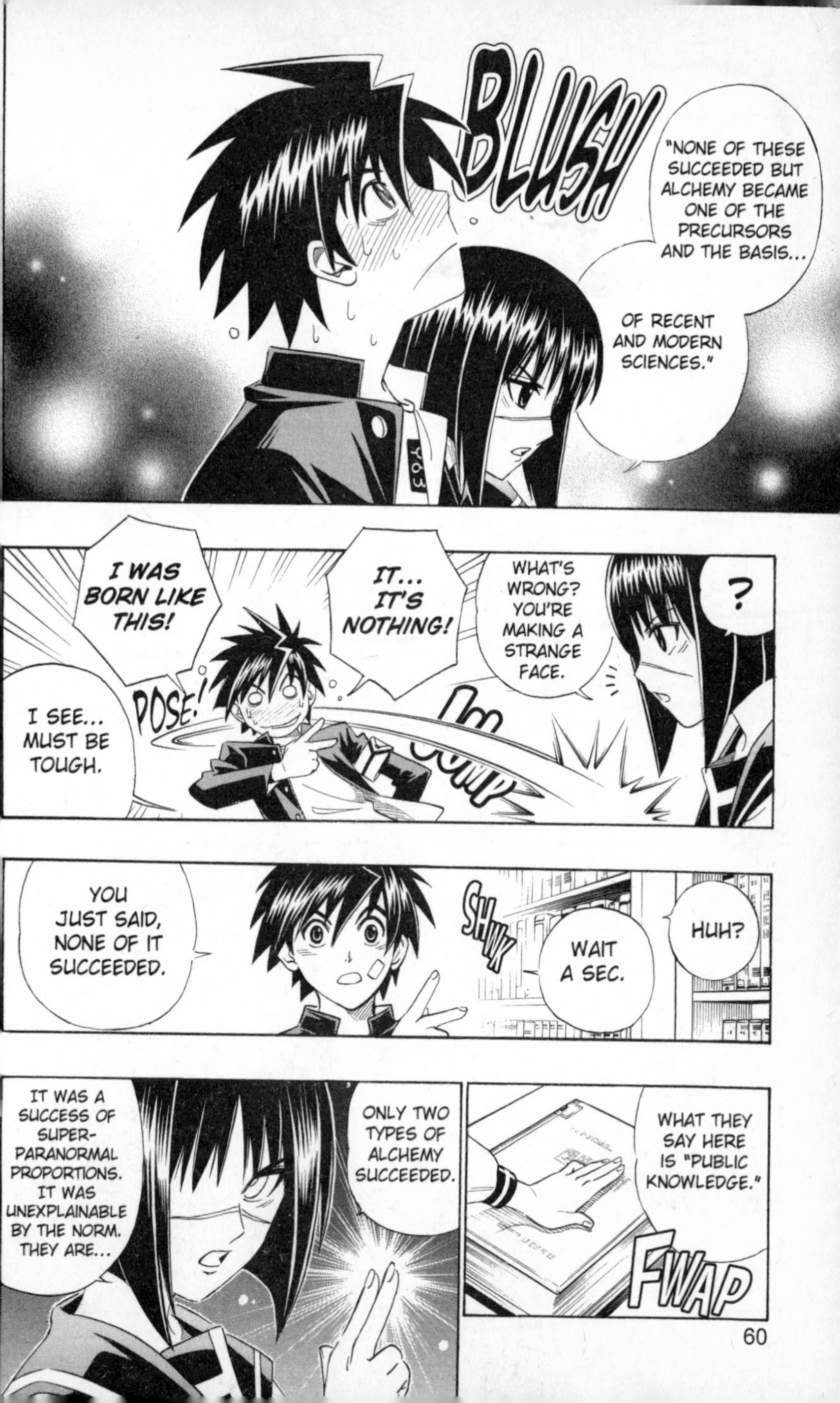
"NONE OF THESE SUCCEEDED BUT ALCHEMY BECAME ONE OF THE PRECURSORS AND THE BASIS...
OF RECENT AND MODERN SCIENCES."
BLUSH
?
WHAT'S WRONG? YOU'RE MAKING A STRANGE FACE.
IT... IT'S NOTHING!
I WAS BORN LIKE THIS!
POSE!
I SEE... MUST BE TOUGH.
HUH?
WAIT A SEC.
YOU JUST SAID, NONE OF IT SUCCEEDED.
WHAT THEY SAY HERE IS "PUBLIC KNOWLEDGE."
FWAP
ONLY TWO TYPES OF ALCHEMY SUCCEEDED.
IT WAS A SUCCESS OF SUPER-PARANORMAL PROPORTIONS. IT WAS UNEXPLAINABLE BY THE NORM. THEY ARE...

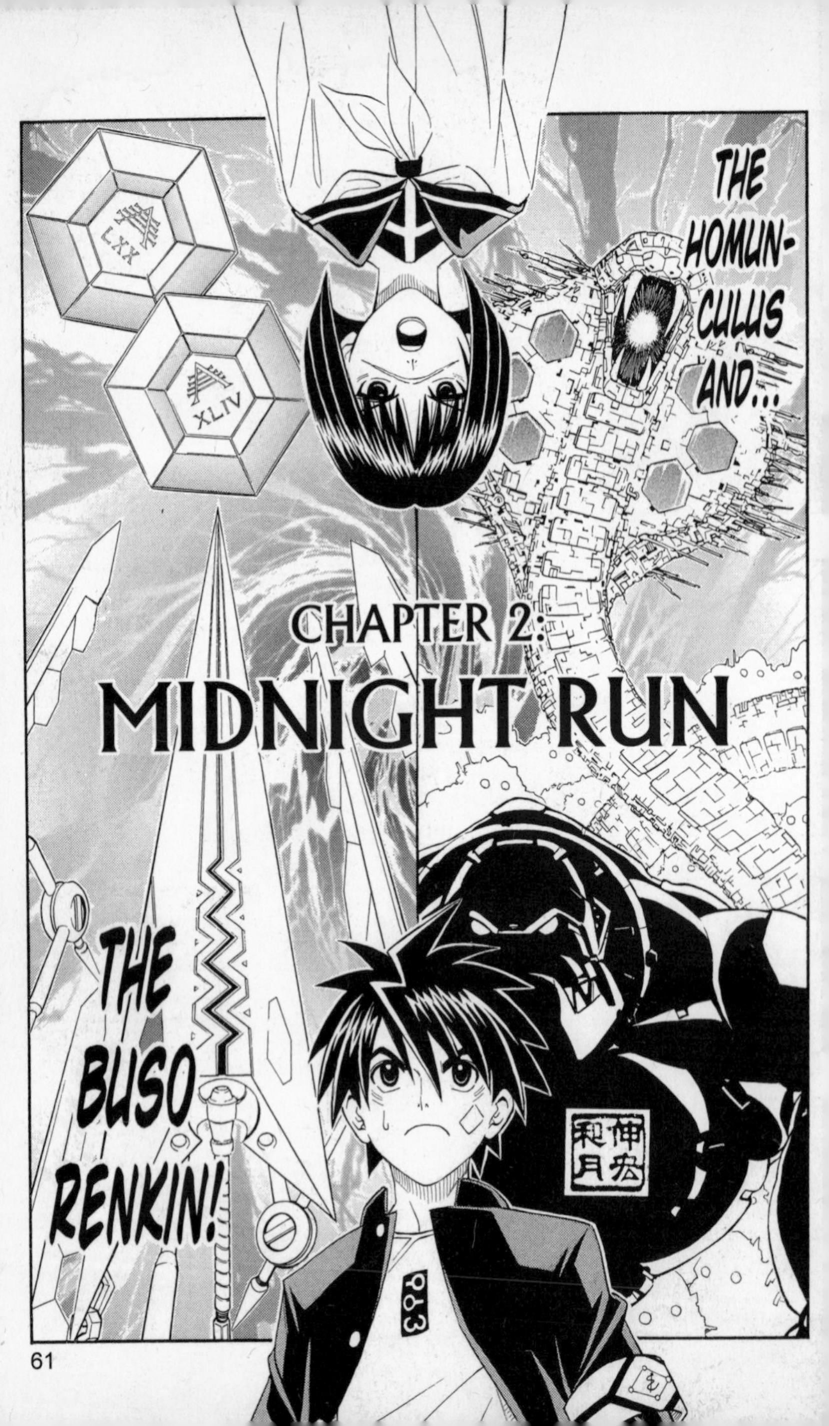
THE HOMUN-CULUS AND...
LXX
XLIV
CHAPTER 2:
MIDNIGHT RUN
THE BUSO RENKIN!

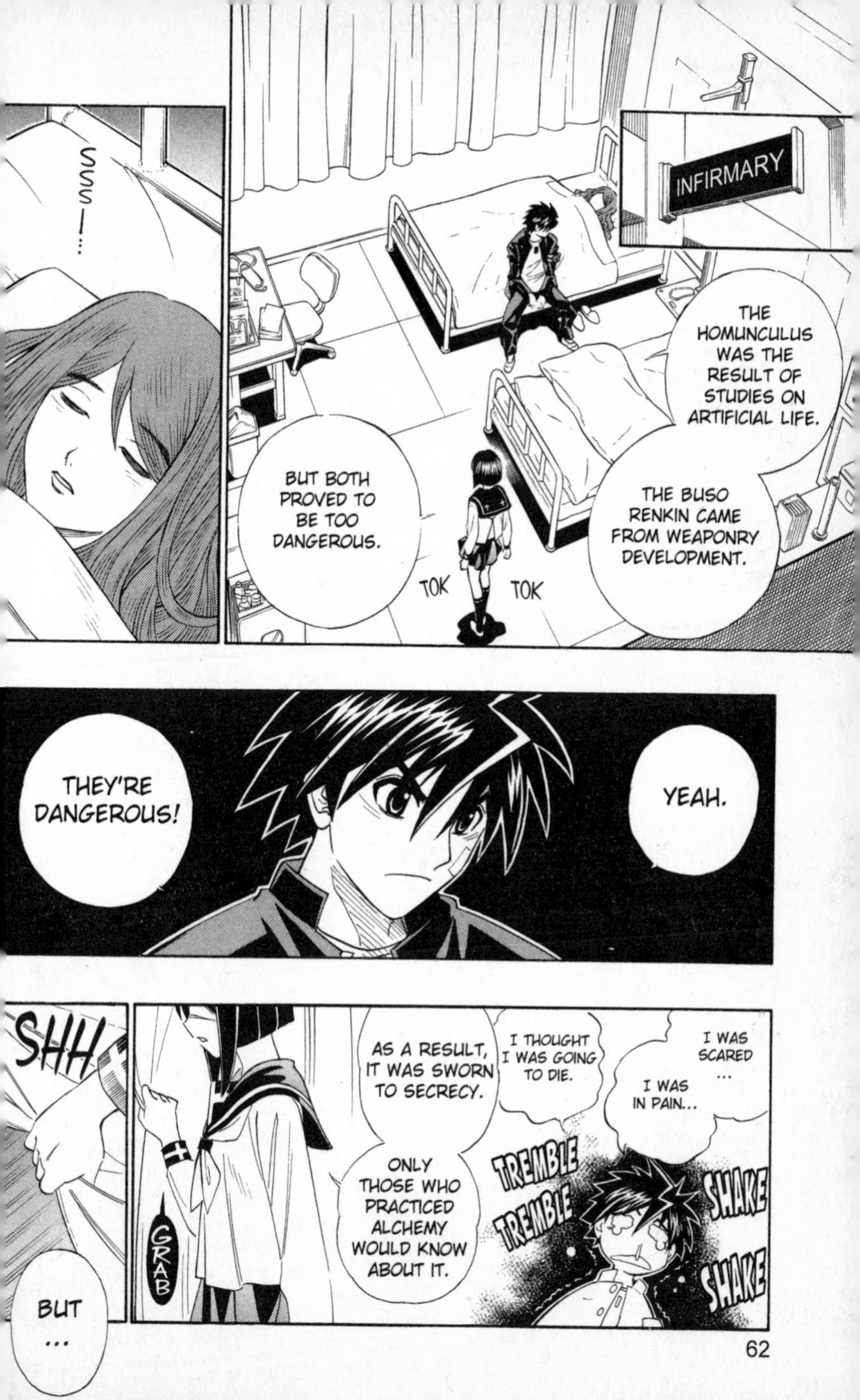
INFIRMARY
THE HOMUNCULUS WAS THE RESULT OF STUDIES ON ARTIFICIAL LIFE.
THE BUSO RENKIN CAME FROM WEAPONRY DEVELOPMENT.
BUT BOTH PROVED TO BE TOO DANGEROUS.
TOK
TOK
SSS—!...
YEAH.
THEY'RE DANGEROUS!
I WAS SCARED ...
I WAS IN PAIN...
I THOUGHT I WAS GOING TO DIE.
SHAKE
SHAKE
TREMBLE
TREMBLE
AS A RESULT, IT WAS SWORN TO SECRECY.
ONLY THOSE WHO PRACTICED ALCHEMY WOULD KNOW ABOUT IT.
GRAB
SHH
BUT ...

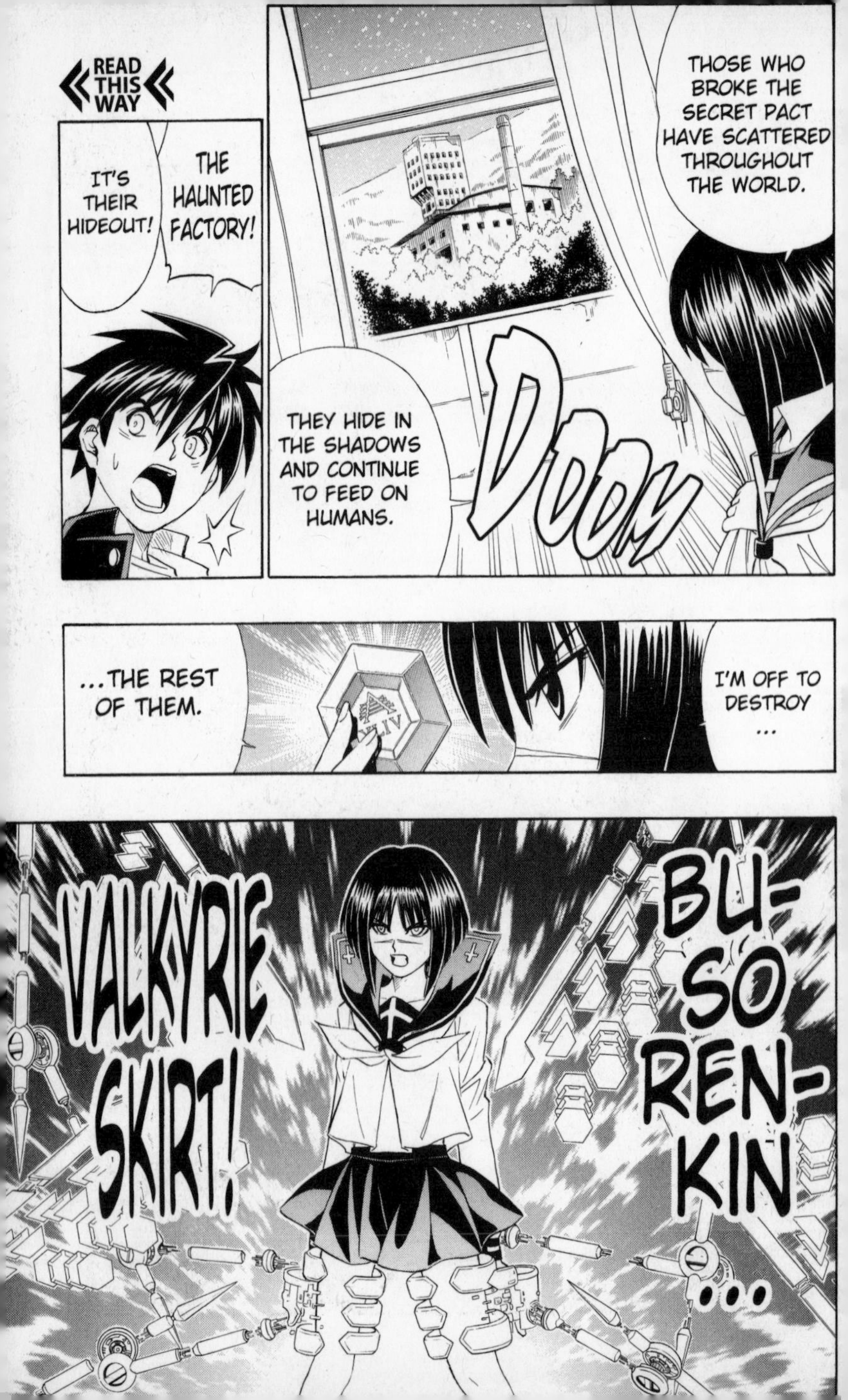
READ THIS WAY
THOSE WHO BROKE THE SECRET PACT HAVE SCATTERED THROUGHOUT THE WORLD.
THEY HIDE IN THE SHADOWS AND CONTINUE TO FEED ON HUMANS.
DOOM
THE HAUNTED FACTORY!
IT'S THEIR HIDEOUT!
I'M OFF TO DESTROY ...
...THE REST OF THEM.
BU-SO REN-KIN...
VALKYRIE SKIRT!

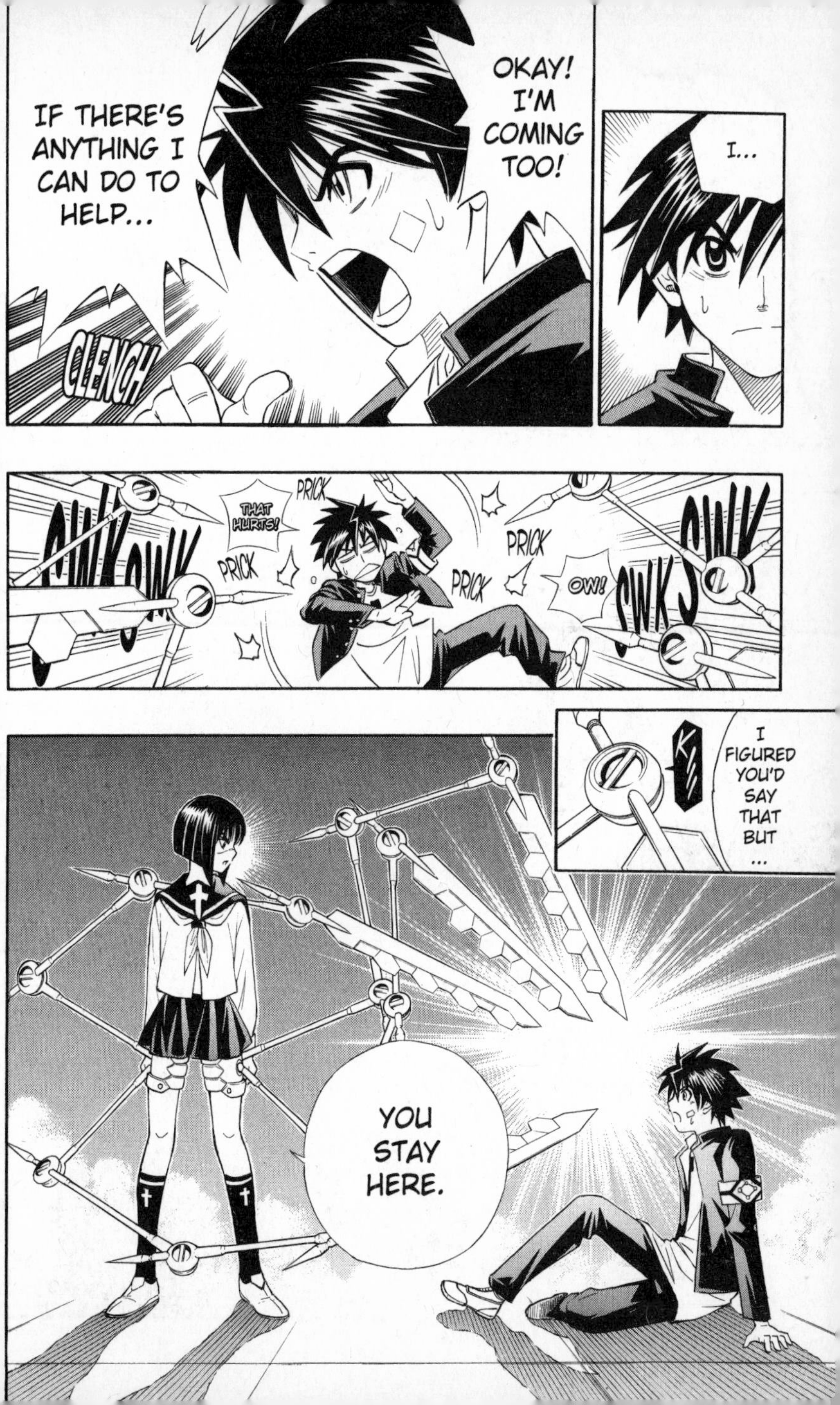
I...
OKAY! I'M COMING TOO!
IF THERE'S ANYTHING I CAN DO TO HELP...
CLENCH
SWK SWK
OW!
PRICK
PRICK
THAT HURTS!
PRICK
PRICK
SWK SWK
I FIGURED YOU'D SAY THAT BUT ...
YOU STAY HERE.

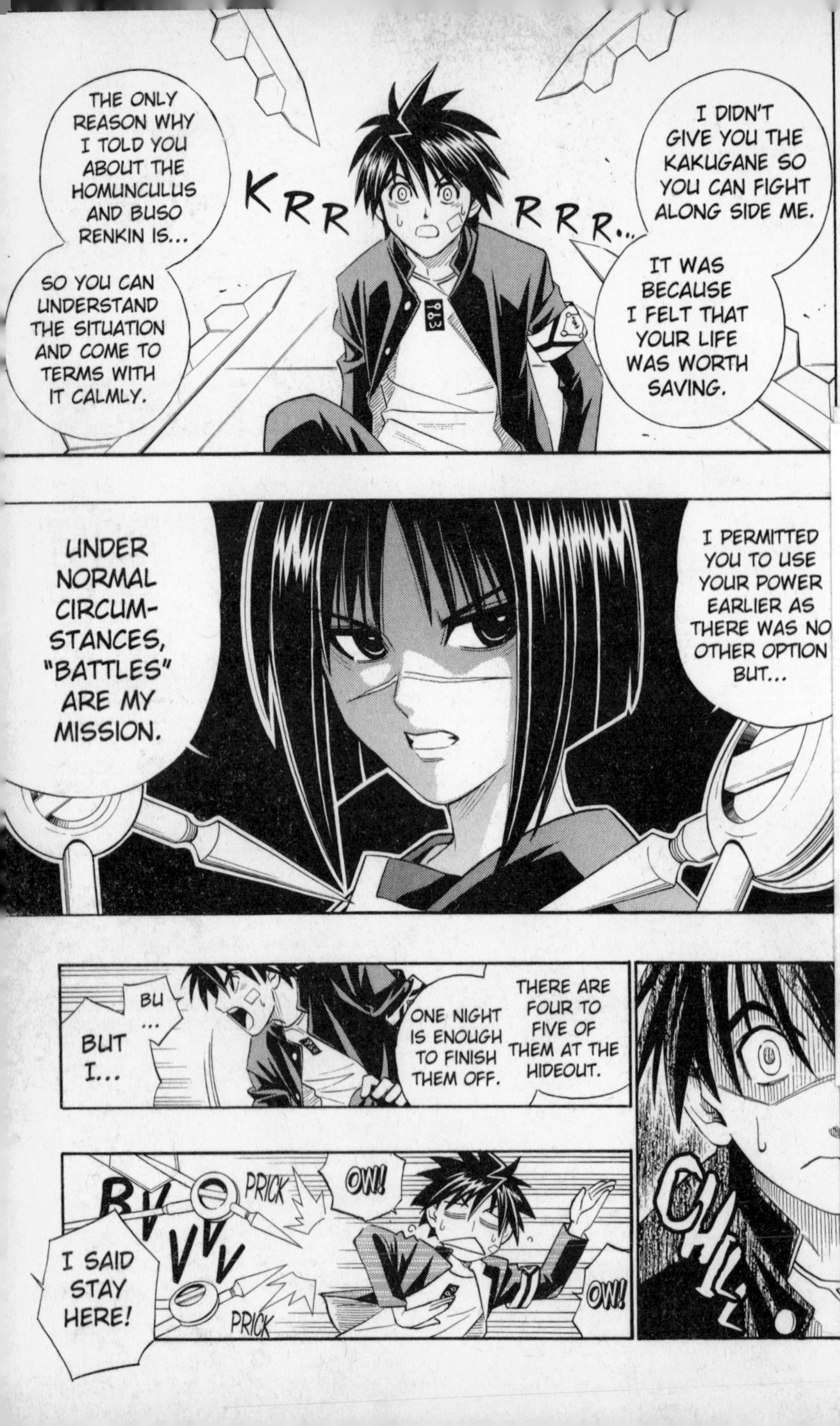
I DIDN'T GIVE YOU THE KAKUGANE SO YOU CAN FIGHT ALONG SIDE ME.
IT WAS BECAUSE I FELT THAT YOUR LIFE WAS WORTH SAVING.
KRRR RRR...
THE ONLY REASON WHY I TOLD YOU ABOUT THE HOMUNCULUS AND BUSO RENKIN IS...
SO YOU CAN UNDERSTAND THE SITUATION AND COME TO TERMS WITH IT CALMLY.
I PERMITTED YOU TO USE YOUR POWER EARLIER AS THERE WAS NO OTHER OPTION BUT...
UNDER NORMAL CIRCUM-STANCES, "BATTLES" ARE MY MISSION.
CHILL.
THERE ARE FOUR TO FIVE OF THEM AT THE HIDEOUT.
ONE NIGHT IS ENOUGH TO FINISH THEM OFF.
BU...
BUT I...
OW!
PRICK
BVVVV
I SAID STAY HERE!
OW!
PRICK

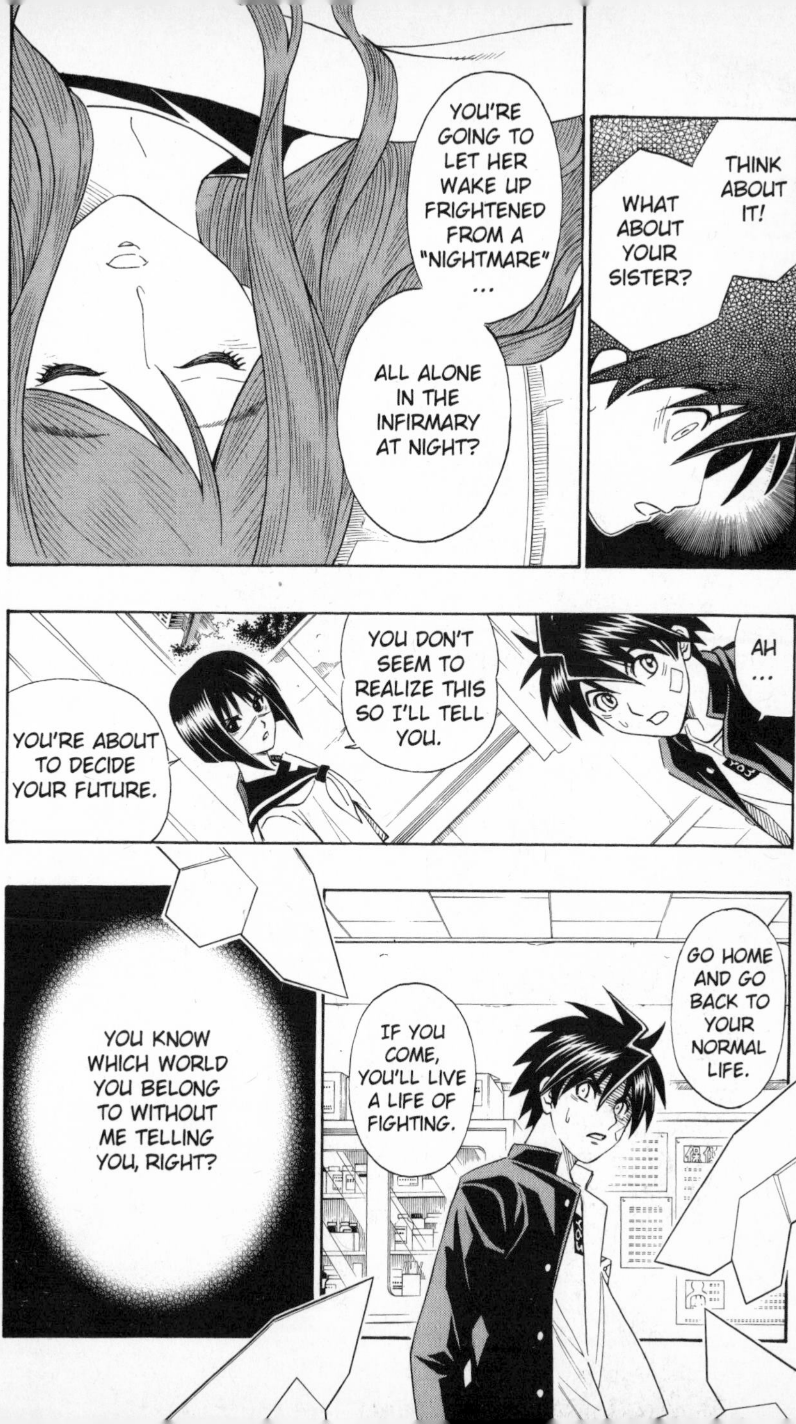
THINK ABOUT IT!
WHAT ABOUT YOUR SISTER?
YOU'RE GOING TO LET HER WAKE UP FRIGHTENED FROM A "NIGHTMARE"...
ALL ALONE IN THE INFIRMARY AT NIGHT?
AH...
YOU DON'T SEEM TO REALIZE THIS SO I'LL TELL YOU.
YOU'RE ABOUT TO DECIDE YOUR FUTURE.
GO HOME AND GO BACK TO YOUR NORMAL LIFE.
IF YOU COME, YOU'LL LIVE A LIFE OF FIGHTING.
YOU KNOW WHICH WORLD YOU BELONG TO WITHOUT ME TELLING YOU, RIGHT?

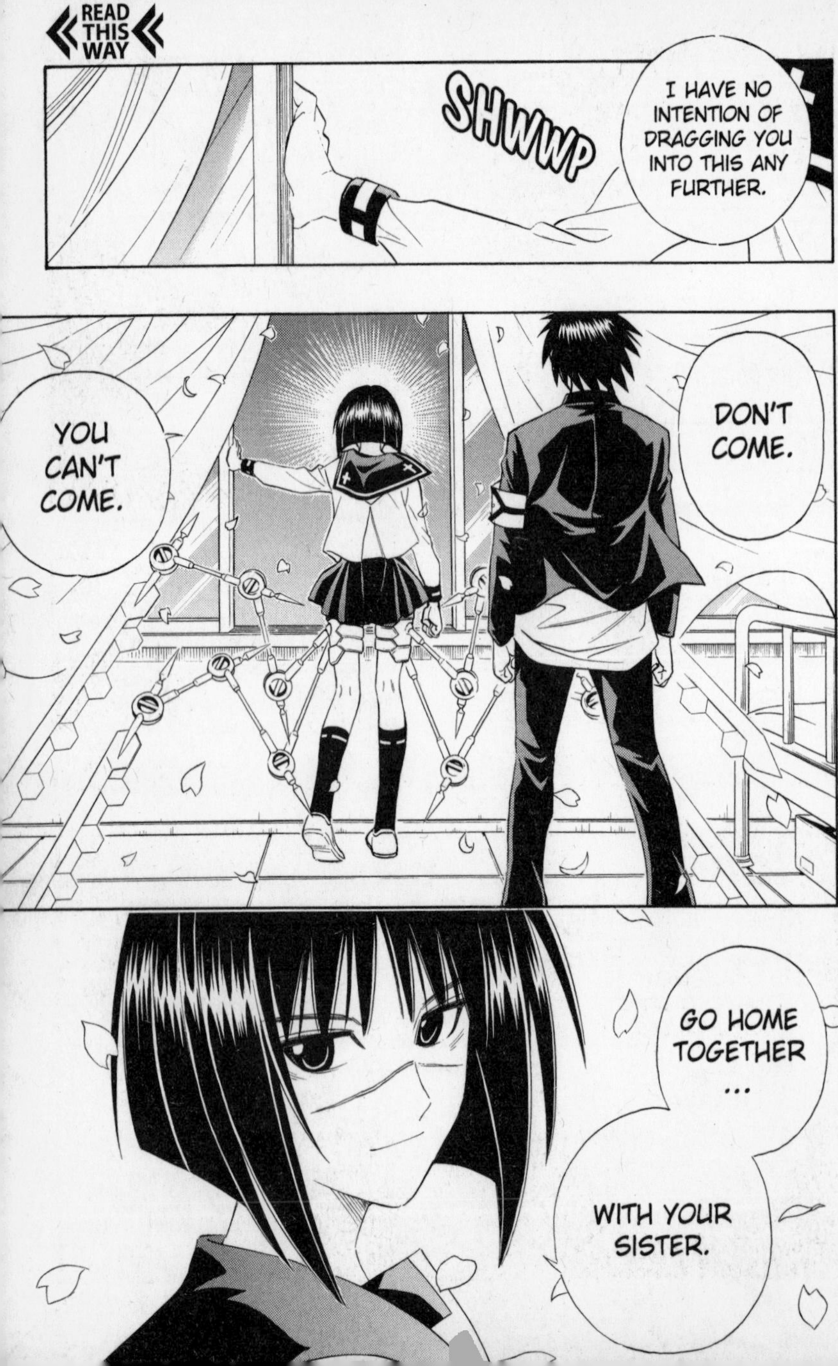
READ THIS WAY
I HAVE NO INTENTION OF DRAGGING YOU INTO THIS ANY FURTHER.
SHWWP
DON'T COME.
YOU CAN'T COME.
GO HOME TOGETHER ...
WITH YOUR SISTER.

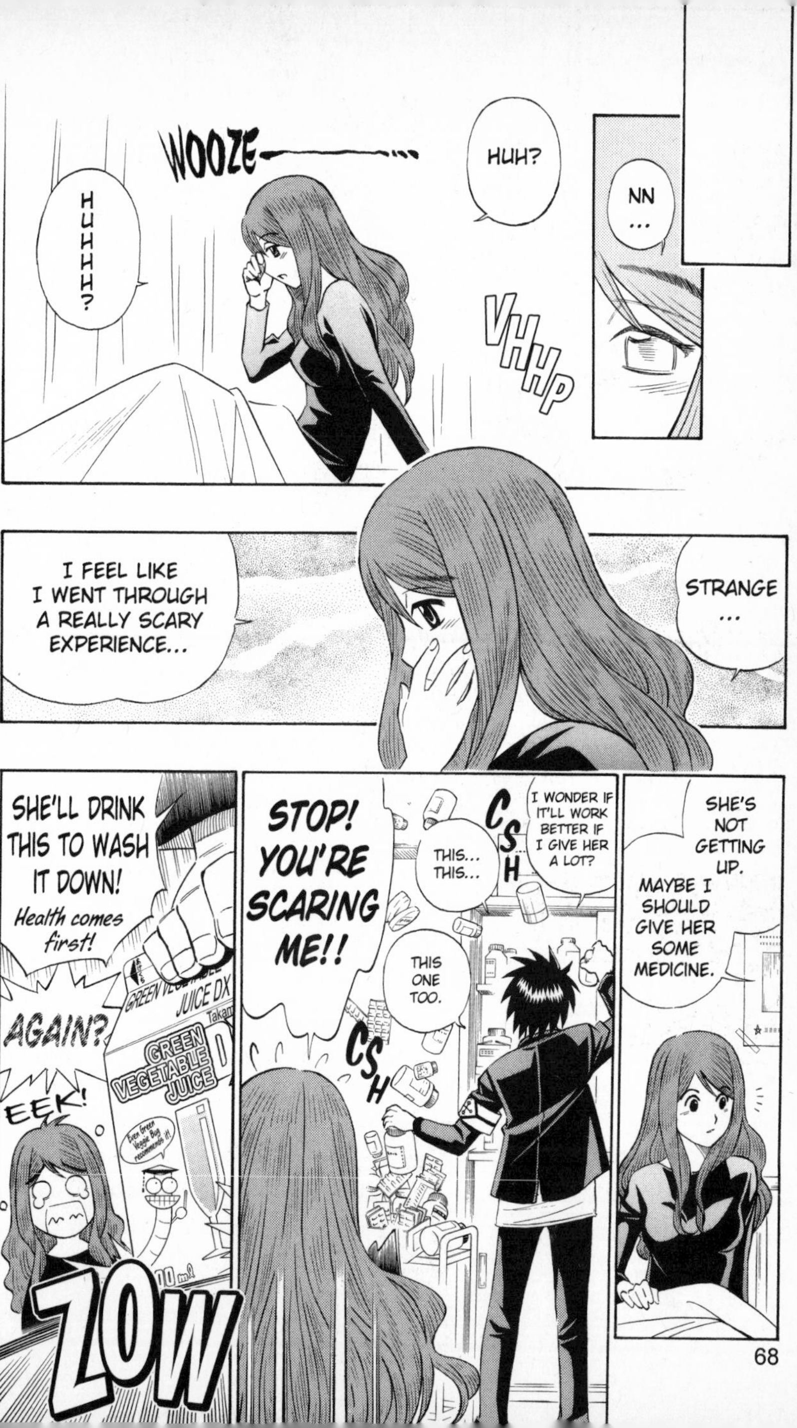

NN ...
VHHP
HUH?
WOOZE
HUHHH?
STRANGE ...
I FEEL LIKE I WENT THROUGH A REALLY SCARY EXPERIENCE...
SHE'S NOT GETTING UP.
MAYBE I SHOULD GIVE HER SOME MEDICINE.
I WONDER IF IT'LL WORK BETTER IF I GIVE HER A LOT?
CSH
THIS... THIS...
THIS ONE TOO.
CSH
STOP! YOU'RE SCARING ME!!
SHE'LL DRINK THIS TO WASH IT DOWN!
Health comes first!
GREEN VEGETABLE JUICE DX
GREEN VEGETABLE JUICE
Even Green Veggie Bug recommends it!
AGAIN?
EEK!
ZOW

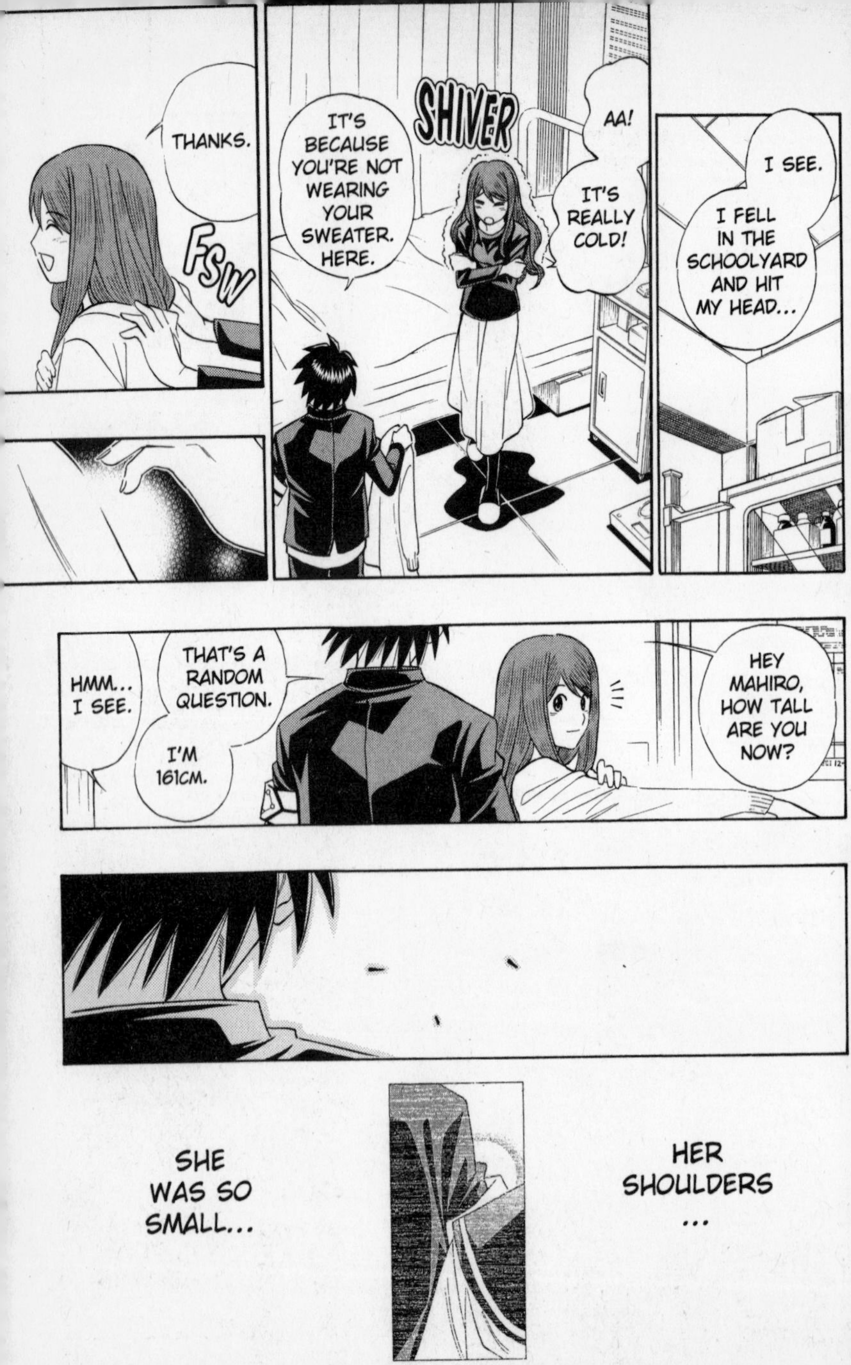
I SEE.
I FELL IN THE SCHOOLYARD AND HIT MY HEAD...
AA!
IT'S REALLY COLD!
SHIVER
IT'S BECAUSE YOU'RE NOT WEARING YOUR SWEATER. HERE.
THANKS.
FSW
HEY MAHIRO, HOW TALL ARE YOU NOW?
THAT'S A RANDOM QUESTION.
I'M 161CM.
HMM... I SEE.
HER SHOULDERS ...
SHE WAS SO SMALL...

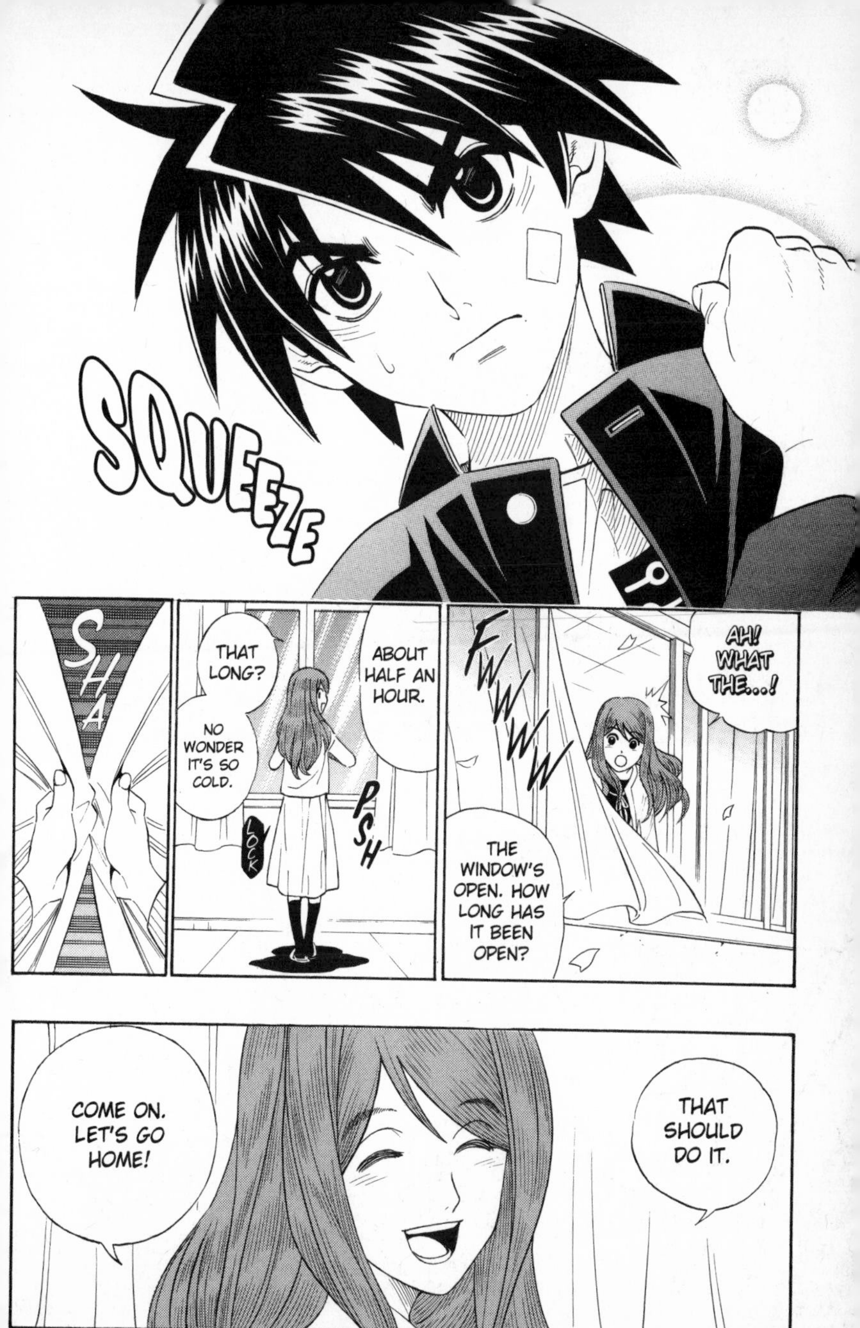
SQUEEZE
AH! WHAT THE...!
FWWWW
THE WINDOW'S OPEN. HOW LONG HAS IT BEEN OPEN?
ABOUT HALF AN HOUR.
THAT LONG?
NO WONDER IT'S SO COLD.
PSH
LOCK
SHA
THAT SHOULD DO IT.
COME ON. LET'S GO HOME!

READ THIS WAY

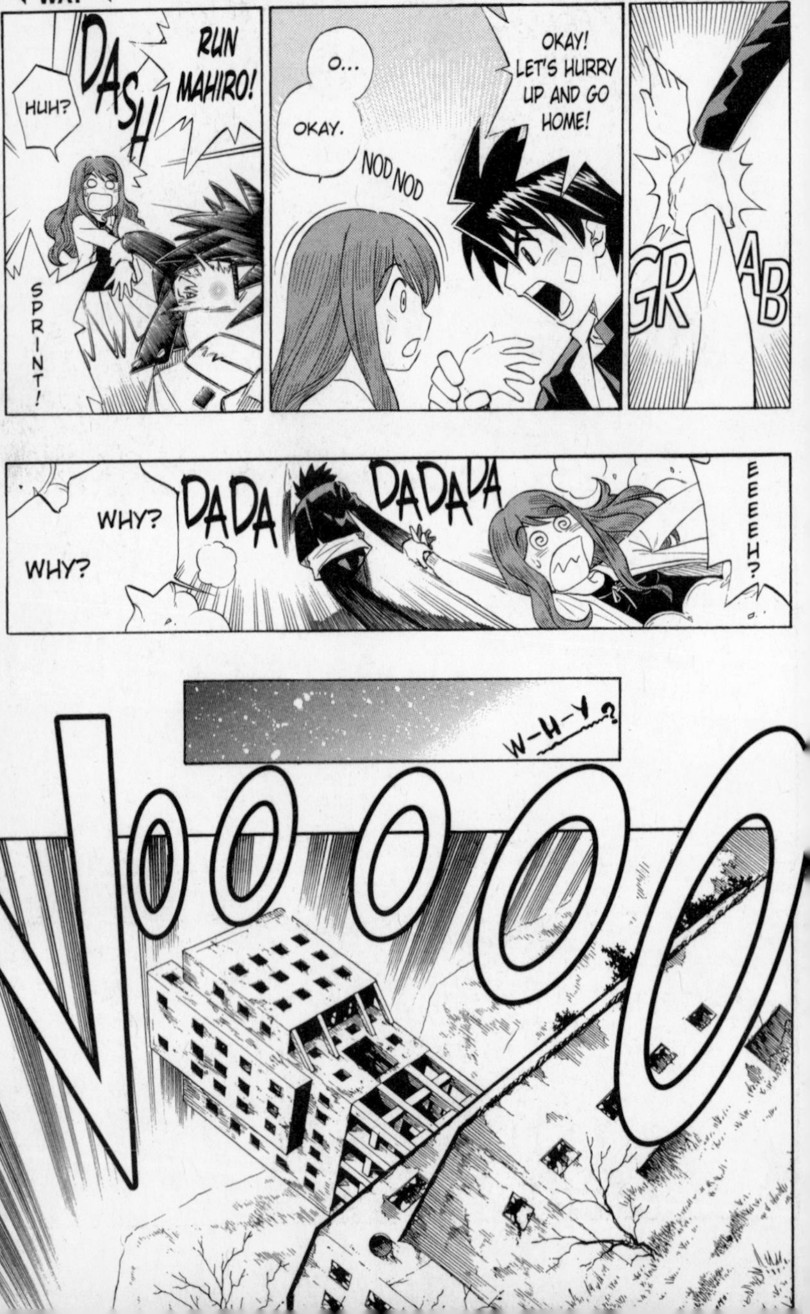

GRAB
OKAY! LET'S HURRY UP AND GO HOME!
O... OKAY.
NOD NOD
RUN MAHIRO!
DASH
HUH?
SPRINT!
EEEEEH?
DADADADA
DADA
WHY?
WHY?
W-H-Y?
NOOOOO

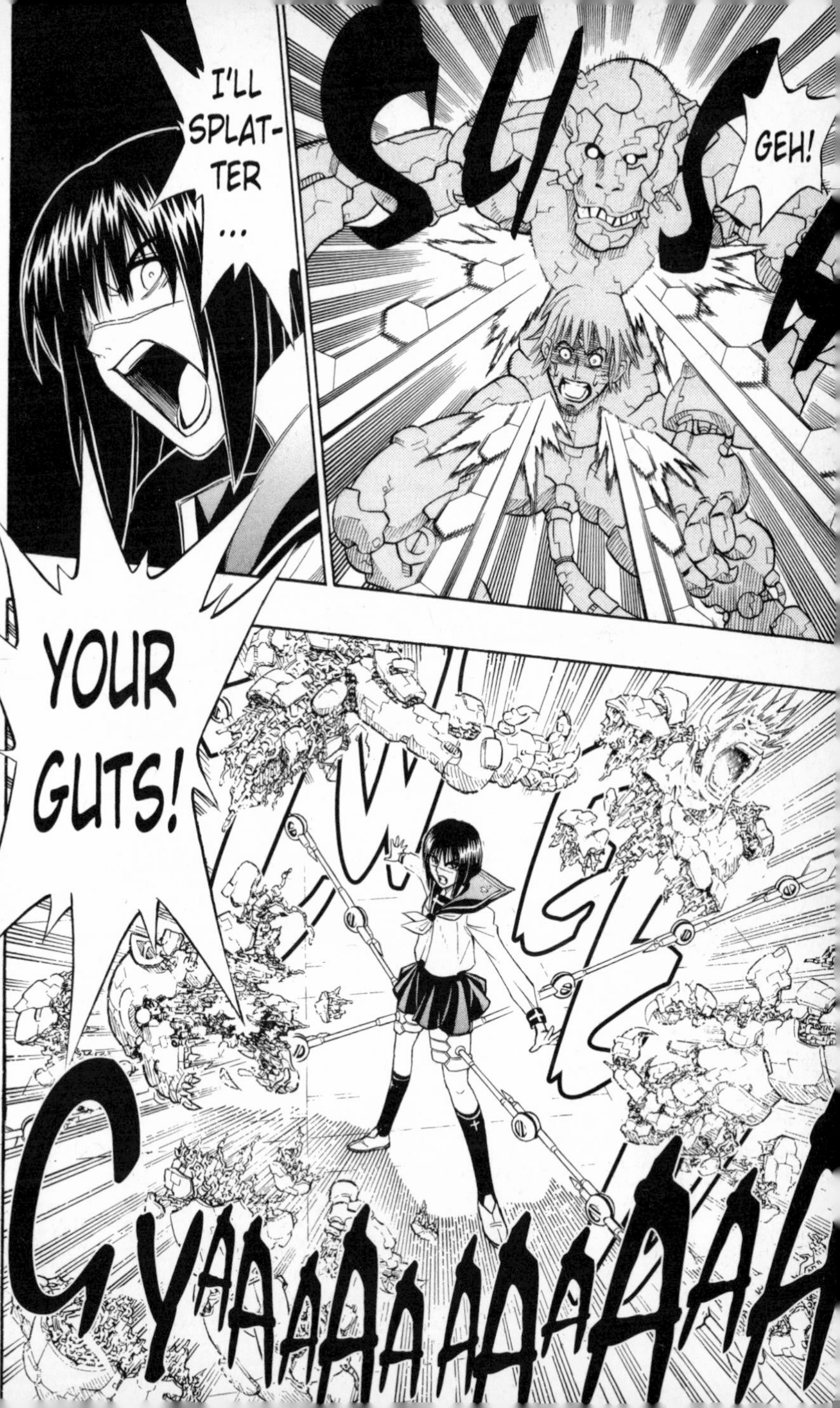
SLISH
GEH!
I'LL SPLATTER...
YOUR GUTS!
GYAAAAAAAAAAH

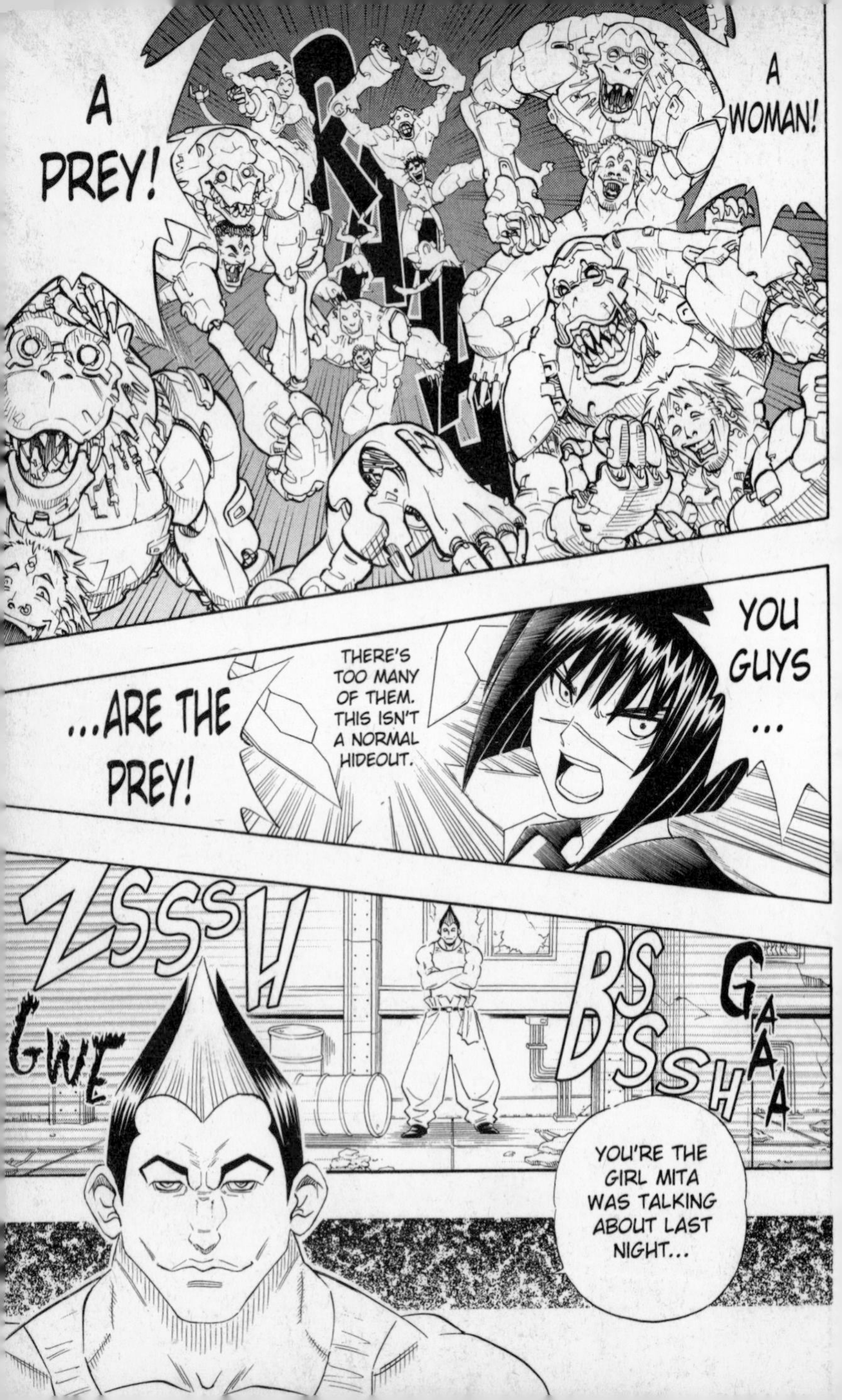
A WOMAN!
A PREY!
YOU GUYS ...
THERE'S TOO MANY OF THEM. THIS ISN'T A NORMAL HIDEOUT.
...ARE THE PREY!
GAAA
BSSSH
YOU'RE THE GIRL MITA WAS TALKING ABOUT LAST NIGHT...
ZSSSH
GWE

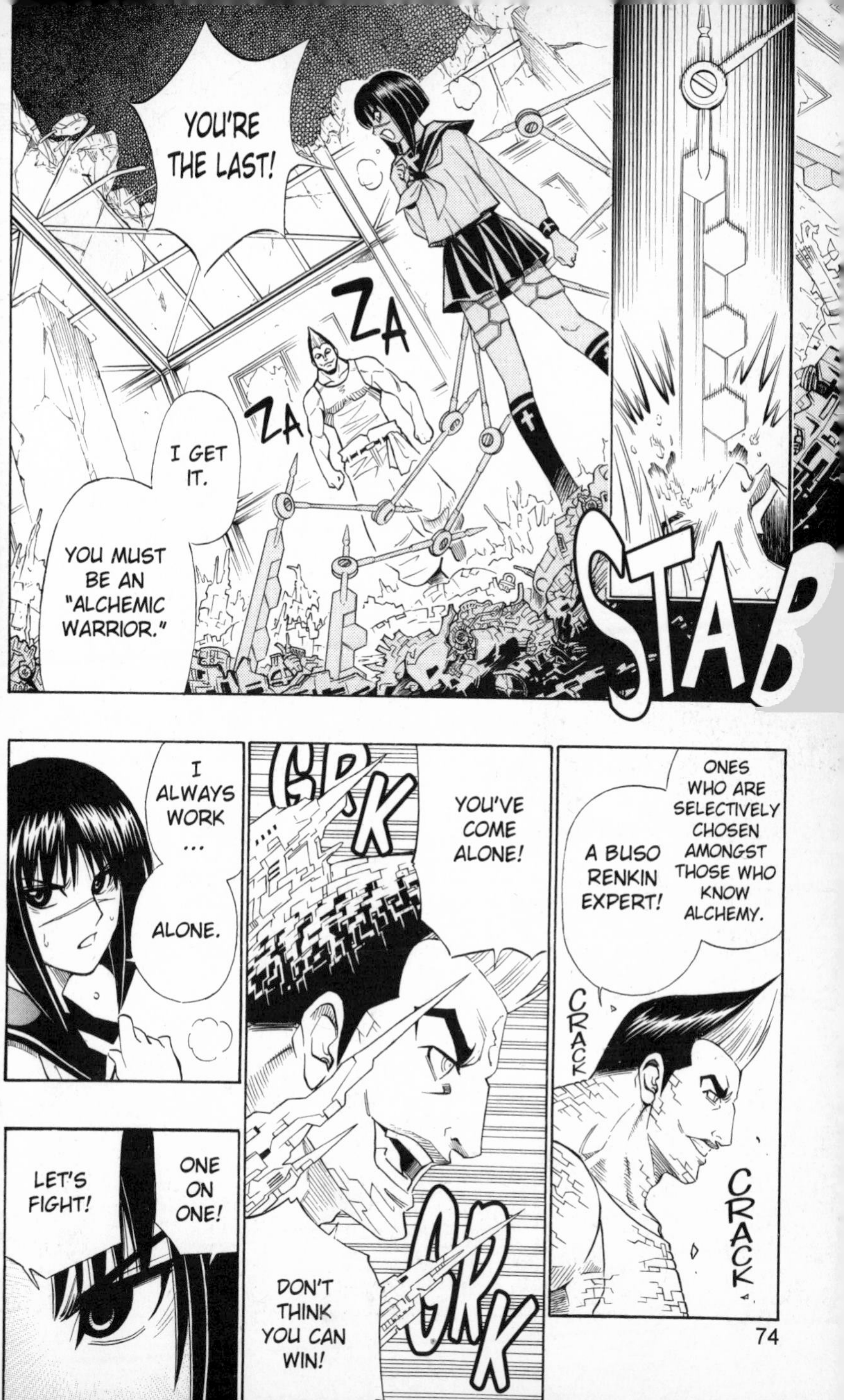
YOU'RE THE LAST!
ZA
ZA
STAB
I GET IT.
YOU MUST BE AN "ALCHEMIC WARRIOR."
ONES WHO ARE SELECTIVELY CHOSEN AMONGST THOSE WHO KNOW ALCHEMY.
A BUSO RENKIN EXPERT!
CRACK
CRACK
YOU'VE COME ALONE!
DON'T THINK YOU CAN WIN!
I ALWAYS WORK ...
ALONE.
ONE ON ONE!
LET'S FIGHT!

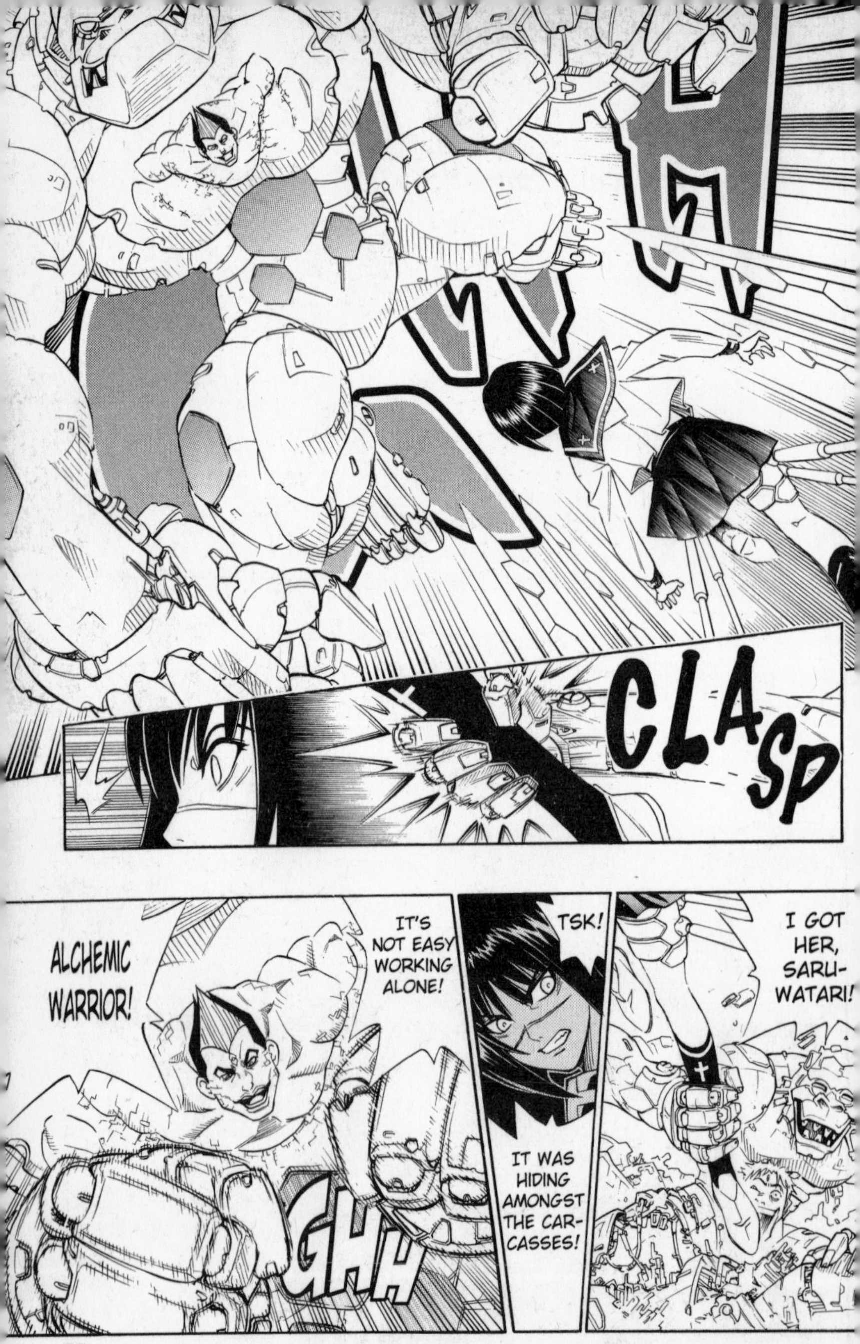
CLASP
I GOT HER, SARU-WATARI!
TSK!
IT WAS HIDING AMONGST THE CAR-CASSES!
IT'S NOT EASY WORKING ALONE!
ALCHEMIC WARRIOR!
GHH

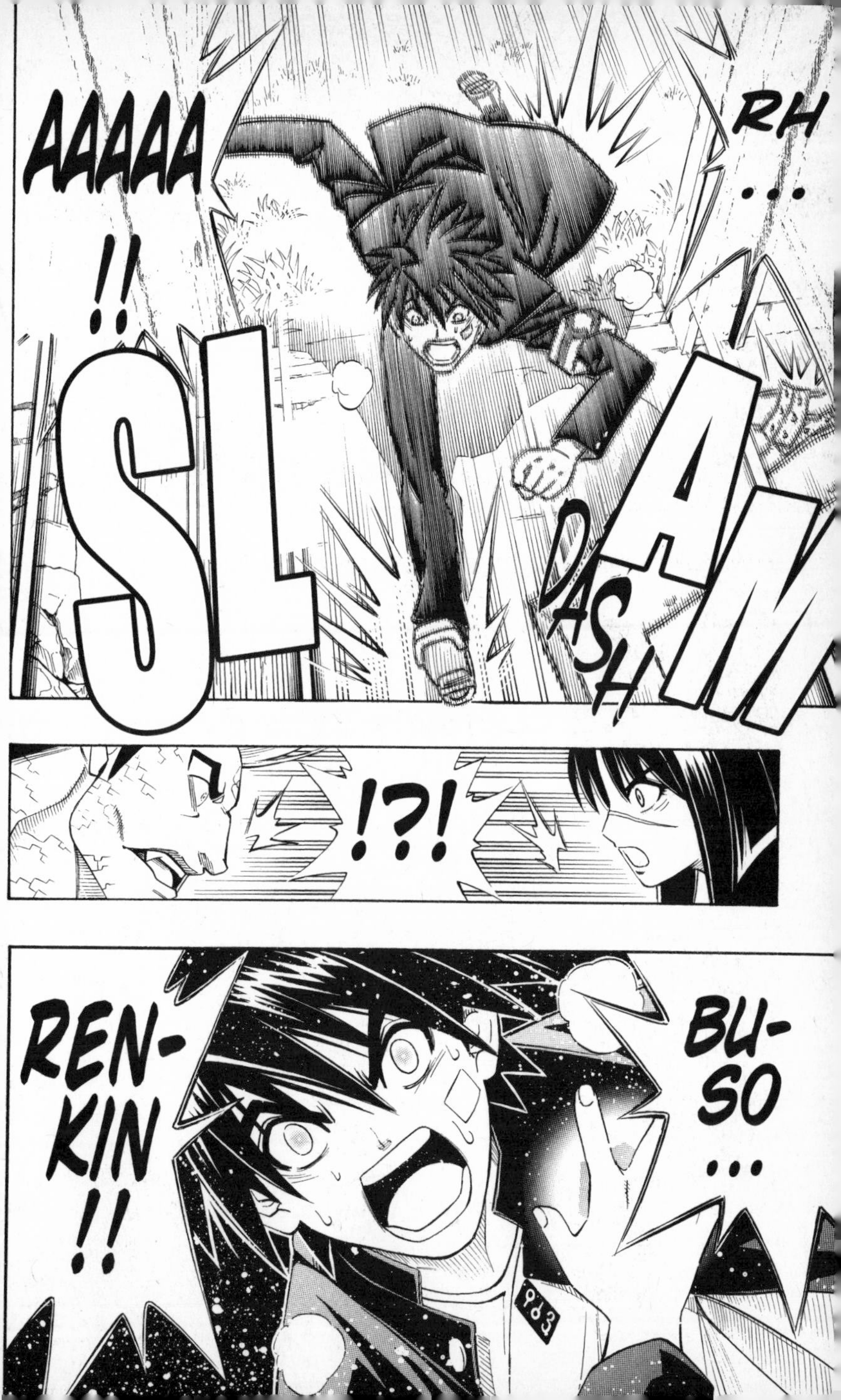
RH...
AAAAA!!
DASH
SLAM
!?!
BU-SO...
REN-KIN!!

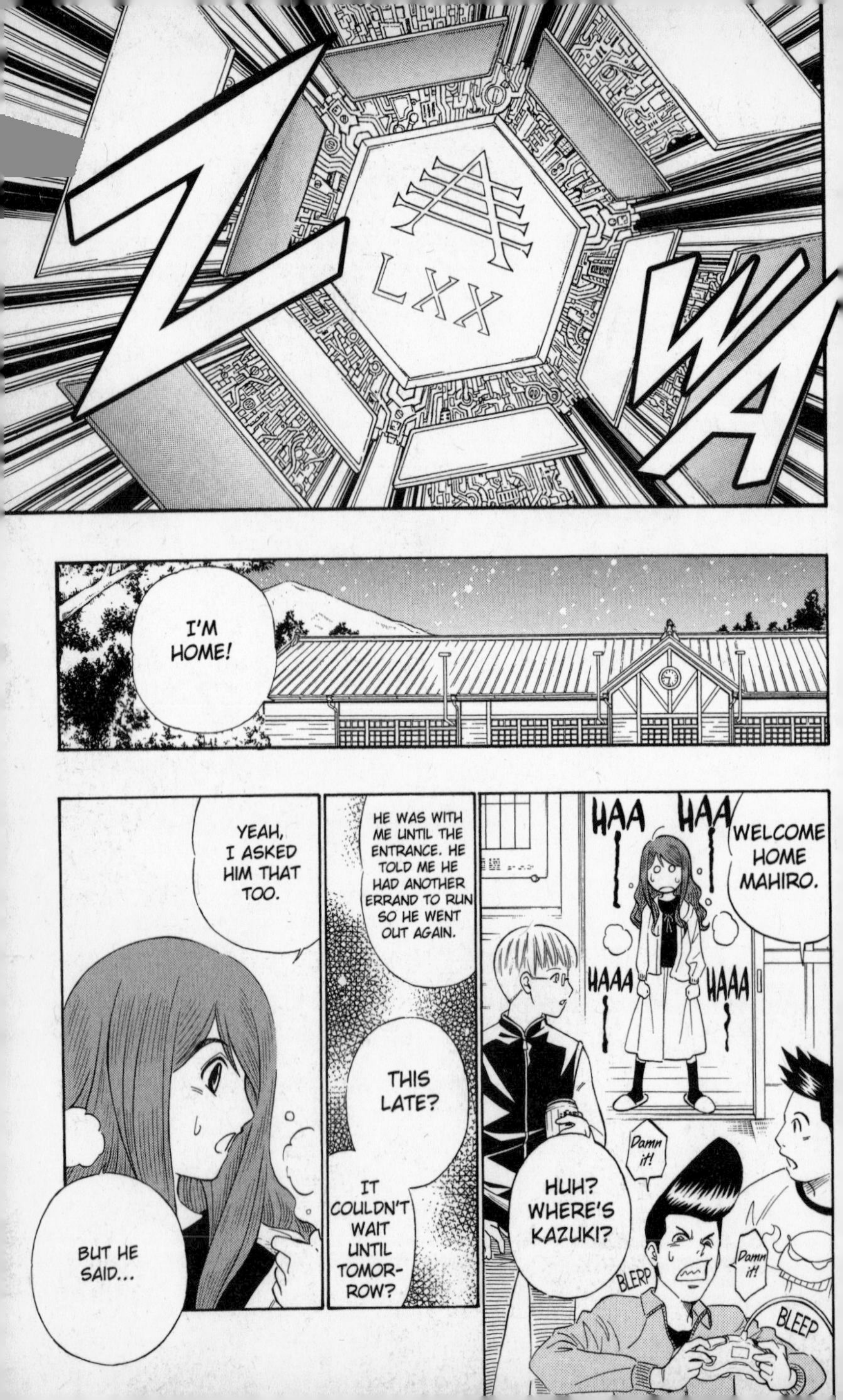
ZWA
I'M HOME!
WELCOME HOME MAHIRO.
HAA HAA
HAAA HAAA
Damn it!
HUH? WHERE'S KAZUKI?
Damn it!
BLERP
BLEEP
HE WAS WITH ME UNTIL THE ENTRANCE. HE TOLD ME HE HAD ANOTHER ERRAND TO RUN SO HE WENT OUT AGAIN.
THIS LATE?
IT COULDN'T WAIT UNTIL TOMOR-ROW?
YEAH, I ASKED HIM THAT TOO.
BUT HE SAID...

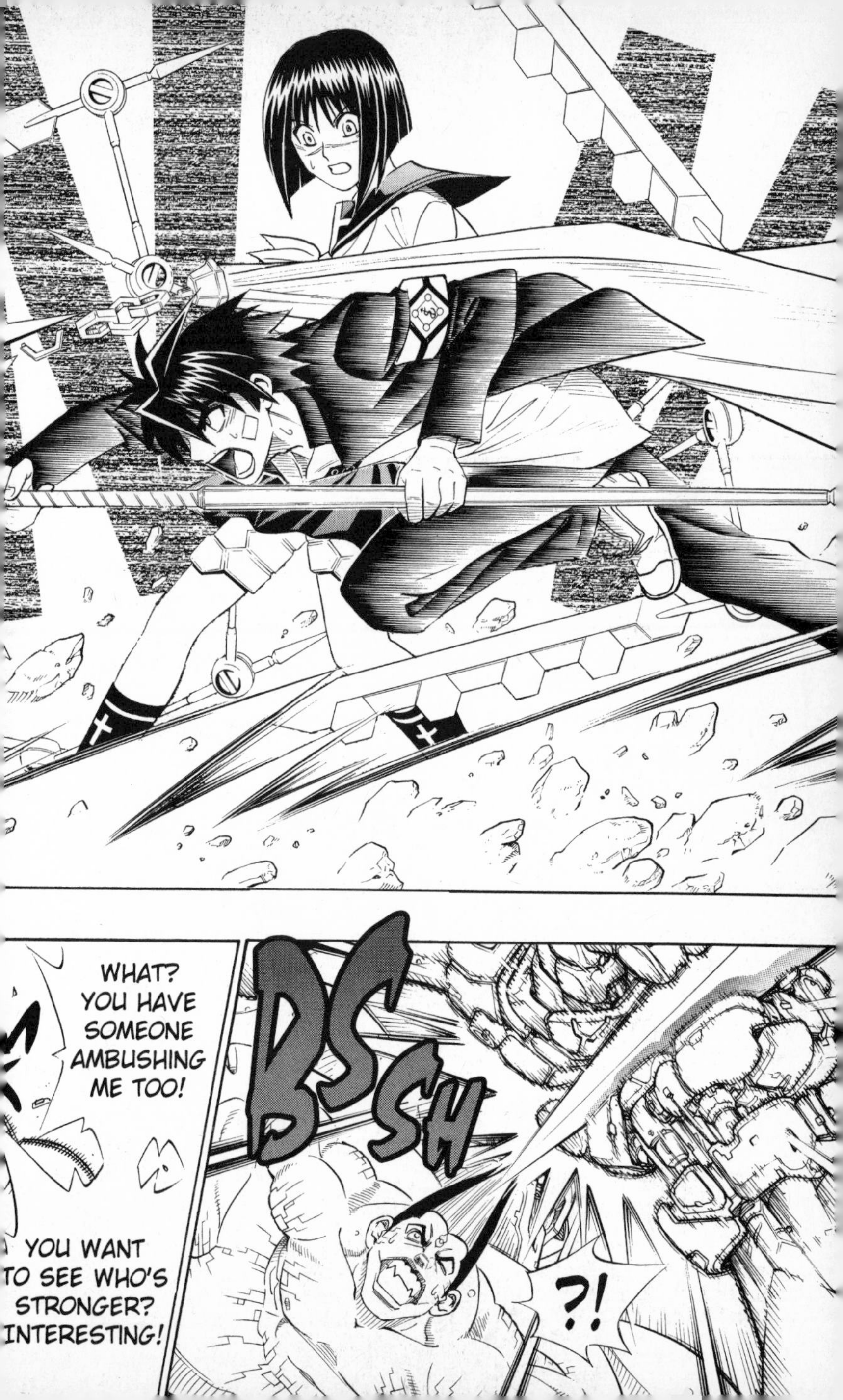
BSSH
?!
WHAT? YOU HAVE SOMEONE AMBUSHING ME TOO!
YOU WANT TO SEE WHO'S STRONGER? INTERESTING!

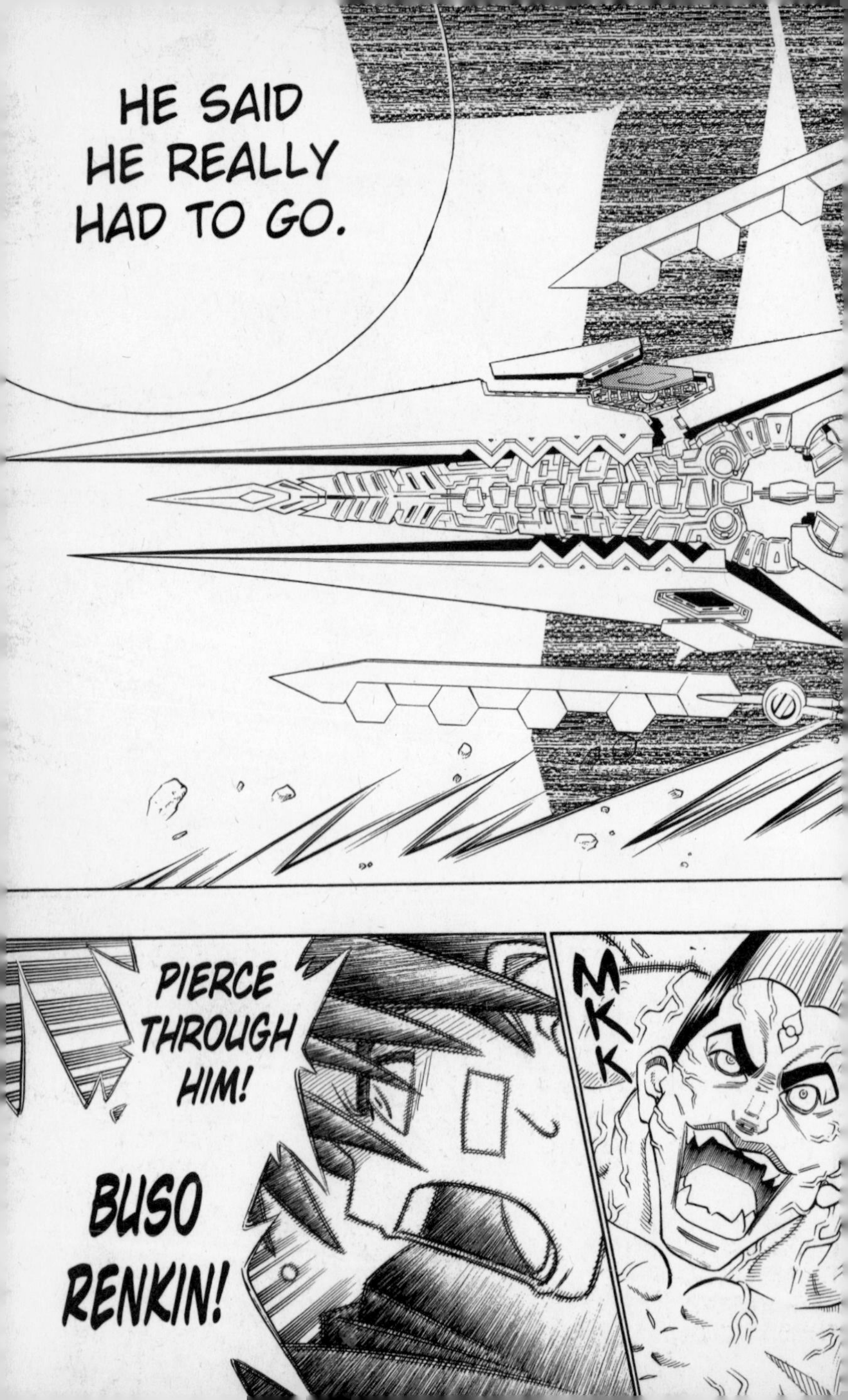
HE SAID HE REALLY HAD TO GO.
MKK
PIERCE THROUGH HIM!
BUSO RENKIN!

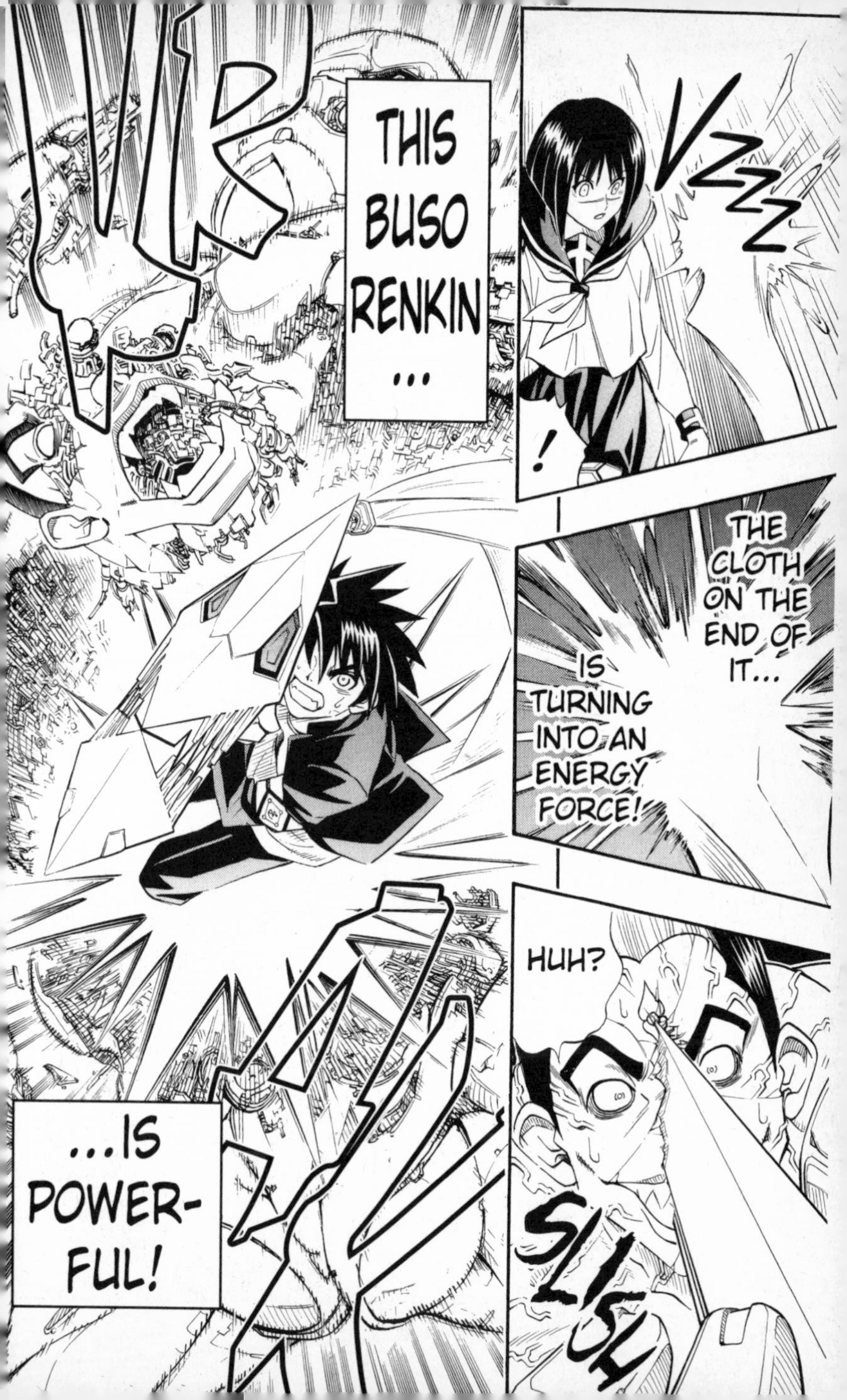
VZZZ
!
THE CLOTH ON THE END OF IT...
IS TURNING INTO AN ENERGY FORCE!
HUH?
SLISH
THIS BUSO RENKIN...
...IS POWER-FUL!

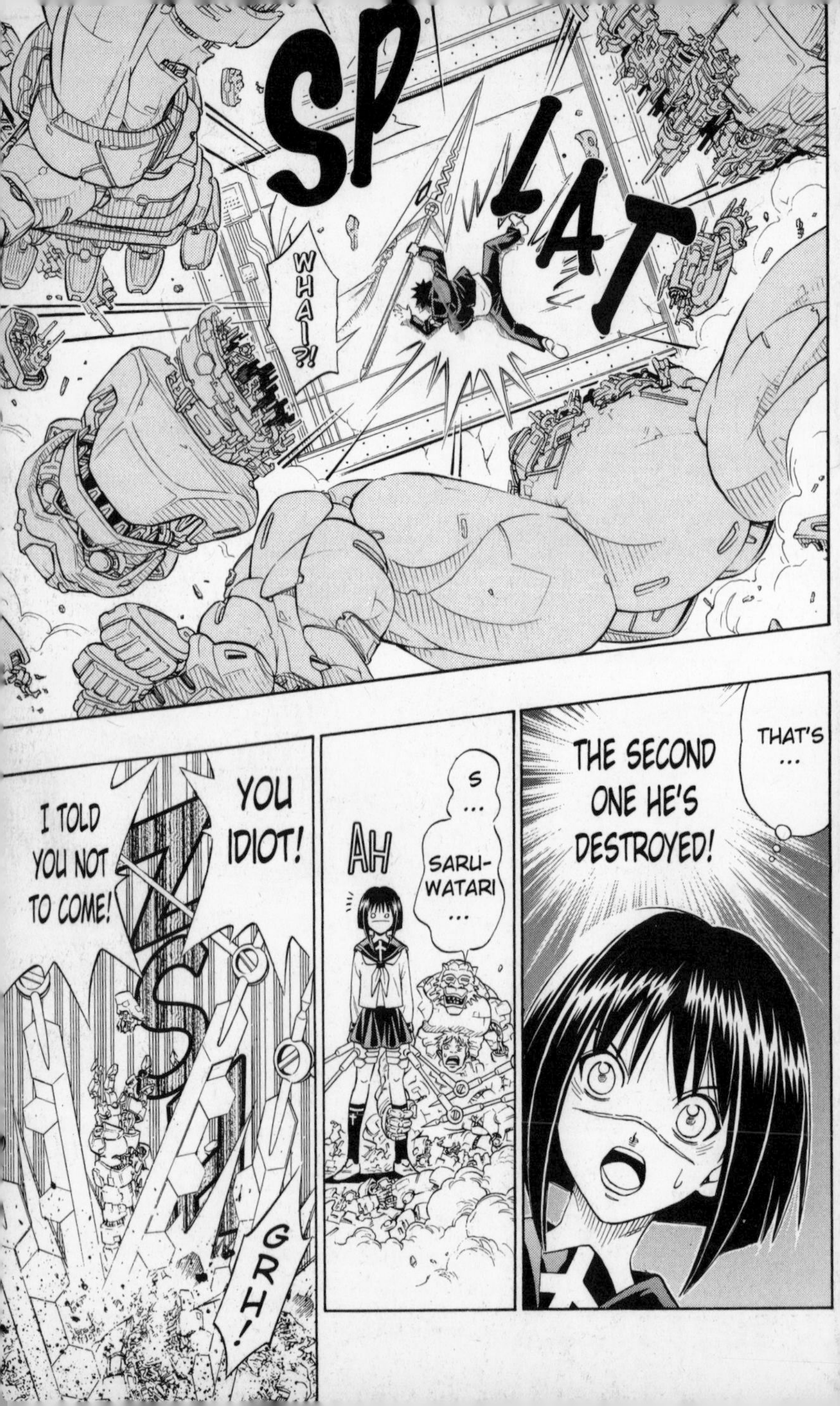
SPLAT
WHA!?!
THAT'S...
THE SECOND ONE HE'S DESTROYED!
S... SARU-WATARI...
AH
YOU IDIOT!
I TOLD YOU NOT TO COME!
GRH!

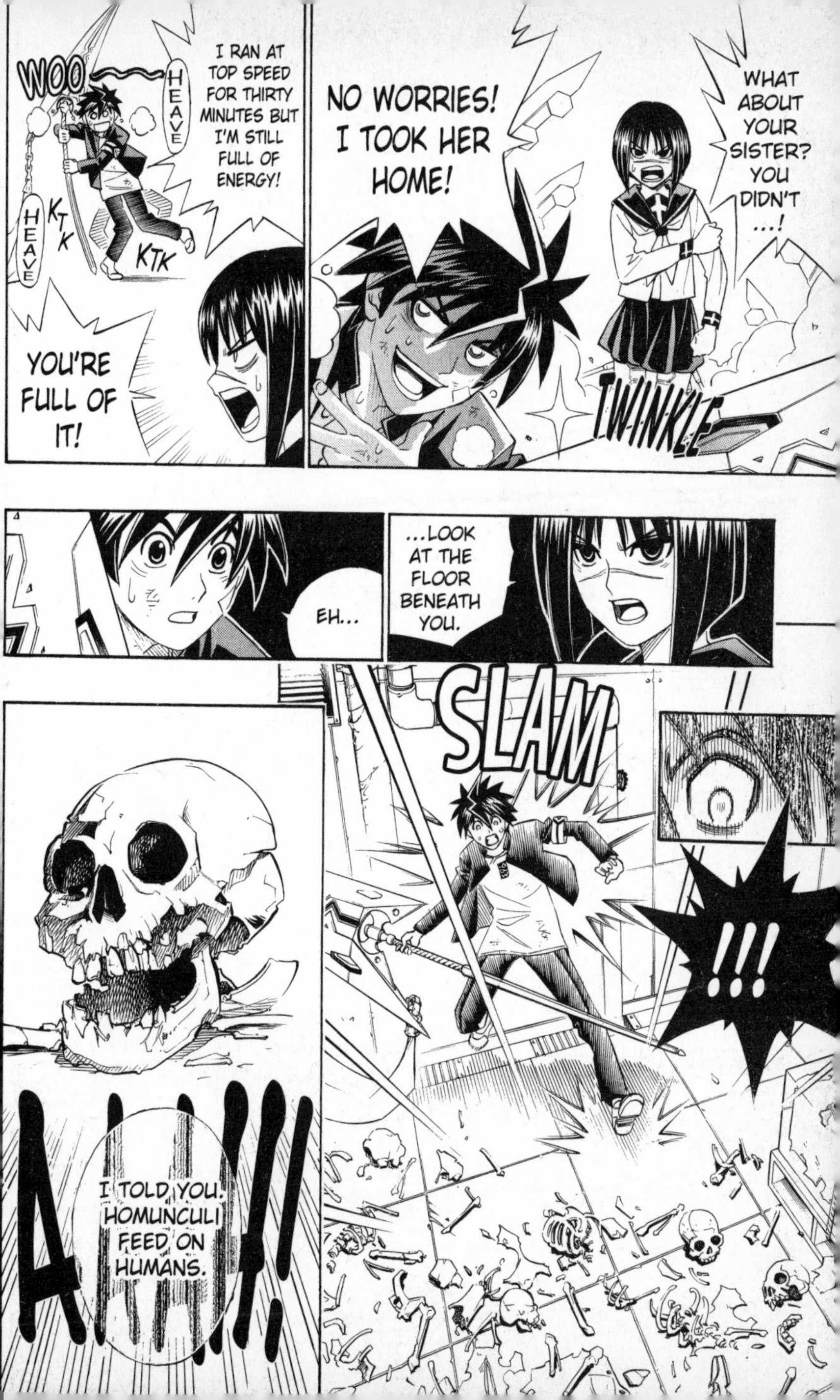
WHAT ABOUT YOUR SISTER? YOU DIDN'T ...!
NO WORRIES! I TOOK HER HOME!
TWINKLE
I RAN AT TOP SPEED FOR THIRTY MINUTES BUT I'M STILL FULL OF ENERGY!
WOO
HEAVE
HEAVE
KTK
KTK
YOU'RE FULL OF IT!
...LOOK AT THE FLOOR BENEATH YOU.
EH...
SLAM
!!!
I TOLD YOU. HOMUNCULI FEED ON HUMANS.

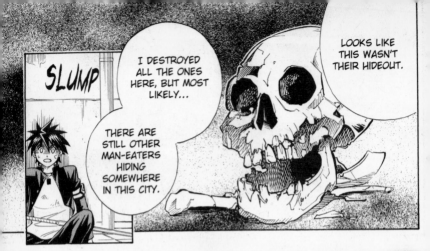

LOOKS LIKE THIS WASN'T THEIR HIDEOUT.
I DESTROYED ALL THE ONES HERE, BUT MOST LIKELY...
THERE ARE STILL OTHER MAN-EATERS HIDING SOMEWHERE IN THIS CITY.
SLUMP
THAT CAN'T BE... THERE'S STILL MORE MONSTERS?
THE SITUATION IS WORSE THAN I THOUGHT.
THIS TIME YOU REALLY NEED TO STAY OUT OF THE WAY!
NO, THAT'S THE REASON I CAN'T BACK OUT.
MAHIRO, ROKUMASU AND THE OTHERS ARE IN DANGER!
...
I HAVE WHAT YOU GAVE TO ME.
I HAVE THE POWER TO FIGHT...

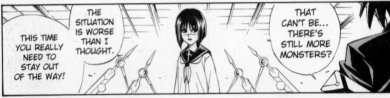

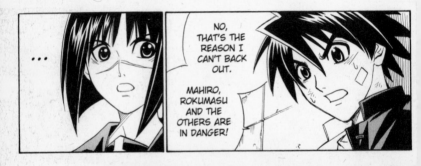

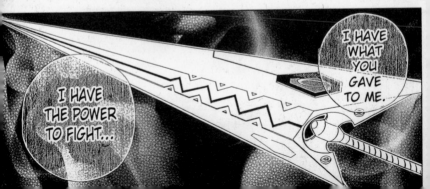

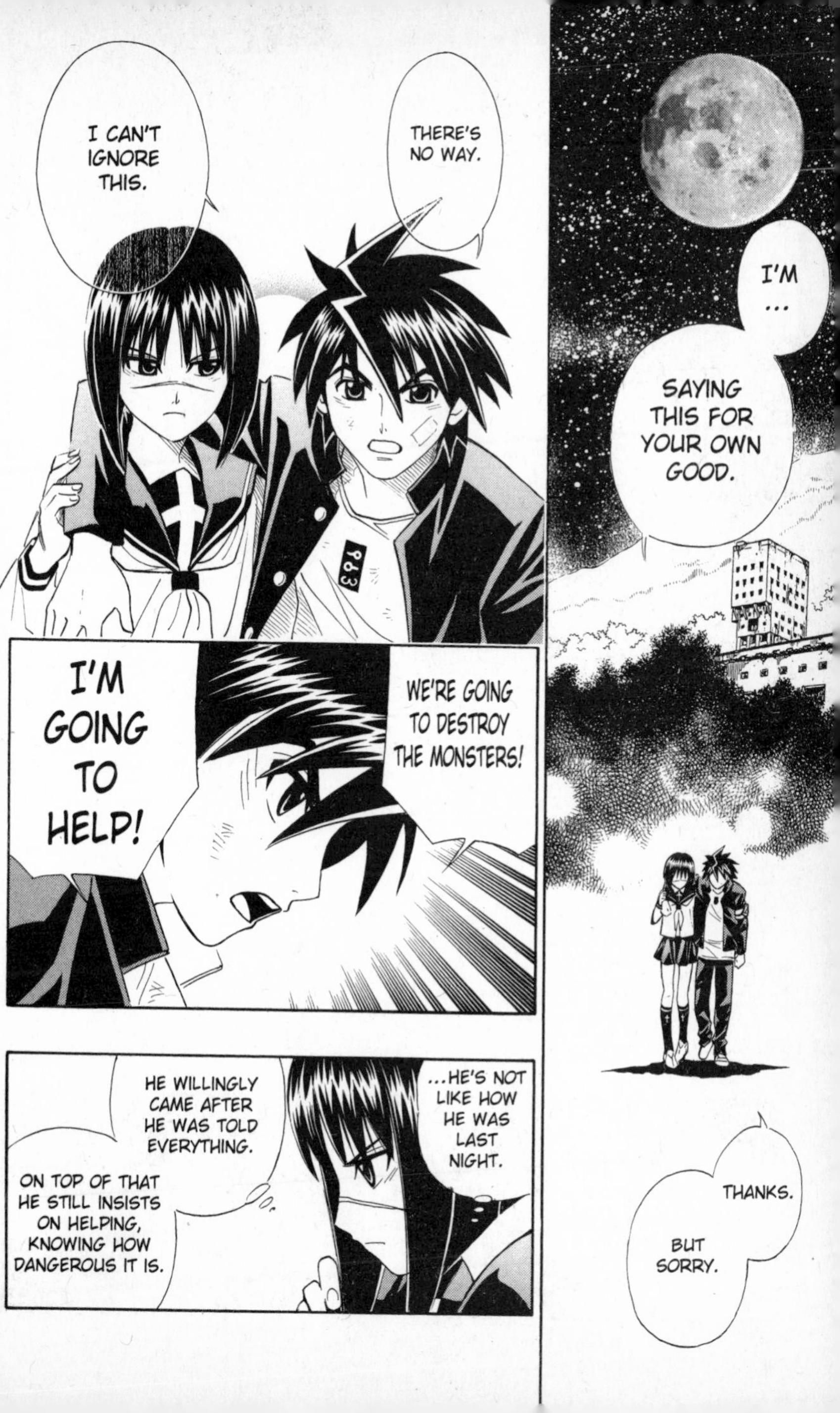
I'M ...
SAYING THIS FOR YOUR OWN GOOD.
THANKS.
BUT SORRY.
THERE'S NO WAY.
I CAN'T IGNORE THIS.
WE'RE GOING TO DESTROY THE MONSTERS!
I'M GOING TO HELP!
...HE'S NOT LIKE HOW HE WAS LAST NIGHT.
HE WILLINGLY CAME AFTER HE WAS TOLD EVERYTHING.
ON TOP OF THAT HE STILL INSISTS ON HELPING, KNOWING HOW DANGEROUS IT IS.

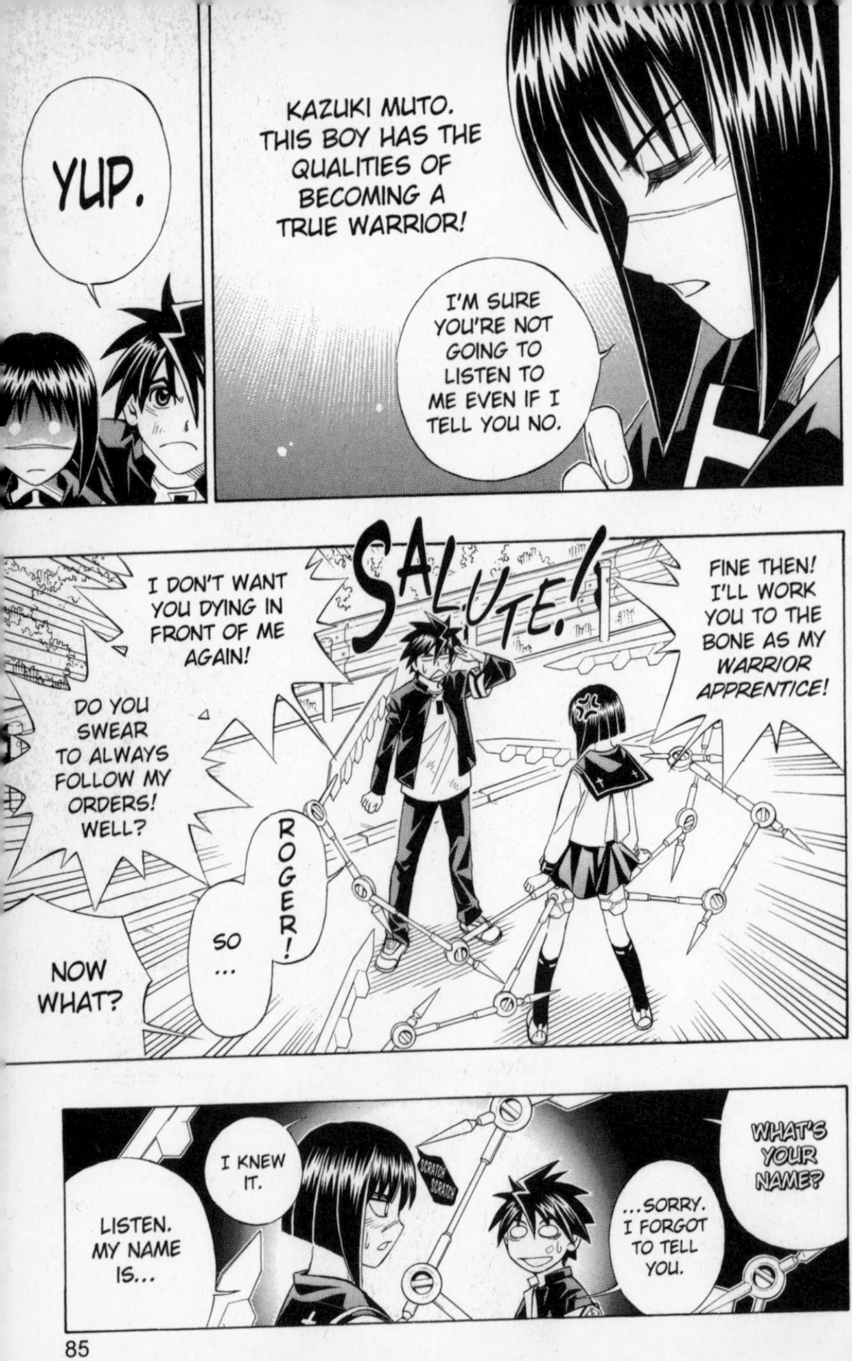

KAZUKI MUTO. THIS BOY HAS THE QUALITIES OF BECOMING A TRUE WARRIOR!
I'M SURE YOU'RE NOT GOING TO LISTEN TO ME EVEN IF I TELL YOU NO.
YUP.
FINE THEN! I'LL WORK YOU TO THE BONE AS MY WARRIOR APPRENTICE!
SALUTE!
I DON'T WANT YOU DYING IN FRONT OF ME AGAIN!
DO YOU SWEAR TO ALWAYS FOLLOW MY ORDERS! WELL?
ROGER!
SO...
NOW WHAT?
WHAT'S YOUR NAME?
...SORRY. I FORGOT TO TELL YOU.
SCRATCH SCRATCH
I KNEW IT.
LISTEN. MY NAME IS...

- King Cobra-type Homunculus
- He used to be a professor at Ginsei Academy. Being an educator was just a job for him and he didn't show any interest in the students. He was the homeroom professor of Papillon Mask, the Homunculi creator. He was turned into a Homunculus for saying, "You should just drop out of school" to Papillon Mask.
- He turned out to be a relatively well balanced Homunculus. After turning into a Homunculus he was able to continue teaching and his social skills improved.

Author's Notes

- Mahiro needed to get eaten by him and get saved. In order to get past this event, I chose a snake that swallows their prey whole.
- I chose to make him into a cold, unsociable character because it took too many pages to build up the characters surrounding Kazuki. He turned out to be more snakelike so it all worked out in the end.

No. 2 Homunculus Mita

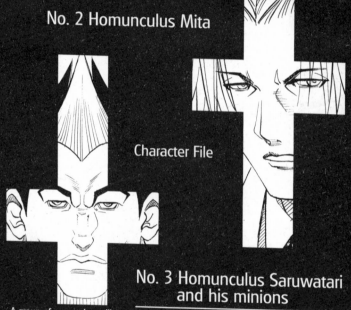

Character File

No. 3 Homunculus Saruwatari and his minions

- A group of mountain gorilla, monkey, baboon, chimp-type Homunculi.
- They used to be Yakuza gang members. Saruwatari's minions were all his yakuza underlings and friends when he used to be in a motorcycle gang. They were turned into Homunculi for trying to mug Papillon Mask one night in town.
- They turned out to be average quality Homunculi. Being monkeys, they strictly follow a social hierarchy based on strength. They are easy to command and manage. The reason why there are so many of them is because they were also research subjects for '???' type Homunculus.

Author's Notes

- Due to the page limitations I created a simple-minded, easy to understand character, a powerhouse gorilla. He also needed underlings so I made them into a pack of monkeys.
- I drew Saruwatari based on John Travolta but... There's no resemblance...

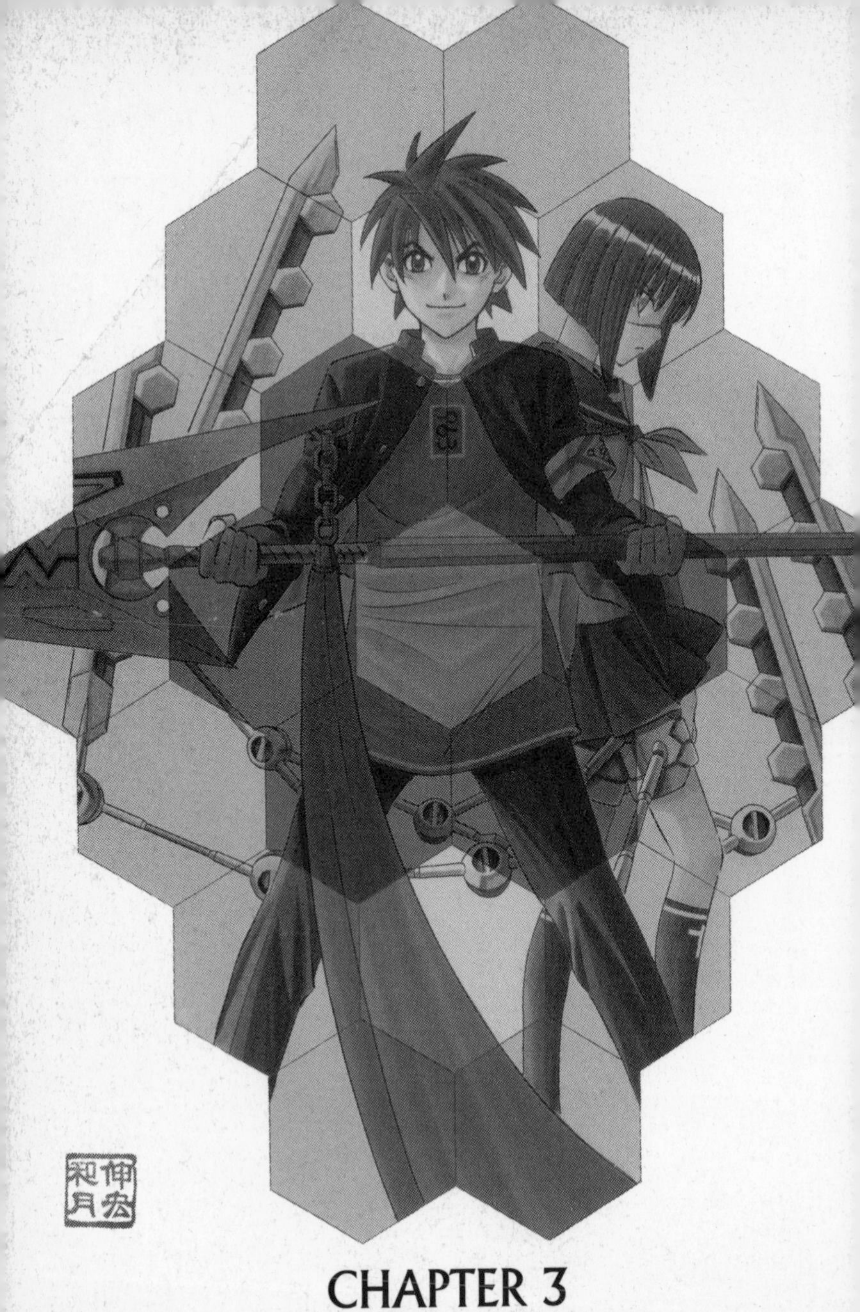

CHAPTER 3
HOMUNCULUS'S IDENTITY

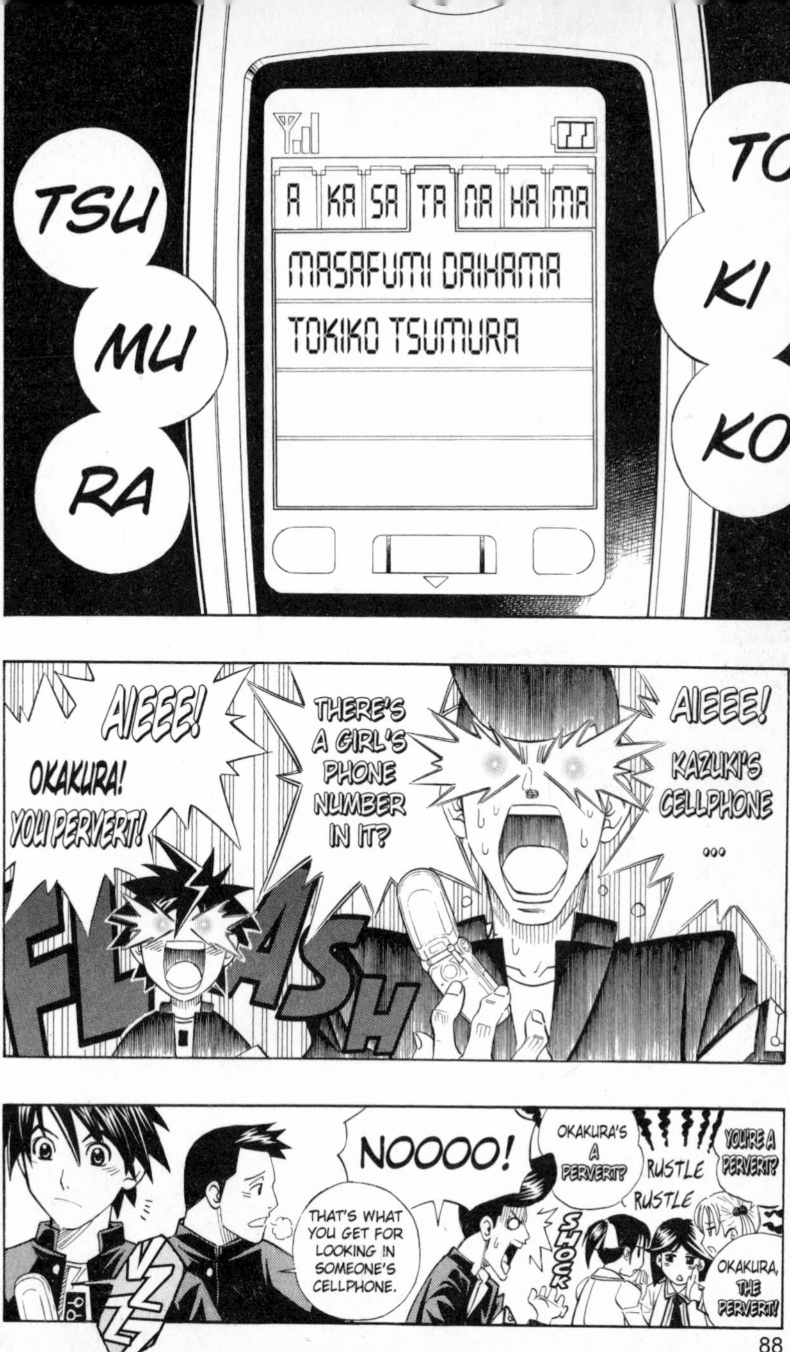
TO KI KO
TSU MU RA
A KA SA TA NA HA MA
MASAFUMI DAIHAMA
TOKIKO TSUMURA
AIEEE!
KAZUKI'S CELLPHONE...
THERE'S A GIRL'S PHONE NUMBER IN IT?
AIEEE!
OKAKURA! YOU PERVERT!
FLASH
YOU'RE A PERVERT?
OKAKURA, THE PERVERT!
RUSTLE
RUSTLE
OKAKURA'S A PERVERT?
SHOCK
NOOOO!
THAT'S WHAT YOU GET FOR LOOKING IN SOMEONE'S CELLPHONE.

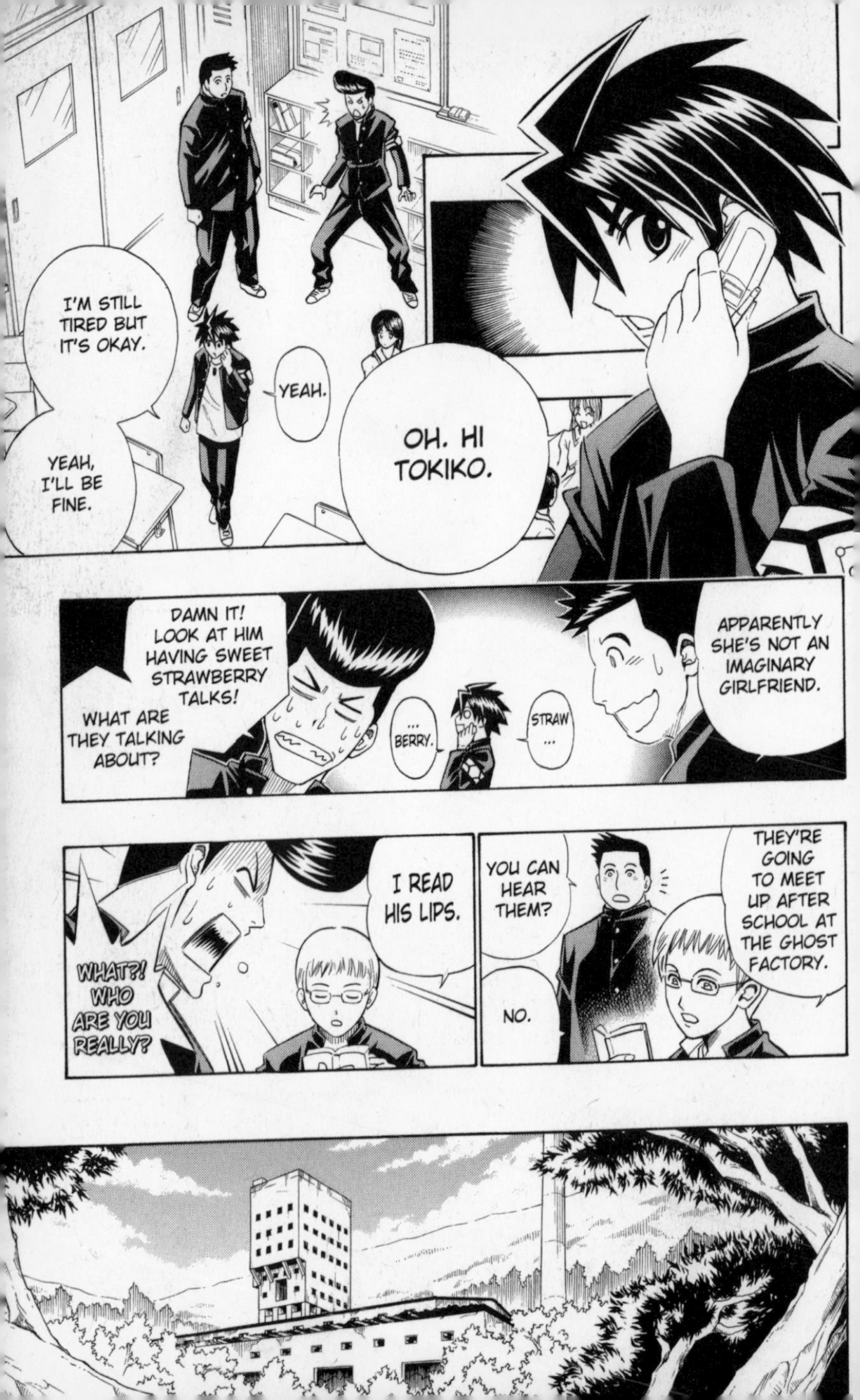
OH. HI TOKIKO.
YEAH.
I'M STILL TIRED BUT IT'S OKAY.
YEAH, I'LL BE FINE.
APPARENTLY SHE'S NOT AN IMAGINARY GIRLFRIEND.
STRAW ...
... BERRY.
DAMN IT! LOOK AT HIM HAVING SWEET STRAWBERRY TALKS!
WHAT ARE THEY TALKING ABOUT?
THEY'RE GOING TO MEET UP AFTER SCHOOL AT THE GHOST FACTORY.
YOU CAN HEAR THEM?
NO.
I READ HIS LIPS.
WHAT?! WHO ARE YOU REALLY?

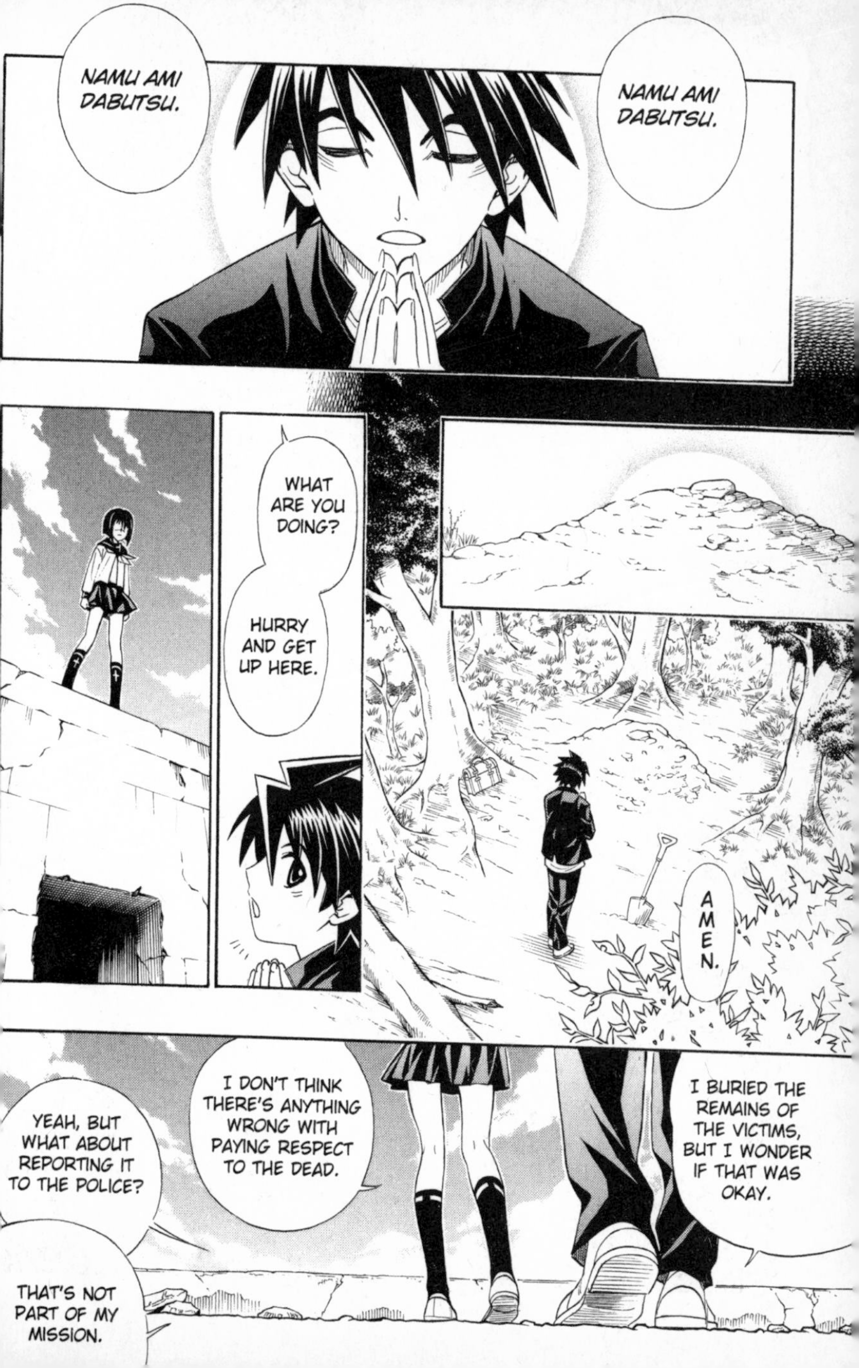
NAMU AMI DABUTSU.
NAMU AMI DABUTSU.
AMEN.
WHAT ARE YOU DOING?
HURRY AND GET UP HERE.
I BURIED THE REMAINS OF THE VICTIMS, BUT I WONDER IF THAT WAS OKAY.
I DON'T THINK THERE'S ANYTHING WRONG WITH PAYING RESPECT TO THE DEAD.
YEAH, BUT WHAT ABOUT REPORTING IT TO THE POLICE?
THAT'S NOT PART OF MY MISSION.

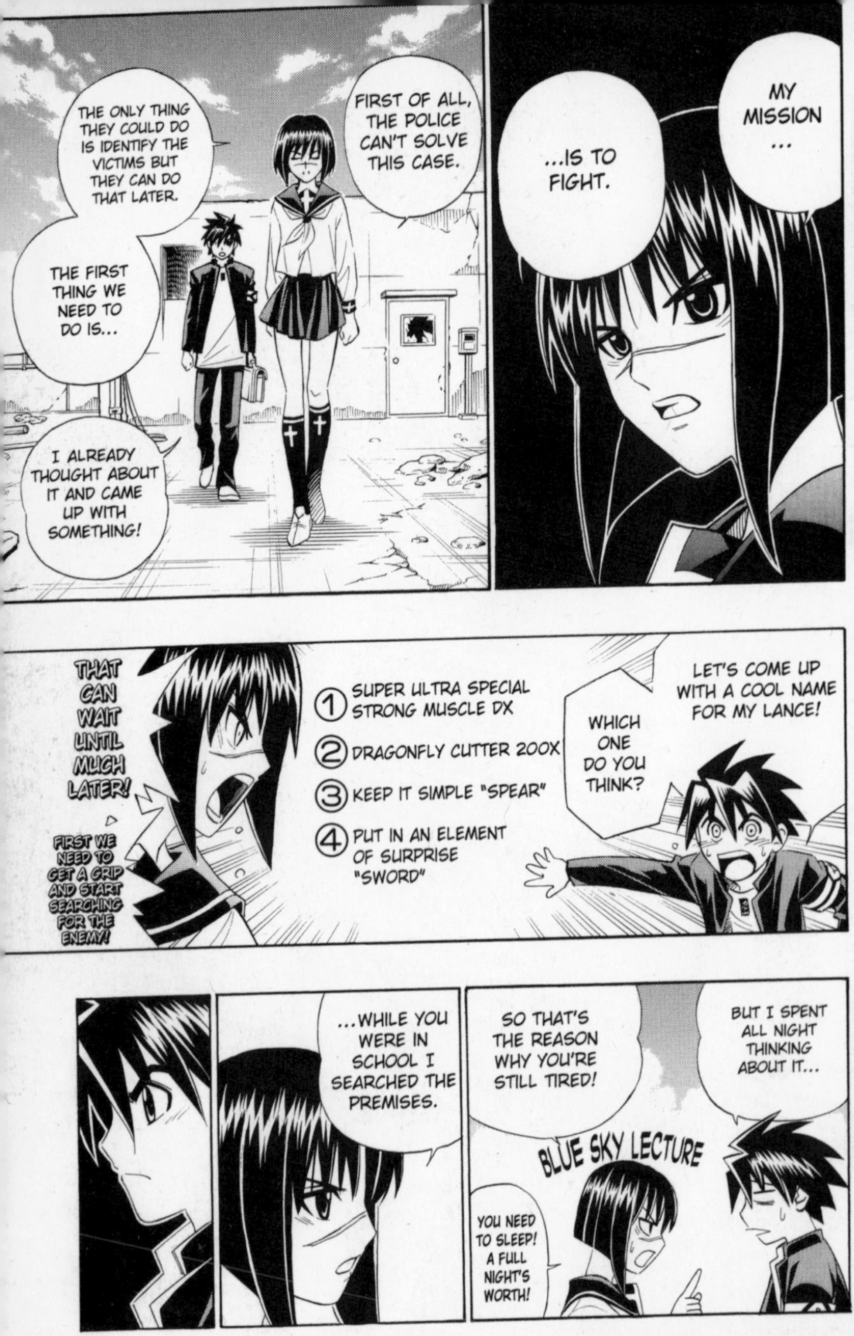
MY MISSION ...
...IS TO FIGHT.
FIRST OF ALL, THE POLICE CAN'T SOLVE THIS CASE.
THE ONLY THING THEY COULD DO IS IDENTIFY THE VICTIMS BUT THEY CAN DO THAT LATER.
THE FIRST THING WE NEED TO DO IS...
I ALREADY THOUGHT ABOUT IT AND CAME UP WITH SOMETHING!
LET'S COME UP WITH A COOL NAME FOR MY LANCE!
WHICH ONE DO YOU THINK?
① SUPER ULTRA SPECIAL STRONG MUSCLE DX
② DRAGONFLY CUTTER 200X
③ KEEP IT SIMPLE "SPEAR"
④ PUT IN AN ELEMENT OF SURPRISE "SWORD"
THAT CAN WAIT UNTIL MUCH LATER!
FIRST WE NEED TO GET A GRIP AND START SEARCHING FOR THE ENEMY!
BUT I SPENT ALL NIGHT THINKING ABOUT IT...
SO THAT'S THE REASON WHY YOU'RE STILL TIRED!
BLUE SKY LECTURE
YOU NEED TO SLEEP! A FULL NIGHT'S WORTH!
...WHILE YOU WERE IN SCHOOL I SEARCHED THE PREMISES.

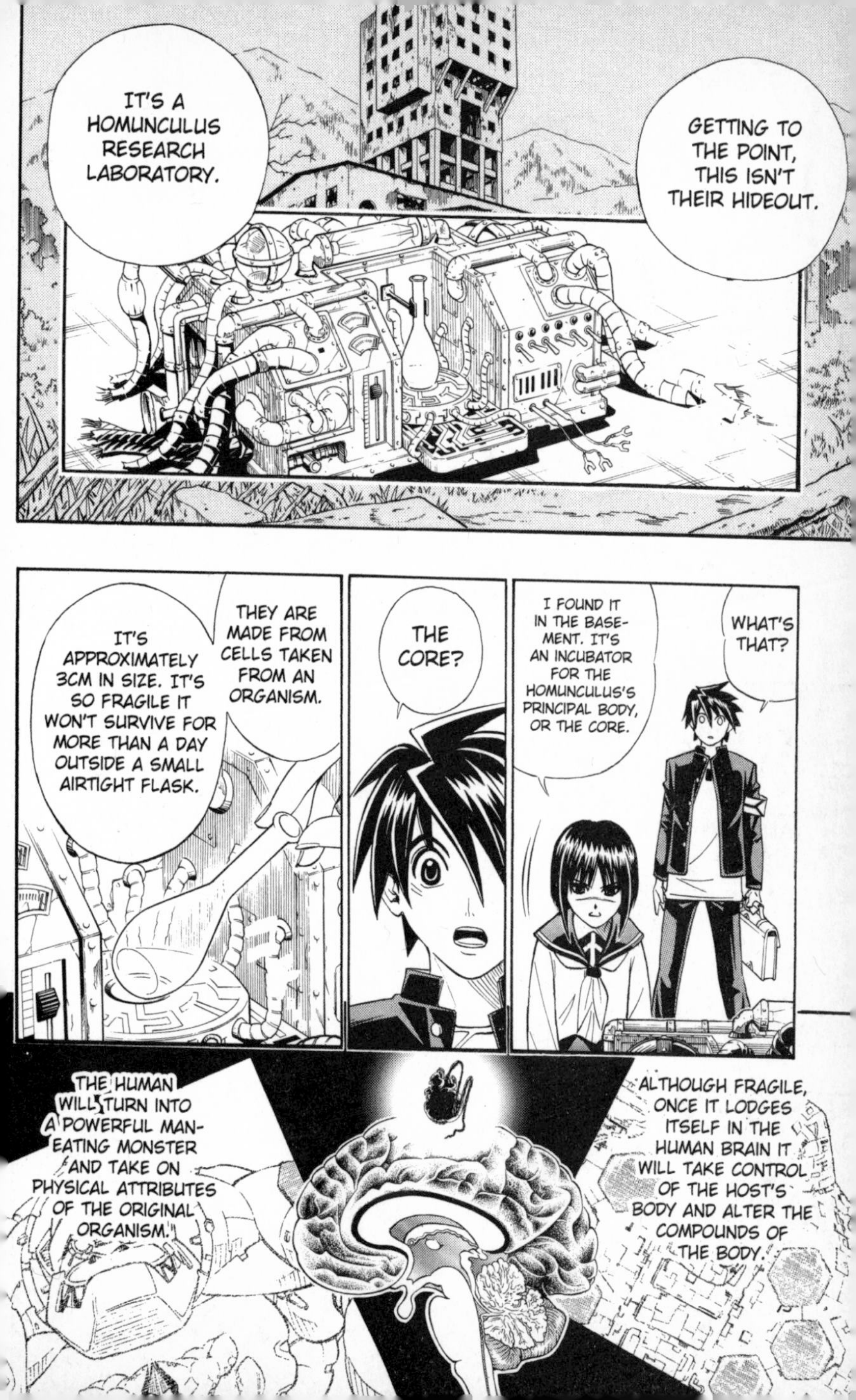
GETTING TO THE POINT, THIS ISN'T THEIR HIDEOUT.
IT'S A HOMUNCULUS RESEARCH LABORATORY.
WHAT'S THAT?
I FOUND IT IN THE BASE-MENT. IT'S AN INCUBATOR FOR THE HOMUNCULUS'S PRINCIPAL BODY, OR THE CORE.
THE CORE?
THEY ARE MADE FROM CELLS TAKEN FROM AN ORGANISM.
IT'S APPROXIMATELY 3CM IN SIZE. IT'S SO FRAGILE IT WON'T SURVIVE FOR MORE THAN A DAY OUTSIDE A SMALL AIRTIGHT FLASK.
ALTHOUGH FRAGILE, ONCE IT LODGES ITSELF IN THE HUMAN BRAIN IT WILL TAKE CONTROL OF THE HOST'S BODY AND ALTER THE COMPOUNDS OF THE BODY.
THE HUMAN WILL TURN INTO A POWERFUL MAN-EATING MONSTER AND TAKE ON PHYSICAL ATTRIBUTES OF THE ORIGINAL ORGANISM.

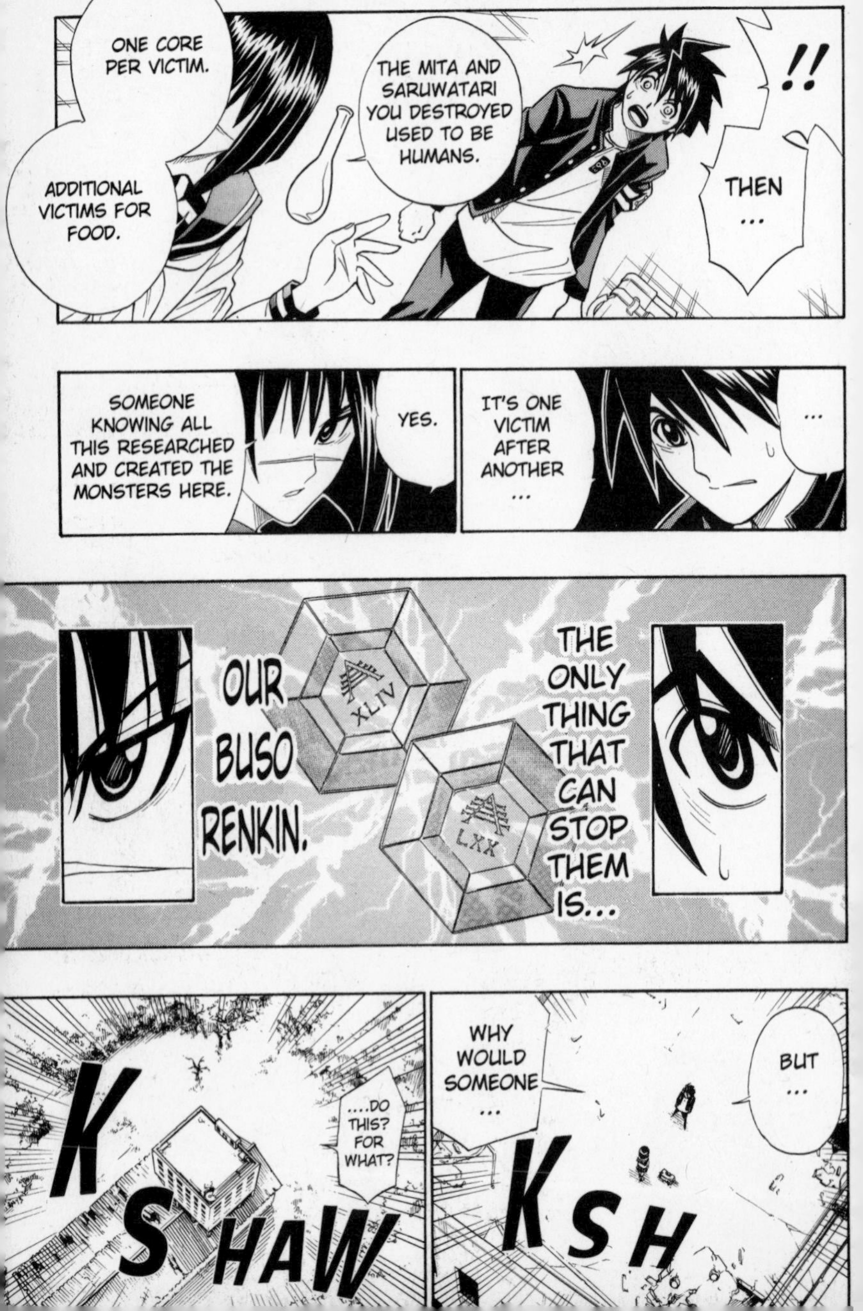
!!
THEN ...
THE MITA AND SARUWATARI YOU DESTROYED USED TO BE HUMANS.
ONE CORE PER VICTIM.
ADDITIONAL VICTIMS FOR FOOD.
...
IT'S ONE VICTIM AFTER ANOTHER ...
YES.
SOMEONE KNOWING ALL THIS RESEARCHED AND CREATED THE MONSTERS HERE.
THE ONLY THING THAT CAN STOP THEM IS...
LXX
XLIV
OUR BUSO RENKIN.
BUT ...
WHY WOULD SOMEONE ...
KSH
....DO THIS? FOR WHAT?
KSHAW

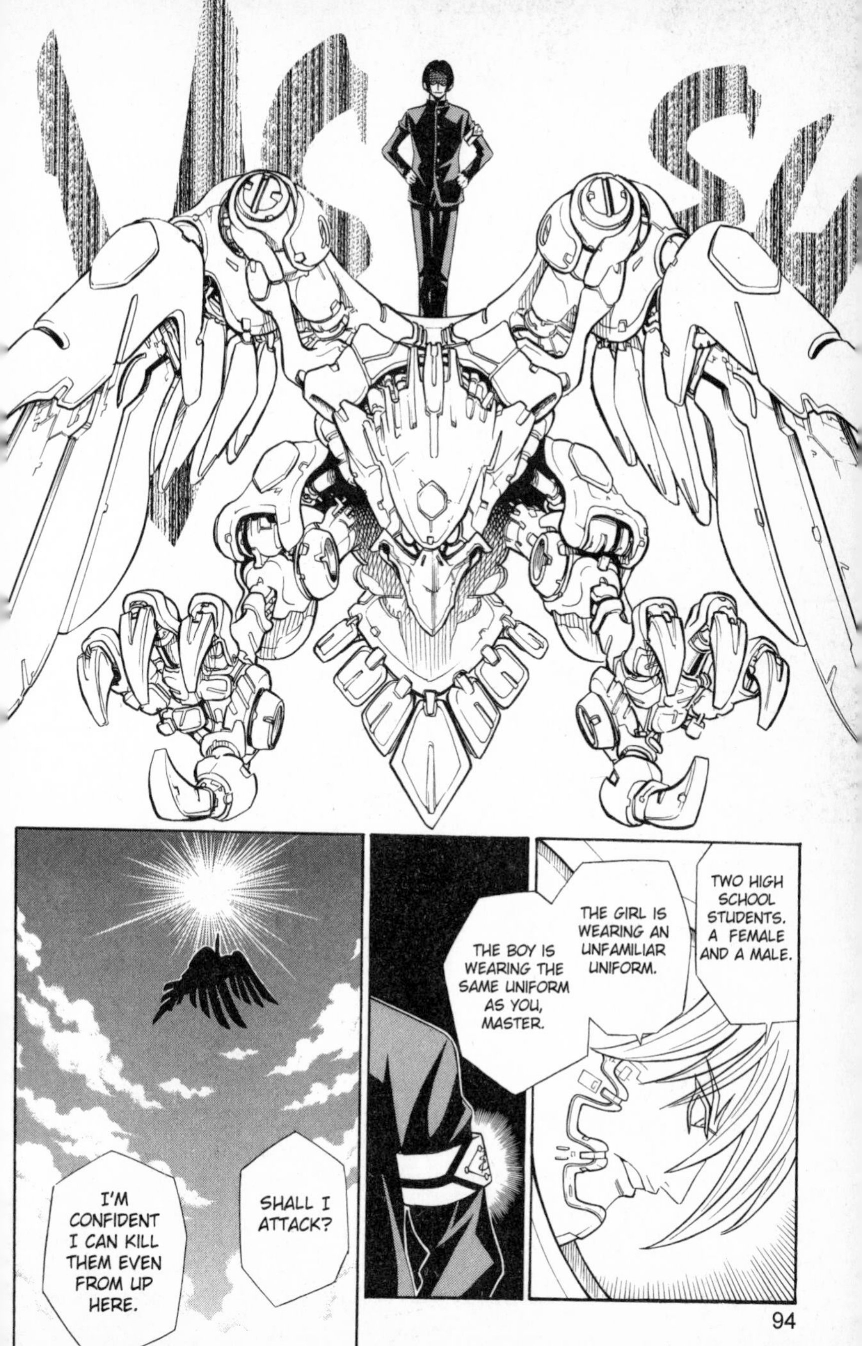
TWO HIGH SCHOOL STUDENTS. A FEMALE AND A MALE.
THE GIRL IS WEARING AN UNFAMILIAR UNIFORM.
THE BOY IS WEARING THE SAME UNIFORM AS YOU, MASTER.
SHALL I ATTACK?
I'M CONFIDENT I CAN KILL THEM EVEN FROM UP HERE.

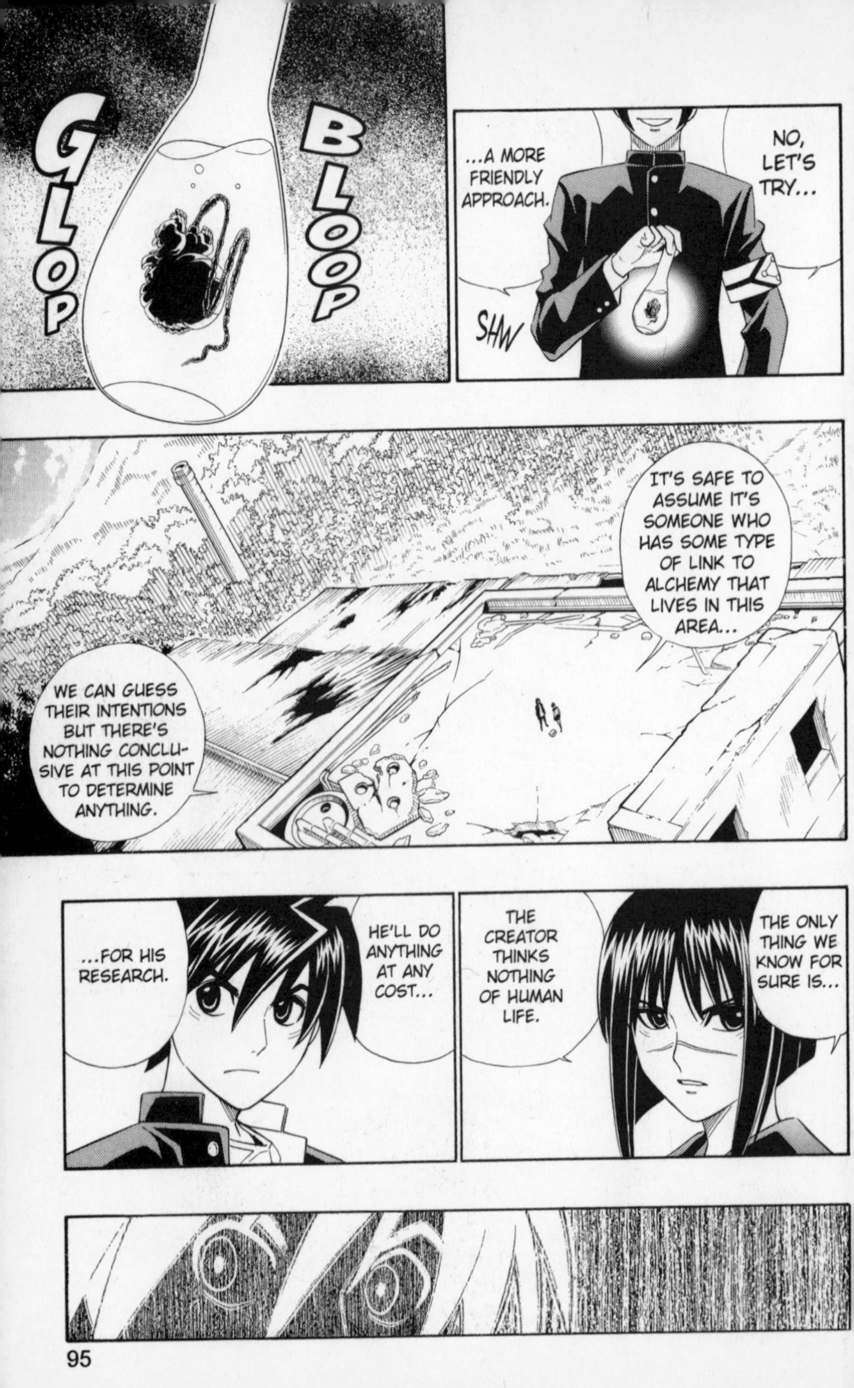
NO, LET'S TRY...
...A MORE FRIENDLY APPROACH.
SHW
BLOOP
GLOP
IT'S SAFE TO ASSUME IT'S SOMEONE WHO HAS SOME TYPE OF LINK TO ALCHEMY THAT LIVES IN THIS AREA...
WE CAN GUESS THEIR INTENTIONS BUT THERE'S NOTHING CONCLUSIVE AT THIS POINT TO DETERMINE ANYTHING.
THE ONLY THING WE KNOW FOR SURE IS...
THE CREATOR THINKS NOTHING OF HUMAN LIFE.
HE'LL DO ANYTHING AT ANY COST...
...FOR HIS RESEARCH.

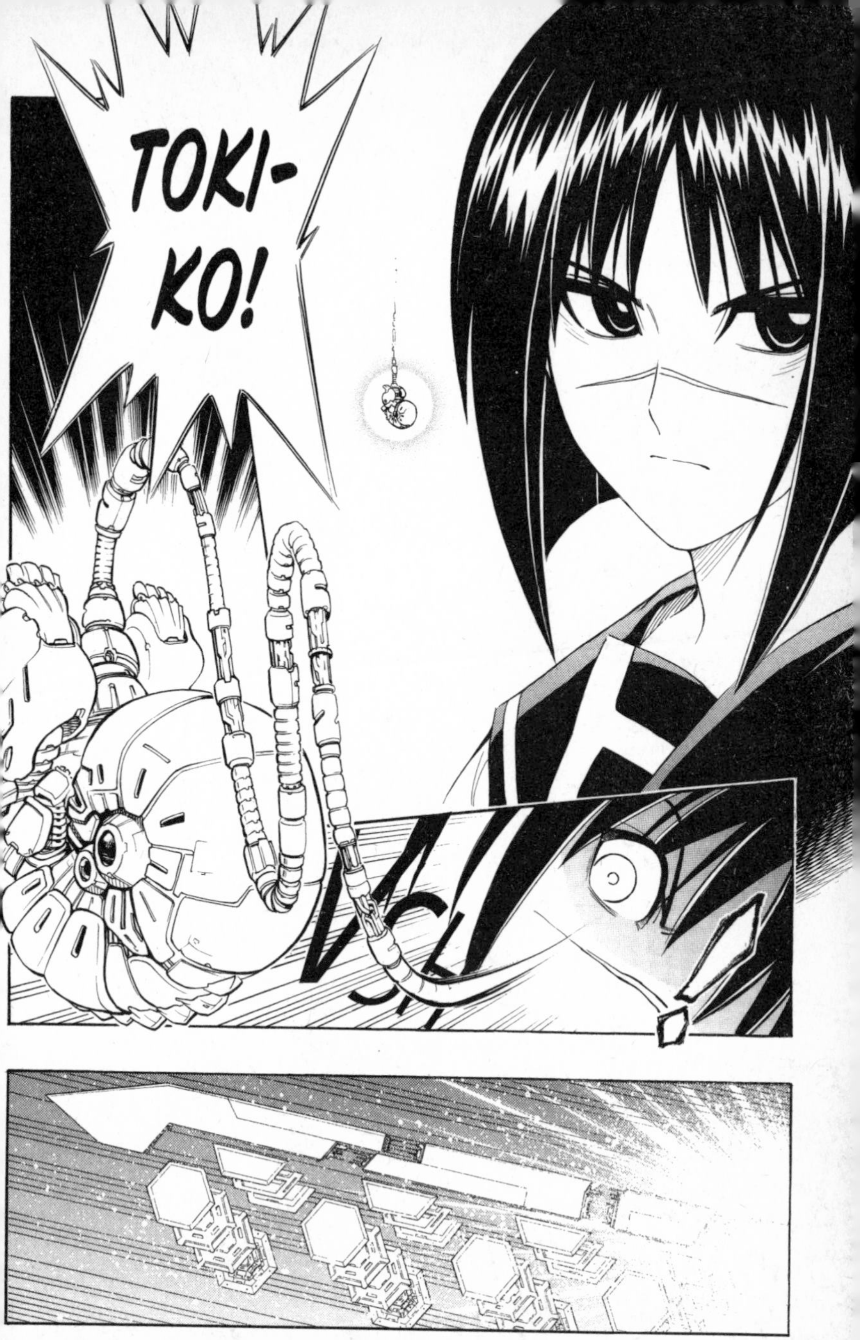
TOKI-
KO!

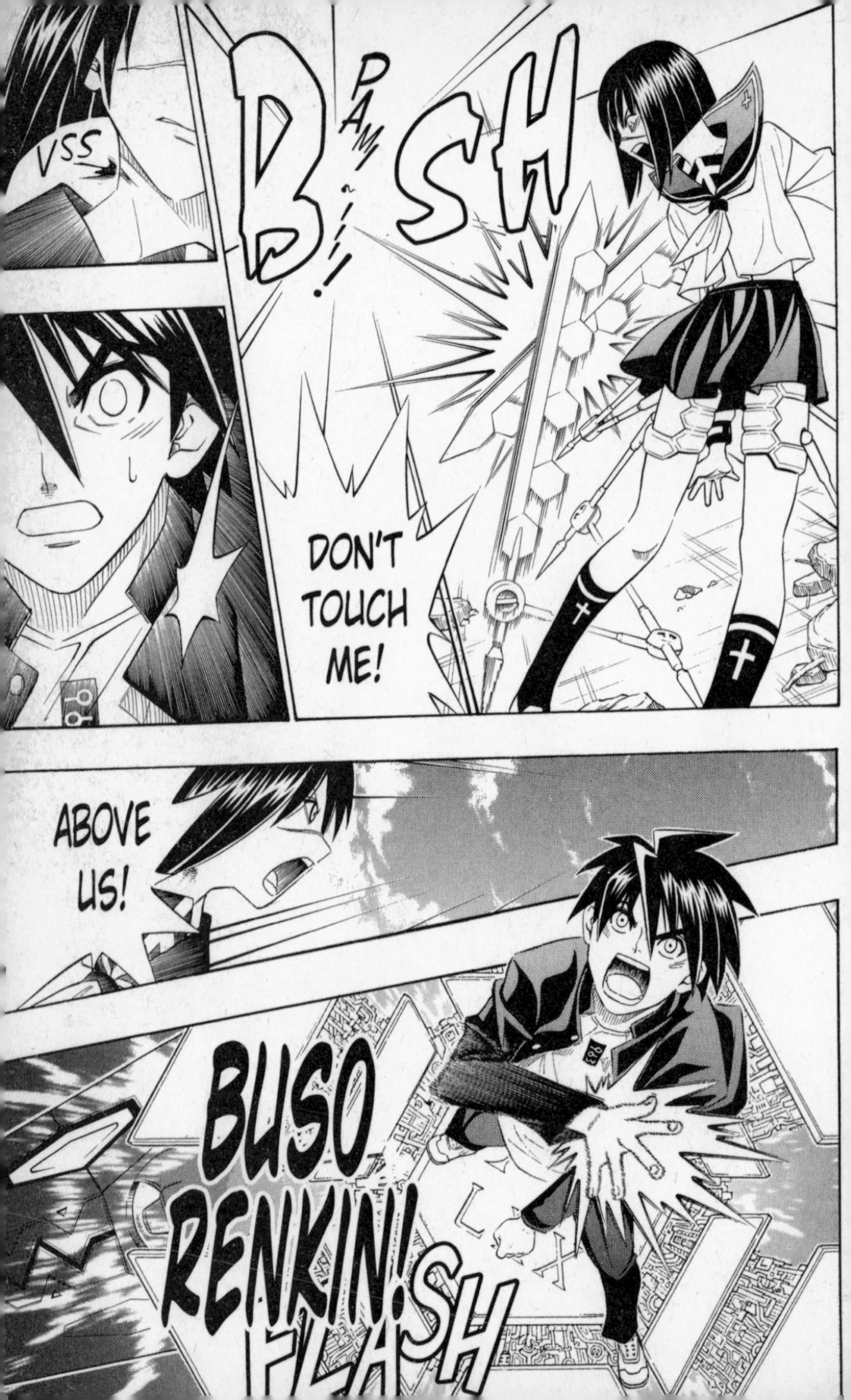
BASH
PAM~!!!
DON'T TOUCH ME!
VSS
BUSO RENKIN!
FLASH
ABOVE US!

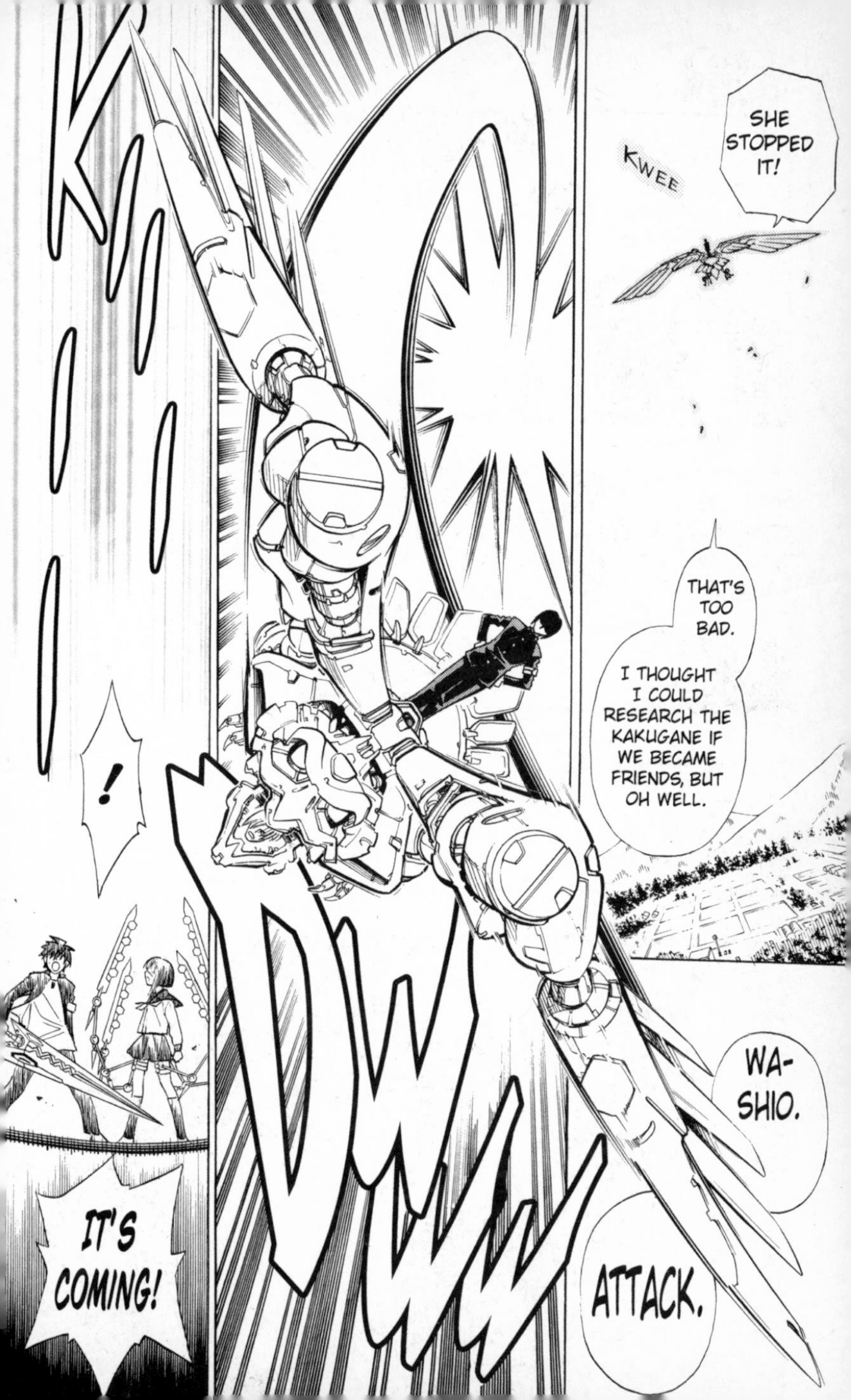
SHE STOPPED IT!
KWEE
THAT'S TOO BAD.
I THOUGHT I COULD RESEARCH THE KAKUGANE IF WE BECAME FRIENDS, BUT OH WELL.
WA-SHIO.
ATTACK.
!
IT'S COMING!

READ THIS WAY

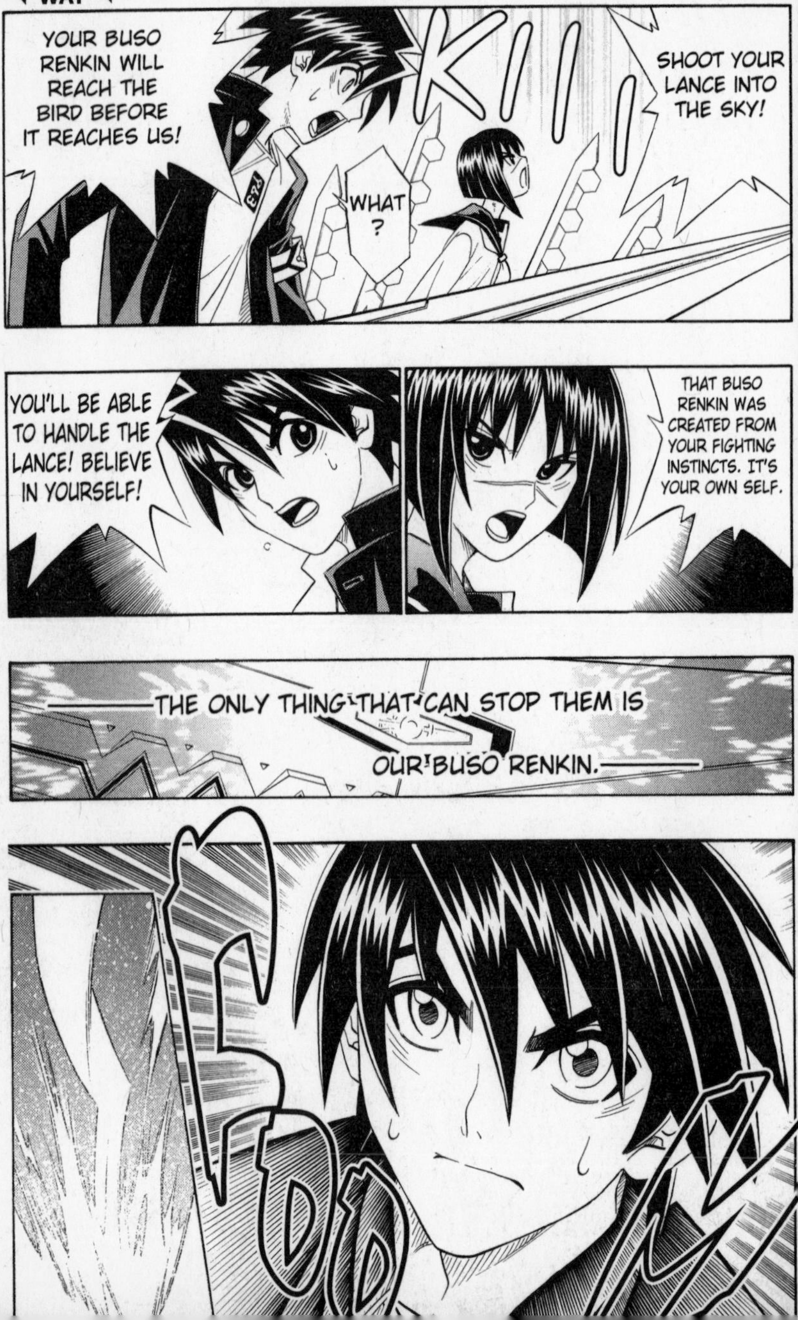
SHOOT YOUR LANCE INTO THE SKY!
KII
WHAT?
YOUR BUSO RENKIN WILL REACH THE BIRD BEFORE IT REACHES US!
THAT BUSO RENKIN WAS CREATED FROM YOUR FIGHTING INSTINCTS. IT'S YOUR OWN SELF.
YOU'LL BE ABLE TO HANDLE THE LANCE! BELIEVE IN YOURSELF!
——THE ONLY THING THAT CAN STOP THEM IS OUR BUSO RENKIN.——

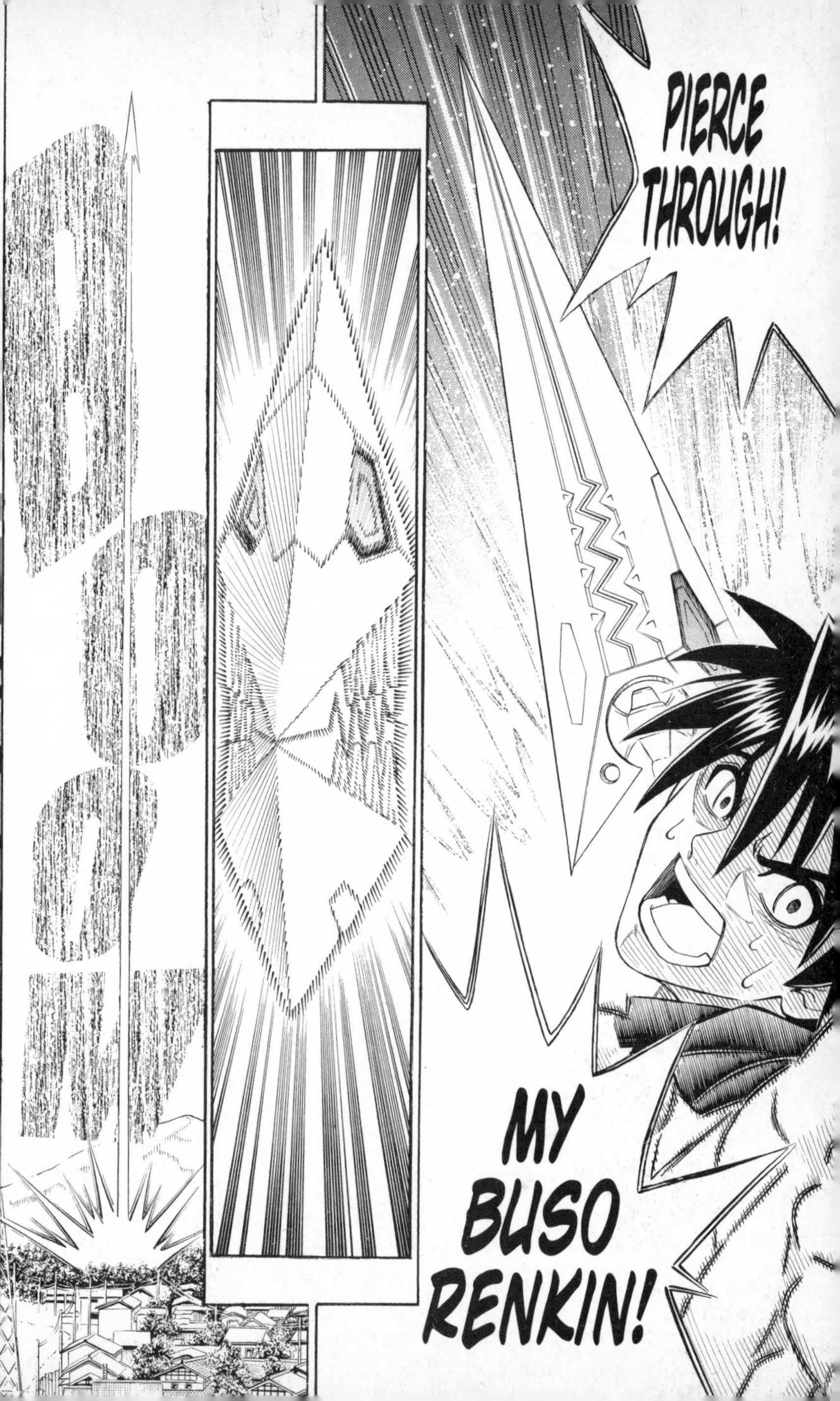
PIERCE THROUGH!
MY BUSO RENKIN!

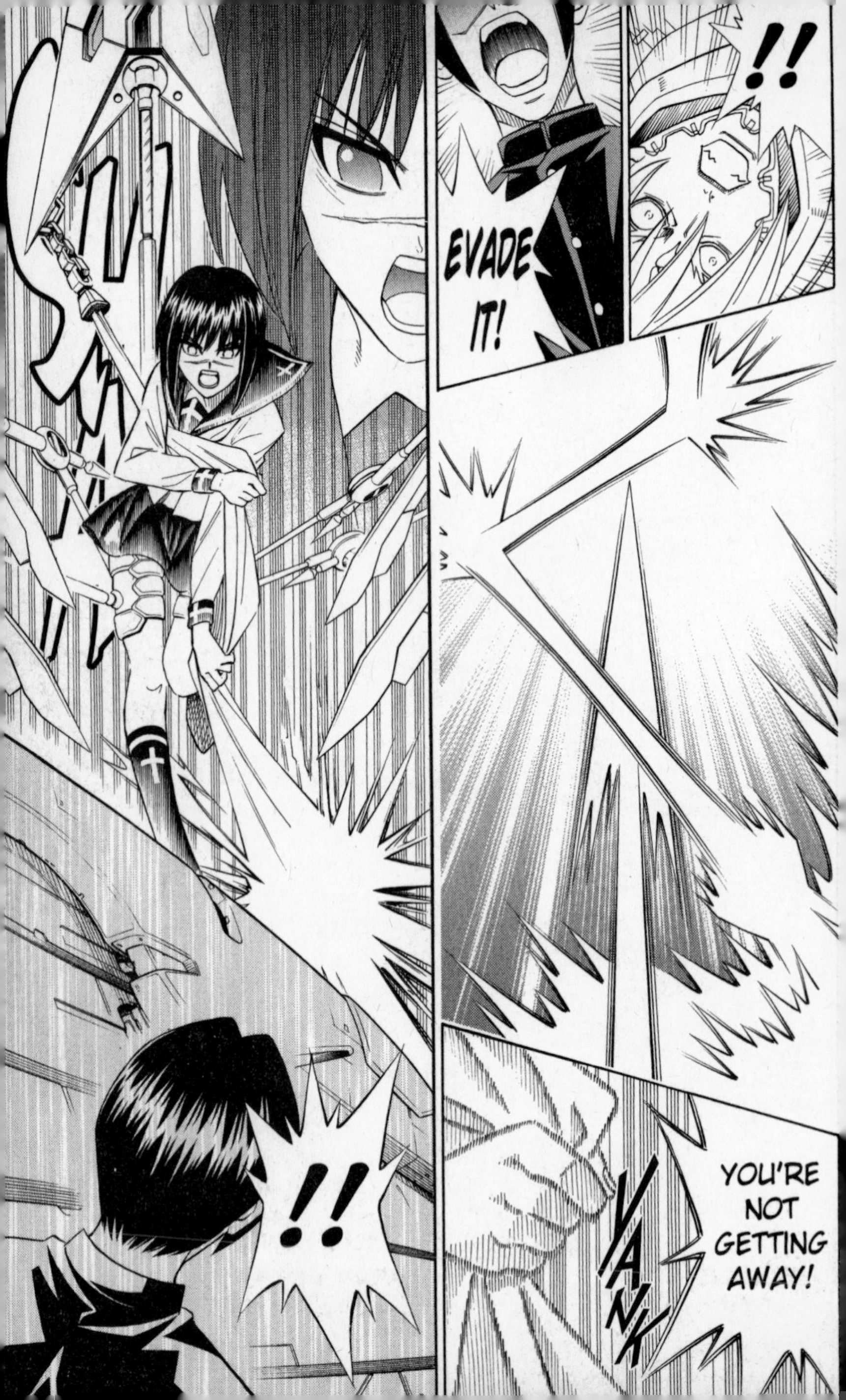
!!
EVADE IT!
YANK
YOU'RE NOT GETTING AWAY!
!!

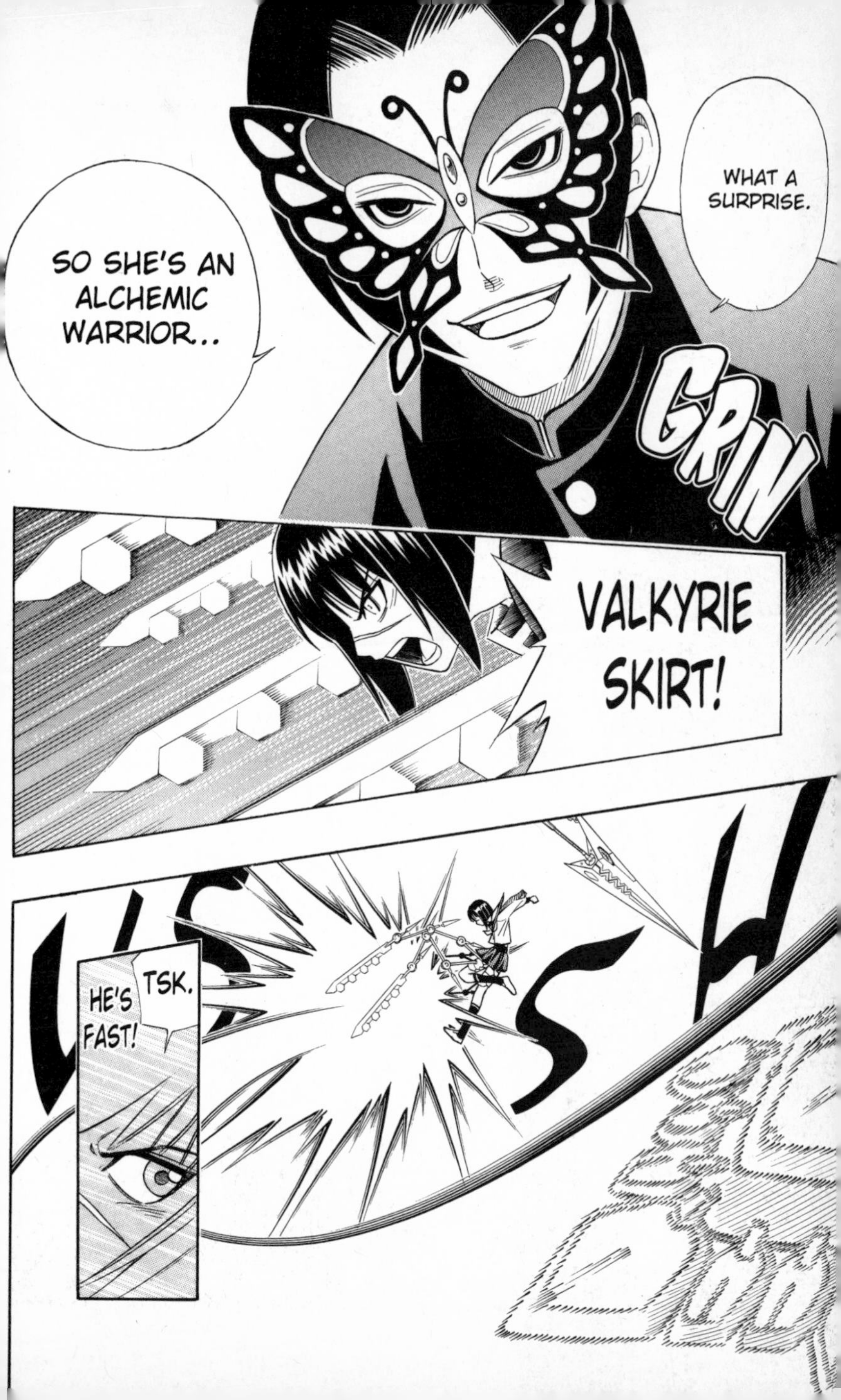
WHAT A SURPRISE.
SO SHE'S AN ALCHEMIC WARRIOR...
GRIN
VALKYRIE SKIRT!
TSK.
HE'S FAST!

READ THIS WAY

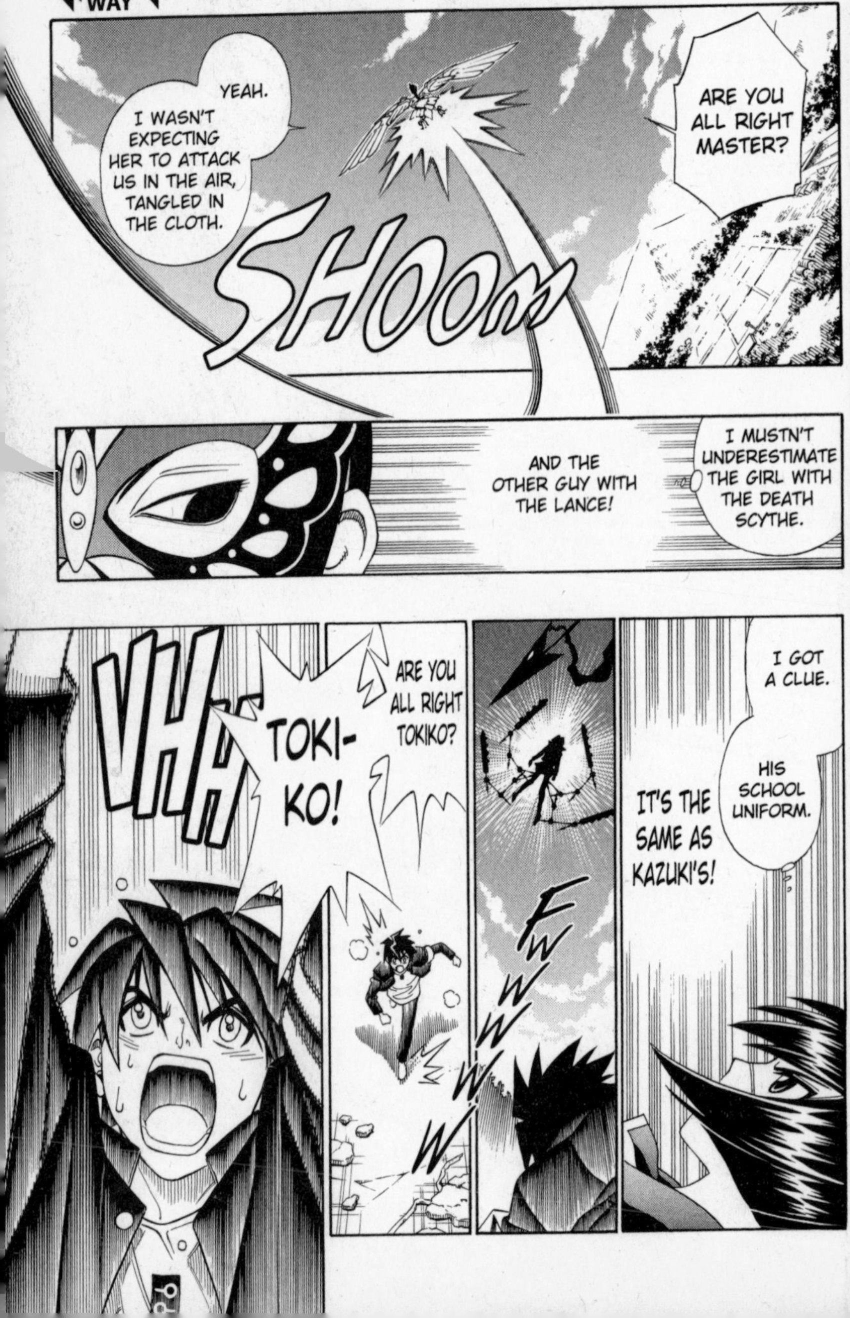
ARE YOU ALL RIGHT MASTER?
YEAH. I WASN'T EXPECTING HER TO ATTACK US IN THE AIR, TANGLED IN THE CLOTH.
SHOOM
I MUSTN'T UNDERESTIMATE THE GIRL WITH THE DEATH SCYTHE.
AND THE OTHER GUY WITH THE LANCE!
I GOT A CLUE.
HIS SCHOOL UNIFORM.
IT'S THE SAME AS KAZUKI'S!
FWWWWWW
ARE YOU ALL RIGHT TOKIKO?
TOKI-KO!
VHA

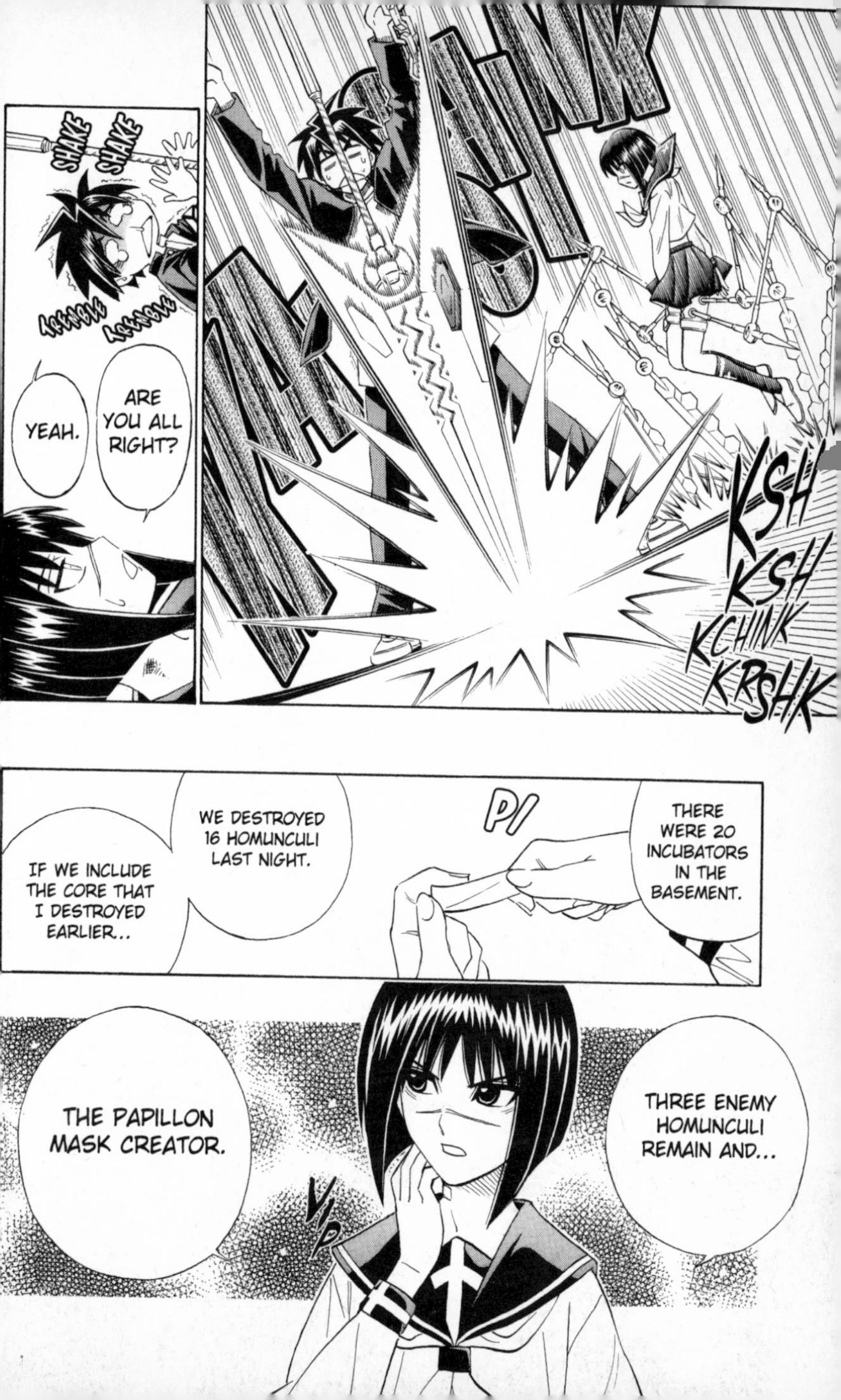
KSH
KSH
KCHINK
KRSHK
SHAKE
SHAKE
ARE YOU ALL RIGHT?
YEAH.
THERE WERE 20 INCUBATORS IN THE BASEMENT.
PI
WE DESTROYED 16 HOMUNCULI LAST NIGHT.
IF WE INCLUDE THE CORE THAT I DESTROYED EARLIER...
THREE ENEMY HOMUNCULI REMAIN AND...
VIP
THE PAPILLON MASK CREATOR.

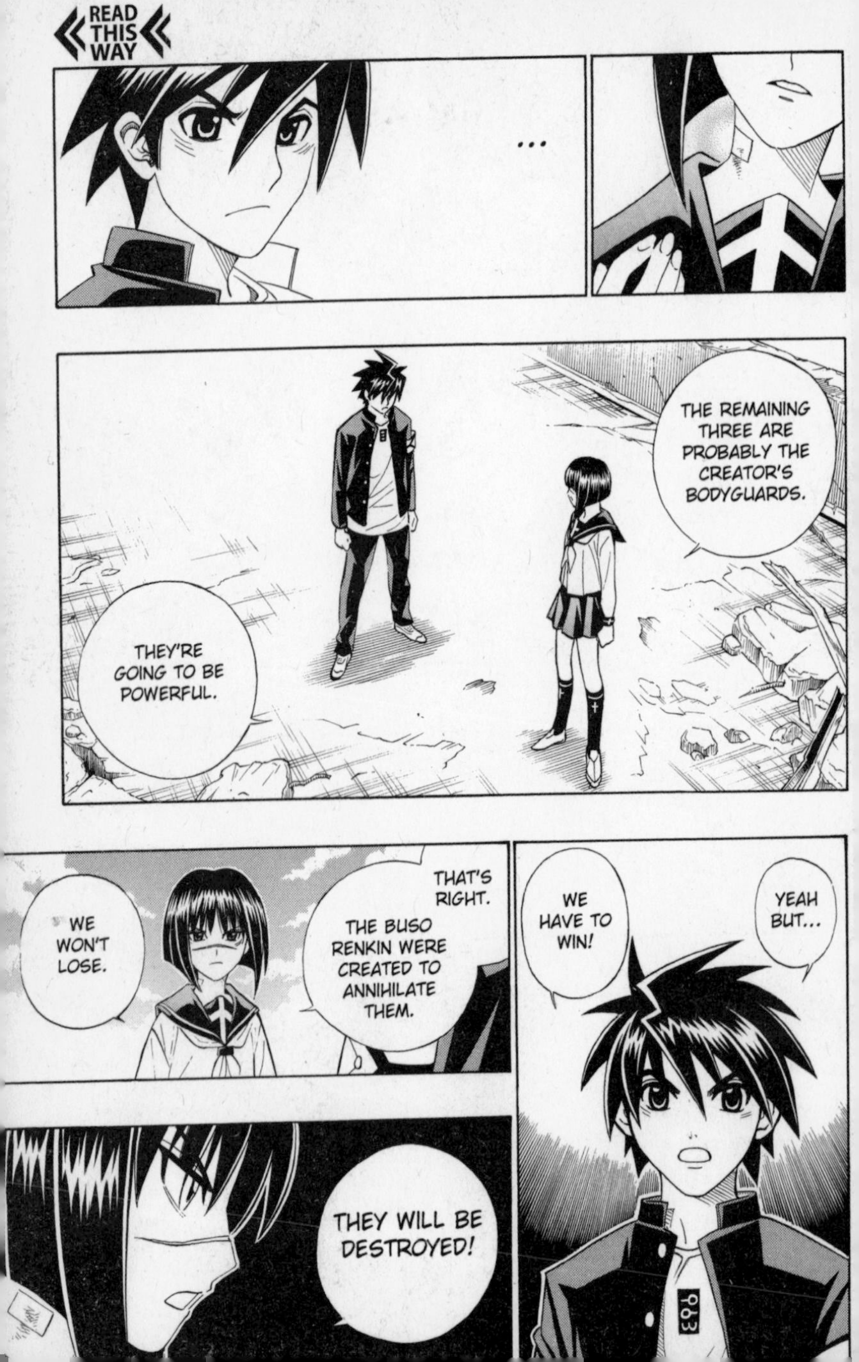
READ THIS WAY
...
THE REMAINING THREE ARE PROBABLY THE CREATOR'S BODYGUARDS.
THEY'RE GOING TO BE POWERFUL.
YEAH BUT...
WE HAVE TO WIN!
THAT'S RIGHT.
THE BUSO RENKIN WERE CREATED TO ANNIHILATE THEM.
WE WON'T LOSE.
THEY WILL BE DESTROYED!

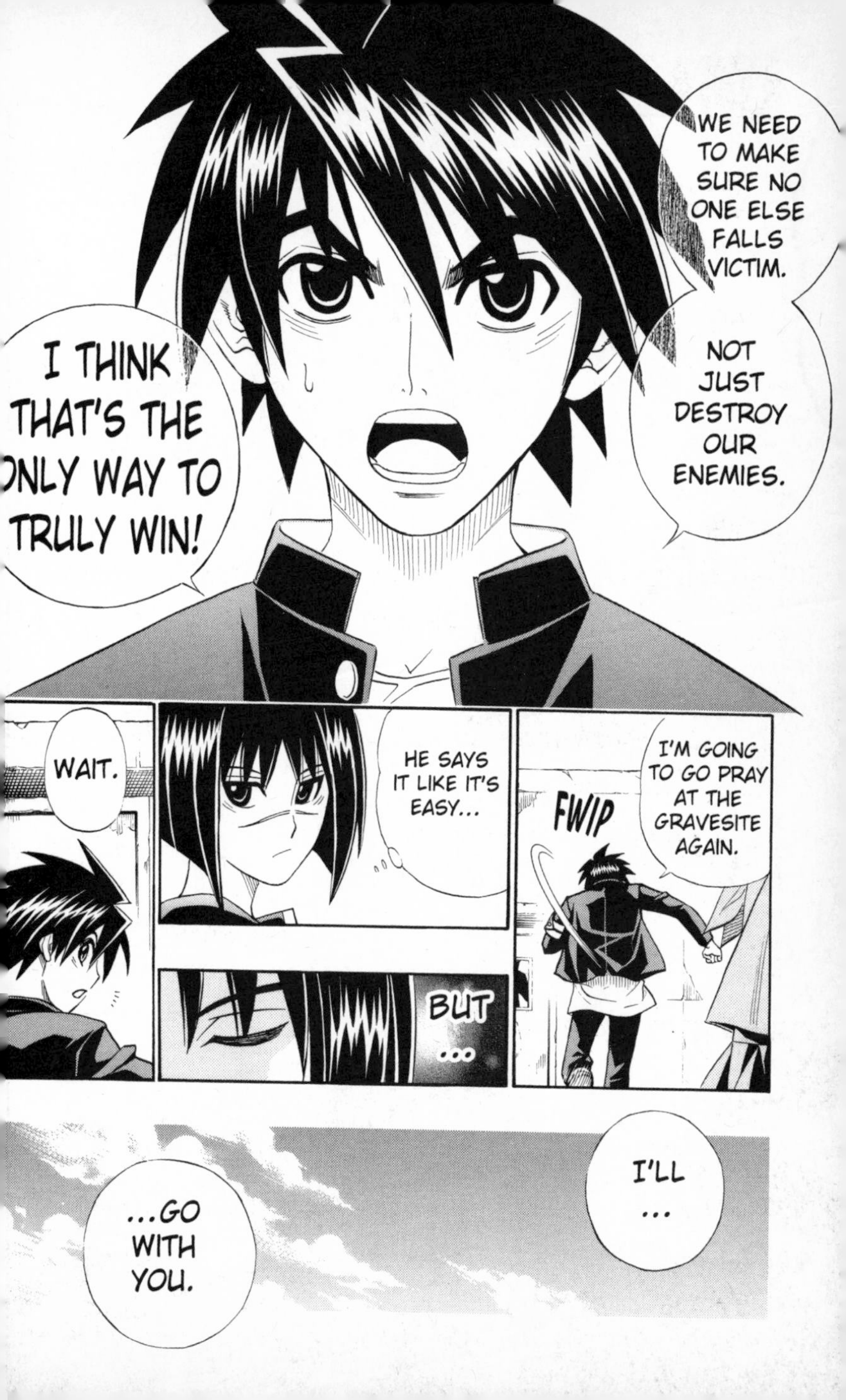
WE NEED TO MAKE SURE NO ONE ELSE FALLS VICTIM.
NOT JUST DESTROY OUR ENEMIES.
I THINK THAT'S THE ONLY WAY TO TRULY WIN!
I'M GOING TO GO PRAY AT THE GRAVESITE AGAIN.
FWIP
HE SAYS IT LIKE IT'S EASY...
BUT ...
WAIT.
I'LL ...
...GO WITH YOU.

READ THIS WAY

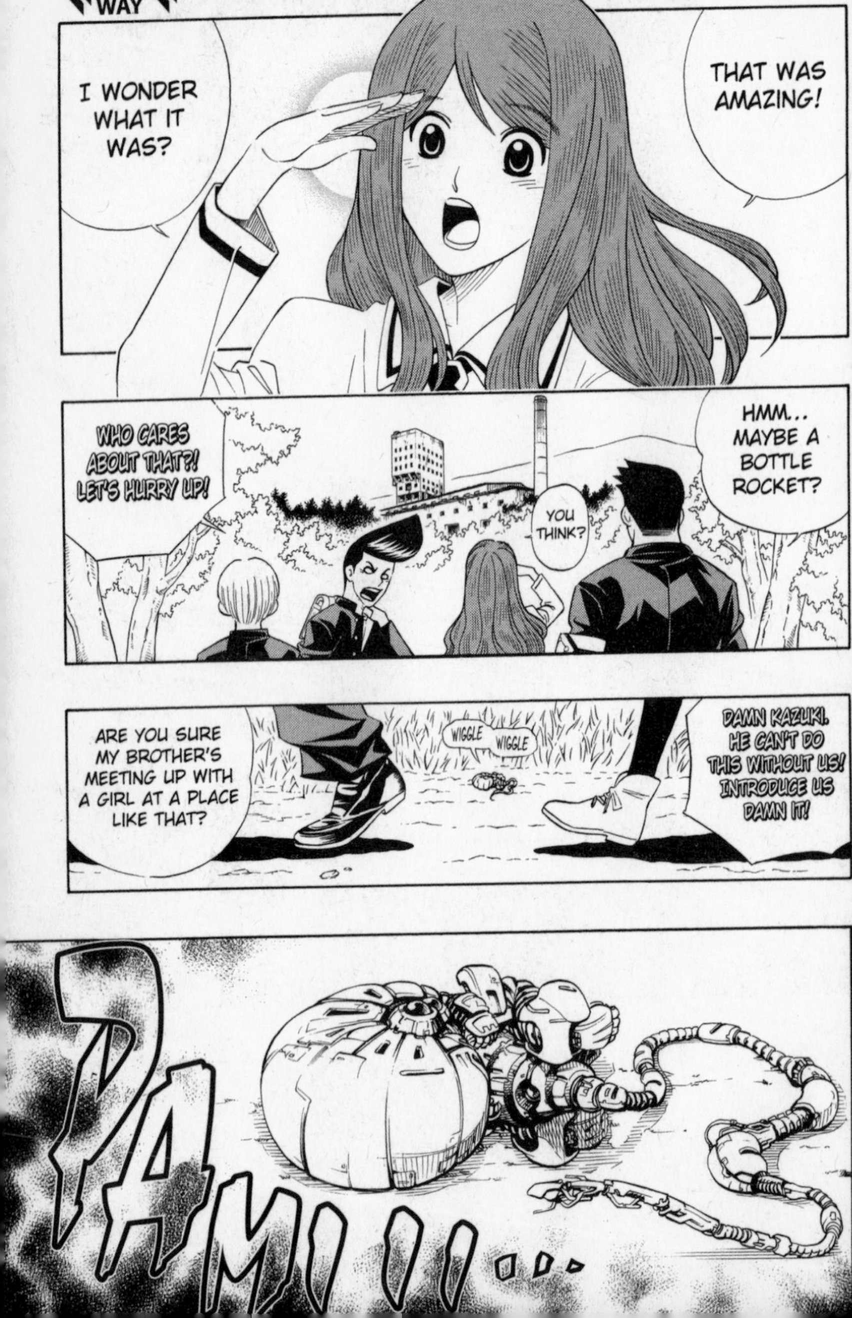
THAT WAS AMAZING!
I WONDER WHAT IT WAS?
HMM.. MAYBE A BOTTLE ROCKET?
YOU THINK?
WHO CARES ABOUT THAT?! LET'S HURRY UP!
DAMN KAZUKI. HE CAN'T DO THIS WITHOUT US! INTRODUCE US DAMN IT!
WIGGLE
WIGGLE
ARE YOU SURE MY BROTHER'S MEETING UP WITH A GIRL AT A PLACE LIKE THAT?
DAM!!!...

Character File No. 4

Tokiko Tsumura

- Bust 78, Waist 55, Hip 79
- Born: August 7th; Leo; Blood type: A; 17 years old.
- Favorites: Rice balls, purple, airy spaces
- Dislikes: Homunculi, unnecessary deaths
- Hobby: Training
- Things she is good at: Getting dressed fast (From uniform to gym clothes in a flash!)
- Affiliation: Organization that governs the Alchemic Warriors (Name has not been revealed at this point)

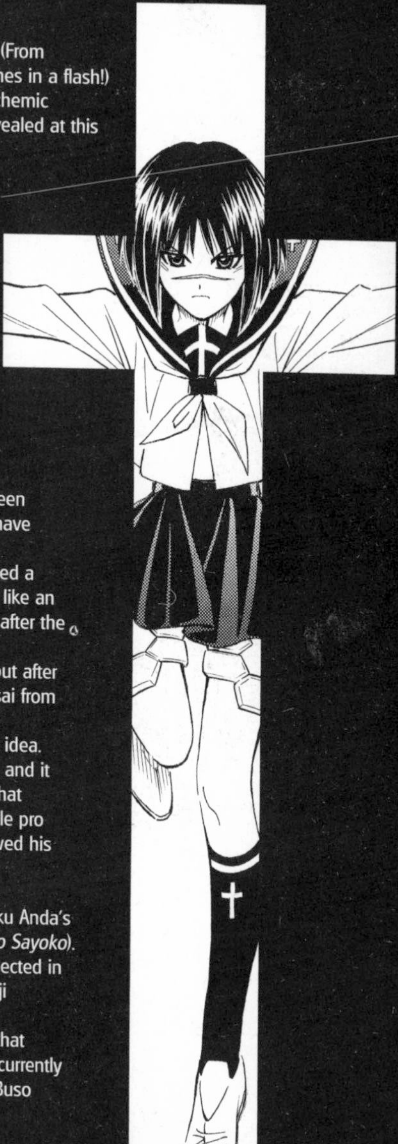

Author's Notes

- She represents the Warrior Heroine I've been wanting to draw for the last four years. I have been continuously conceptualizing her.
- As she is the one guiding Kazuki I've added a sisterly quality to her. (I imagine her to be like an after-school club president that is looking after the younger members)
- I kept thinking how easy she is to draw but after taking a closer look she looks like Battousai from Rurouni Kenshin...
- The scar on her nose is Kurosaki Sensei's idea. We were just talking about random things and it came up while we were talking about "What would you do if you were to draw a female pro wrestling story?" With his consent I borrowed his idea.
- I borrowed her last name Tsumura from a character named Sayoko Tsumura from Riku Anda's novel, "The Sixth Sayoko" (*Rokuban me no Sayoko*). Sayoko's mysteriousness is somewhat reflected in Tokiko's character. I came up with the kanji combination for the name "Tokiko".
- I was hoping she'd be a Warrior Heroine that equals the male character's presence but currently he's by far the most popular character in Buso Renkin... You can do it, Kazuki!

CHAPTER 4: PARASITIC HOMUNCULUS

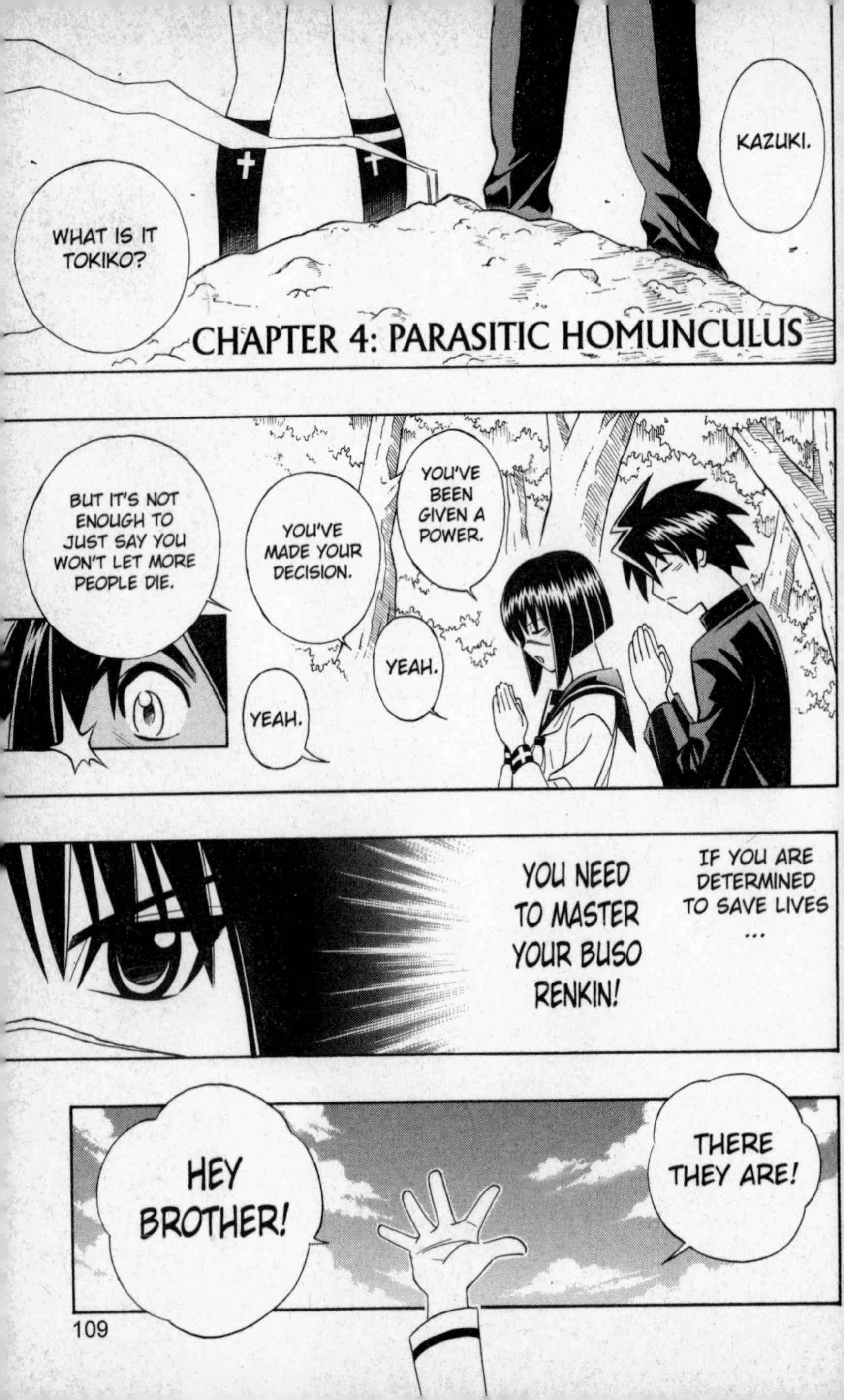
KAZUKI.
WHAT IS IT TOKIKO?
YOU'VE BEEN GIVEN A POWER.
YEAH.
YOU'VE MADE YOUR DECISION.
YEAH.
BUT IT'S NOT ENOUGH TO JUST SAY YOU WON'T LET MORE PEOPLE DIE.
IF YOU ARE DETERMINED TO SAVE LIVES ...
YOU NEED TO MASTER YOUR BUSO RENKIN!
THERE THEY ARE!
HEY BROTHER!

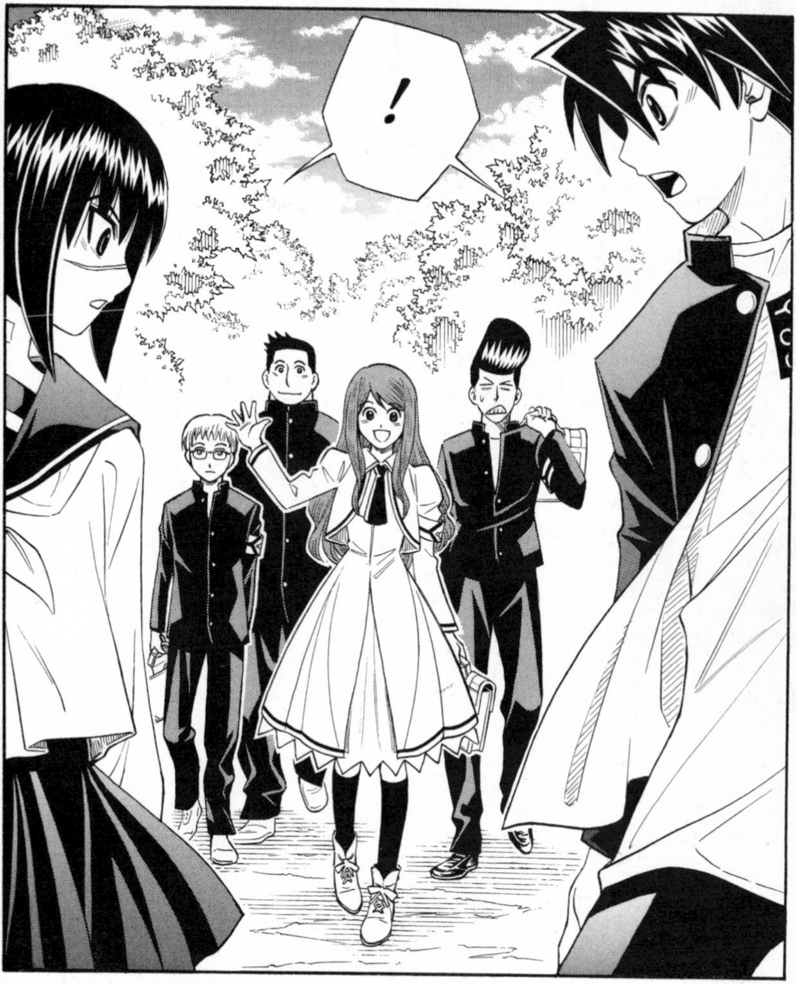
!

CHAPTER 4:
PARASITIC HOMUNCULUS

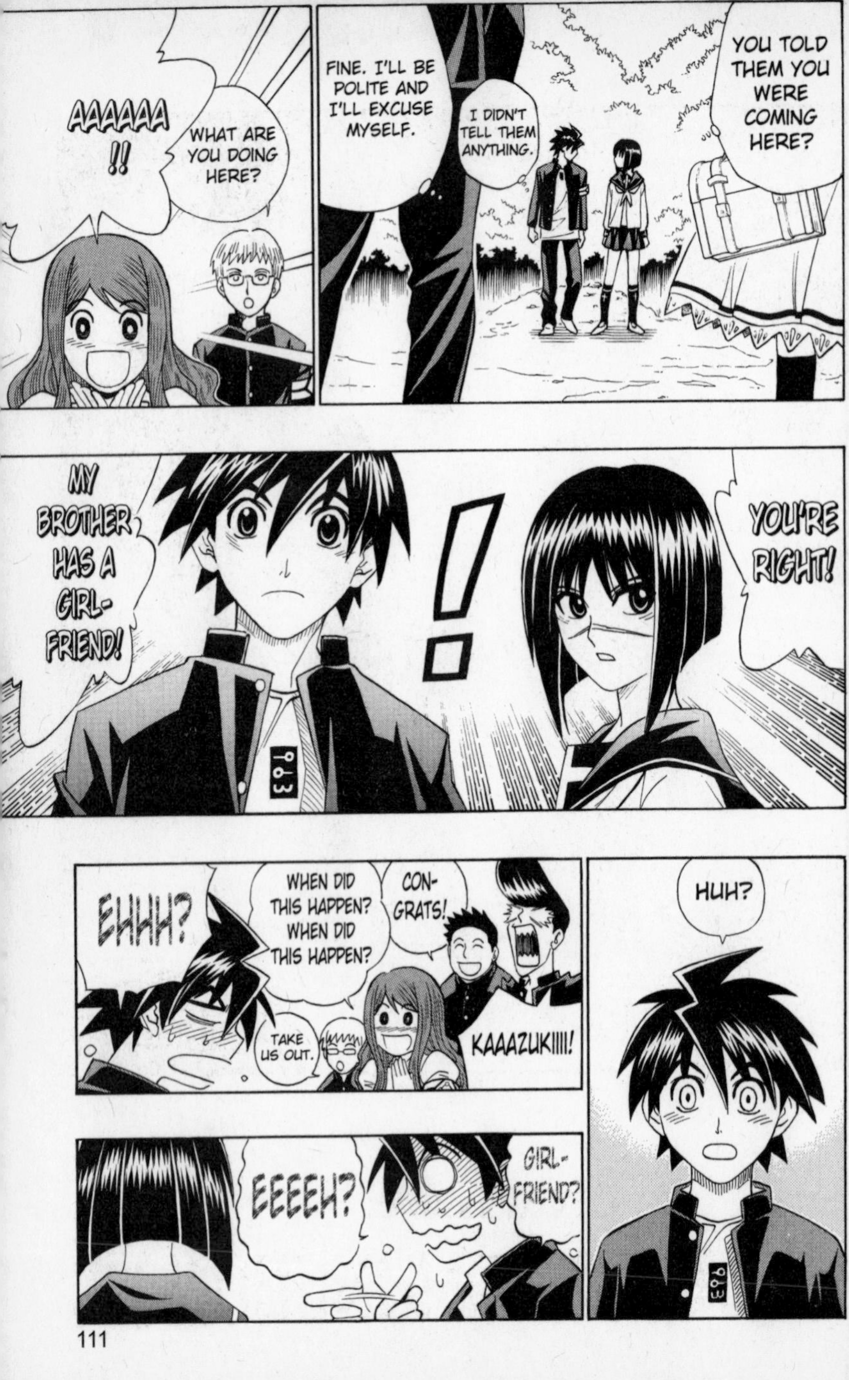
YOU TOLD THEM YOU WERE COMING HERE?
I DIDN'T TELL THEM ANYTHING.
FINE. I'LL BE POLITE AND I'LL EXCUSE MYSELF.
WHAT ARE YOU DOING HERE?
AAAAAA!!
YOU'RE RIGHT!
!
MY BROTHER HAS A GIRL-FRIEND!
HUH?
CON-GRATS!
KAAAZUKIIII!
WHEN DID THIS HAPPEN? WHEN DID THIS HAPPEN?
TAKE US OUT.
EHHH?
GIRL-FRIEND?
EEEEH?

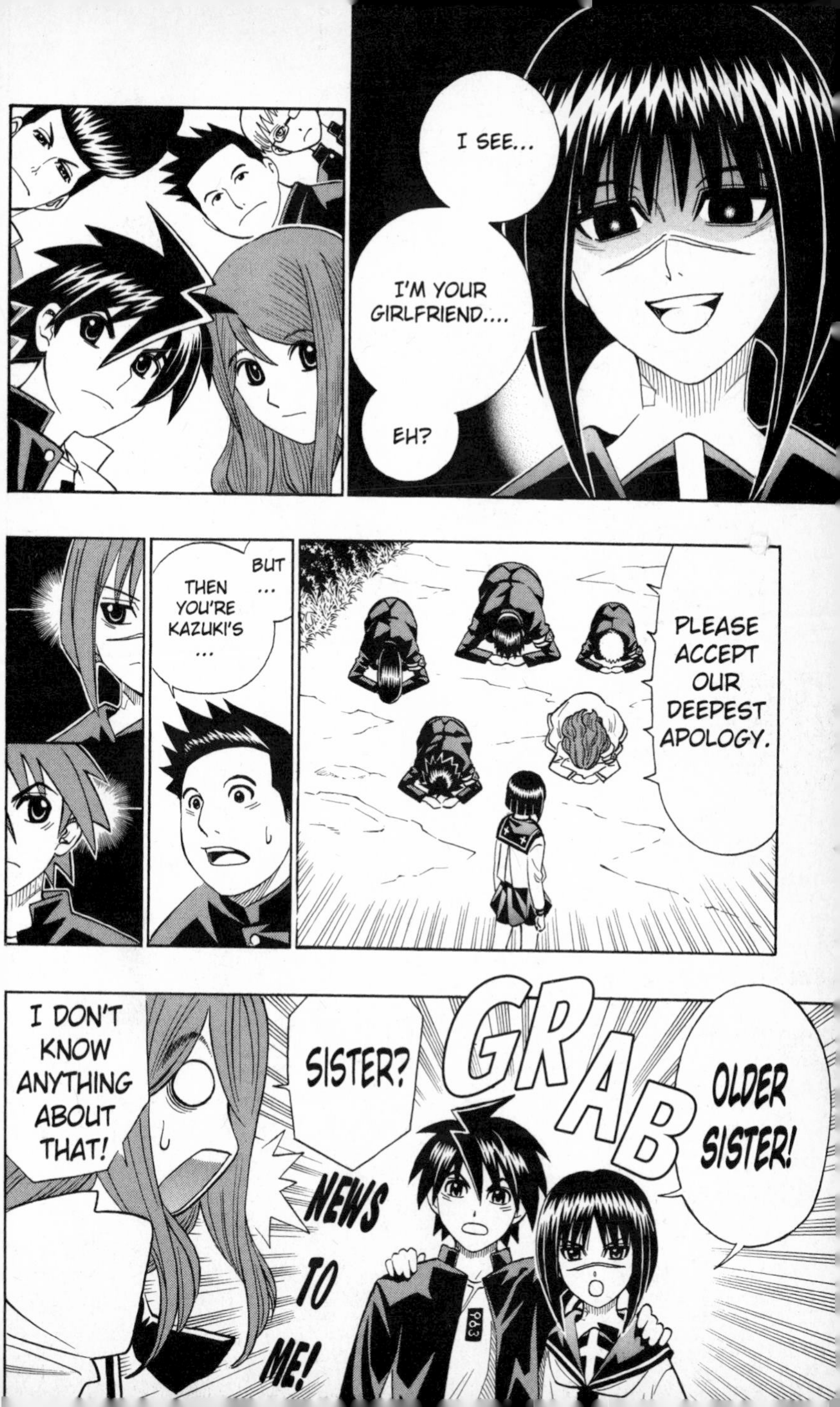

I SEE...
I'M YOUR GIRLFRIEND....
EH?
PLEASE ACCEPT OUR DEEPEST APOLOGY.
BUT... THEN YOU'RE KAZUKI'S...
OLDER SISTER!
GRAB
SISTER?
I DON'T KNOW ANYTHING ABOUT THAT!
NEWS TO ME!

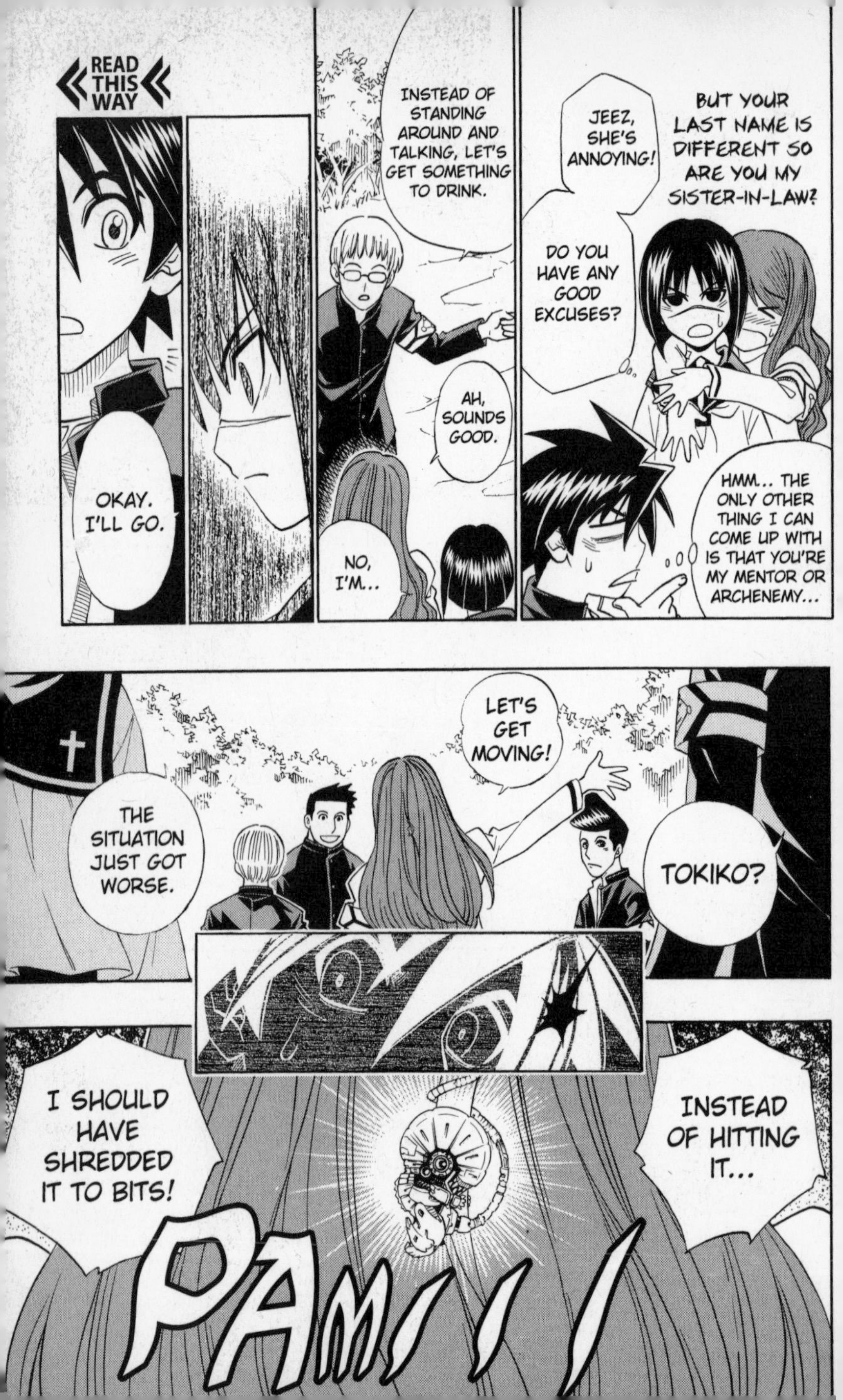
READ THIS WAY
BUT YOUR LAST NAME IS DIFFERENT SO ARE YOU MY SISTER-IN-LAW?
JEEZ, SHE'S ANNOYING!
DO YOU HAVE ANY GOOD EXCUSES?
HMM... THE ONLY OTHER THING I CAN COME UP WITH IS THAT YOU'RE MY MENTOR OR ARCHENEMY...
INSTEAD OF STANDING AROUND AND TALKING, LET'S GET SOMETHING TO DRINK.
AH, SOUNDS GOOD.
NO, I'M...
OKAY. I'LL GO.
TOKIKO?
LET'S GET MOVING!
THE SITUATION JUST GOT WORSE.
INSTEAD OF HITTING IT...
I SHOULD HAVE SHREDDED IT TO BITS!
PAM!

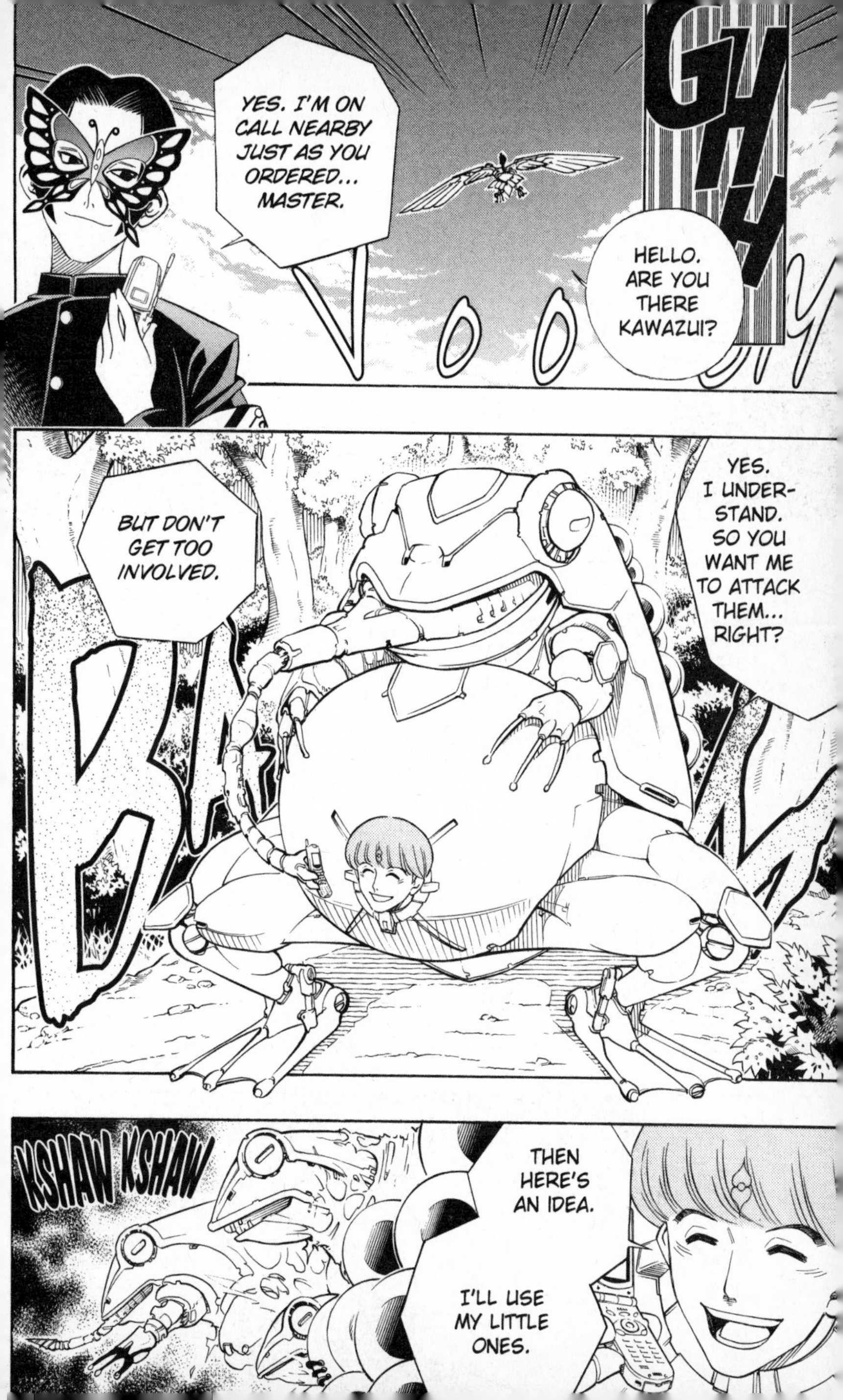
HELLO. ARE YOU THERE KAWAZUI?
YES. I'M ON CALL NEARBY JUST AS YOU ORDERED... MASTER.
YES. I UNDER-STAND. SO YOU WANT ME TO ATTACK THEM... RIGHT?
BUT DON'T GET TOO INVOLVED.
THEN HERE'S AN IDEA.
I'LL USE MY LITTLE ONES.
KSHAW KSHAW

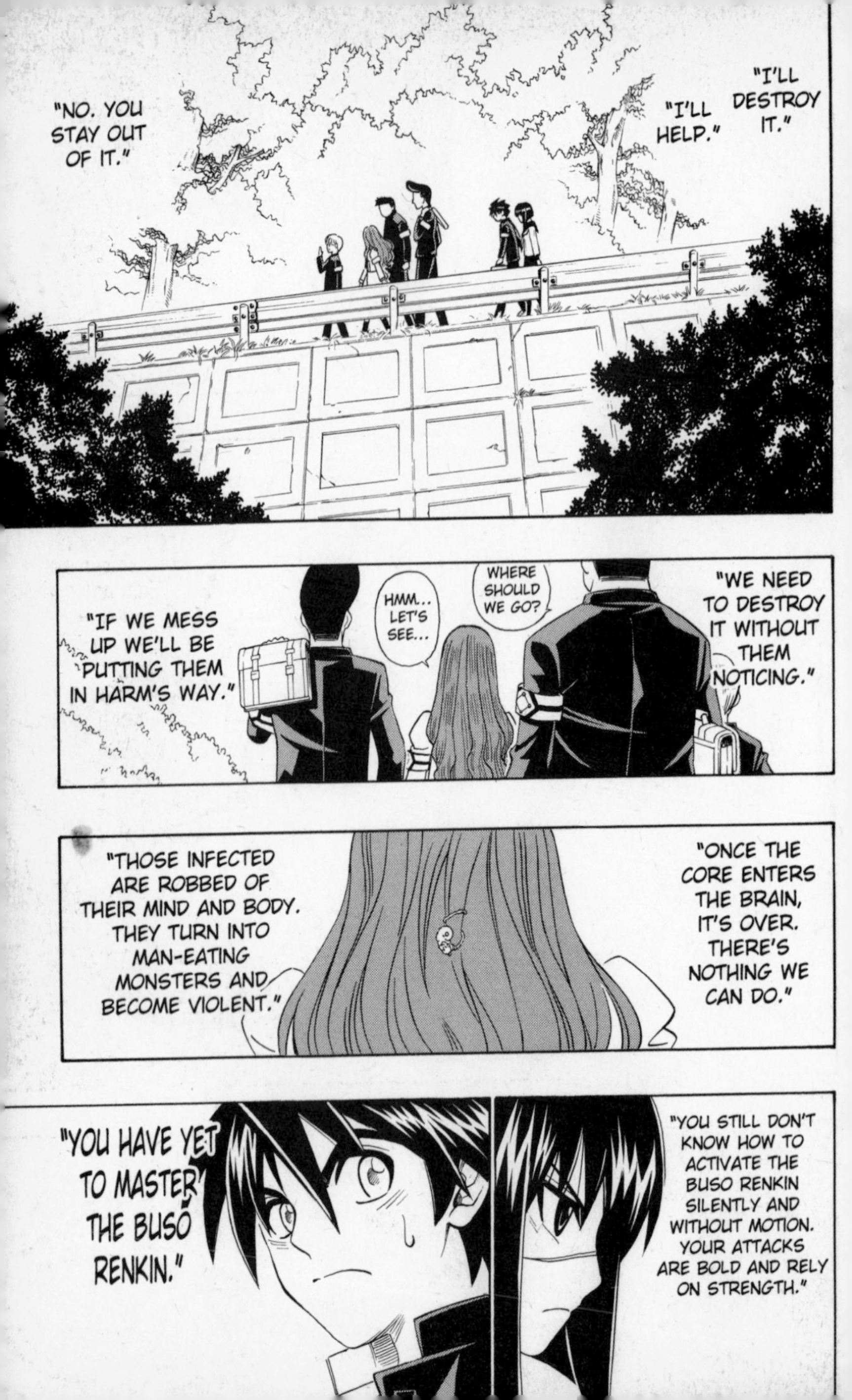
"I'LL DESTROY IT."
"I'LL HELP."
"NO. YOU STAY OUT OF IT."
"WE NEED TO DESTROY IT WITHOUT THEM NOTICING."
WHERE SHOULD WE GO?
HMM... LET'S SEE...
"IF WE MESS UP WE'LL BE PUTTING THEM IN HARM'S WAY."
"ONCE THE CORE ENTERS THE BRAIN, IT'S OVER. THERE'S NOTHING WE CAN DO."
"THOSE INFECTED ARE ROBBED OF THEIR MIND AND BODY. THEY TURN INTO MAN-EATING MONSTERS AND BECOME VIOLENT."
"YOU STILL DON'T KNOW HOW TO ACTIVATE THE BUSO RENKIN SILENTLY AND WITHOUT MOTION. YOUR ATTACKS ARE BOLD AND RELY ON STRENGTH."
"YOU HAVE YET TO MASTER THE BUSŌ RENKIN."

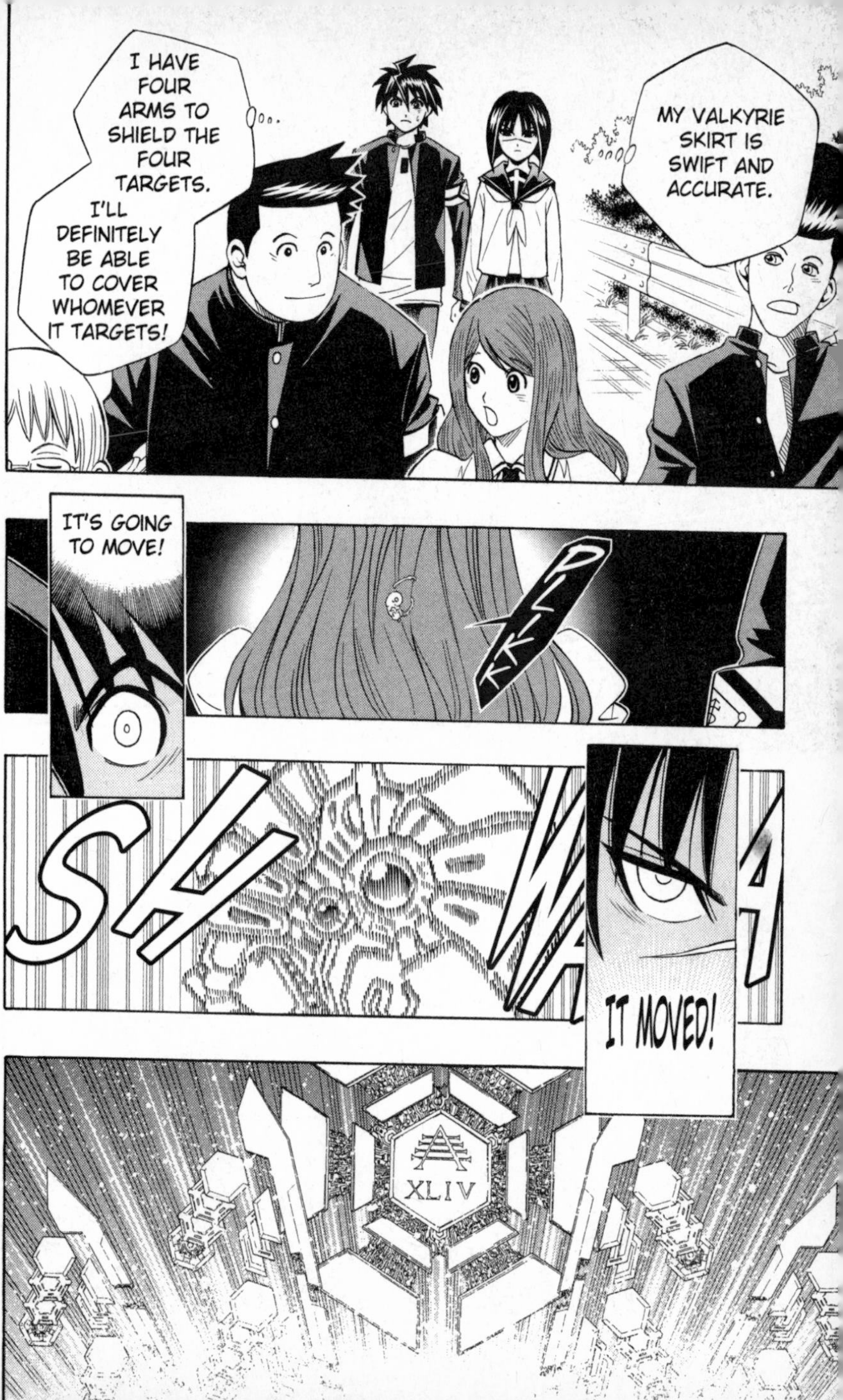
MY VALKYRIE SKIRT IS SWIFT AND ACCURATE.
I HAVE FOUR ARMS TO SHIELD THE FOUR TARGETS.
I'LL DEFINITELY BE ABLE TO COVER WHOMEVER IT TARGETS!
PLIKK
IT'S GOING TO MOVE!
IT MOVED!
SHWA
XLIV

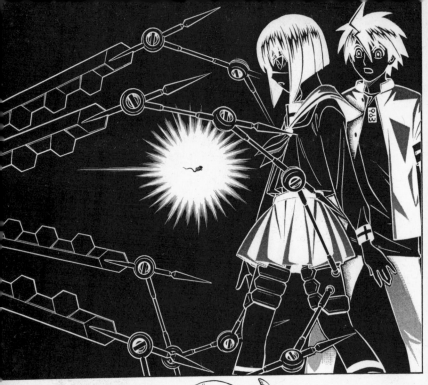

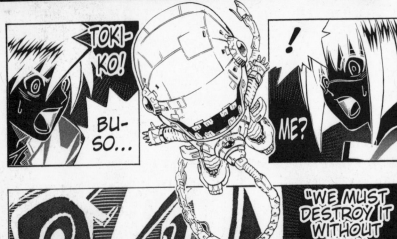

TOKI-KO!

BU-SO...

!

ME?

"WE MUST DESTROY IT WITHOUT THEM NOTICING."

117

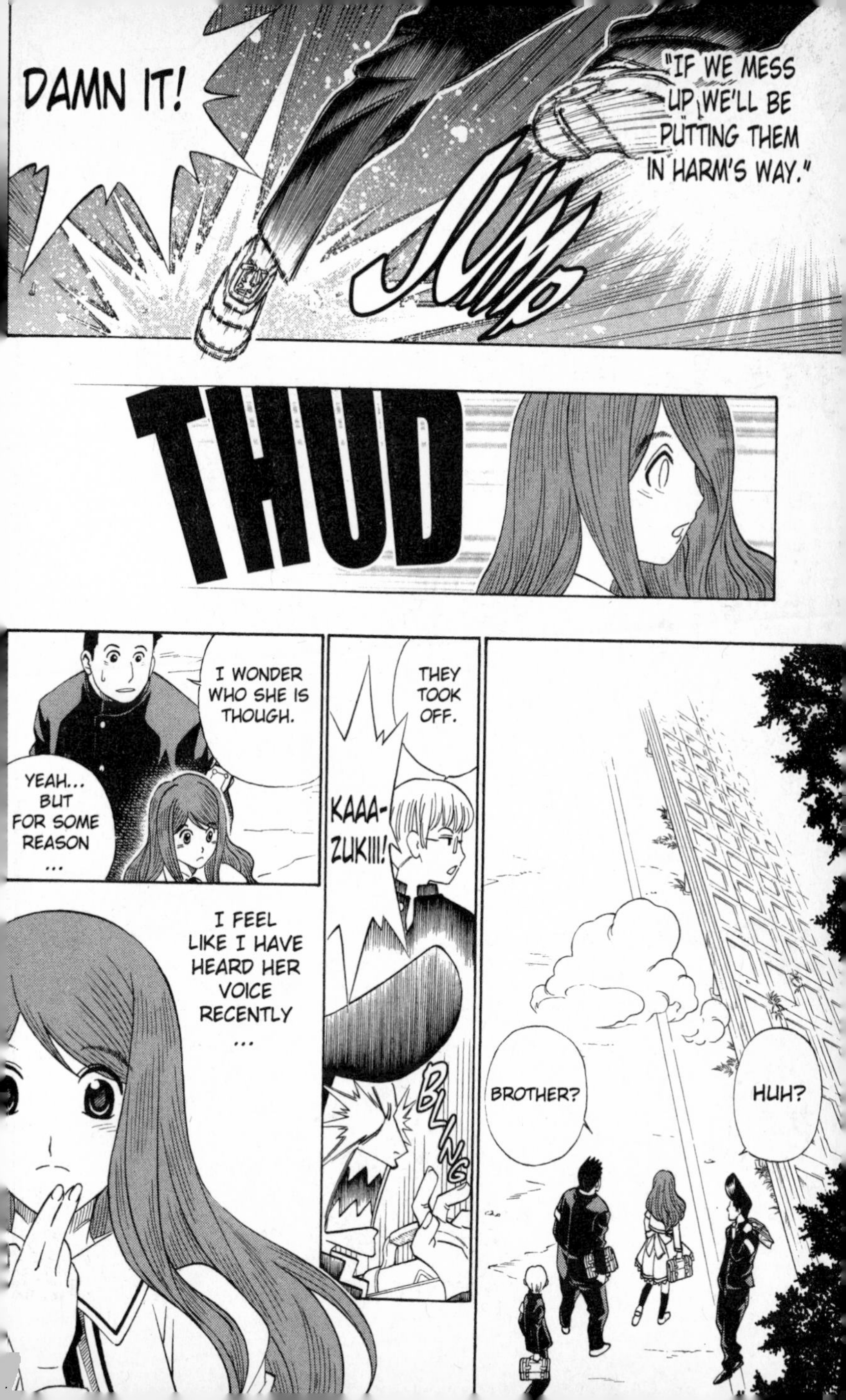
"IF WE MESS UP WE'LL BE PUTTING THEM IN HARM'S WAY."
DAMN IT!
THUD
HUH?
BROTHER?
THEY TOOK OFF.
KAAA-ZUKIII!
I WONDER WHO SHE IS THOUGH.
YEAH... BUT FOR SOME REASON ...
I FEEL LIKE I HAVE HEARD HER VOICE RECENTLY ...

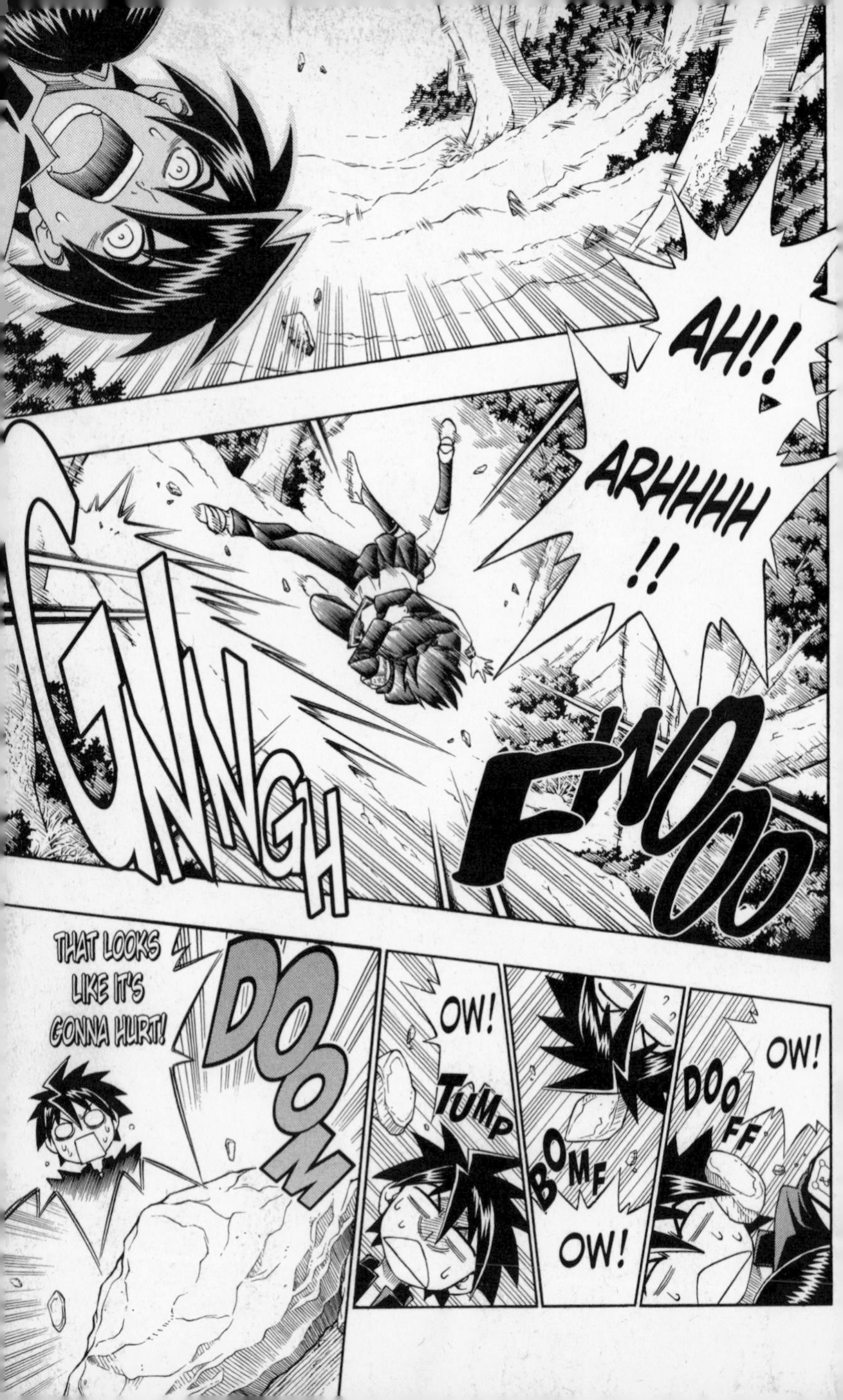
AH!!
ARHHHH!!
FWOOO
GWNNGH
OW!
DOOFF
BOMF
OW!
OW!
TUMP
DOOOM
THAT LOOKS LIKE IT'S GONNA HURT!

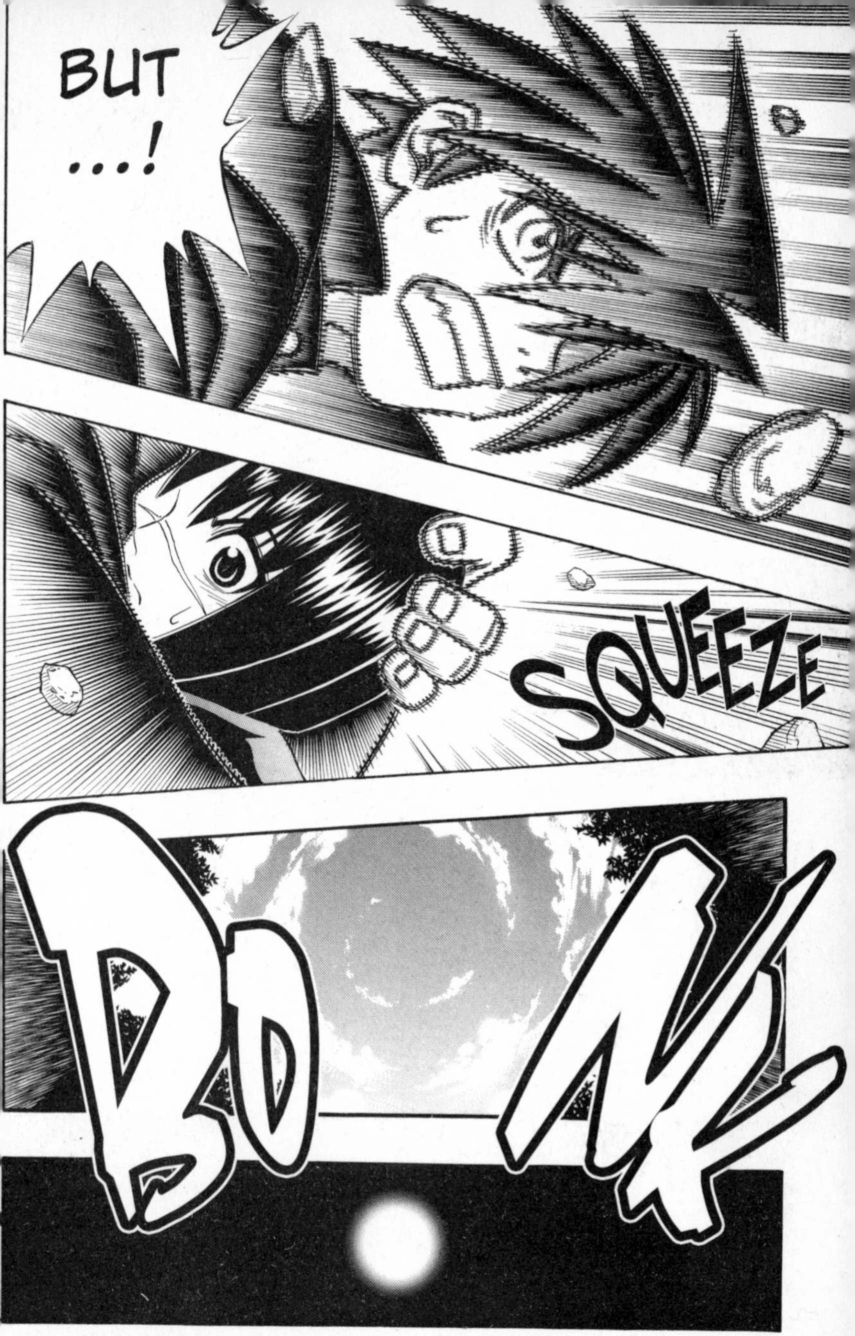
BUT ...!
SQUEEZE
BOOM

READ THIS WAY

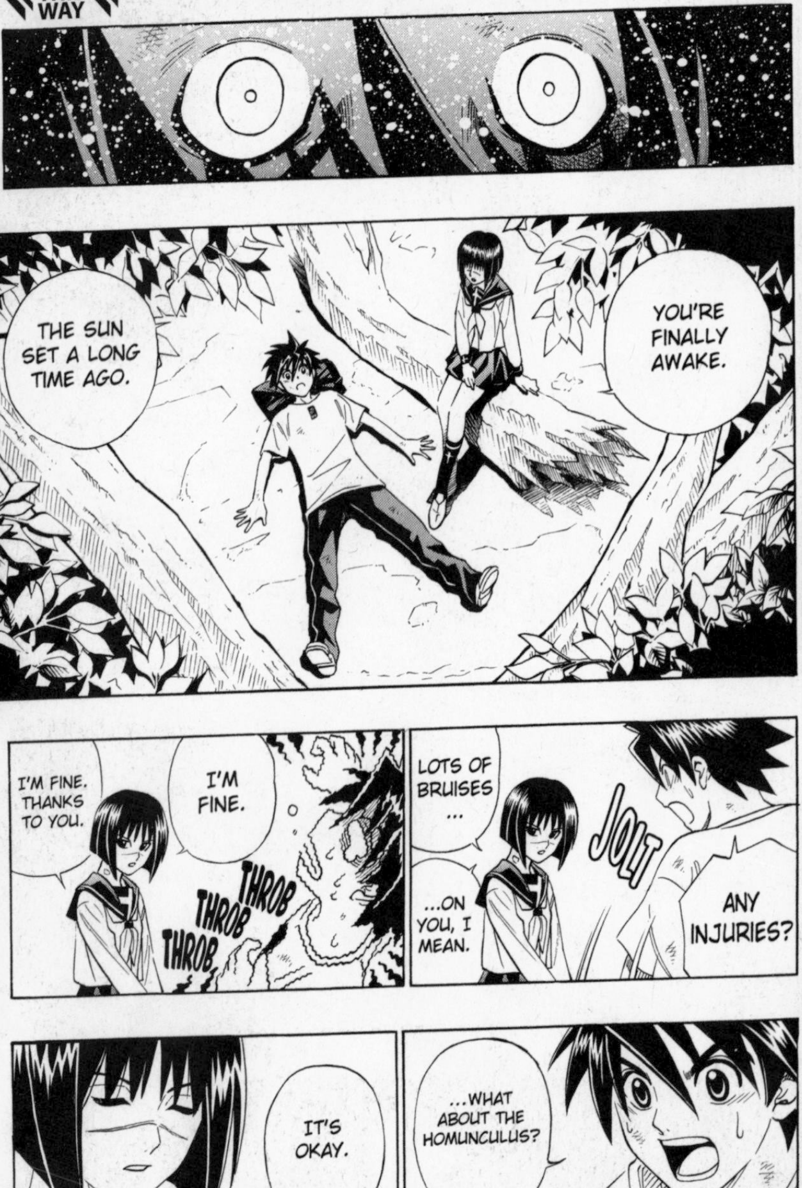
YOU'RE FINALLY AWAKE.
THE SUN SET A LONG TIME AGO.
JOLT
ANY INJURIES?
LOTS OF BRUISES ...
...ON YOU, I MEAN.
I'M FINE.
THROB THROB THROB
I'M FINE. THANKS TO YOU.
...WHAT ABOUT THE HOMUNCULUS?
IT'S OKAY.

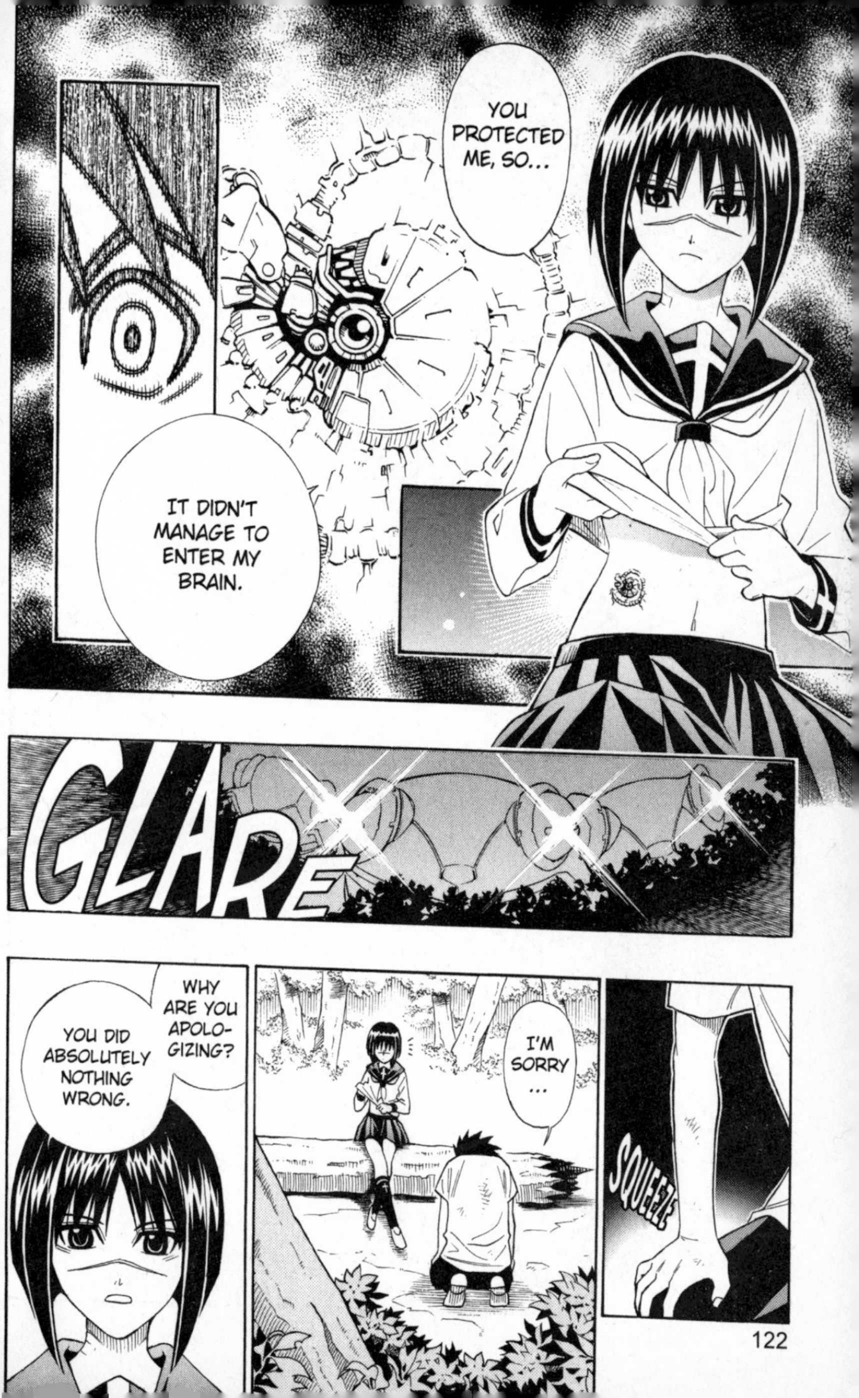
YOU PROTECTED ME, SO...
IT DIDN'T MANAGE TO ENTER MY BRAIN.
GLARE
SQUEEZE
I'M SORRY...
WHY ARE YOU APOLOGIZING?
YOU DID ABSOLUTELY NOTHING WRONG.

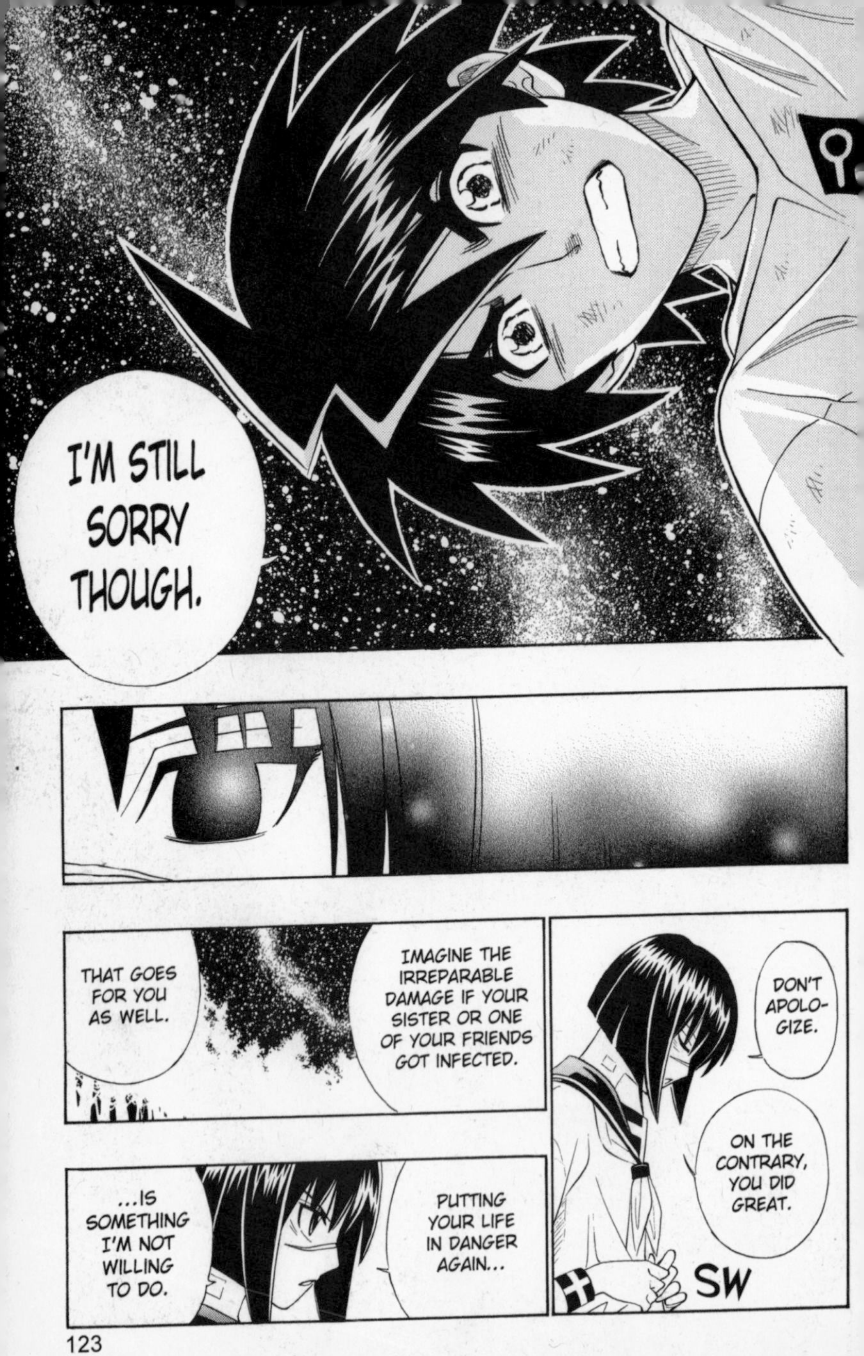
I'M STILL SORRY THOUGH.
DON'T APOLOGIZE.
ON THE CONTRARY, YOU DID GREAT.
SW
IMAGINE THE IRREPARABLE DAMAGE IF YOUR SISTER OR ONE OF YOUR FRIENDS GOT INFECTED.
THAT GOES FOR YOU AS WELL.
PUTTING YOUR LIFE IN DANGER AGAIN...
...IS SOMETHING I'M NOT WILLING TO DO.

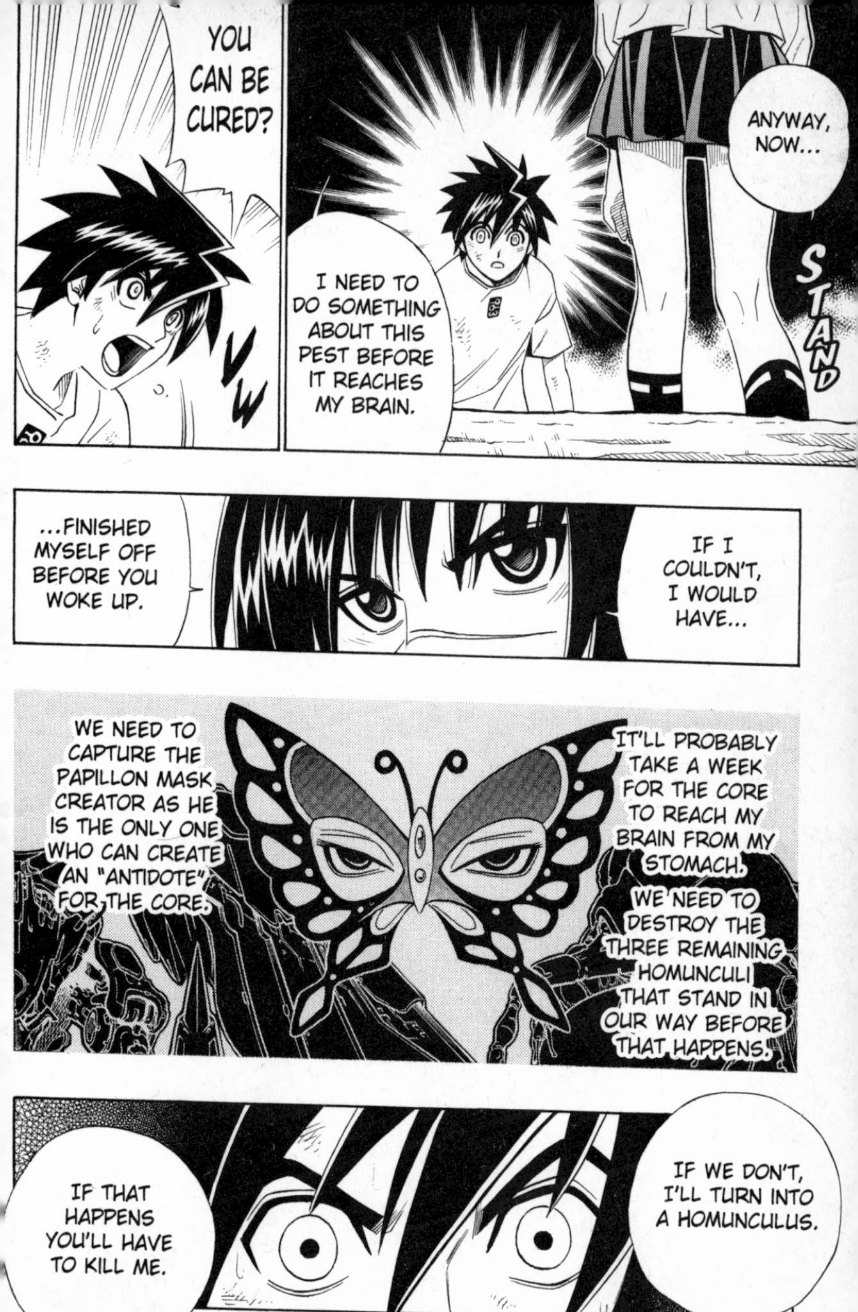
ANYWAY, NOW...
STAND
I NEED TO DO SOMETHING ABOUT THIS PEST BEFORE IT REACHES MY BRAIN.
YOU CAN BE CURED?
VW
IF I COULDN'T, I WOULD HAVE...
...FINISHED MYSELF OFF BEFORE YOU WOKE UP.
IT'LL PROBABLY TAKE A WEEK FOR THE CORE TO REACH MY BRAIN FROM MY STOMACH.
WE NEED TO DESTROY THE THREE REMAINING HOMUNCULI THAT STAND IN OUR WAY BEFORE THAT HAPPENS.
WE NEED TO CAPTURE THE PAPILLON MASK CREATOR AS HE IS THE ONLY ONE WHO CAN CREATE AN "ANTIDOTE" FOR THE CORE.
IF WE DON'T, I'LL TURN INTO A HOMUNCULUS.
IF THAT HAPPENS YOU'LL HAVE TO KILL ME.

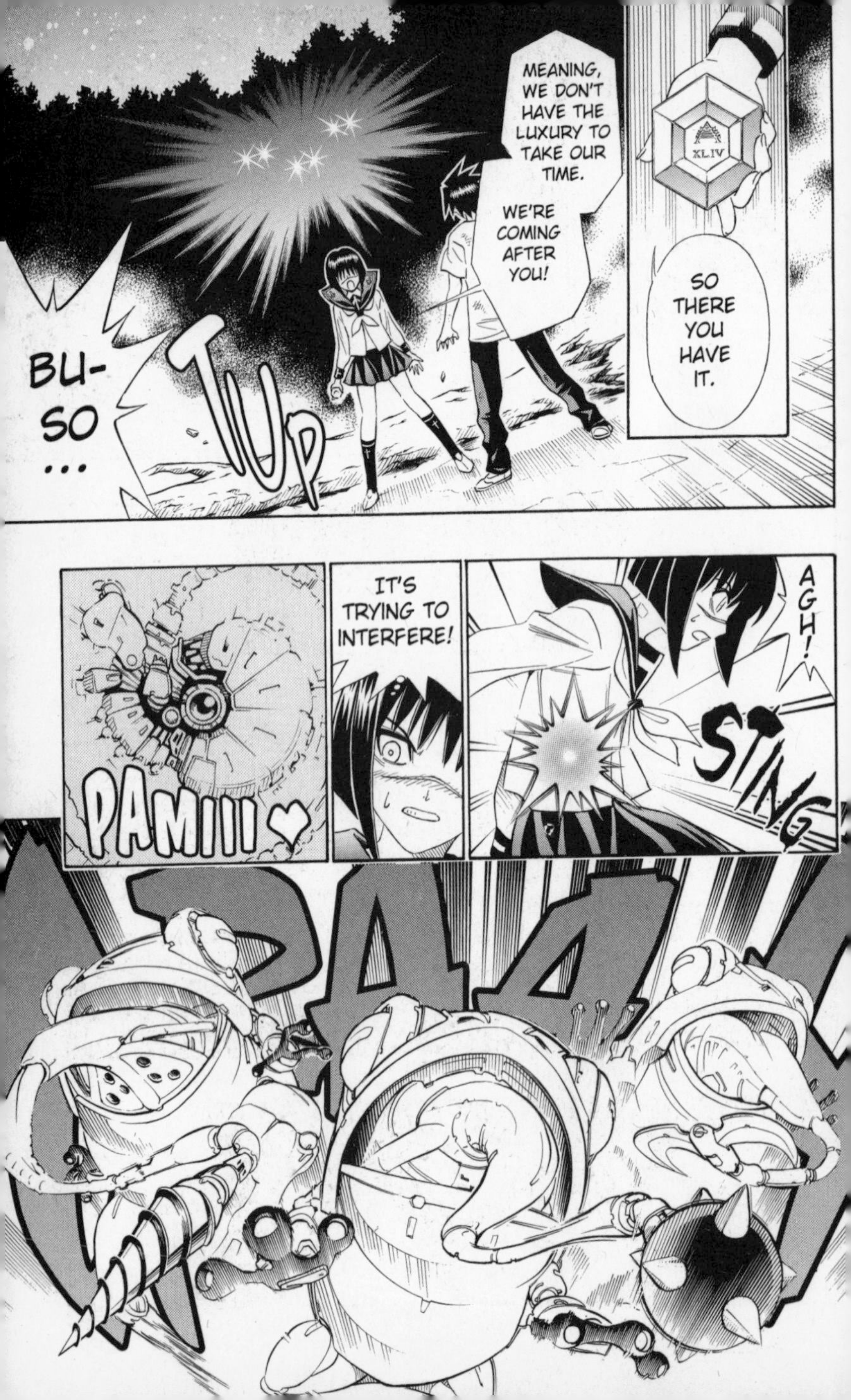
XLIV
SO THERE YOU HAVE IT.
MEANING, WE DON'T HAVE THE LUXURY TO TAKE OUR TIME.
WE'RE COMING AFTER YOU!
TIUP
BU-SO...
AGH!
STING
IT'S TRYING TO INTERFERE!
PAMIII ♥

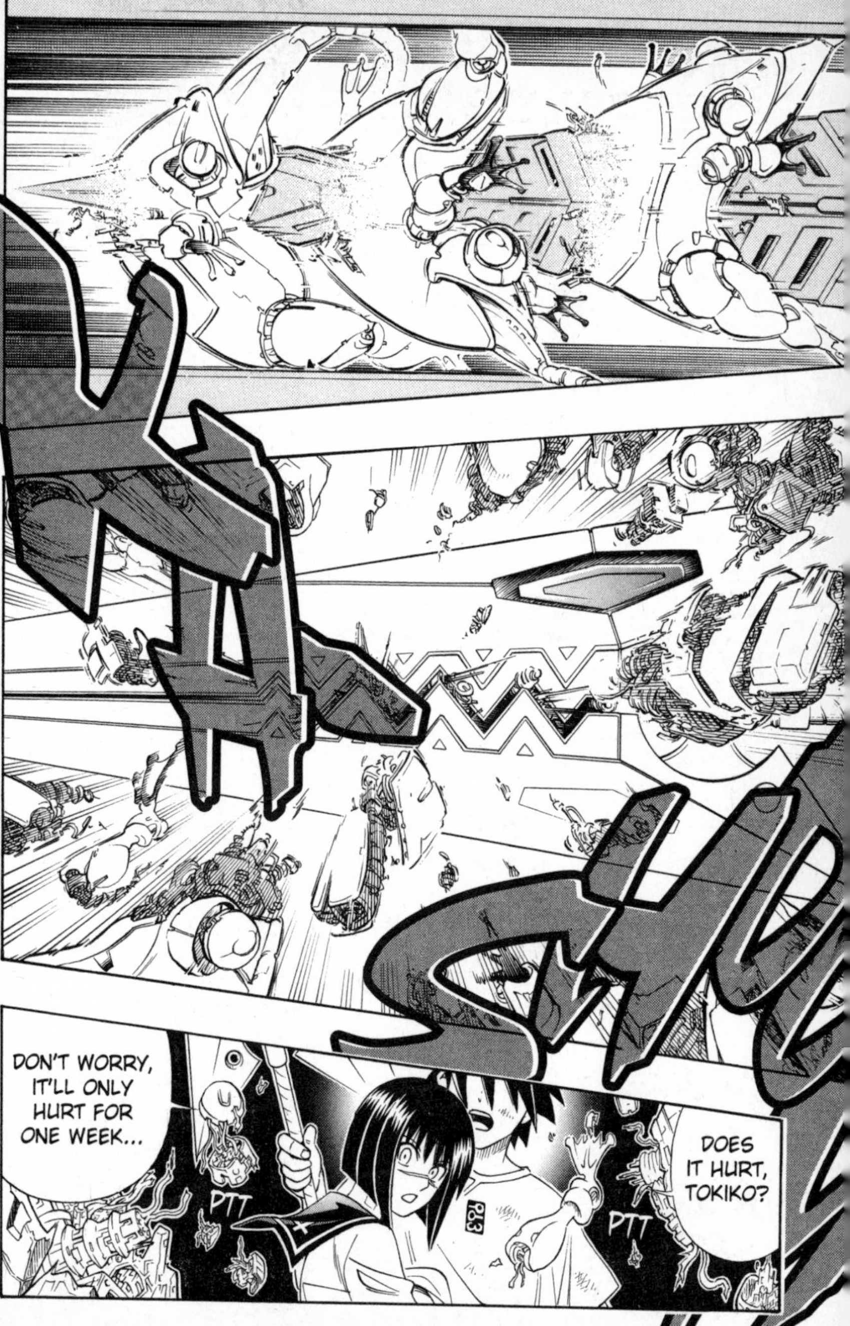
DOES IT HURT, TOKIKO?
PTT
PTT
DON'T WORRY, IT'LL ONLY HURT FOR ONE WEEK...

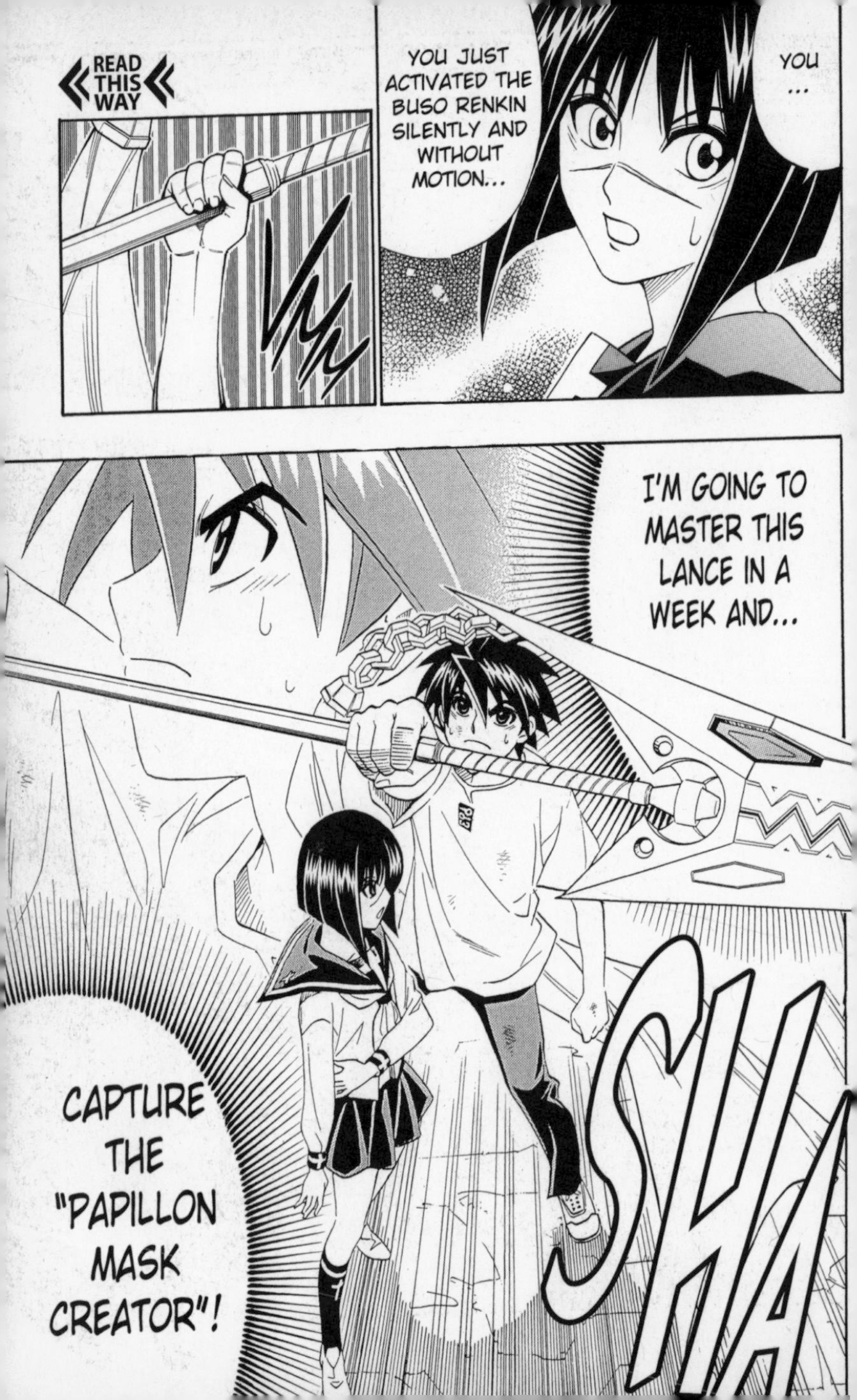
READ THIS WAY
YOU ...
YOU JUST ACTIVATED THE BUSO RENKIN SILENTLY AND WITHOUT MOTION...
I'M GOING TO MASTER THIS LANCE IN A WEEK AND...
SHA
CAPTURE THE "PAPILLON MASK CREATOR"!

Character File No. 5

Mahiro Muto

- Height: 161 cm; Weight: 49kg
- Bust 85, Waist 59, Hip 88
- Born: February 29th; Pisces; Blood type: 0; 15 years old
- Favorites: Mentaiko spaghetti, earth tones, Chi-chin, Sa-chan & Tokiko, reading manga
- Dislikes: Green veggie juice, marathons
- Hobbies: Checking out new candy products
- Things she is good at: Being outgoing (she can have a friendly chit-chat with someone who she's known for five minutes!)
- Affiliation: Private Ginsei Academy First Year High School Student Classroom A, Dorm Resident

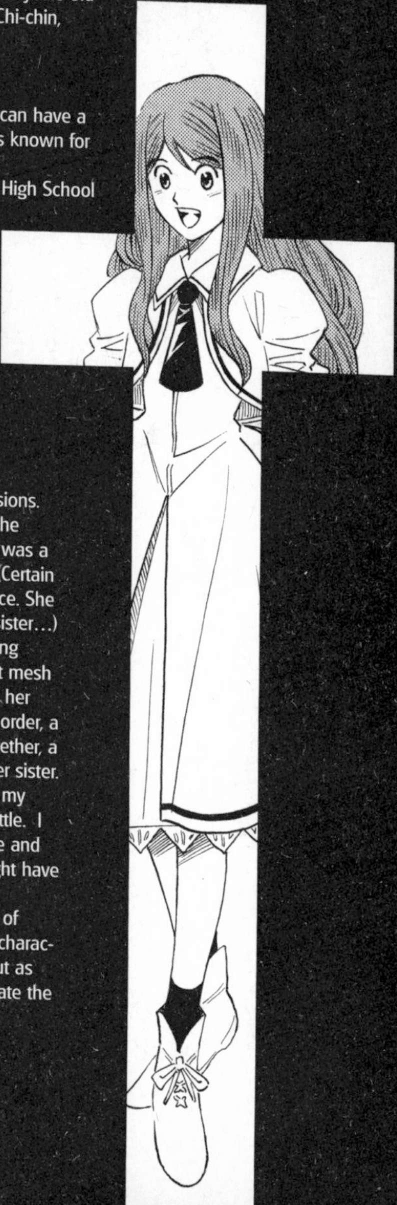

Author's Notes

- She was the character with the most revisions. She was first cast as an older classmate, the "Heroine who got left behind a year." She was a very challenging character to manipulate. (Certain things haven't changed, like her appearance. She doesn't look like she is Kazuki's younger sister...) I planned her to be the Heroine representing normalcy, opposite of Tokiko, but I couldn't mesh it well together. Instead I decided to make her relationship with Kazuki simpler! She is in order, a classmate, a girl who he grew up with together, a cousin, an older sister, and lastly, a younger sister.
- Her uniform is a typical sailor uniform but my friend advised me I should play with it a little. I used a Gothic Lolita Magazine as reference and designed it. Now looking at it, I think I might have had too much fun with the design?
- She was supposed to complement a side of Kazuki's daily life and be a well-balanced character that would feed off of Kazuki's jokes but as the chapters went on... Never underestimate the Muto family genetics.

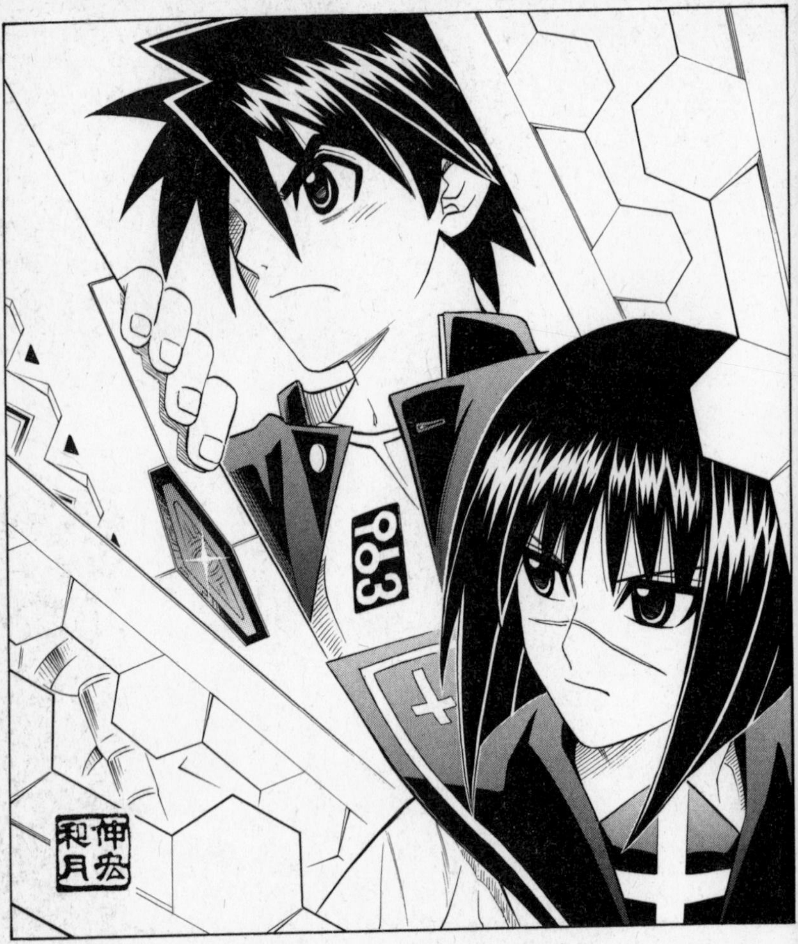

CHAPTER 5:
VS. KAWAZUI (Part 1)

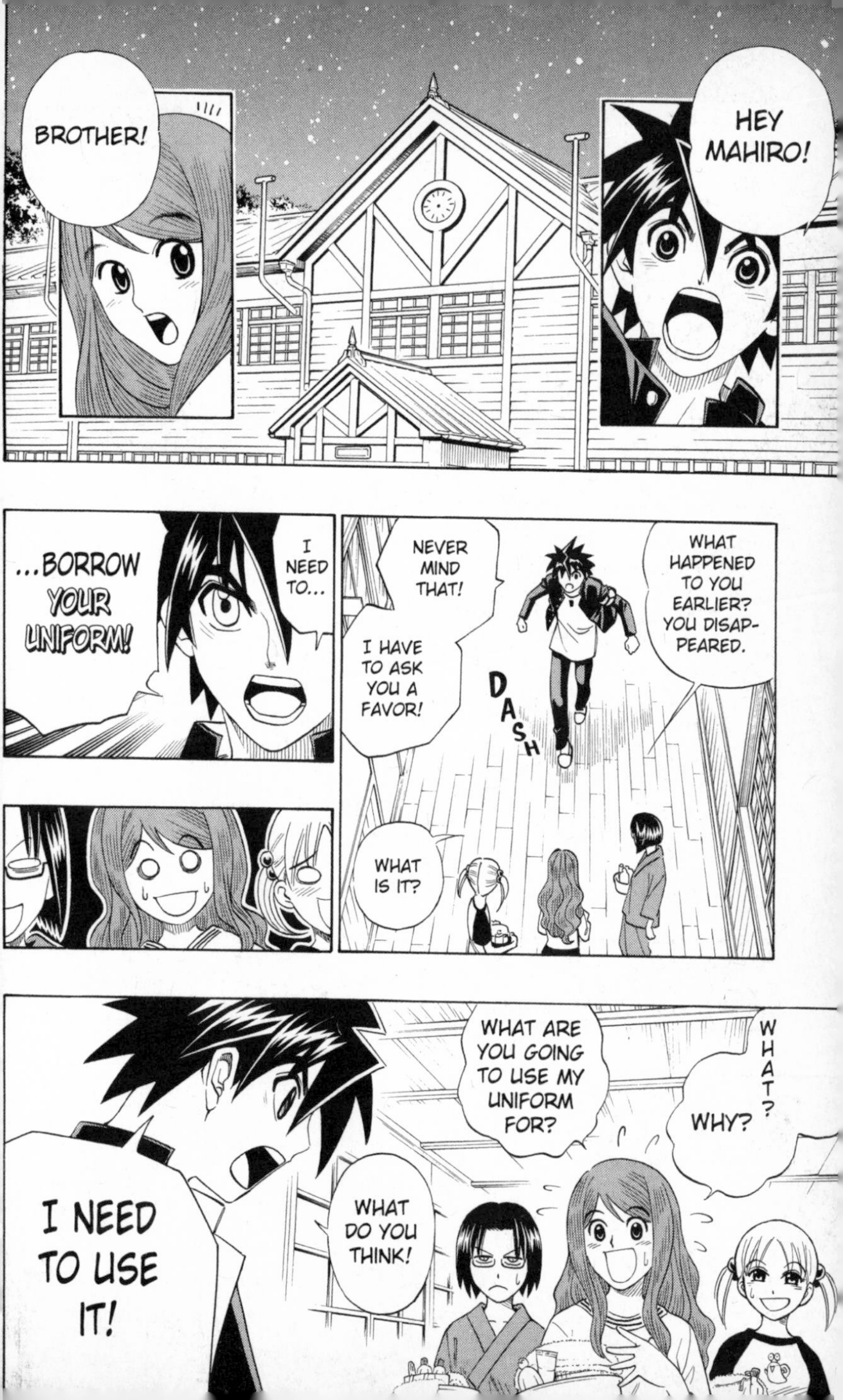

HEY MAHIRO!
BROTHER!
WHAT HAPPENED TO YOU EARLIER? YOU DISAPPEARED.
NEVER MIND THAT!
I HAVE TO ASK YOU A FAVOR!
DASH
WHAT IS IT?
I NEED TO...
...BORROW YOUR UNIFORM!
WHAT? WHAT?
WHY?
WHAT ARE YOU GOING TO USE MY UNIFORM FOR?
WHAT DO YOU THINK!
I NEED TO USE IT!

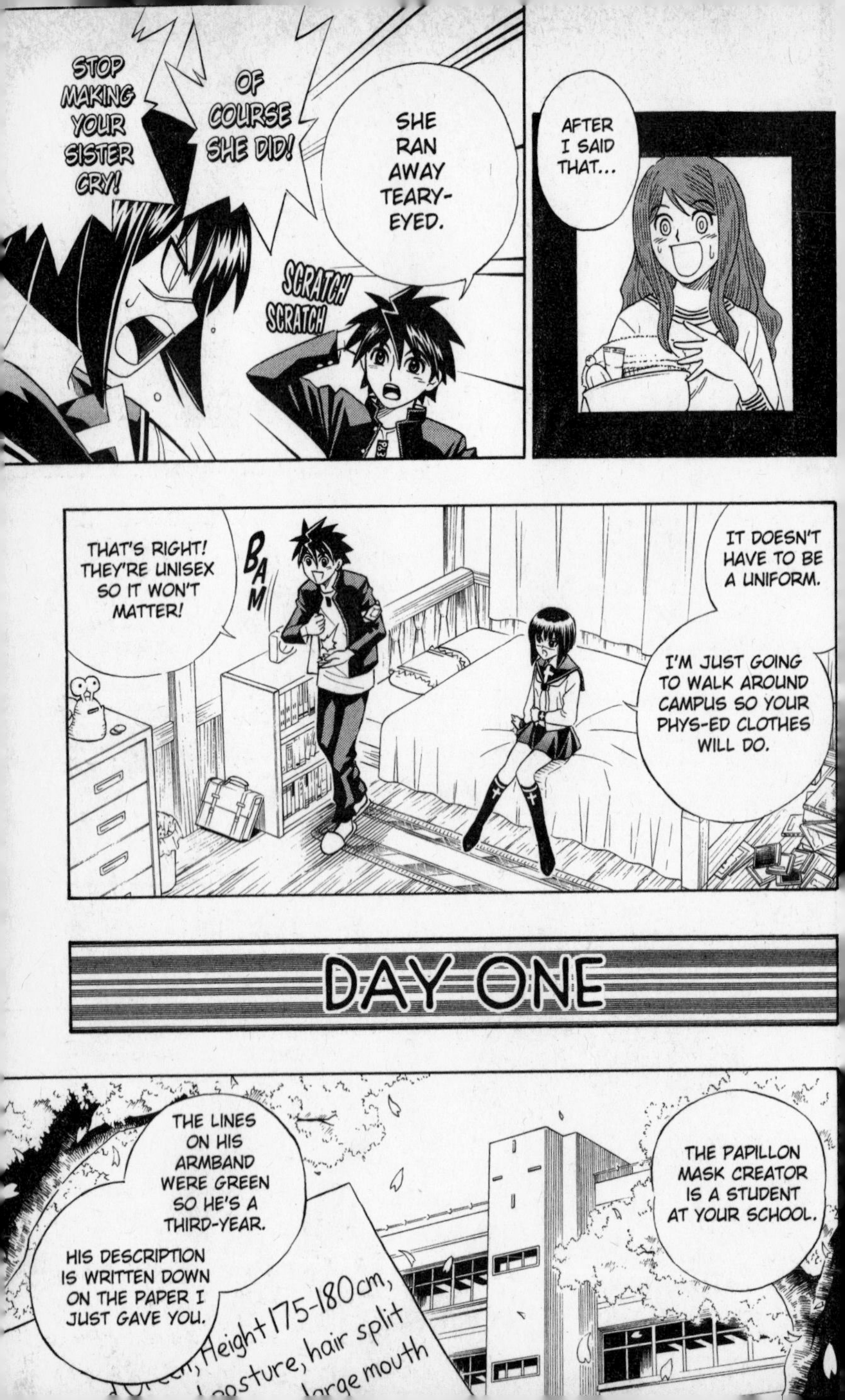
AFTER I SAID THAT...
SHE RAN AWAY TEARY-EYED.
OF COURSE SHE DID!
STOP MAKING YOUR SISTER CRY!
SCRATCH SCRATCH
IT DOESN'T HAVE TO BE A UNIFORM.
I'M JUST GOING TO WALK AROUND CAMPUS SO YOUR PHYS-ED CLOTHES WILL DO.
BAM
THAT'S RIGHT! THEY'RE UNISEX SO IT WON'T MATTER!
DAY ONE
THE PAPILLON MASK CREATOR IS A STUDENT AT YOUR SCHOOL.
THE LINES ON HIS ARMBAND WERE GREEN SO HE'S A THIRD-YEAR.
HIS DESCRIPTION IS WRITTEN DOWN ON THE PAPER I JUST GAVE YOU.
Height 175-180cm, hair split
posture,
large mouth

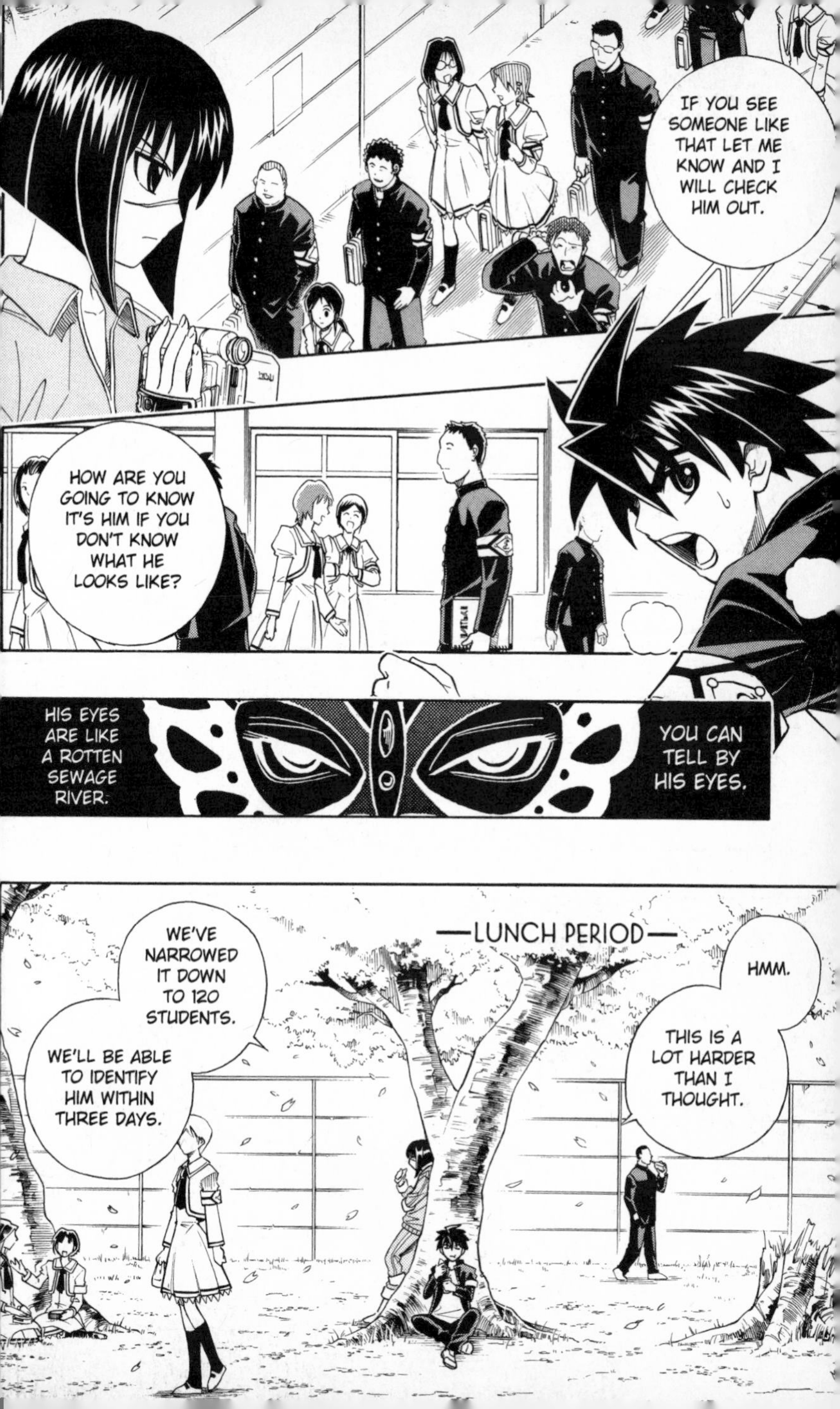
IF YOU SEE SOMEONE LIKE THAT LET ME KNOW AND I WILL CHECK HIM OUT.
HOW ARE YOU GOING TO KNOW IT'S HIM IF YOU DON'T KNOW WHAT HE LOOKS LIKE?
YOU CAN TELL BY HIS EYES.
HIS EYES ARE LIKE A ROTTEN SEWAGE RIVER.
—LUNCH PERIOD—
HMM.
THIS IS A LOT HARDER THAN I THOUGHT.
WE'VE NARROWED IT DOWN TO 120 STUDENTS.
WE'LL BE ABLE TO IDENTIFY HIM WITHIN THREE DAYS.

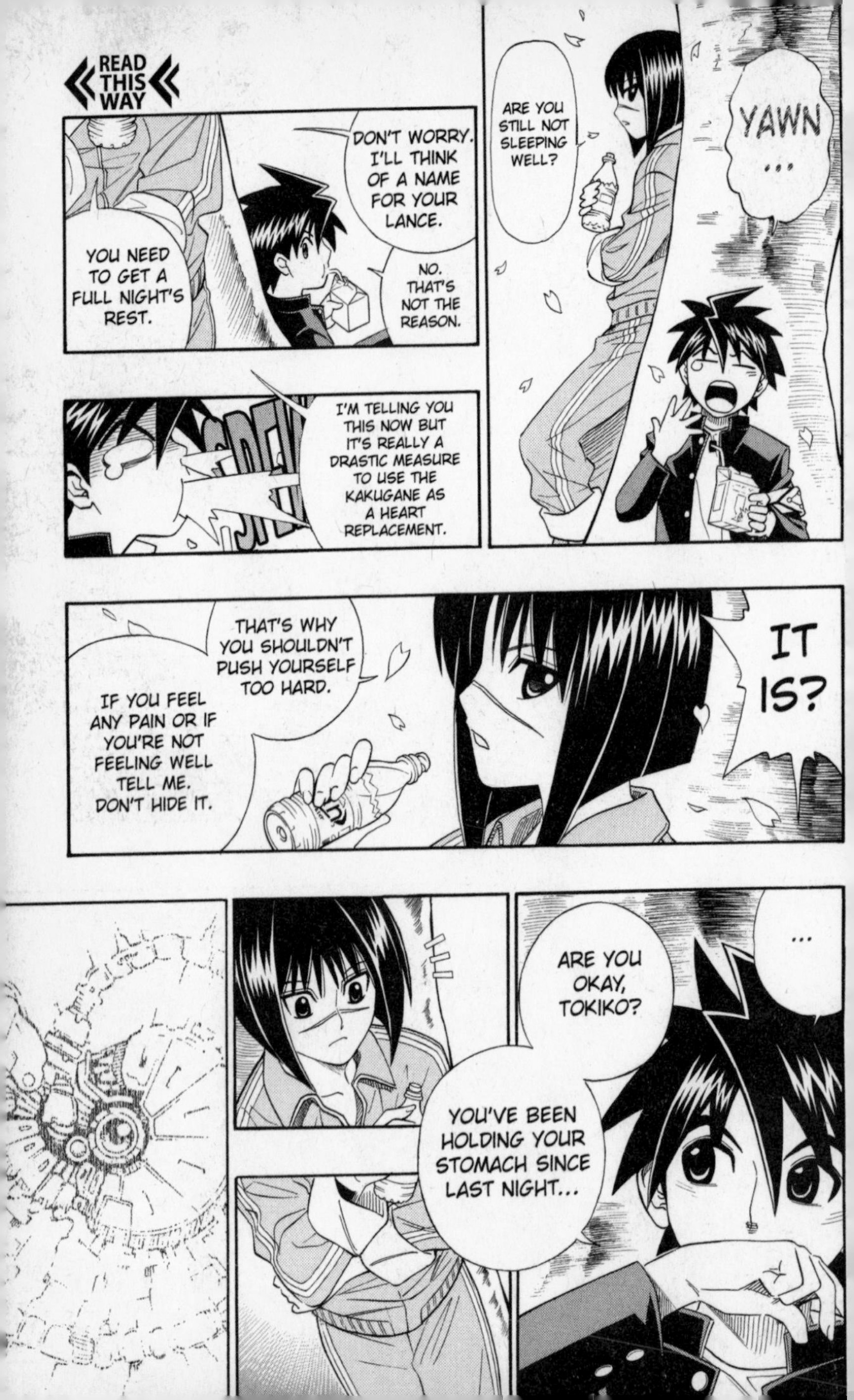
READ THIS WAY
YAWN...
ARE YOU STILL NOT SLEEPING WELL?
DON'T WORRY. I'LL THINK OF A NAME FOR YOUR LANCE.
NO. THAT'S NOT THE REASON.
YOU NEED TO GET A FULL NIGHT'S REST.
I'M TELLING YOU THIS NOW BUT IT'S REALLY A DRASTIC MEASURE TO USE THE KAKUGANE AS A HEART REPLACEMENT.
IT IS?
THAT'S WHY YOU SHOULDN'T PUSH YOURSELF TOO HARD.
IF YOU FEEL ANY PAIN OR IF YOU'RE NOT FEELING WELL TELL ME. DON'T HIDE IT.
...
ARE YOU OKAY, TOKIKO?
YOU'VE BEEN HOLDING YOUR STOMACH SINCE LAST NIGHT...

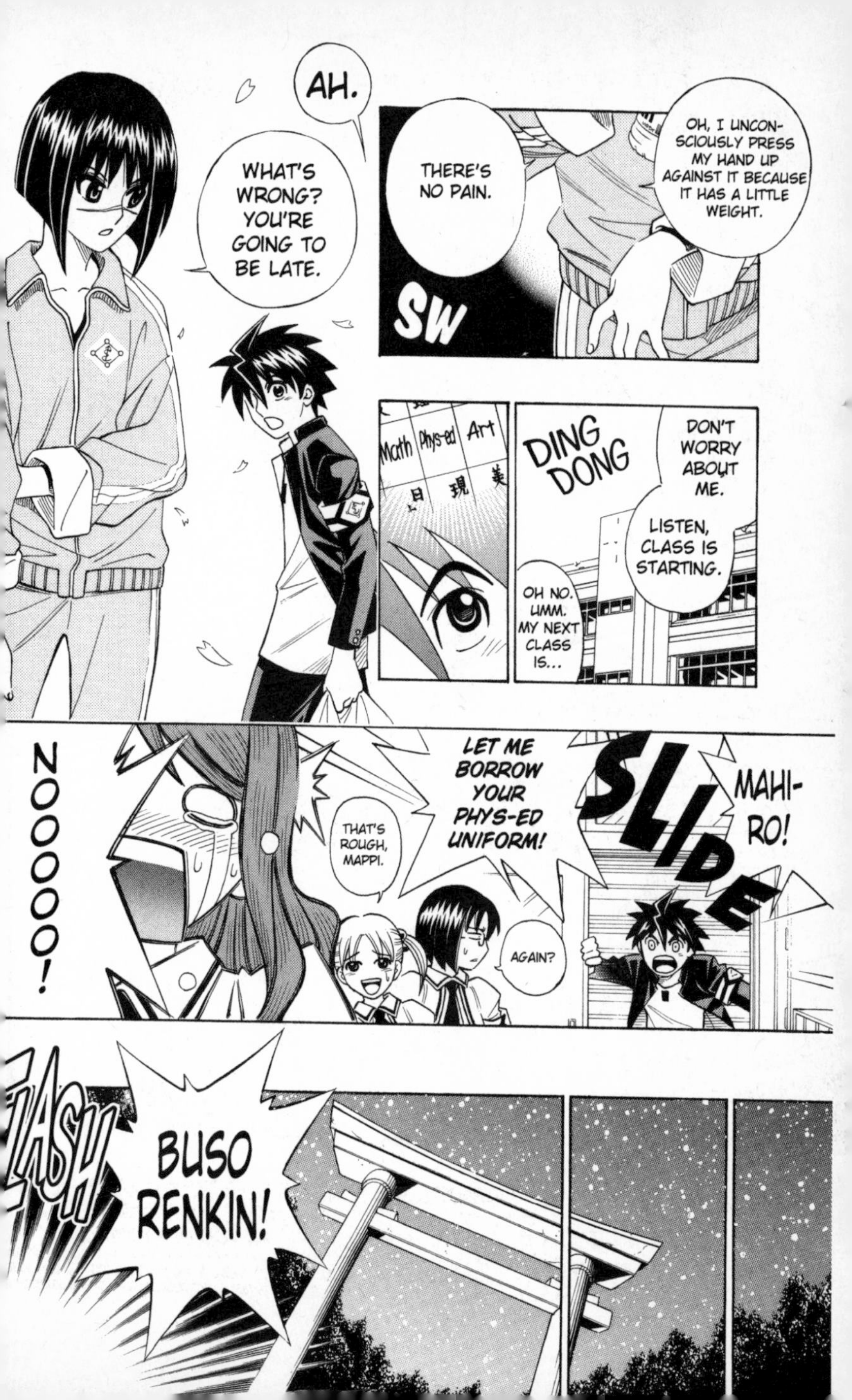
OH, I UNCON-SCIOUSLY PRESS MY HAND UP AGAINST IT BECAUSE IT HAS A LITTLE WEIGHT.
THERE'S NO PAIN.
SW
DON'T WORRY ABOUT ME.
LISTEN, CLASS IS STARTING.
DING DONG
OH NO. UMM. MY NEXT CLASS IS...
Math Phys-ed Art
日 現 美
AH.
WHAT'S WRONG? YOU'RE GOING TO BE LATE.
MAHI-RO!
SLIDE
LET ME BORROW YOUR PHYS-ED UNIFORM!
AGAIN?
THAT'S ROUGH, MAPPI.
NOOOOOO!
BUSO RENKIN!

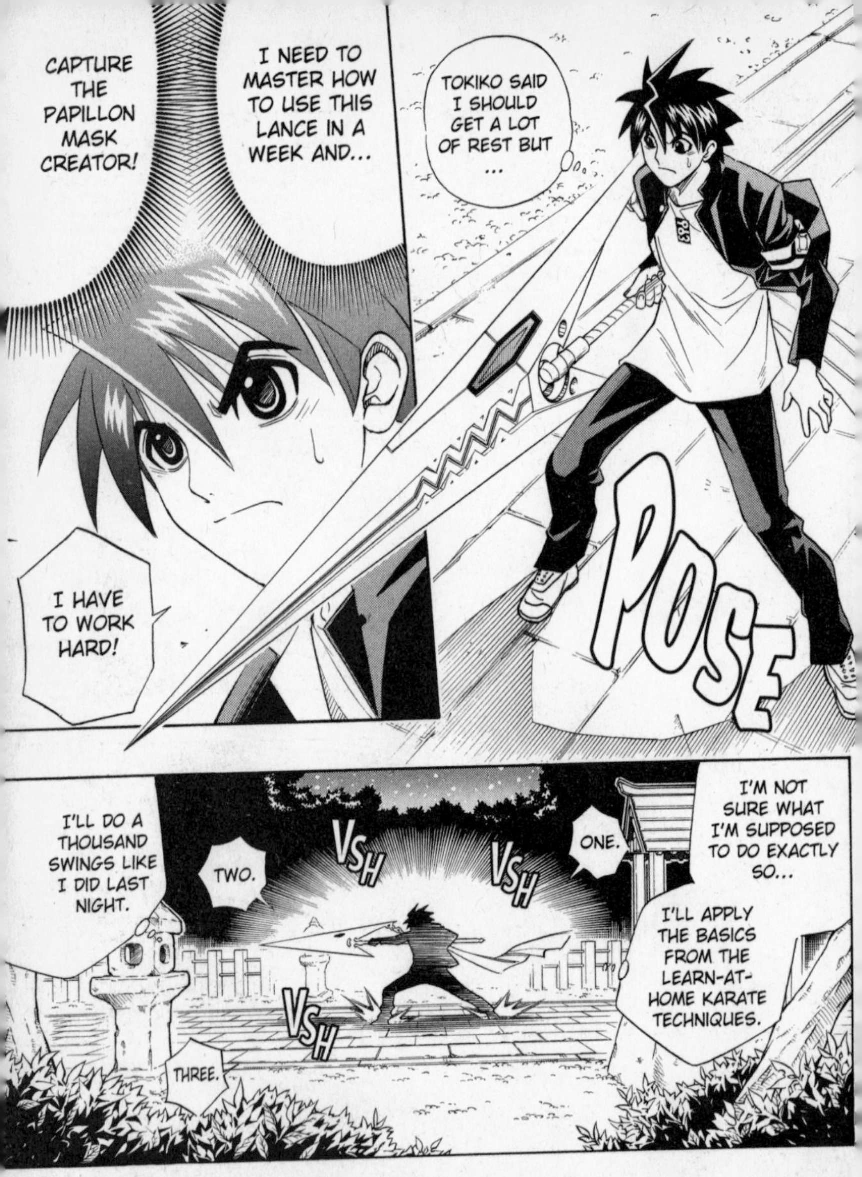
TOKIKO SAID I SHOULD GET A LOT OF REST BUT ...
POSE
I NEED TO MASTER HOW TO USE THIS LANCE IN A WEEK AND...
CAPTURE THE PAPILLON MASK CREATOR!
I HAVE TO WORK HARD!
I'M NOT SURE WHAT I'M SUPPOSED TO DO EXACTLY SO...
I'LL APPLY THE BASICS FROM THE LEARN-AT-HOME KARATE TECHNIQUES.
ONE.
VSH
TWO.
VSH
I'LL DO A THOUSAND SWINGS LIKE I DID LAST NIGHT.
VSH
THREE.

DAY TWO

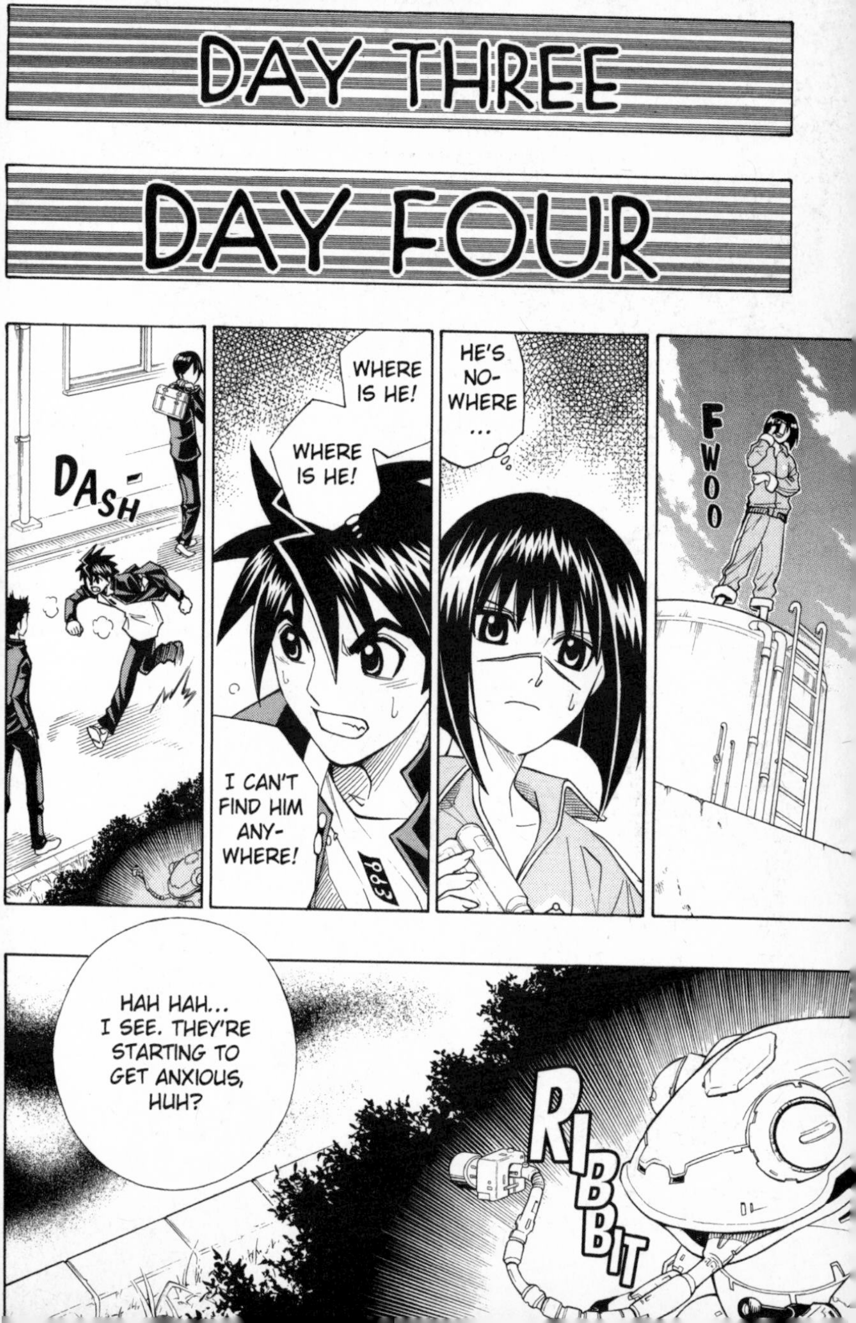
DAY THREE
DAY FOUR
FWOO
HE'S NO-WHERE...
WHERE IS HE!
WHERE IS HE!
I CAN'T FIND HIM ANY-WHERE!
DASH
RIBBIT
HAH HAH... I SEE. THEY'RE STARTING TO GET ANXIOUS, HUH?

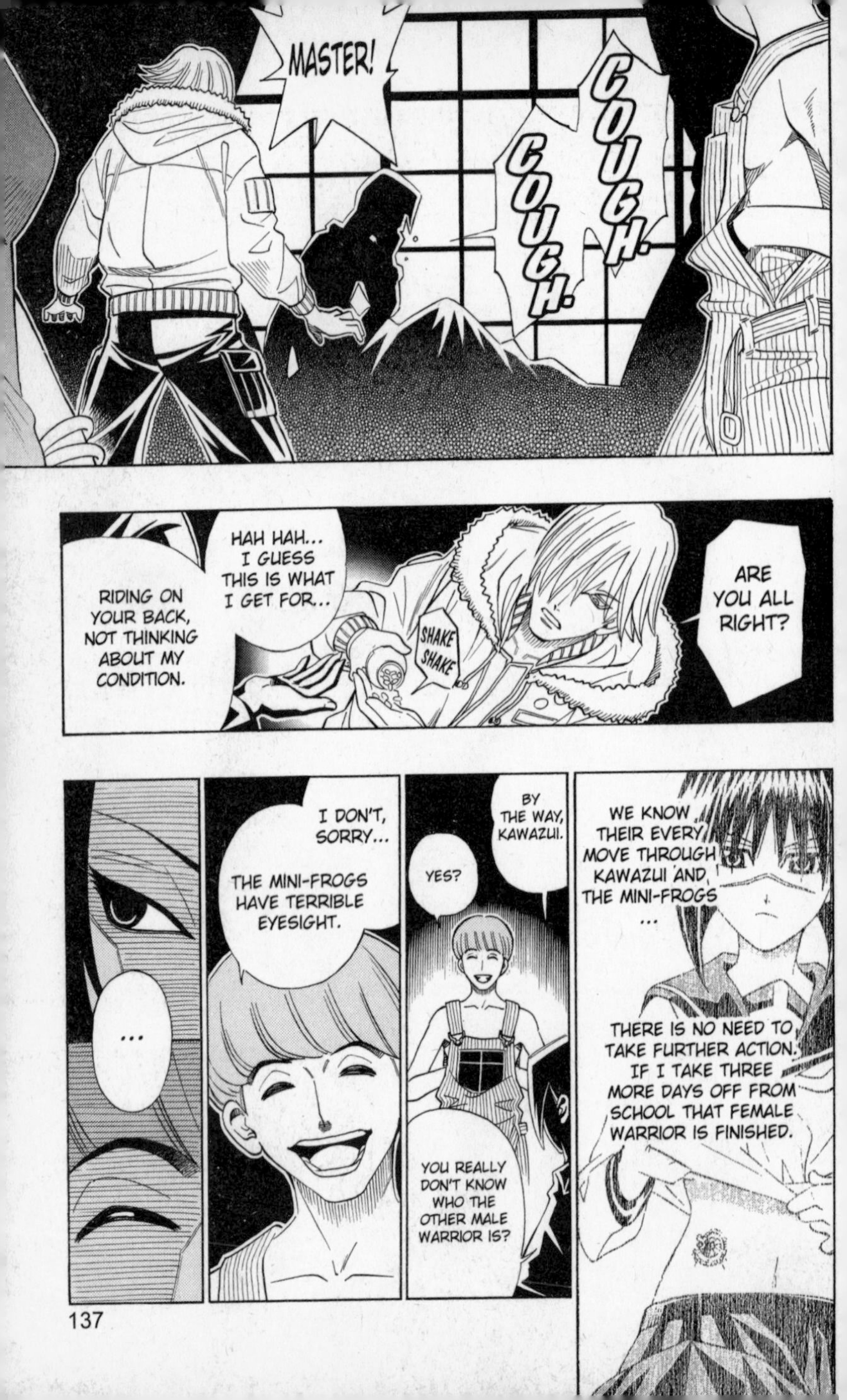
MASTER!
COUGH.
COUGH.
ARE YOU ALL RIGHT?
SHAKE SHAKE
HAH HAH... I GUESS THIS IS WHAT I GET FOR...
RIDING ON YOUR BACK, NOT THINKING ABOUT MY CONDITION.
WE KNOW THEIR EVERY MOVE THROUGH KAWAZUI AND THE MINI-FROGS ...
THERE IS NO NEED TO TAKE FURTHER ACTION. IF I TAKE THREE MORE DAYS OFF FROM SCHOOL THAT FEMALE WARRIOR IS FINISHED.
BY THE WAY, KAWAZUI.
YES?
YOU REALLY DON'T KNOW WHO THE OTHER MALE WARRIOR IS?
I DON'T, SORRY...
THE MINI-FROGS HAVE TERRIBLE EYESIGHT.
...

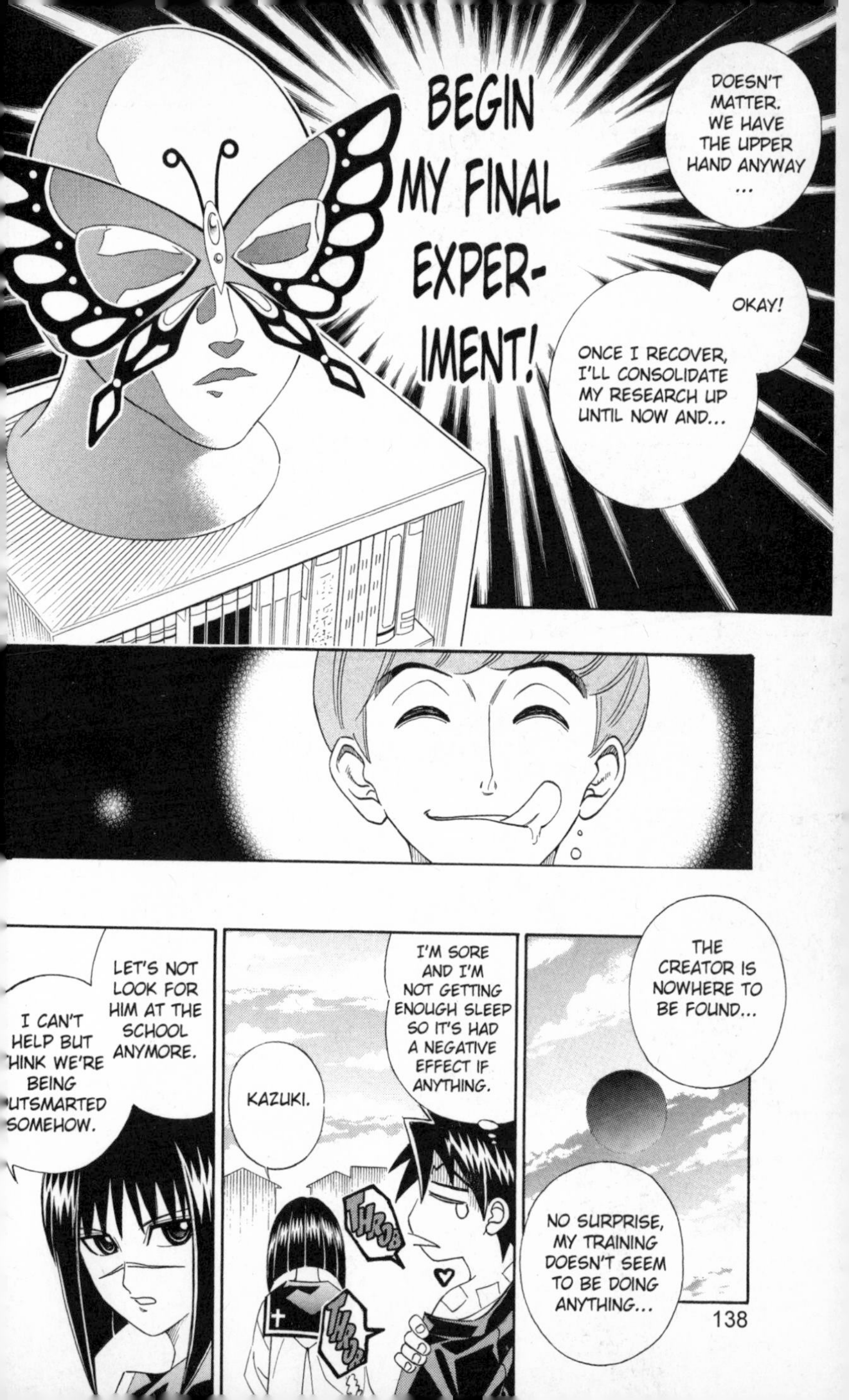
DOESN'T MATTER. WE HAVE THE UPPER HAND ANYWAY ...
OKAY!
ONCE I RECOVER, I'LL CONSOLIDATE MY RESEARCH UP UNTIL NOW AND...
BEGIN MY FINAL EXPER-IMENT!
THE CREATOR IS NOWHERE TO BE FOUND...
NO SURPRISE, MY TRAINING DOESN'T SEEM TO BE DOING ANYTHING...
I'M SORE AND I'M NOT GETTING ENOUGH SLEEP SO IT'S HAD A NEGATIVE EFFECT IF ANYTHING.
THROB
THROB
KAZUKI.
LET'S NOT LOOK FOR HIM AT THE SCHOOL ANYMORE.
I CAN'T HELP BUT HINK WE'RE BEING UTSMARTED SOMEHOW.

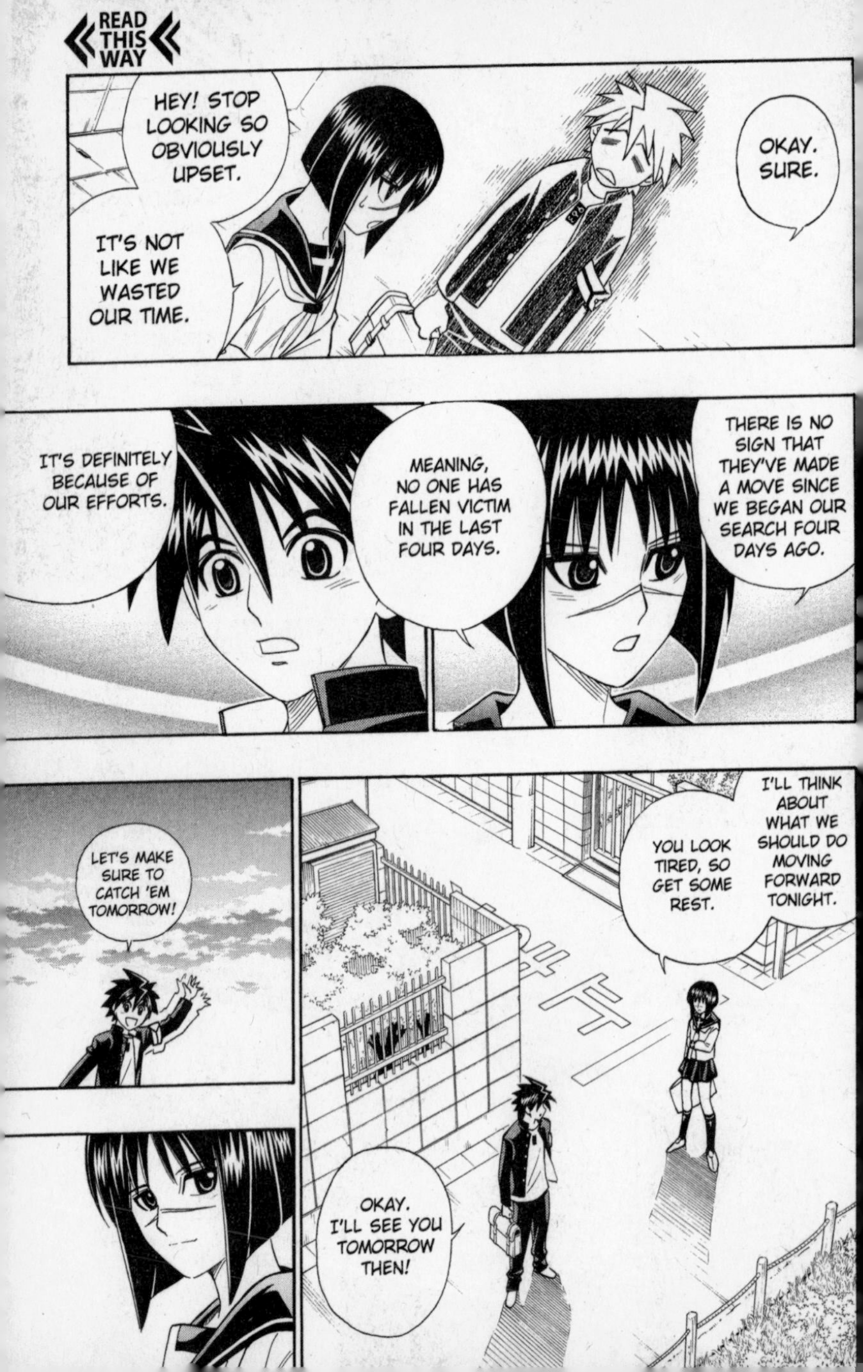
READ THIS WAY
HEY! STOP LOOKING SO OBVIOUSLY UPSET.
IT'S NOT LIKE WE WASTED OUR TIME.
OKAY. SURE.
THERE IS NO SIGN THAT THEY'VE MADE A MOVE SINCE WE BEGAN OUR SEARCH FOUR DAYS AGO.
MEANING, NO ONE HAS FALLEN VICTIM IN THE LAST FOUR DAYS.
IT'S DEFINITELY BECAUSE OF OUR EFFORTS.
I'LL THINK ABOUT WHAT WE SHOULD DO MOVING FORWARD TONIGHT.
YOU LOOK TIRED, SO GET SOME REST.
OKAY. I'LL SEE YOU TOMORROW THEN!
LET'S MAKE SURE TO CATCH 'EM TOMORROW!

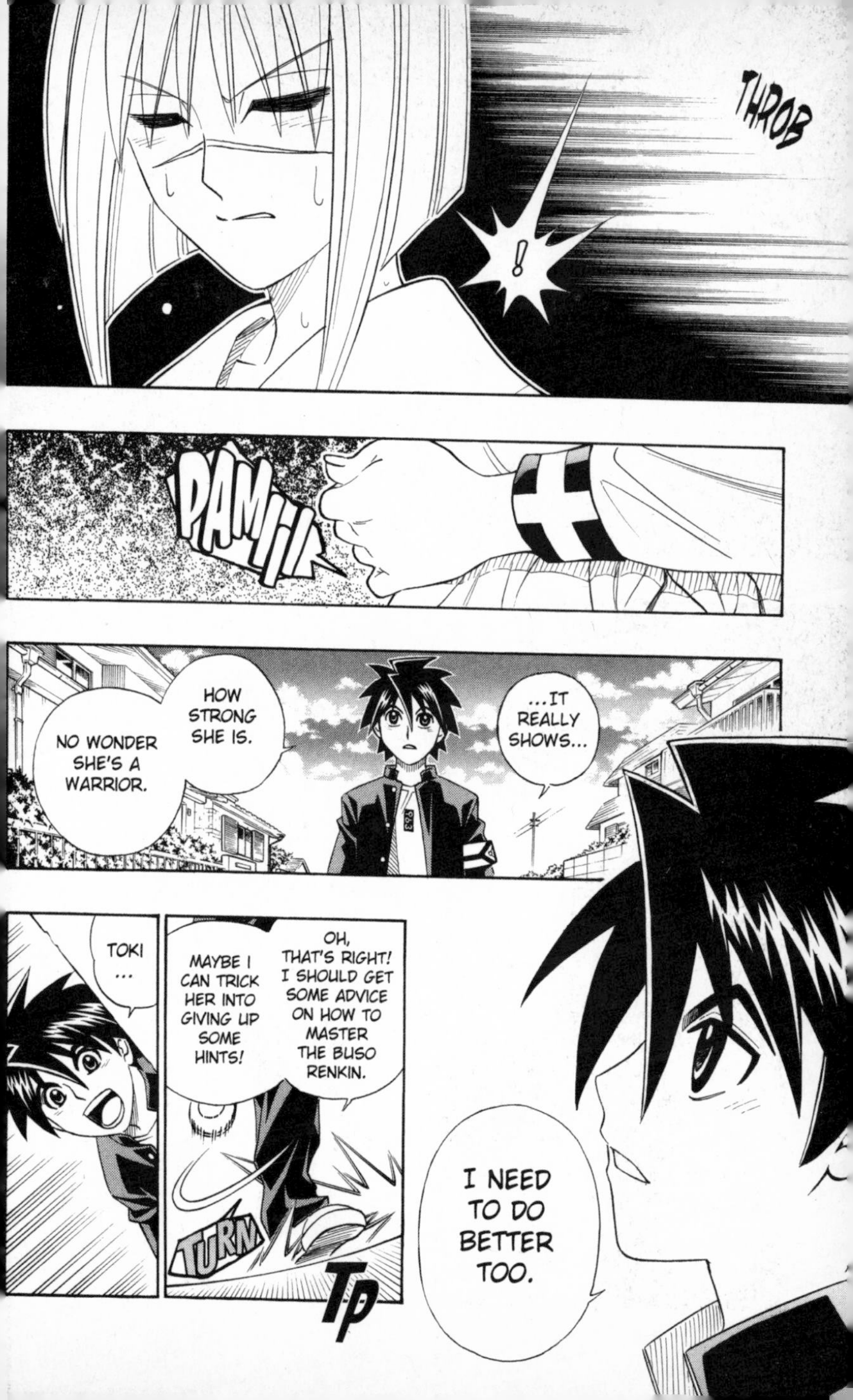
THROB
!
PAMIII
...IT REALLY SHOWS...
HOW STRONG SHE IS.
NO WONDER SHE'S A WARRIOR.
I NEED TO DO BETTER TOO.
OH, THAT'S RIGHT! I SHOULD GET SOME ADVICE ON HOW TO MASTER THE BUSO RENKIN.
MAYBE I CAN TRICK HER INTO GIVING UP SOME HINTS!
TURN
TP
TOKI ...

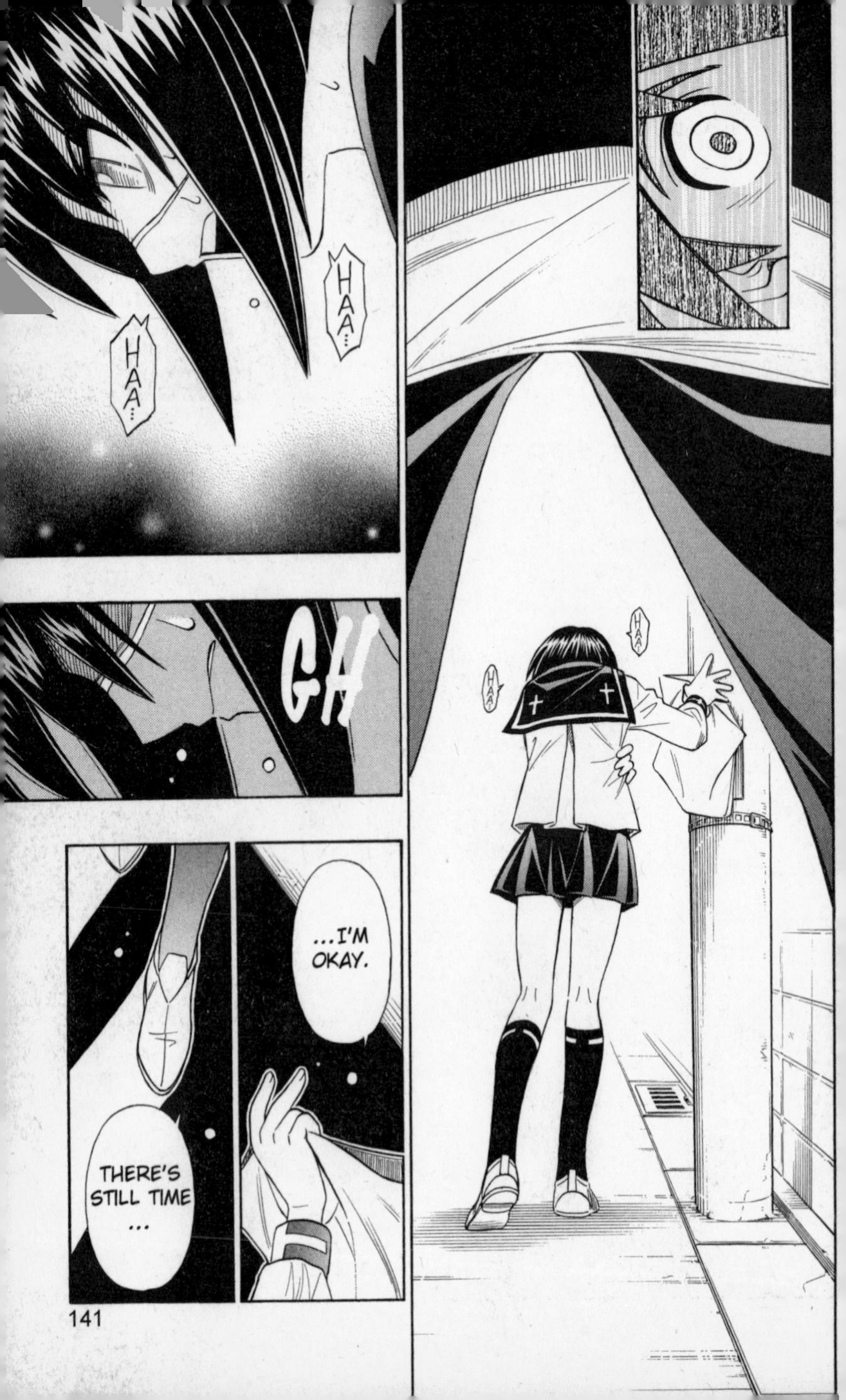

HAA...
HAA...
HAA...
HAA...
GH
...I'M OKAY.
THERE'S STILL TIME ...

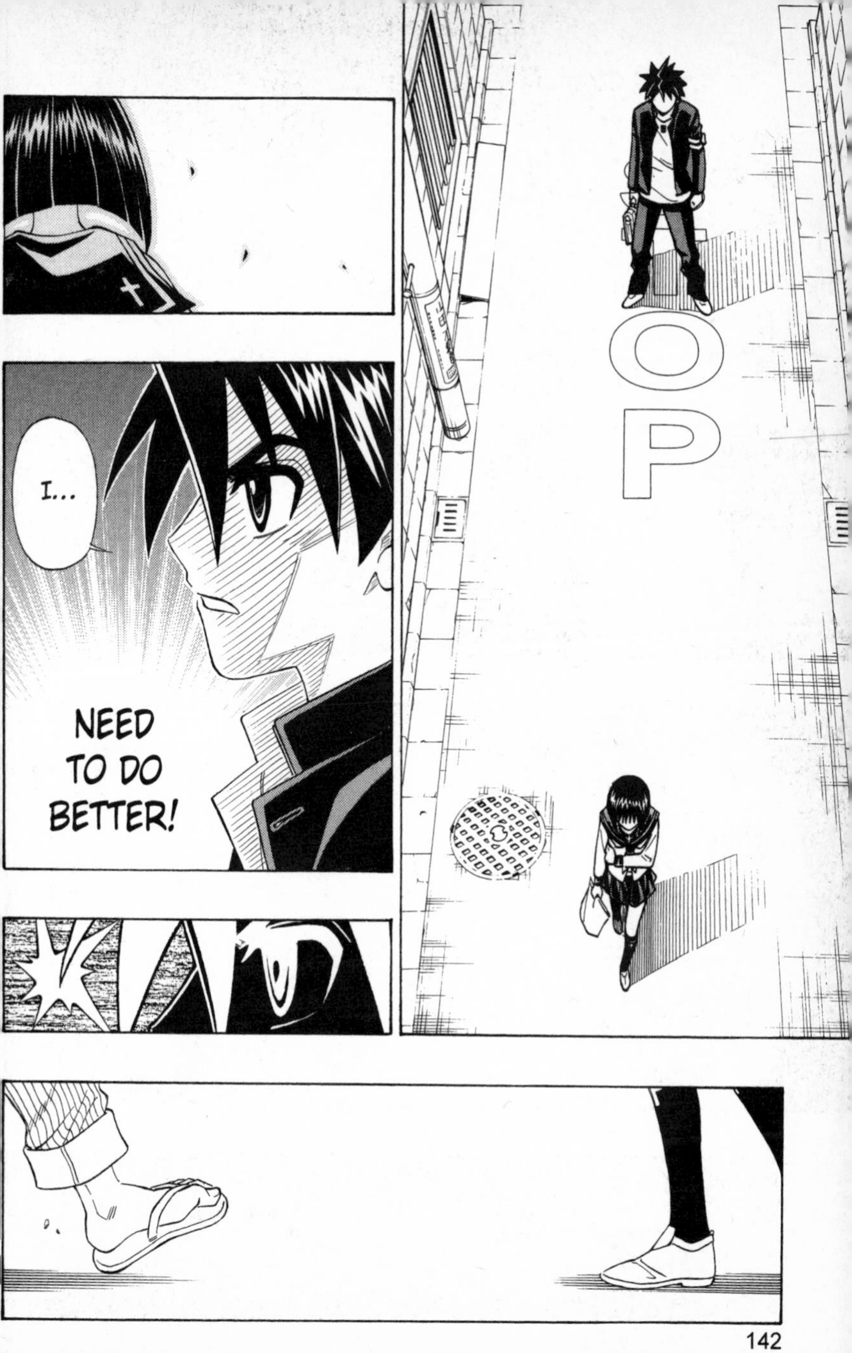

O
P
I...
NEED TO DO BETTER!

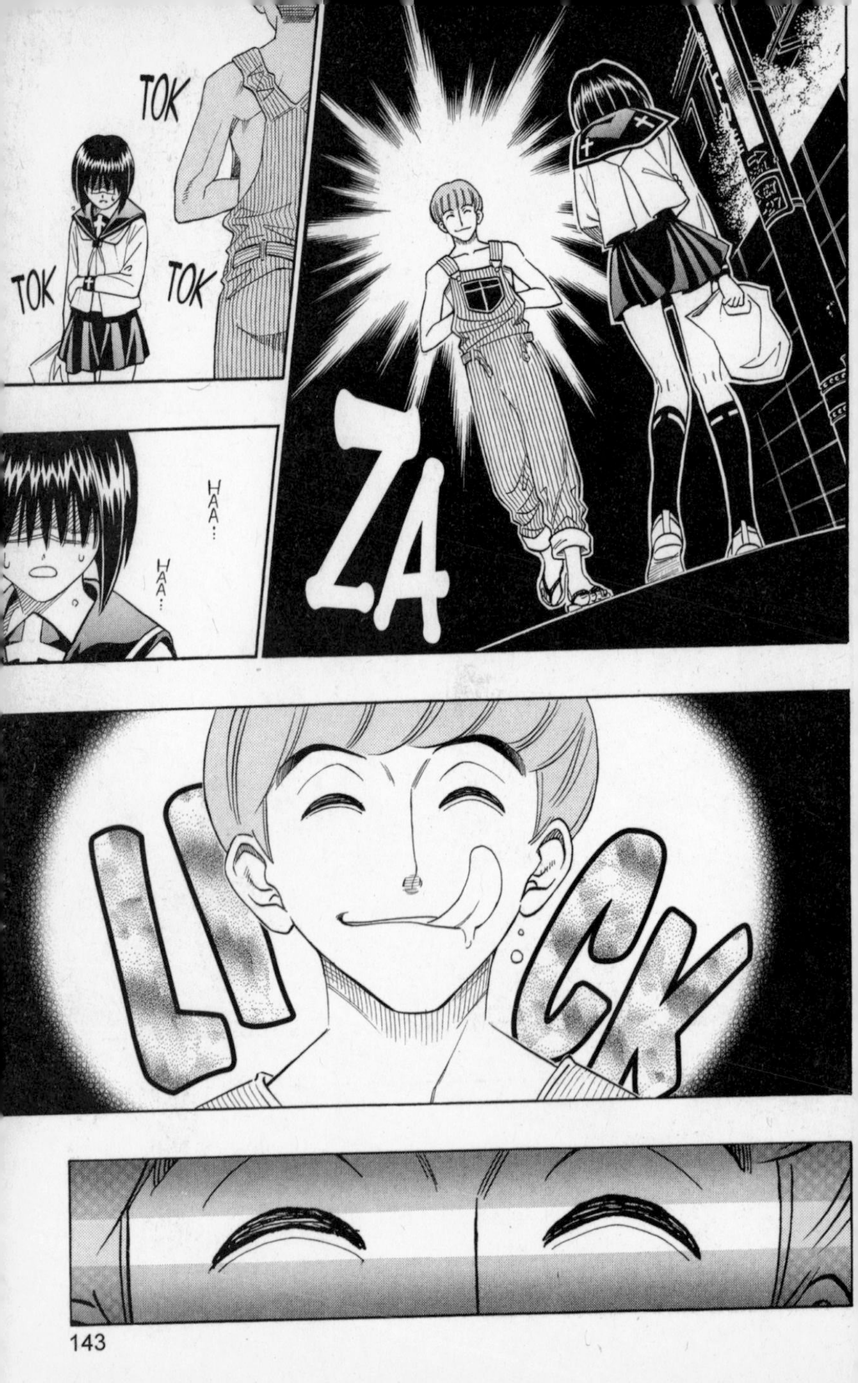
ZA
TOK
TOK
TOK
HAA...
HAA...
LICK

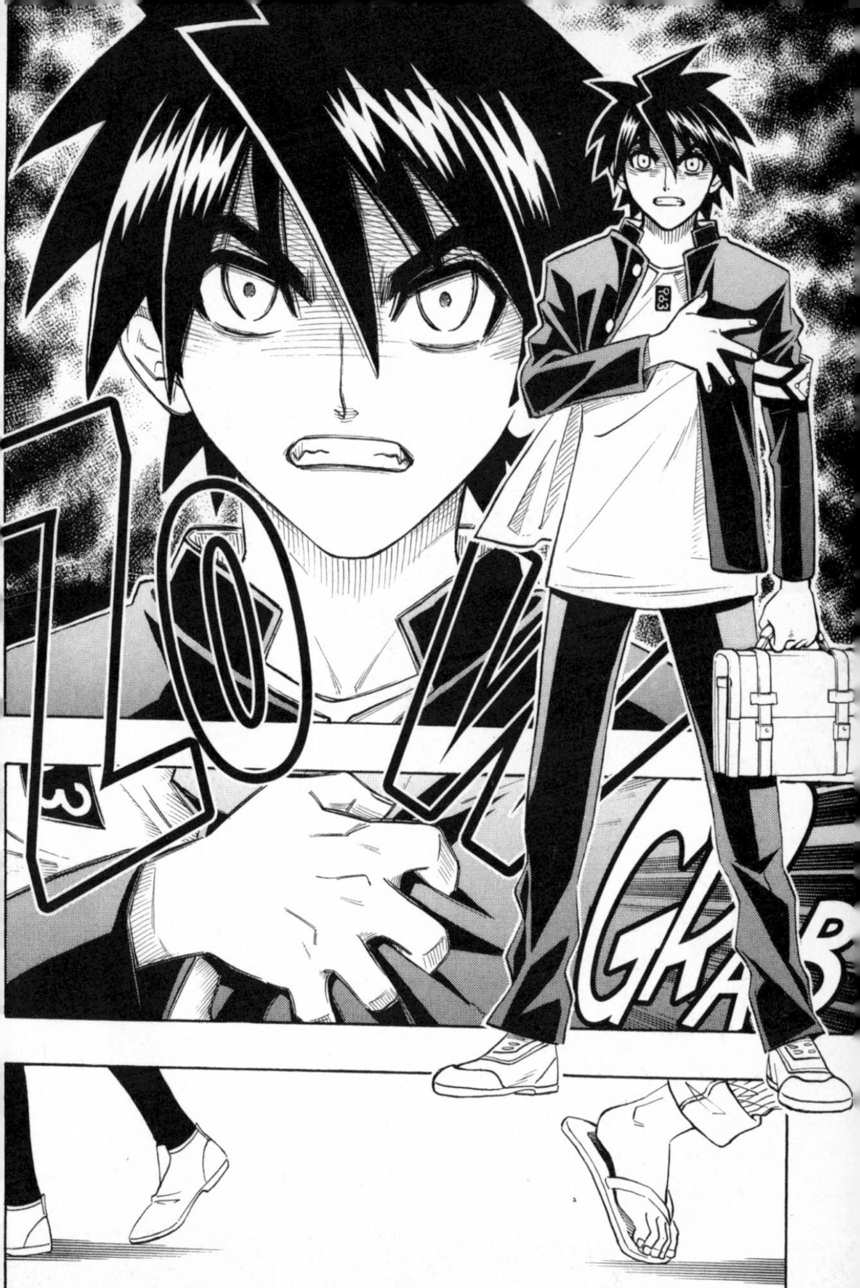

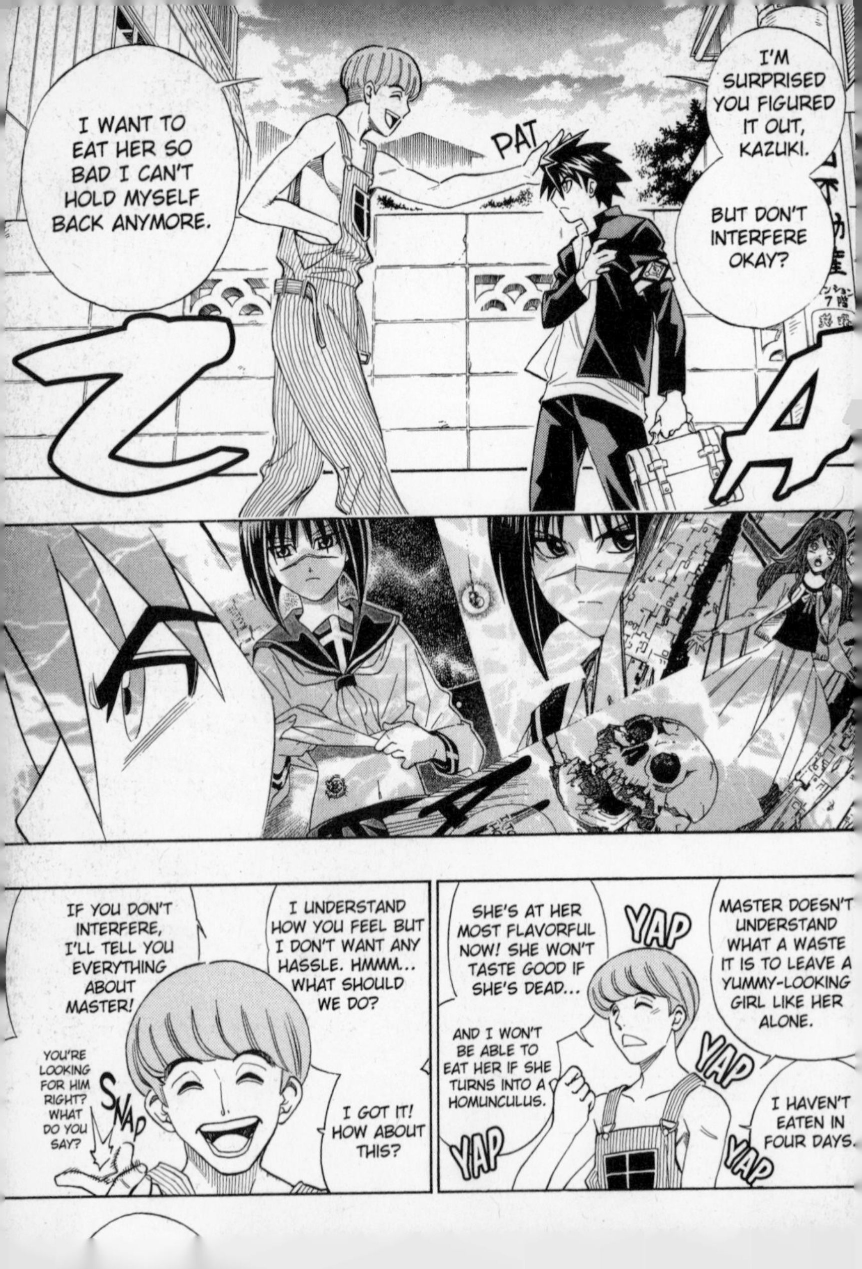
I'M SURPRISED YOU FIGURED IT OUT, KAZUKI.
BUT DON'T INTERFERE OKAY?
PAT
I WANT TO EAT HER SO BAD I CAN'T HOLD MYSELF BACK ANYMORE.
ZA
A
MASTER DOESN'T UNDERSTAND WHAT A WASTE IT IS TO LEAVE A YUMMY-LOOKING GIRL LIKE HER ALONE.
YAP
SHE'S AT HER MOST FLAVORFUL NOW! SHE WON'T TASTE GOOD IF SHE'S DEAD...
YAP
I HAVEN'T EATEN IN FOUR DAYS.
AND I WON'T BE ABLE TO EAT HER IF SHE TURNS INTO A HOMUNCULUS.
YAP
YAP
I UNDERSTAND HOW YOU FEEL BUT I DON'T WANT ANY HASSLE. HMMM... WHAT SHOULD WE DO?
I GOT IT! HOW ABOUT THIS?
IF YOU DON'T INTERFERE, I'LL TELL YOU EVERYTHING ABOUT MASTER!
YOU'RE LOOKING FOR HIM RIGHT? WHAT DO YOU SAY?
SNAP

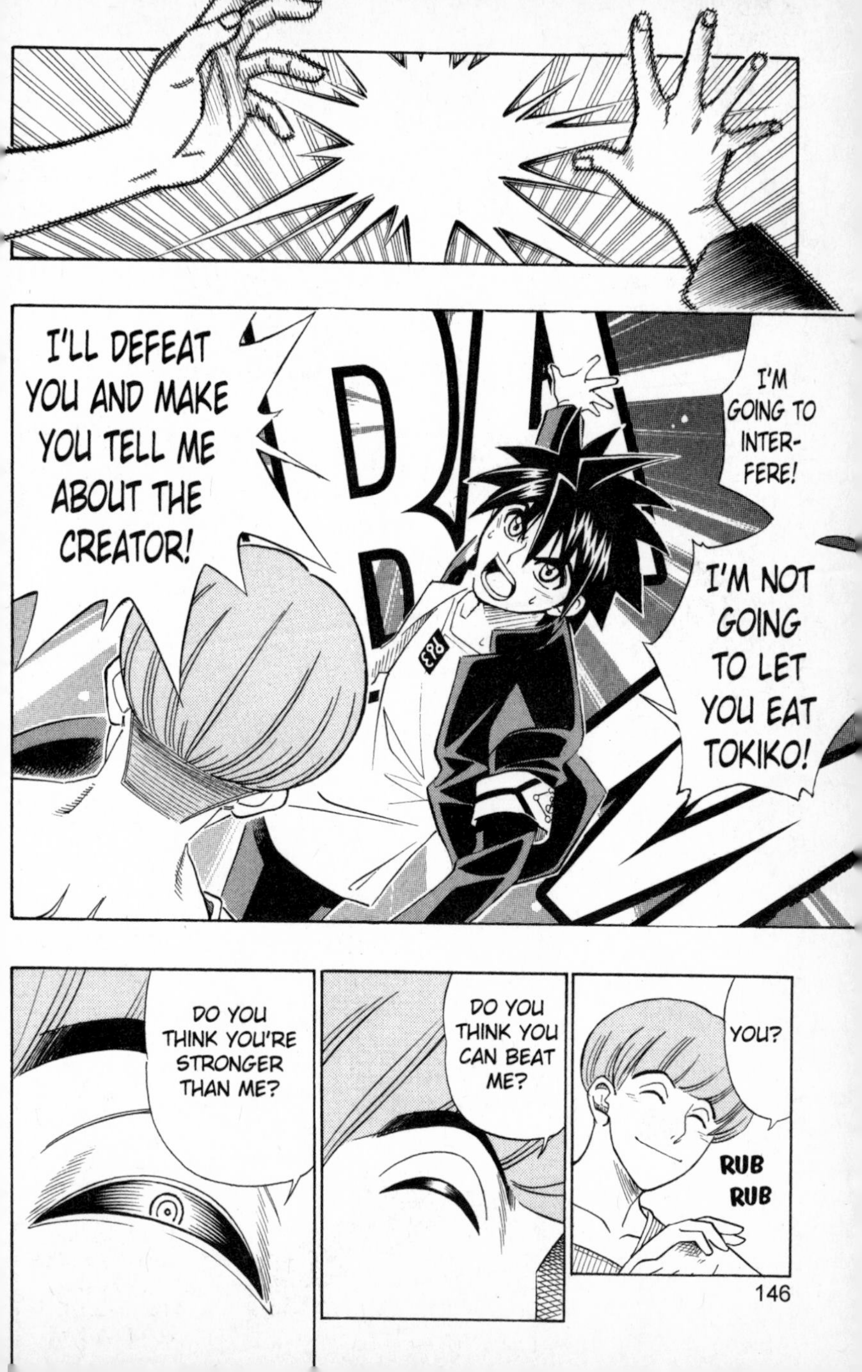
I'M GOING TO INTER-FERE!
I'M NOT GOING TO LET YOU EAT TOKIKO!
I'LL DEFEAT YOU AND MAKE YOU TELL ME ABOUT THE CREATOR!
YOU?
RUB RUB
DO YOU THINK YOU CAN BEAT ME?
DO YOU THINK YOU'RE STRONGER THAN ME?

READ THIS WAY

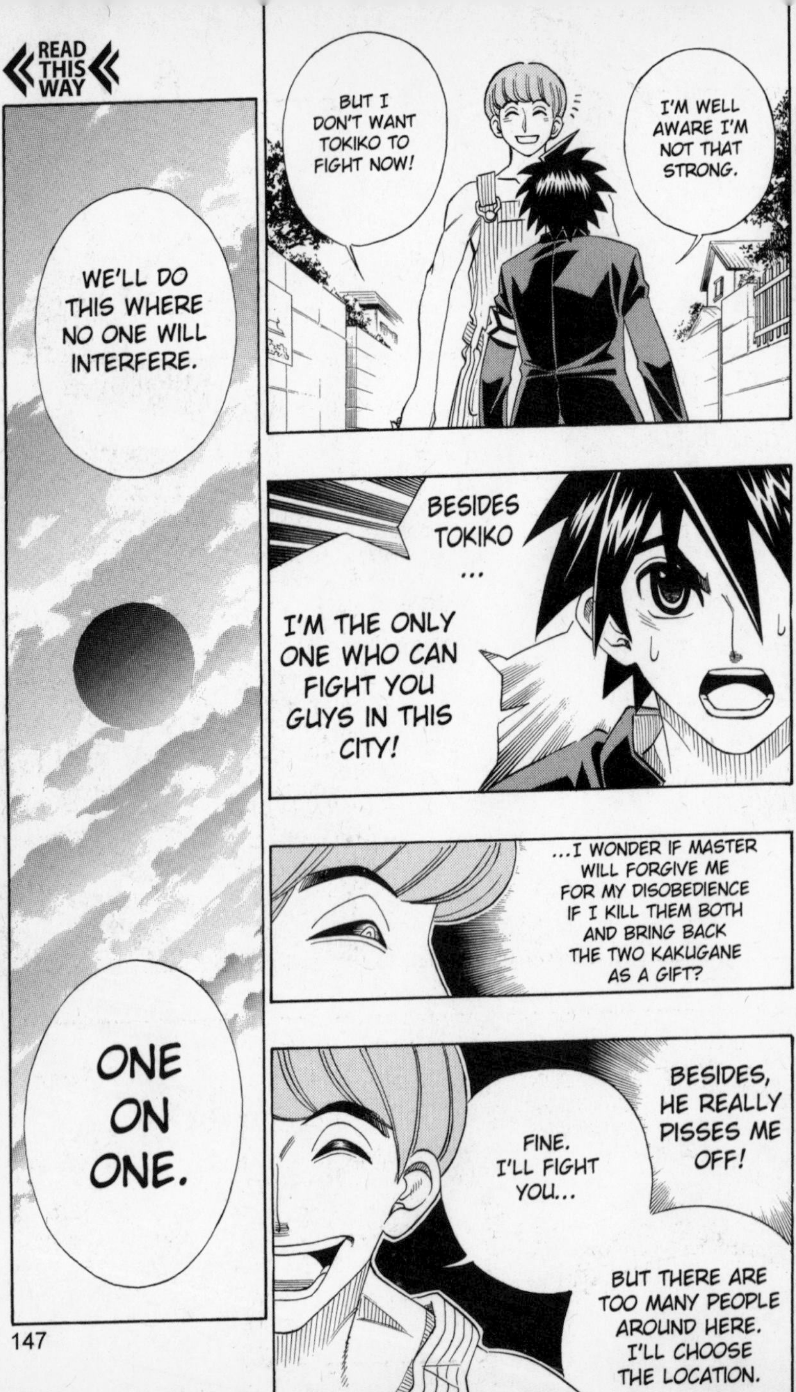
I'M WELL AWARE I'M NOT THAT STRONG.
BUT I DON'T WANT TOKIKO TO FIGHT NOW!
BESIDES TOKIKO ...
I'M THE ONLY ONE WHO CAN FIGHT YOU GUYS IN THIS CITY!
...I WONDER IF MASTER WILL FORGIVE ME FOR MY DISOBEDIENCE IF I KILL THEM BOTH AND BRING BACK THE TWO KAKUGANE AS A GIFT?
BESIDES, HE REALLY PISSES ME OFF!
FINE. I'LL FIGHT YOU...
BUT THERE ARE TOO MANY PEOPLE AROUND HERE. I'LL CHOOSE THE LOCATION.
WE'LL DO THIS WHERE NO ONE WILL INTERFERE.
ONE ON ONE.

· A Surinam Toad Homunculus.
· He used to be the Creator's online buddy and a fellow recluse. They got along at first but they got in an argument stemming from something small. He sent hate mails to the Creator so he turned him into a Homunculus.
· An inferior-quality Homunculus. It has useful abilities such as creating mini-frogs and making them do his bidding but Kawazui himself is rather questionable.

Author's Notes

· The story required a sneaky character who spies on people so after putting some thought into it I decided to use a Surinam Toad.
· To my surprise Kawazui turned out to have a lot of character. I enjoyed drawing this character a lot. I felt like I had a small revelation about the future Creator character while drawing Kawazui.

No. 6 Homunculus Kawazui

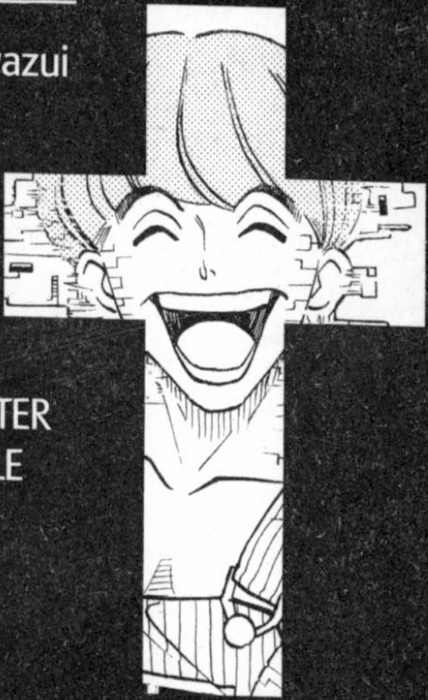

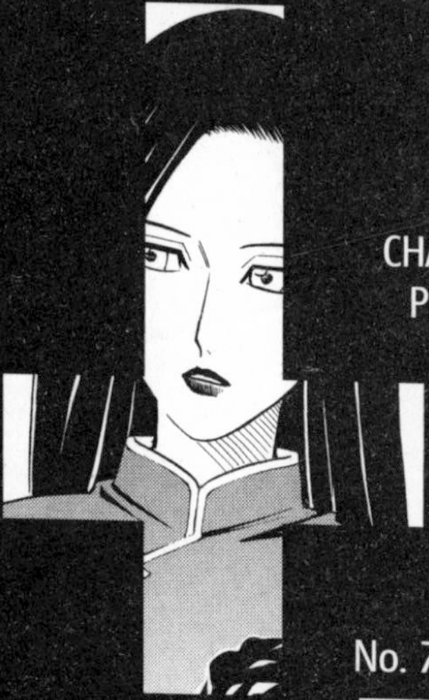

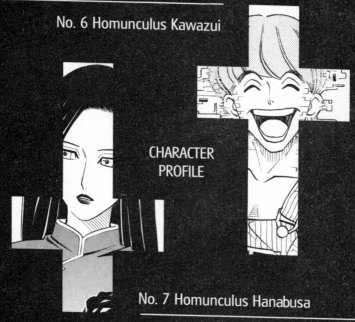

CHARACTER PROFILE

No. 7 Homunculus Hanabusa

· A rose Homunculus.
· She was a tutor the Creator's father hired for him. She tried seducing the Creator for his family fortune but the Creator saw through her and turned her into a Homunculus.
· She was the first Homunculus the Papillon Mask created. Using Hanafusa's vines, the Creator collected samples from the zoo for his latter Homunculus creations.

Author's Notes

· I made her into a rose in order to use a plant's ability to expand and grow. I had an idea to cover the dorm with vines but that idea got cut due to the storyline.
· Due to the tight schedule I had to design her impromptu. I wish I could have made her sexier with wavy hair.

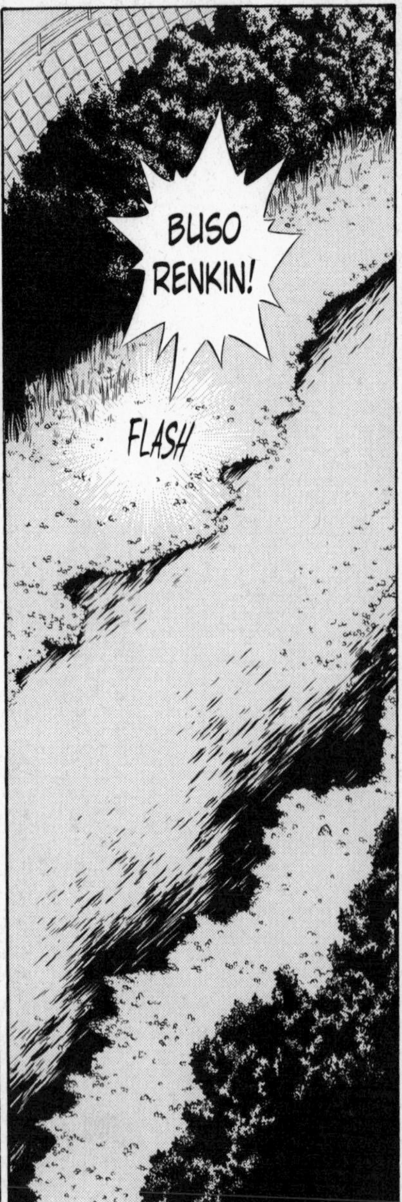
BUSO RENKIN!
FLASH

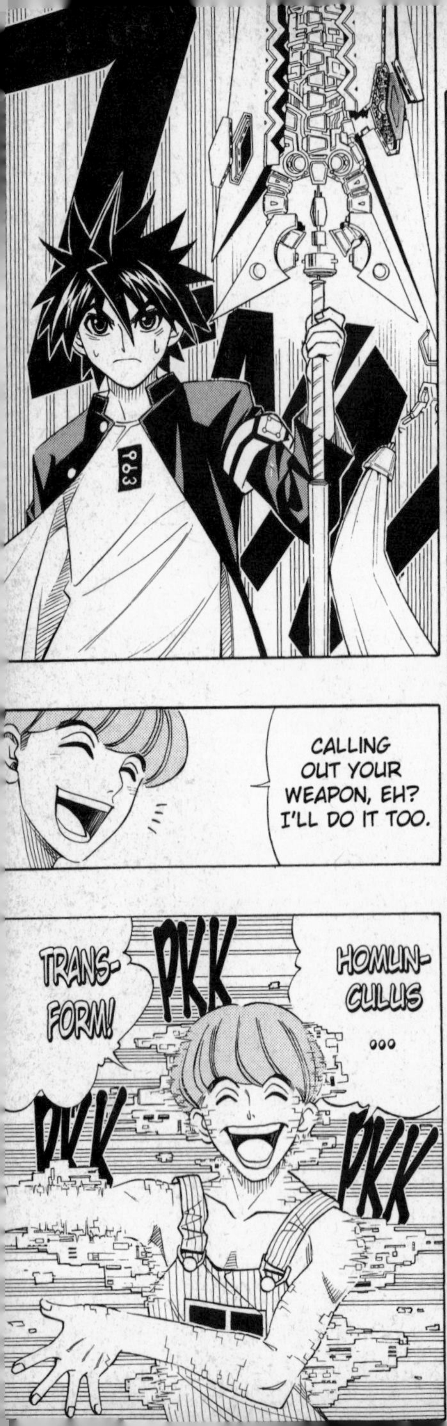
CALLING OUT YOUR WEAPON, EH? I'LL DO IT TOO.
HOMUN-CULUS ...
PKK
PKK
TRANS-FORM!
PKK

CHAPTER 6:
VS. KAWAZUI (PART 2)

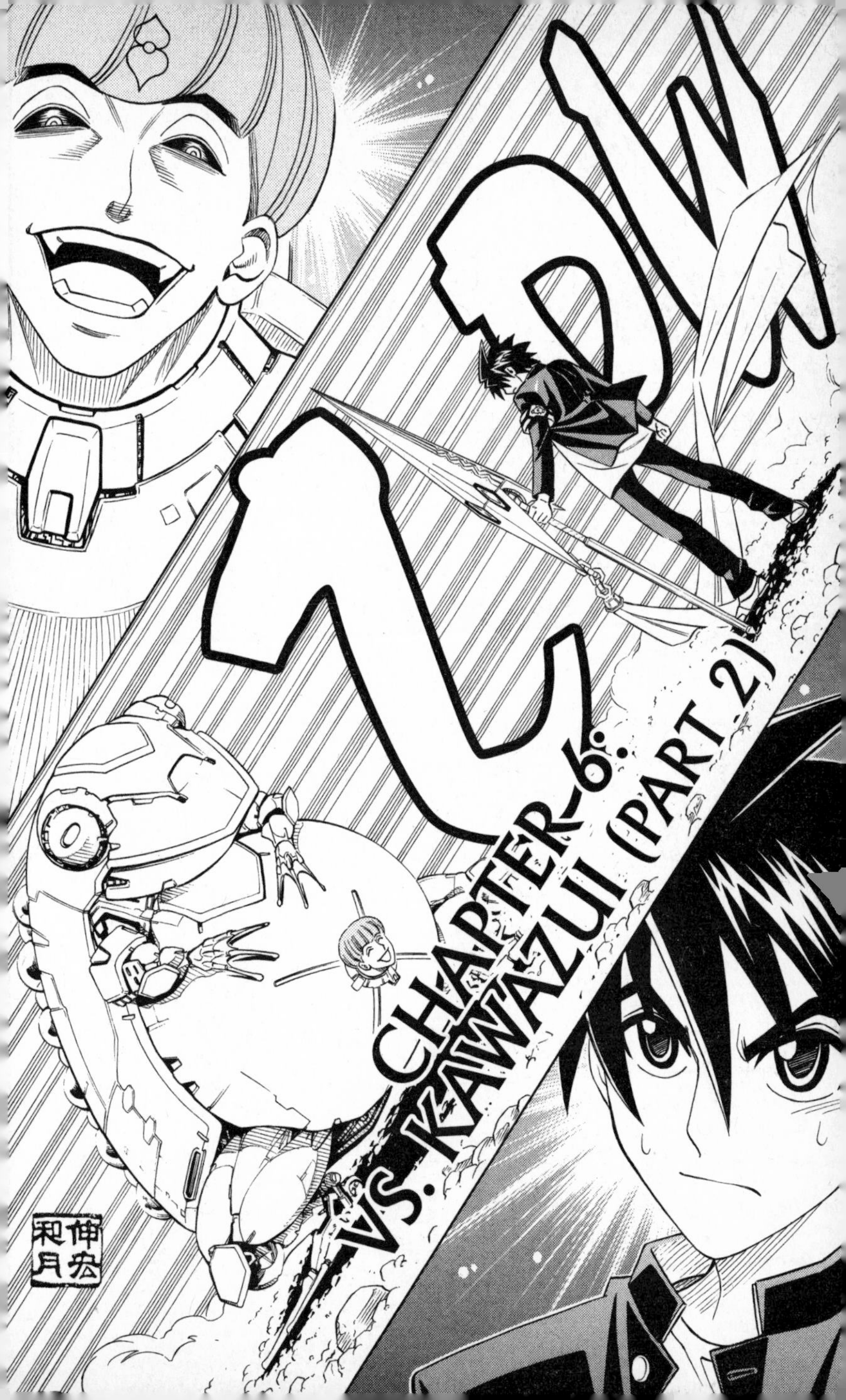
CHAPTER 6:
VS. KAWAZUI (PART 2)
伸宏
和月

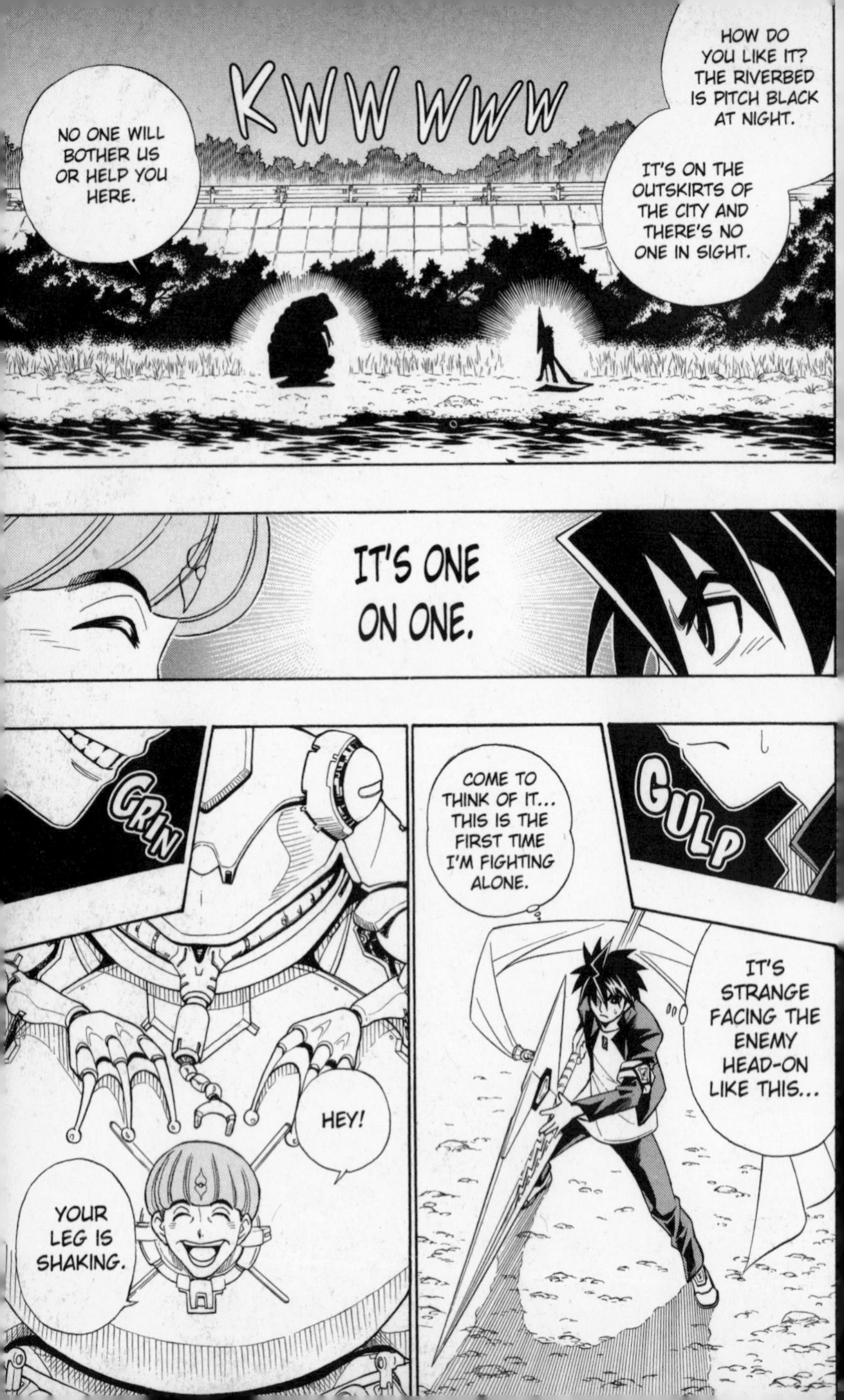
HOW DO YOU LIKE IT? THE RIVERBED IS PITCH BLACK AT NIGHT.
KWWWWWW
IT'S ON THE OUTSKIRTS OF THE CITY AND THERE'S NO ONE IN SIGHT.
NO ONE WILL BOTHER US OR HELP YOU HERE.
IT'S ONE ON ONE.
GULP
COME TO THINK OF IT... THIS IS THE FIRST TIME I'M FIGHTING ALONE.
IT'S STRANGE FACING THE ENEMY HEAD-ON LIKE THIS...
GRIN
HEY!
YOUR LEG IS SHAKING.

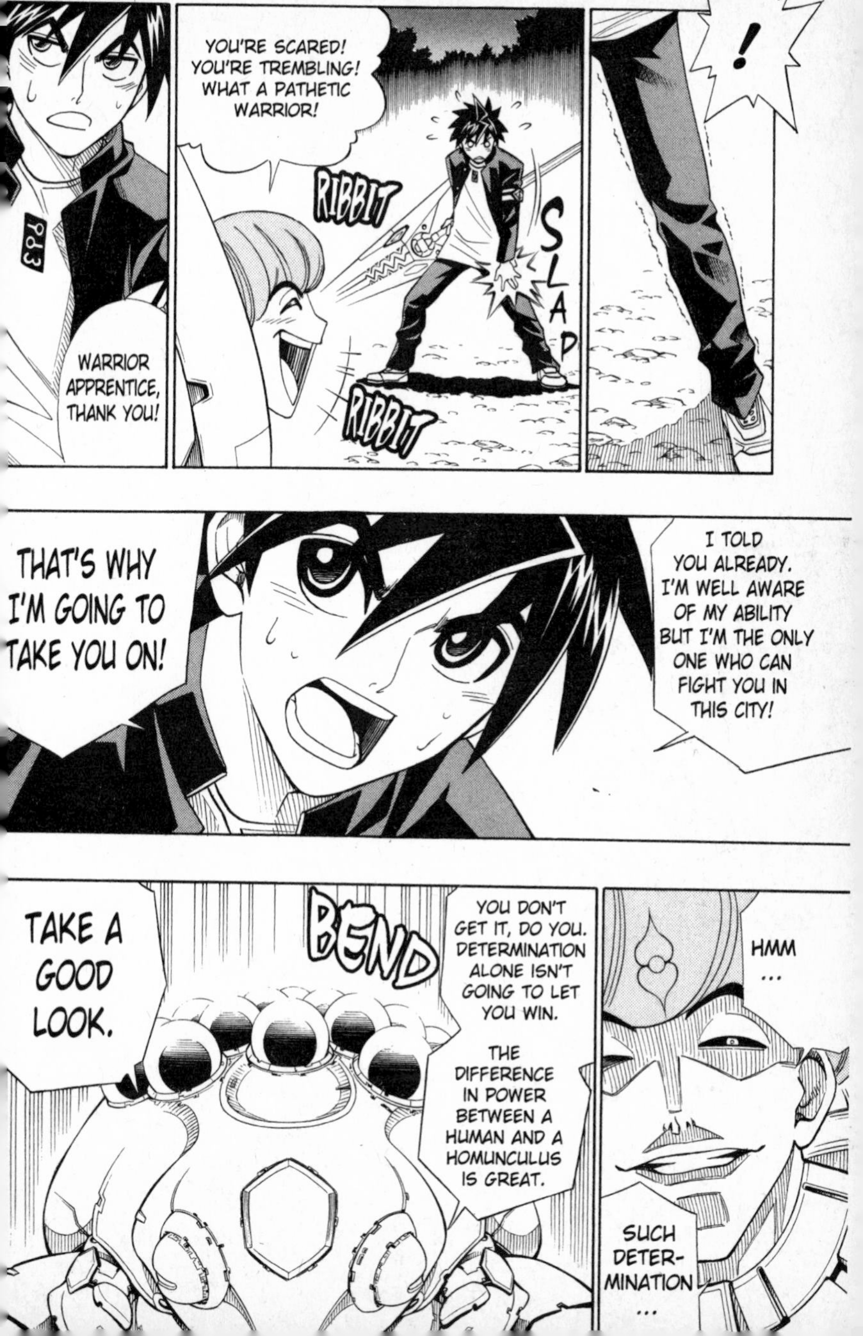
!
YOU'RE SCARED! YOU'RE TREMBLING! WHAT A PATHETIC WARRIOR!
RIBBIT
SLAP
RIBBIT
WARRIOR APPRENTICE, THANK YOU!
I TOLD YOU ALREADY. I'M WELL AWARE OF MY ABILITY BUT I'M THE ONLY ONE WHO CAN FIGHT YOU IN THIS CITY!
THAT'S WHY I'M GOING TO TAKE YOU ON!
HMM ...
SUCH DETER-MINATION ...
BEND
YOU DON'T GET IT, DO YOU. DETERMINATION ALONE ISN'T GOING TO LET YOU WIN.
THE DIFFERENCE IN POWER BETWEEN A HUMAN AND A HOMUNCULUS IS GREAT.
TAKE A GOOD LOOK.

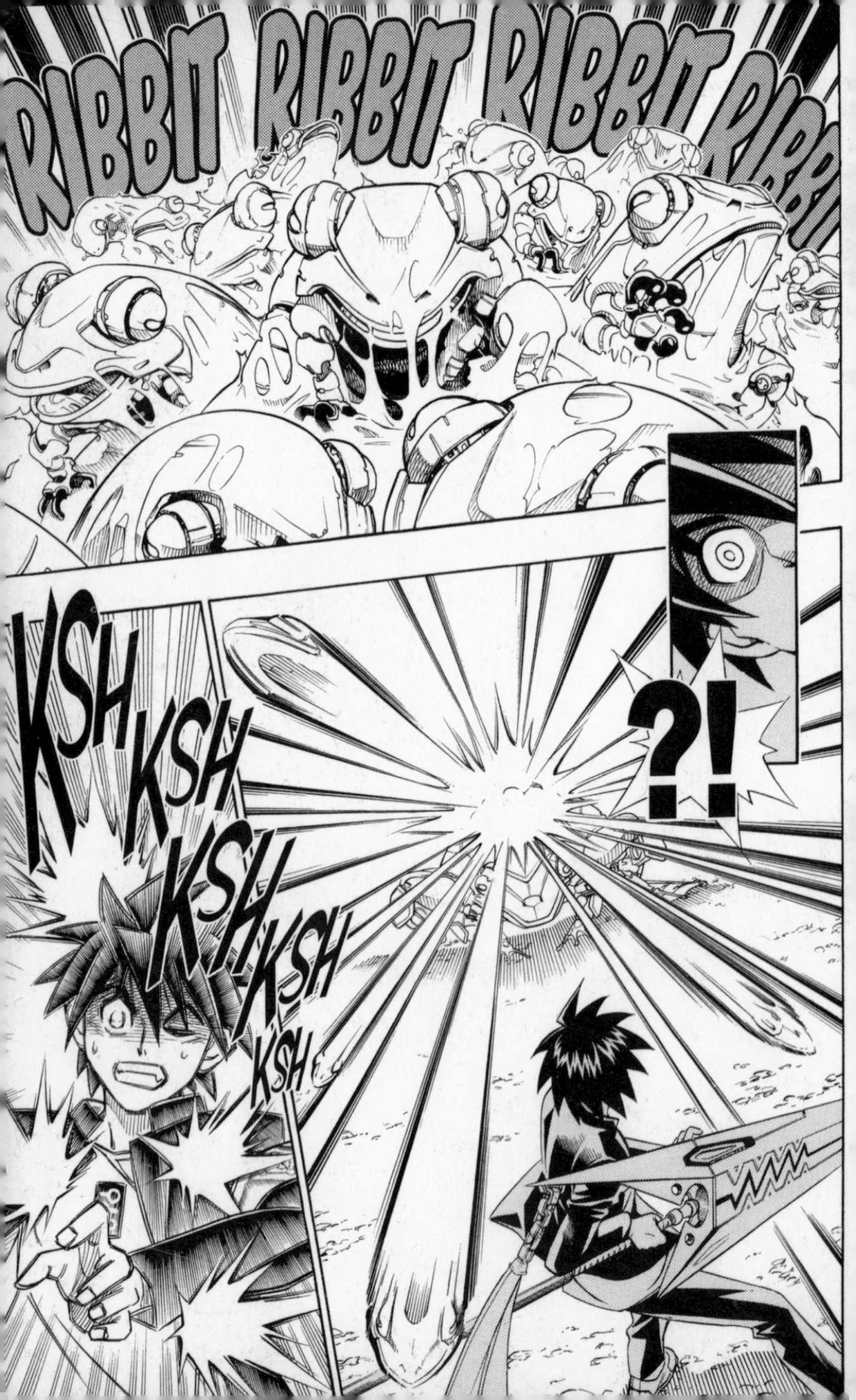
RIBBIT RIBBIT RIBBIT RIBBI
?!
KSH KSH KSH KSH KSH KSH

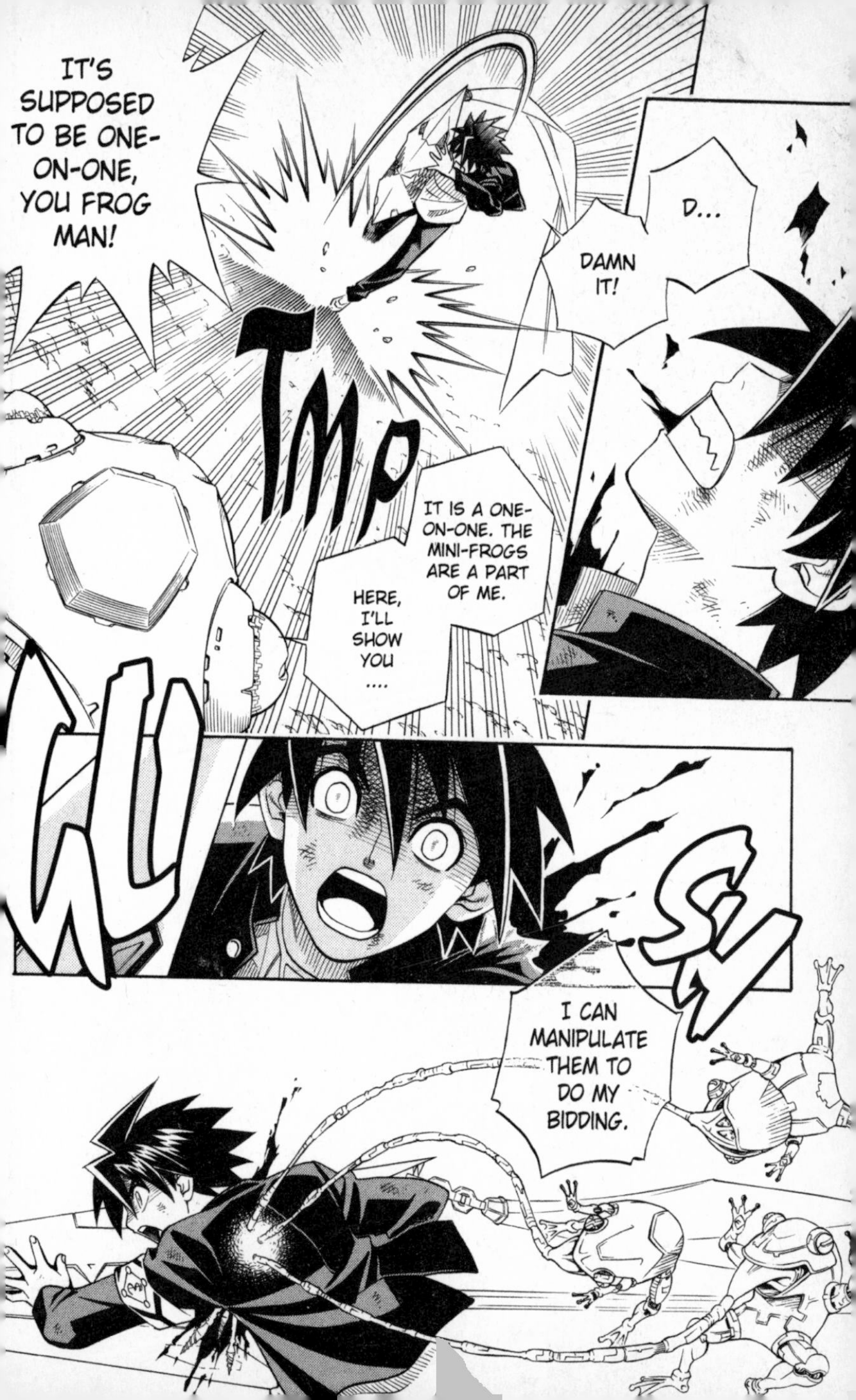
D...
DAMN IT!
IT'S SUPPOSED TO BE ONE-ON-ONE, YOU FROG MAN!
TMP
IT IS A ONE-ON-ONE. THE MINI-FROGS ARE A PART OF ME.
HERE, I'LL SHOW YOU....
SY
WU
I CAN MANIPULATE THEM TO DO MY BIDDING.

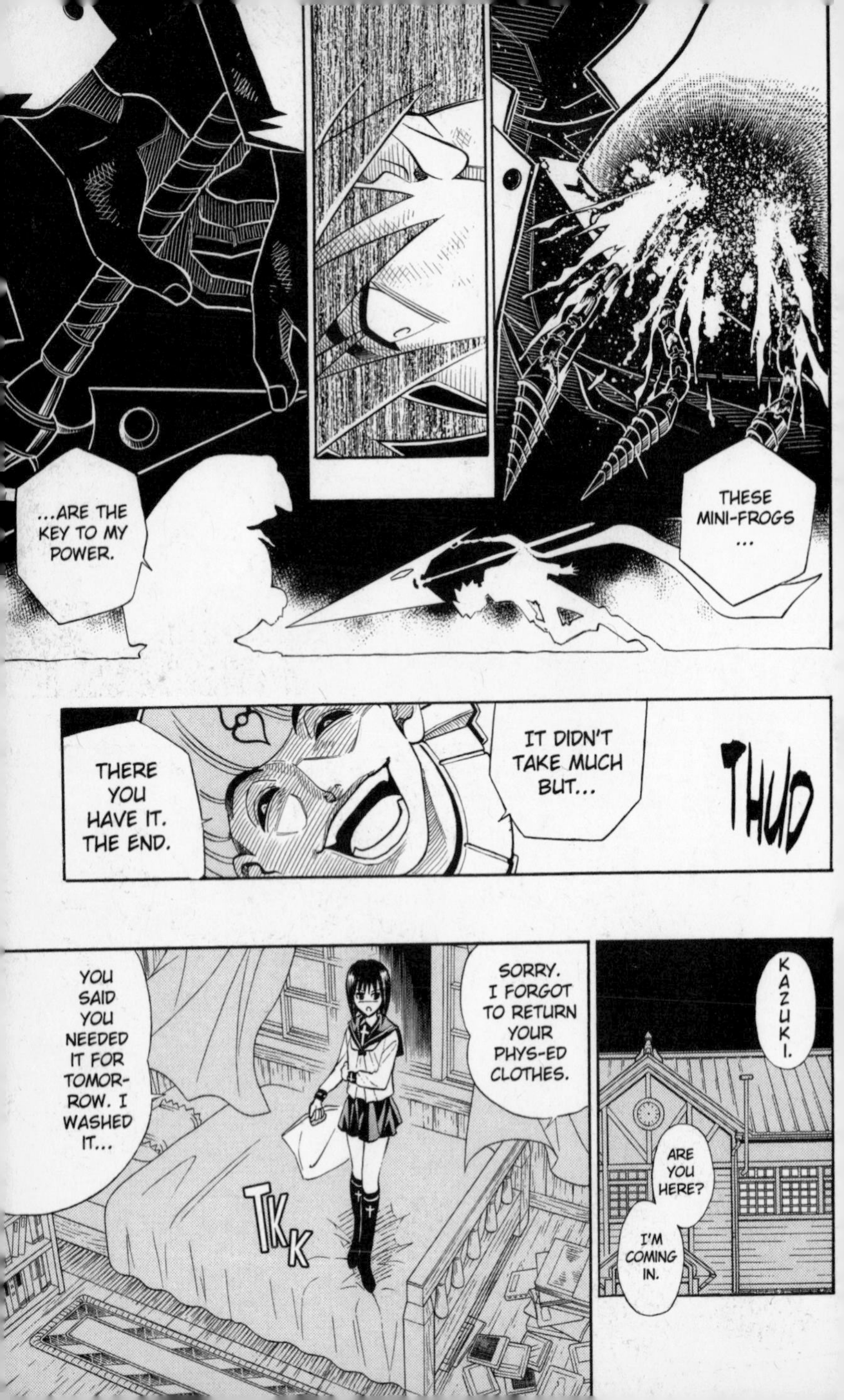
THESE MINI-FROGS ...
...ARE THE KEY TO MY POWER.
THUD
IT DIDN'T TAKE MUCH BUT...
THERE YOU HAVE IT. THE END.
KAZUKI.
ARE YOU HERE?
I'M COMING IN.
SORRY. I FORGOT TO RETURN YOUR PHYS-ED CLOTHES.
YOU SAID YOU NEEDED IT FOR TOMORROW. I WASHED IT...
TKK

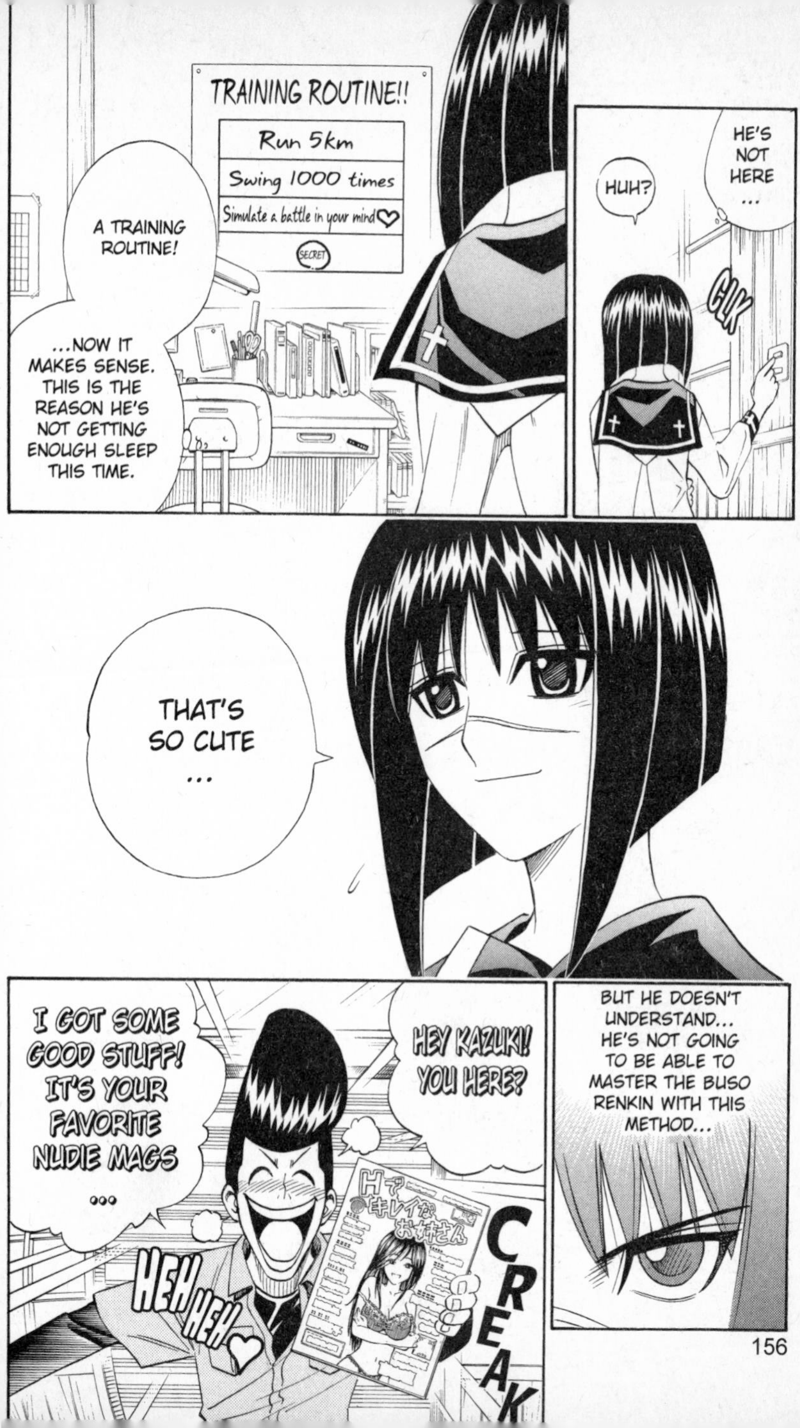
HE'S NOT HERE ...
HUH?
CLK
TRAINING ROUTINE!!
Run 5km
Swing 1000 times
Simulate a battle in your mind♡
SECRET
A TRAINING ROUTINE!
...NOW IT MAKES SENSE. THIS IS THE REASON HE'S NOT GETTING ENOUGH SLEEP THIS TIME.
THAT'S SO CUTE ...
BUT HE DOESN'T UNDERSTAND... HE'S NOT GOING TO BE ABLE TO MASTER THE BUSO RENKIN WITH THIS METHOD...
HEY KAZUKI! YOU HERE?
I GOT SOME GOOD STUFF! IT'S YOUR FAVORITE NUDIE MAGS ...
Hでキレイなお姉さん
HEH HEH♡
CREAK

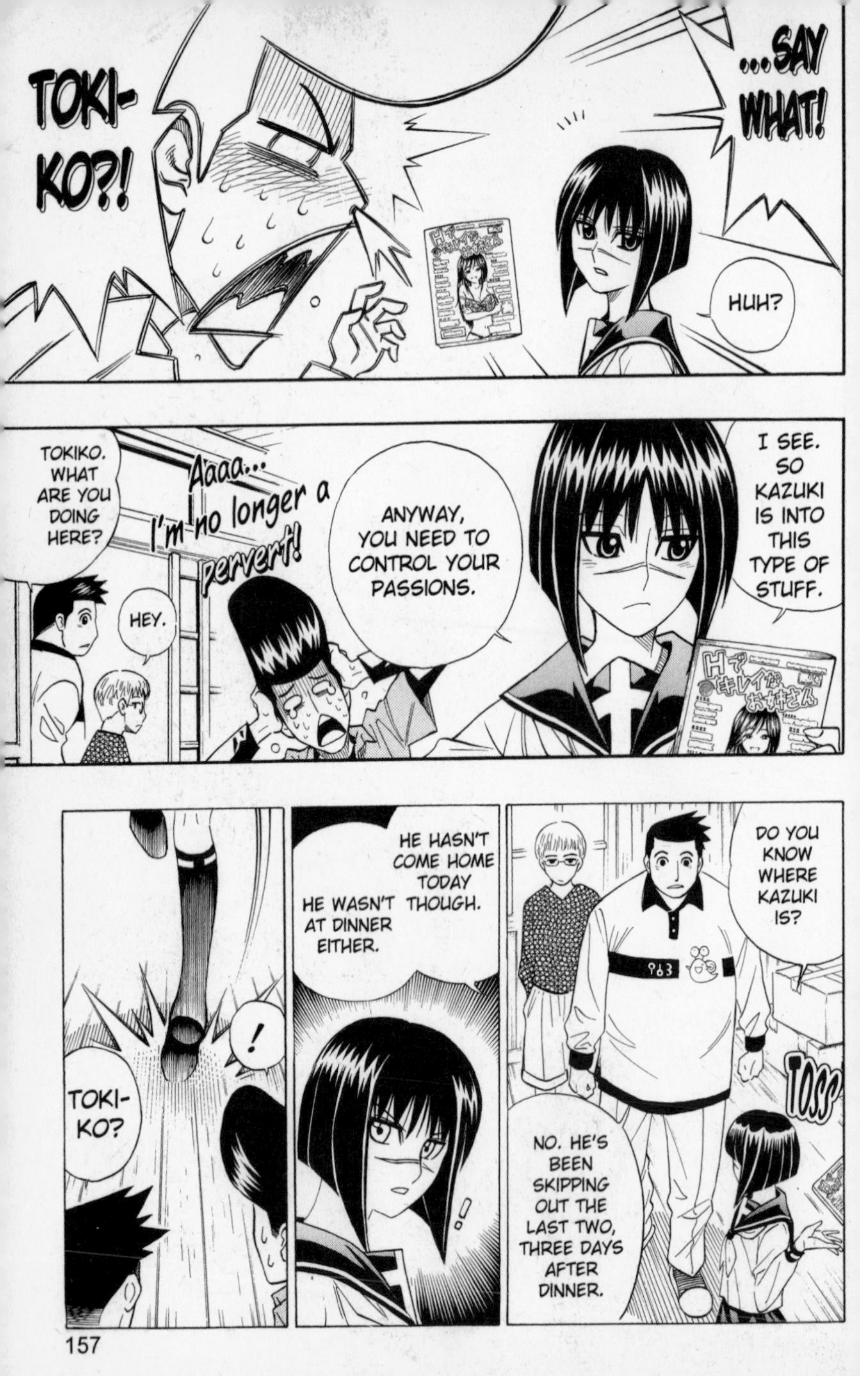
...SAY WHAT!
HUH?
TOKI-KO?!
I SEE. SO KAZUKI IS INTO THIS TYPE OF STUFF.
ANYWAY, YOU NEED TO CONTROL YOUR PASSIONS.
Aaaa... I'm no longer a pervert!
TOKIKO. WHAT ARE YOU DOING HERE?
HEY.
DO YOU KNOW WHERE KAZUKI IS?
TOSS
NO. HE'S BEEN SKIPPING OUT THE LAST TWO, THREE DAYS AFTER DINNER.
HE HASN'T COME HOME TODAY THOUGH.
HE WASN'T AT DINNER EITHER.
!
!
TOKI-KO?

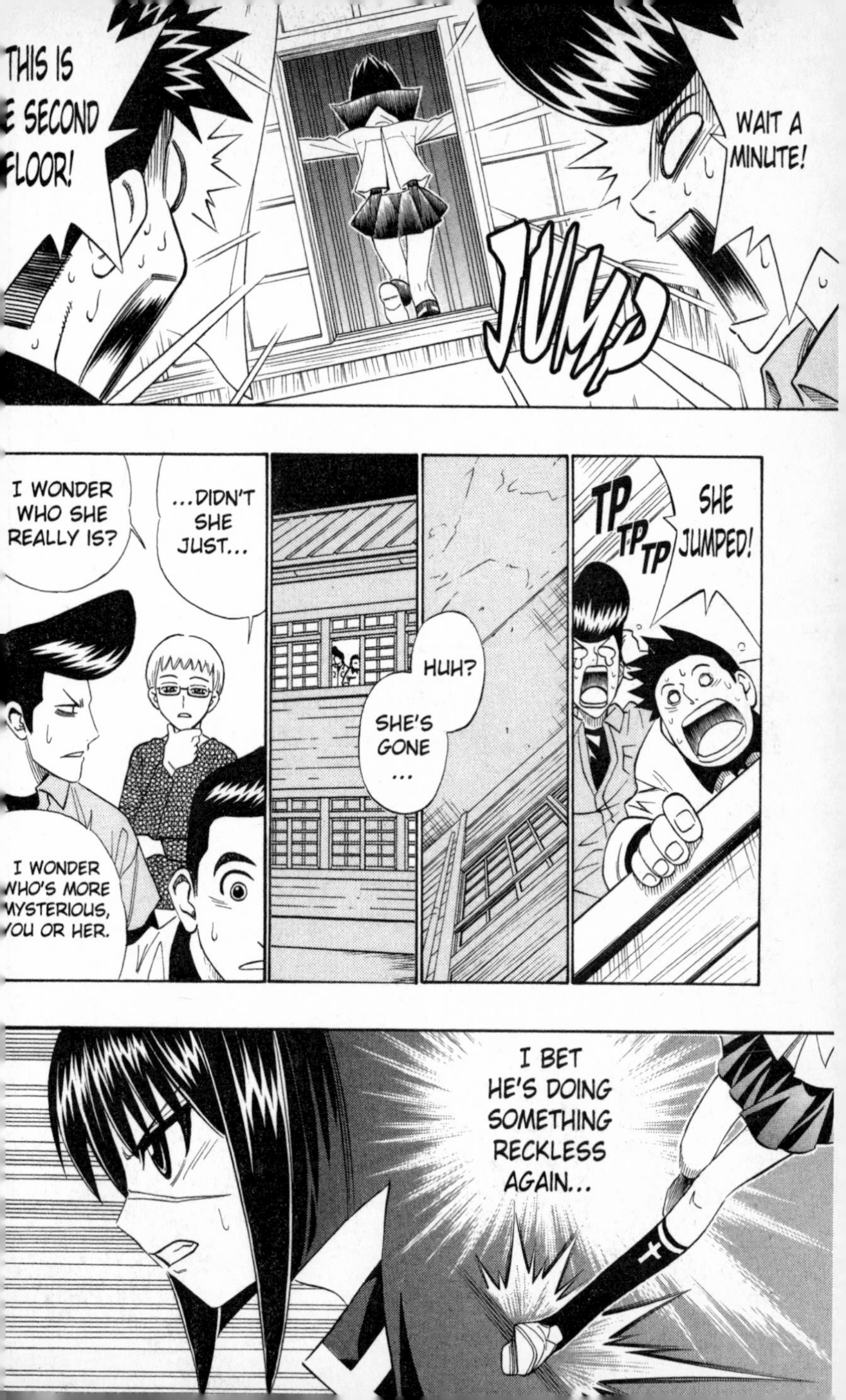
WAIT A MINUTE!
JUMP
THIS IS
E SECOND FLOOR!
TP TP TP
SHE JUMPED!
HUH?
SHE'S GONE ...
...DIDN'T SHE JUST...
I WONDER WHO SHE REALLY IS?
I WONDER
HO'S MORE
YSTERIOUS,
OU OR HER.
I BET HE'S DOING SOMETHING RECKLESS AGAIN...

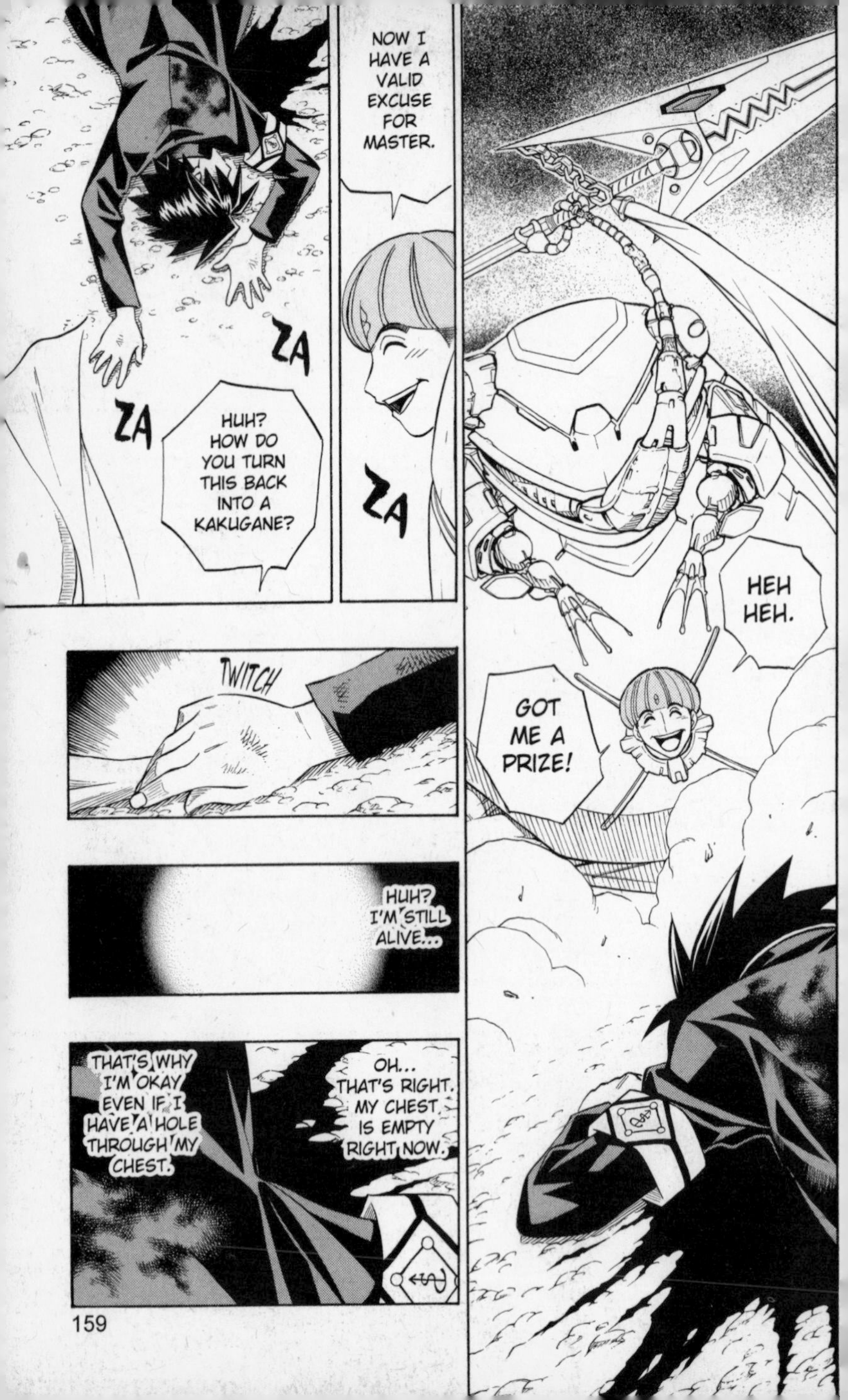
HEH HEH.
GOT ME A PRIZE!
NOW I HAVE A VALID EXCUSE FOR MASTER.
ZA
ZA
HUH? HOW DO YOU TURN THIS BACK INTO A KAKUGANE?
ZA
TWITCH
HUH? I'M STILL ALIVE...
OH... THAT'S RIGHT. MY CHEST IS EMPTY RIGHT NOW.
THAT'S WHY I'M OKAY EVEN IF I HAVE A HOLE THROUGH MY CHEST.

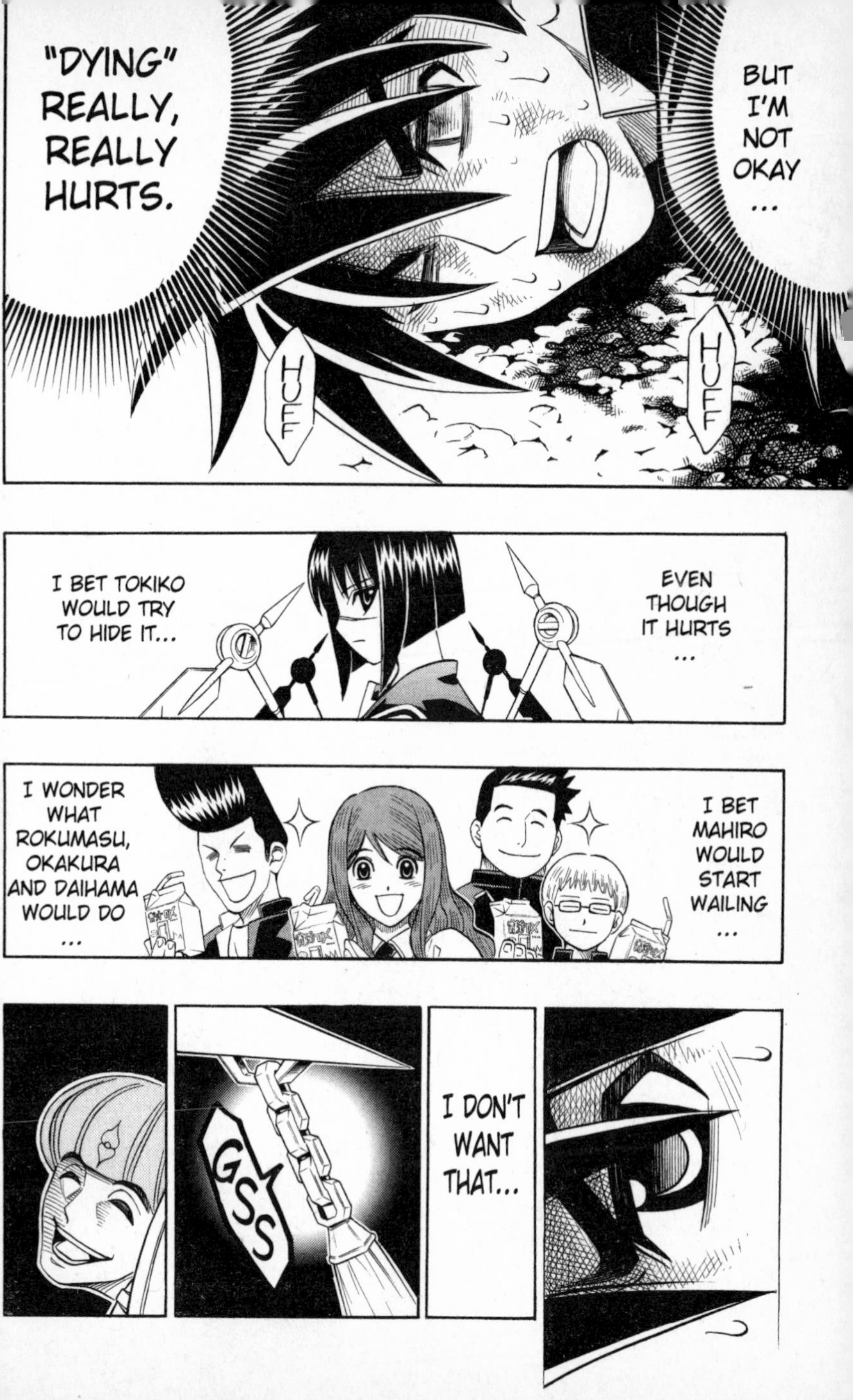
BUT I'M NOT OKAY ...
"DYING" REALLY, REALLY HURTS.
HUFF
HUFF
EVEN THOUGH IT HURTS ...
I BET TOKIKO WOULD TRY TO HIDE IT...
I BET MAHIRO WOULD START WAILING ...
I WONDER WHAT ROKUMASU, OKAKURA AND DAIHAMA WOULD DO ...
I DON'T WANT THAT...
GSS

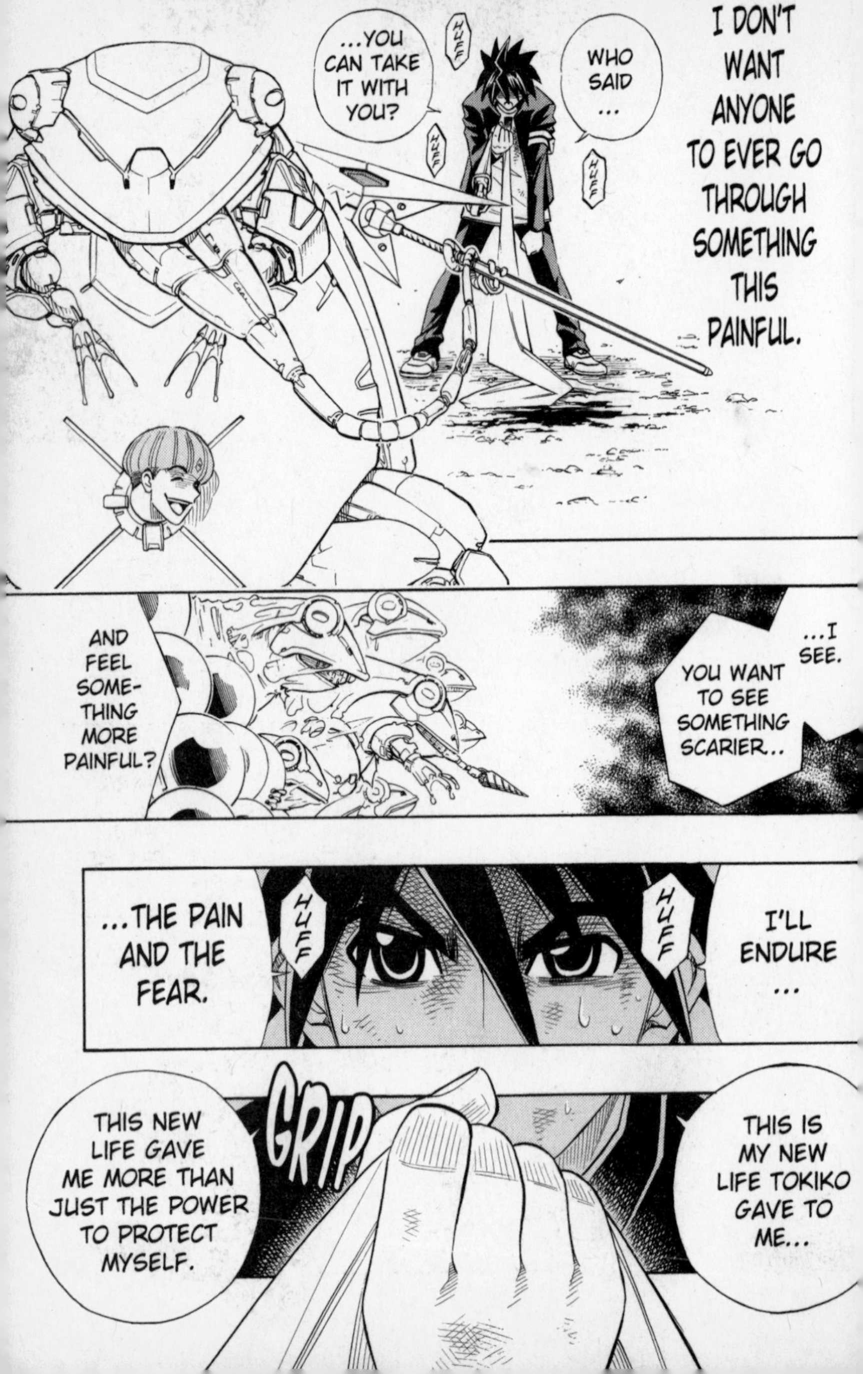
I DON'T WANT ANYONE TO EVER GO THROUGH SOMETHING THIS PAINFUL.
WHO SAID ...
HUFF
HUFF
HUFF
...YOU CAN TAKE IT WITH YOU?
...I SEE.
YOU WANT TO SEE SOMETHING SCARIER...
AND FEEL SOME-THING MORE PAINFUL?
I'LL ENDURE ...
HUFF
HUFF
...THE PAIN AND THE FEAR.
THIS IS MY NEW LIFE TOKIKO GAVE TO ME...
GRIP
THIS NEW LIFE GAVE ME MORE THAN JUST THE POWER TO PROTECT MYSELF.

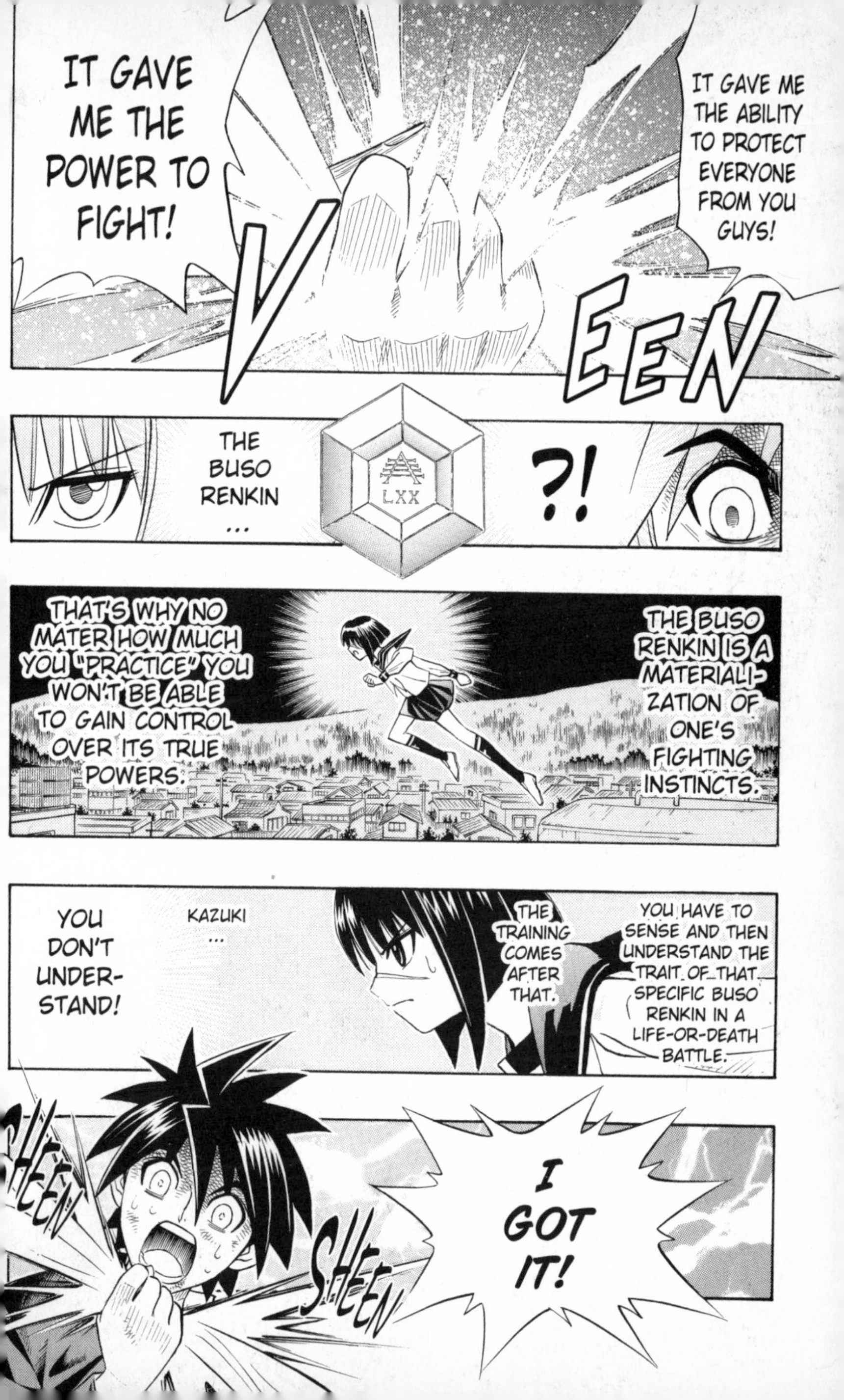

IT GAVE ME THE ABILITY TO PROTECT EVERYONE FROM YOU GUYS!
IT GAVE ME THE POWER TO FIGHT!
VEEN
?!
THE BUSO RENKIN ...
LXX
THE BUSO RENKIN IS A MATERIALI-ZATION OF ONE'S FIGHTING INSTINCTS.
THAT'S WHY NO MATER HOW MUCH YOU "PRACTICE" YOU WON'T BE ABLE TO GAIN CONTROL OVER ITS TRUE POWERS.
YOU HAVE TO SENSE AND THEN UNDERSTAND THE TRAIT OF THAT SPECIFIC BUSO RENKIN IN A LIFE-OR-DEATH BATTLE.
THE TRAINING COMES AFTER THAT.
KAZUKI ...
YOU DON'T UNDER-STAND!
I GOT IT!
SHEEN
SHEEN

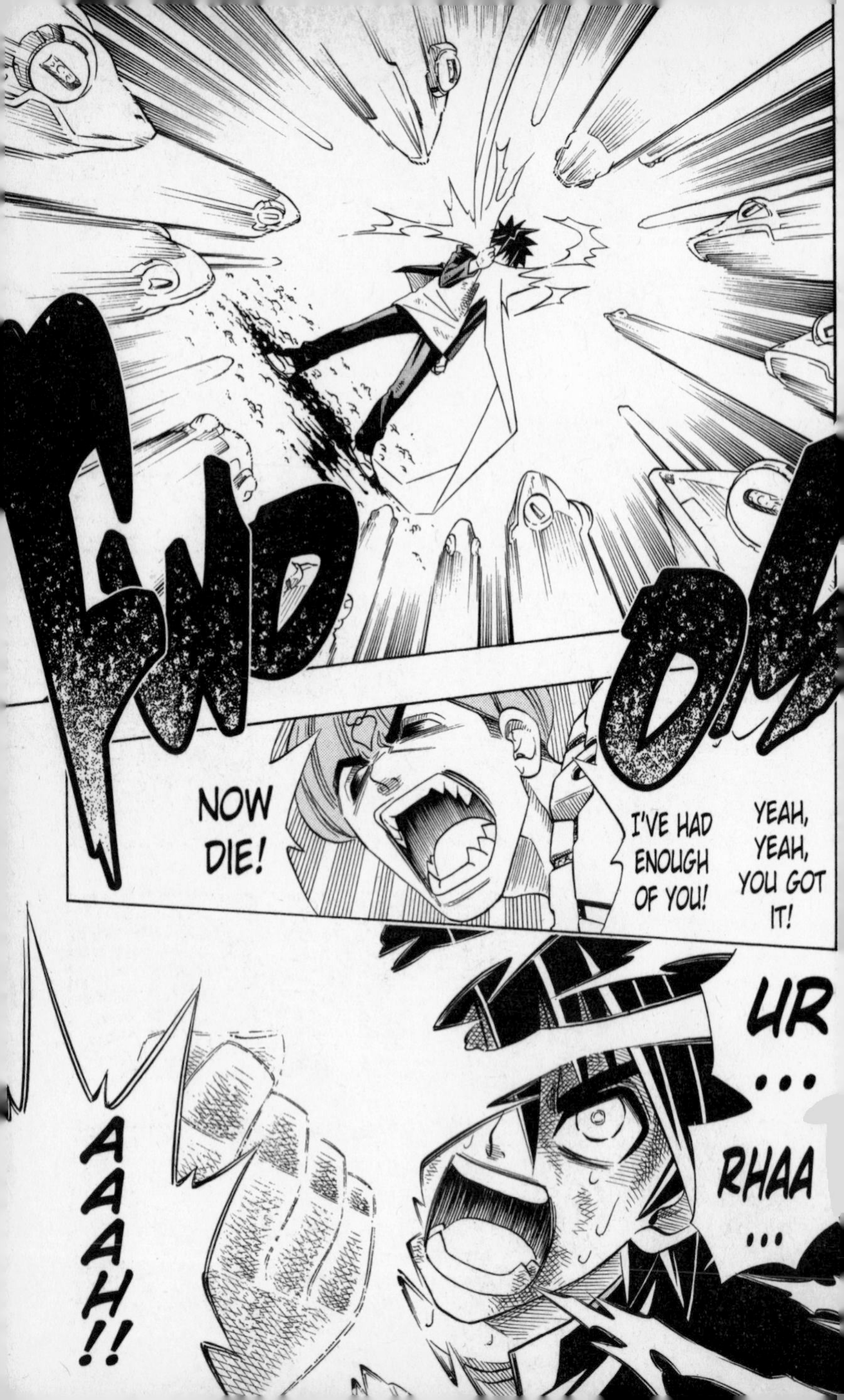
YEAH, YEAH, YOU GOT IT!
I'VE HAD ENOUGH OF YOU!
NOW DIE!
UR... RHAA...
AAAAH!!

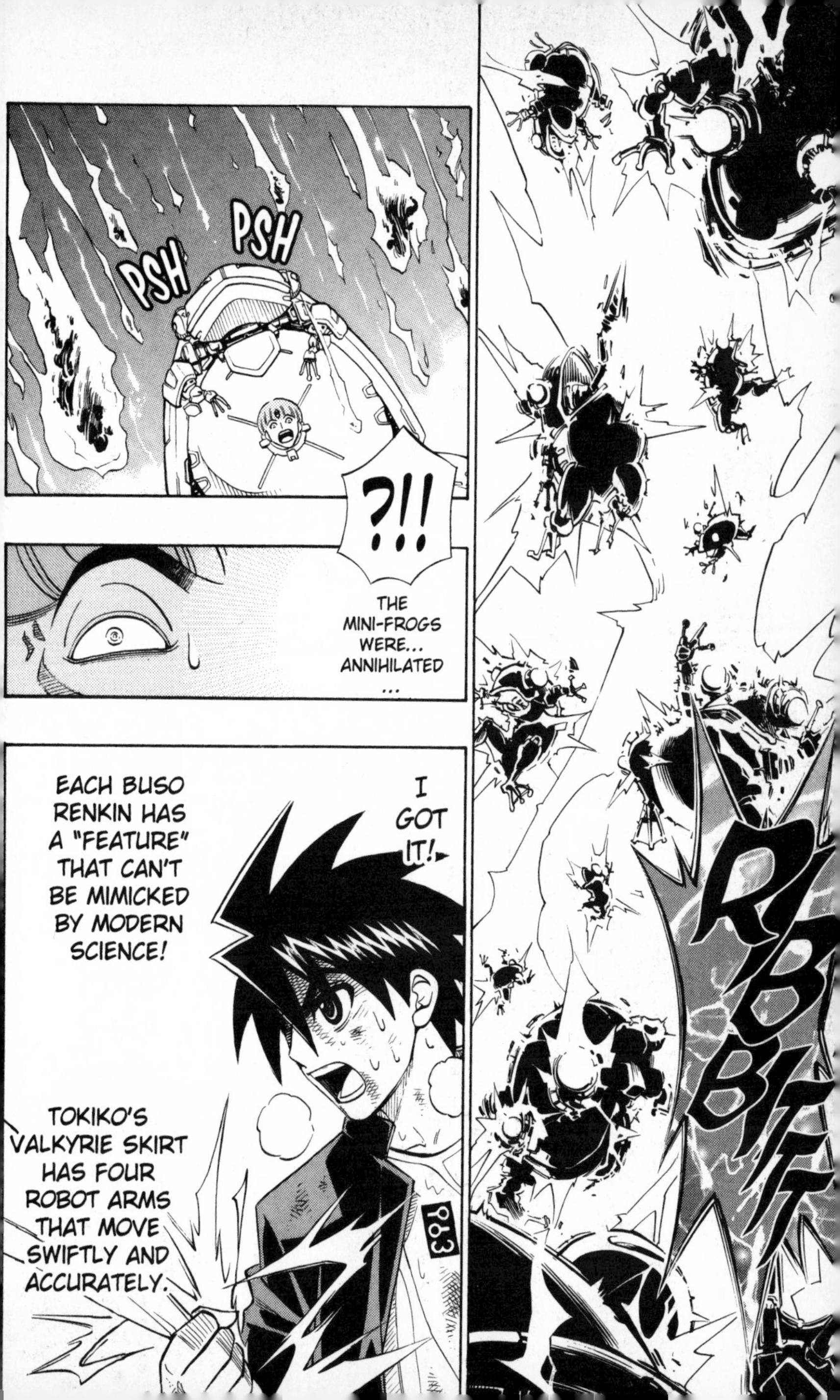

RIBBIT
PSH
PSH
?!!
THE MINI-FROGS WERE... ANNIHILATED ...
I GOT IT!
EACH BUSO RENKIN HAS A "FEATURE" THAT CAN'T BE MIMICKED BY MODERN SCIENCE!
TOKIKO'S VALKYRIE SKIRT HAS FOUR ROBOT ARMS THAT MOVE SWIFTLY AND ACCURATELY.

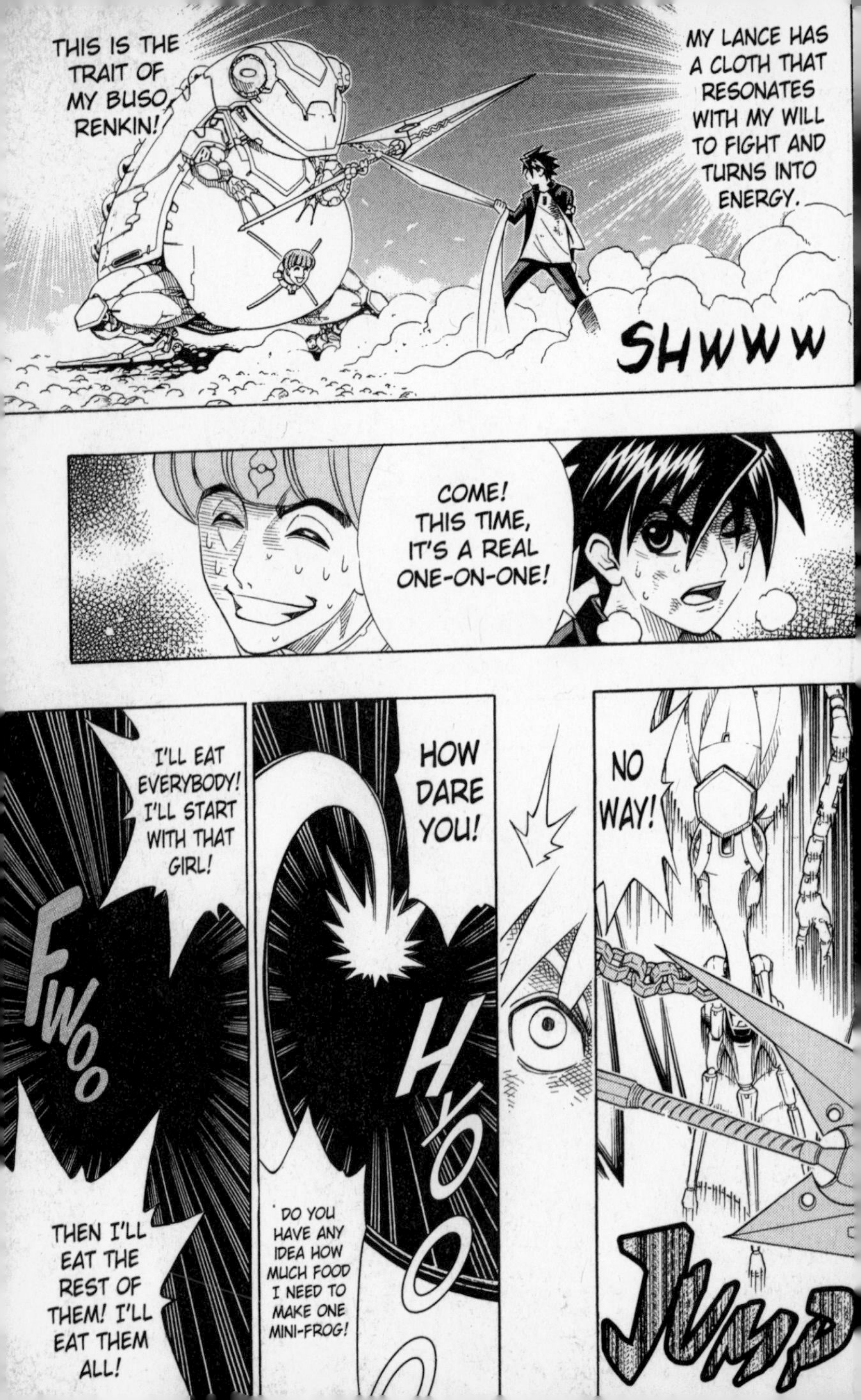
MY LANCE HAS A CLOTH THAT RESONATES WITH MY WILL TO FIGHT AND TURNS INTO ENERGY.
THIS IS THE TRAIT OF MY BUSO RENKIN!
SHWWW
COME! THIS TIME, IT'S A REAL ONE-ON-ONE!
NO WAY!
JUMP
HOW DARE YOU!
DO YOU HAVE ANY IDEA HOW MUCH FOOD I NEED TO MAKE ONE MINI-FROG!
HYOOO
I'LL EAT EVERYBODY! I'LL START WITH THAT GIRL!
FWOO
THEN I'LL EAT THE REST OF THEM! I'LL EAT THEM ALL!

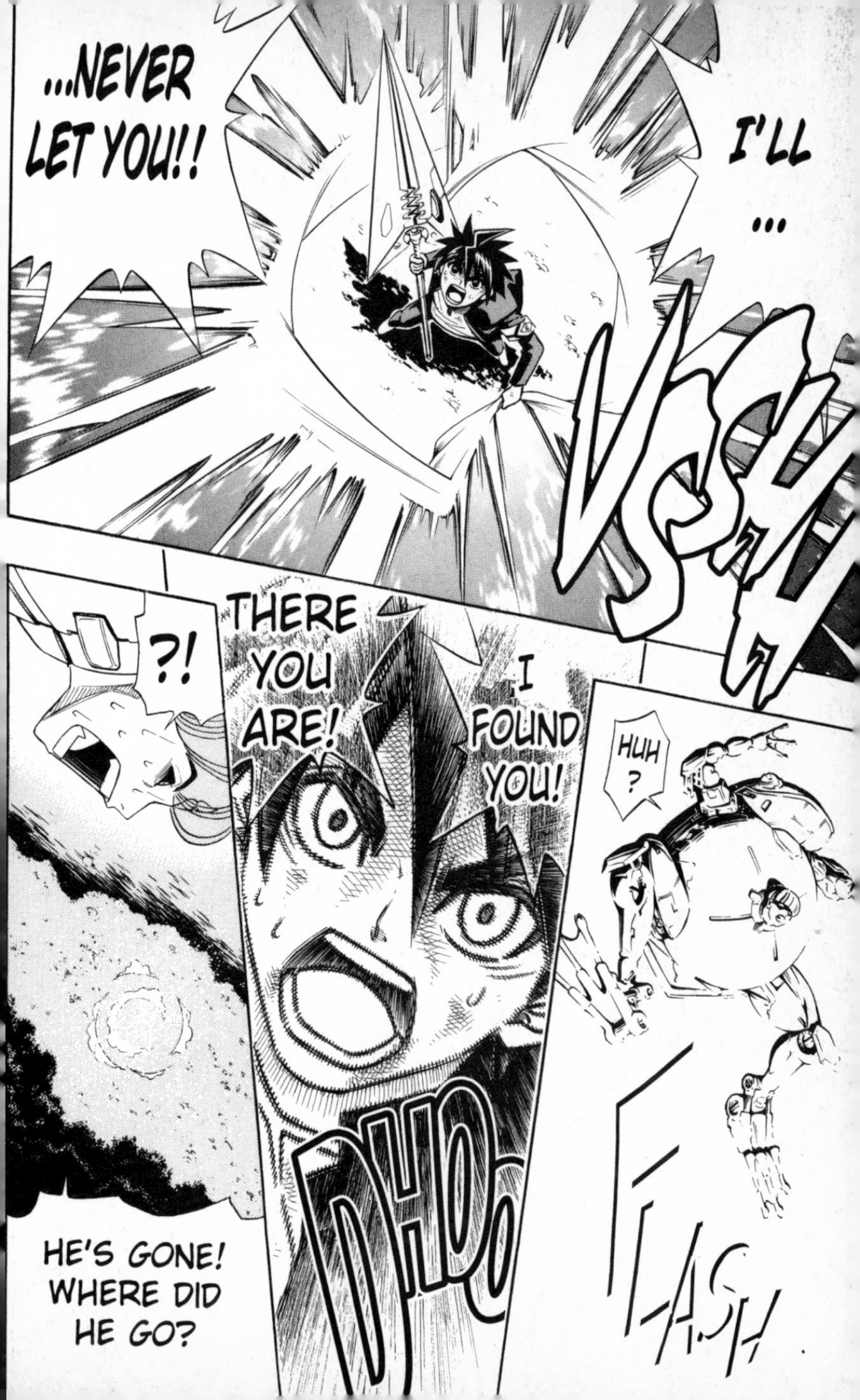
I'LL ...
...NEVER LET YOU!!
VSHH
HUH ?
FLASH
I FOUND YOU!
THERE YOU ARE!
DHOO
?!
HE'S GONE! WHERE DID HE GO?

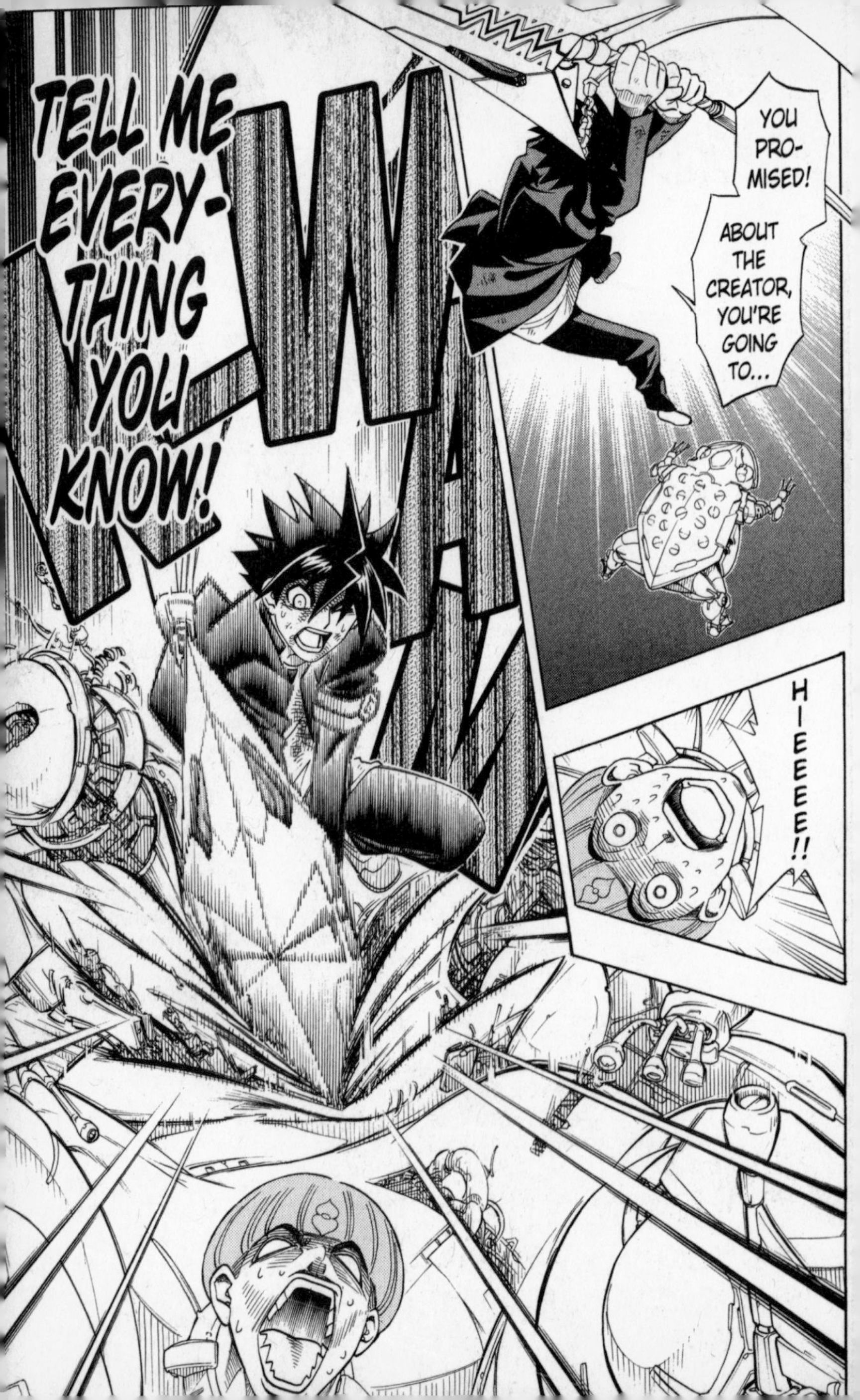
YOU PROMISED!
ABOUT THE CREATOR, YOU'RE GOING TO...
HIEEEE!!
TELL ME EVERYTHING YOU KNOW!

Chapter 1: New Life

· The series began with the concept of "Incredible and strange beings battling it out" but then I realized, it was a "Romantic Comedy Wannabe"…. I was full of anxieties.

· I tried changing the art style a bit so you can tell where I was drawing with great agony in several sections. The artwork juuust isn't right. Mahiro looks completely different now compared to the beginning…

· I created the page flow right around when I bought a cellphone so I ended up using the cellphone a lot. I was thinking how useful it was at first but I realized it was too useful. I ended up stressing over how to use it in several places…

· This is a commonly used structural format. Maybe that's why people would ask where I got the idea from, or point out that I copied it from XYZ in their letters. I got it from Ultraman. (I'm an old man so I know very little about the anime and videogames that are out now…) My first editor figured it out right away.

Chapter 2: Midnight Run

· I wanted to state that the Alchemy in my manga is different from Alchemy in the traditional sense so I ended up squishing my explanation in there. Unfortunately, I don't think a lot of people know what Alchemy really is.

· Kazuki's attack from this chapter is my favorite scene in the whole volume.

· The reason why I didn't reveal Tokiko's name in the first two chapters is because I didn't have the opportunity. It was a complete structural blunder.

· I got the title from one of my favorite movies.

Chapter 3: Homunculus's Identity

· This chapter continued to set the stage. I know making the setting too complicated equates to a boring manga but… I paid very close attention.

· In the introduction of the Papillon Mask Creator, my editor at the time was like, "I'm not sure about this mask…" It was an obvious critique but I ended up agonizing over it. With my friends and assistants' encouragement I decided to go with it. At this point, I had no idea things would turn out like that later…

· This is the chapter I started to feel like I grasped Kazuki's "space cadet" character.

Chapter 4: Parasitic Homunculus

· In order to create a "time limit" and "suppress Tokiko's power for the time being" she becomes ill from the parasitic Homunculus.

· I tried a touch of "Passion" by showing Tokiko's stomach a little bit! I was so embarrassed I drew it while my assistants were asleep. Thoughts such as "I wonder if they'll say something?" and "Will they make a comment?" were racing through my head while I nervously handed them the pages but no response. The pink typhoon ended up passing through only my head.

· The scene where Kazuki is protecting Tokiko from the boulder was an idea that came up suddenly when I was creating the page flow. I think the only person who would do something like this instinctively is Kazuki. It's a side of him that I'd really like to expand.

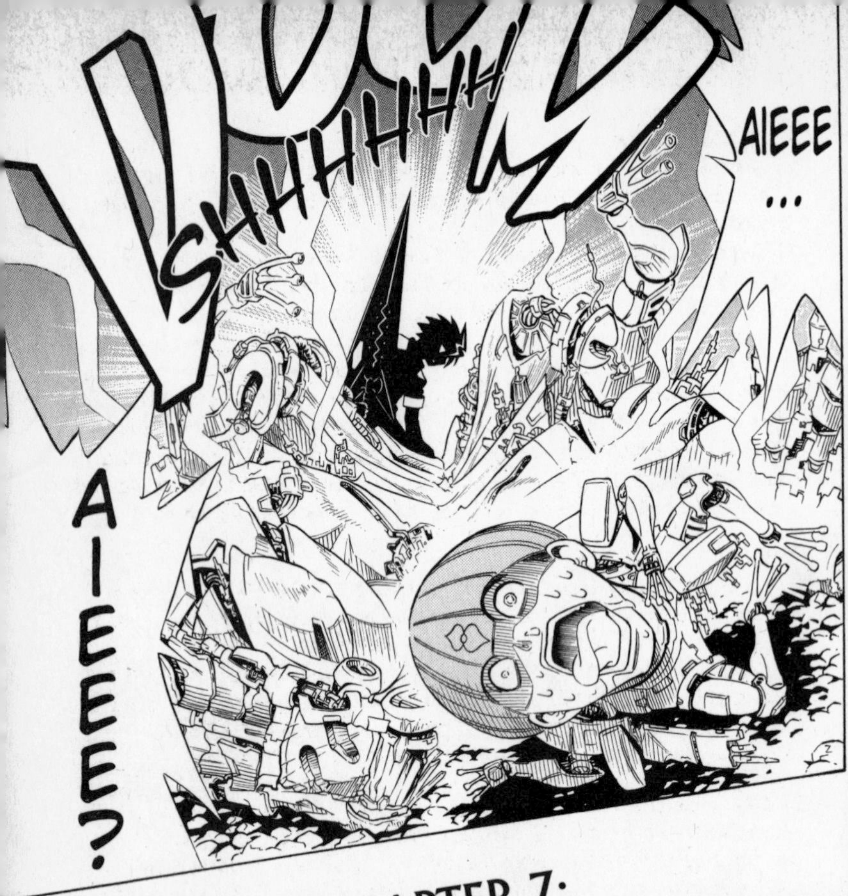
SHHHHHHH
AIEEE ...
AIEEE?

CHAPTER 7: YOU'RE A LITTLE STRONGER

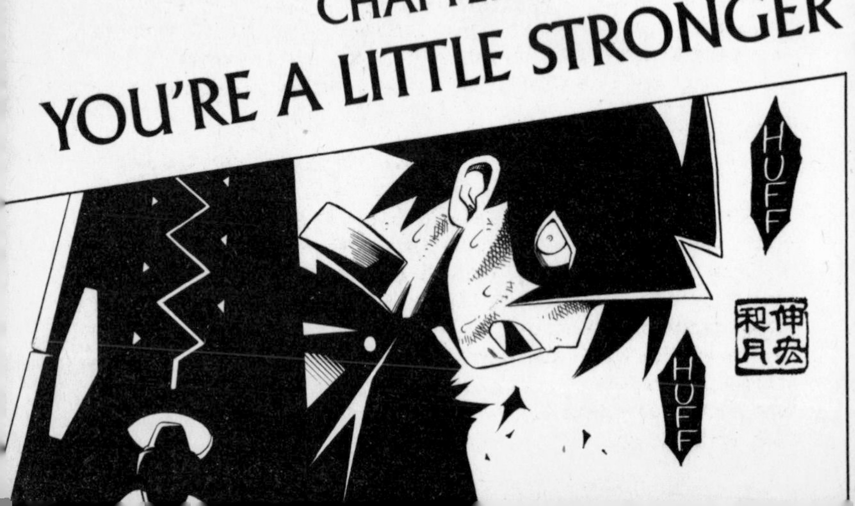
HUFF
HUFF
伸宏
和月

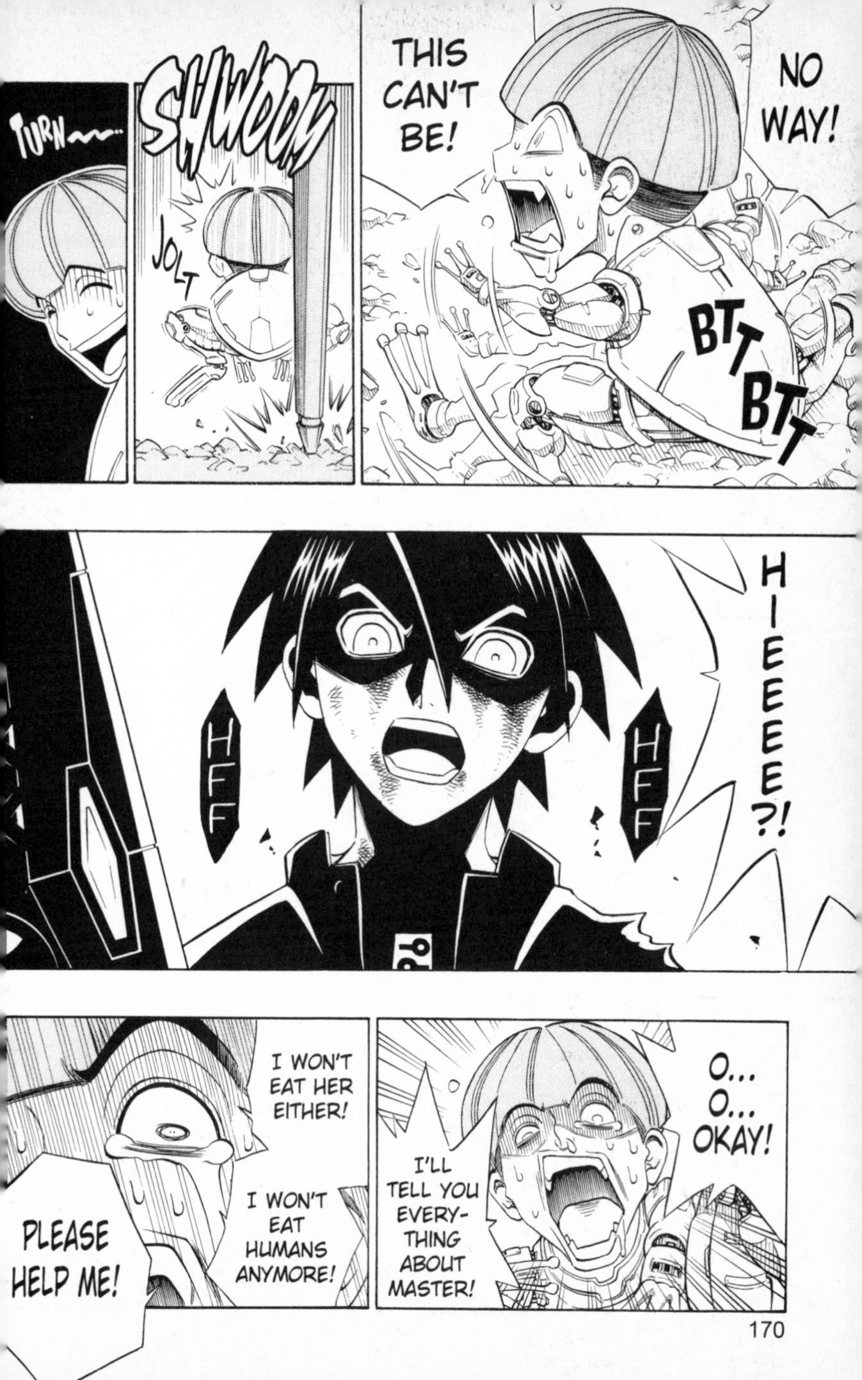
NO WAY!
THIS CAN'T BE!
BTT BTT
SHWOOM
JOLT
TURN~~~...
HIEEEEE?!
HFF
HFF
O... O... OKAY!
I'LL TELL YOU EVERY-THING ABOUT MASTER!
I WON'T EAT HER EITHER!
I WON'T EAT HUMANS ANYMORE!
PLEASE HELP ME!

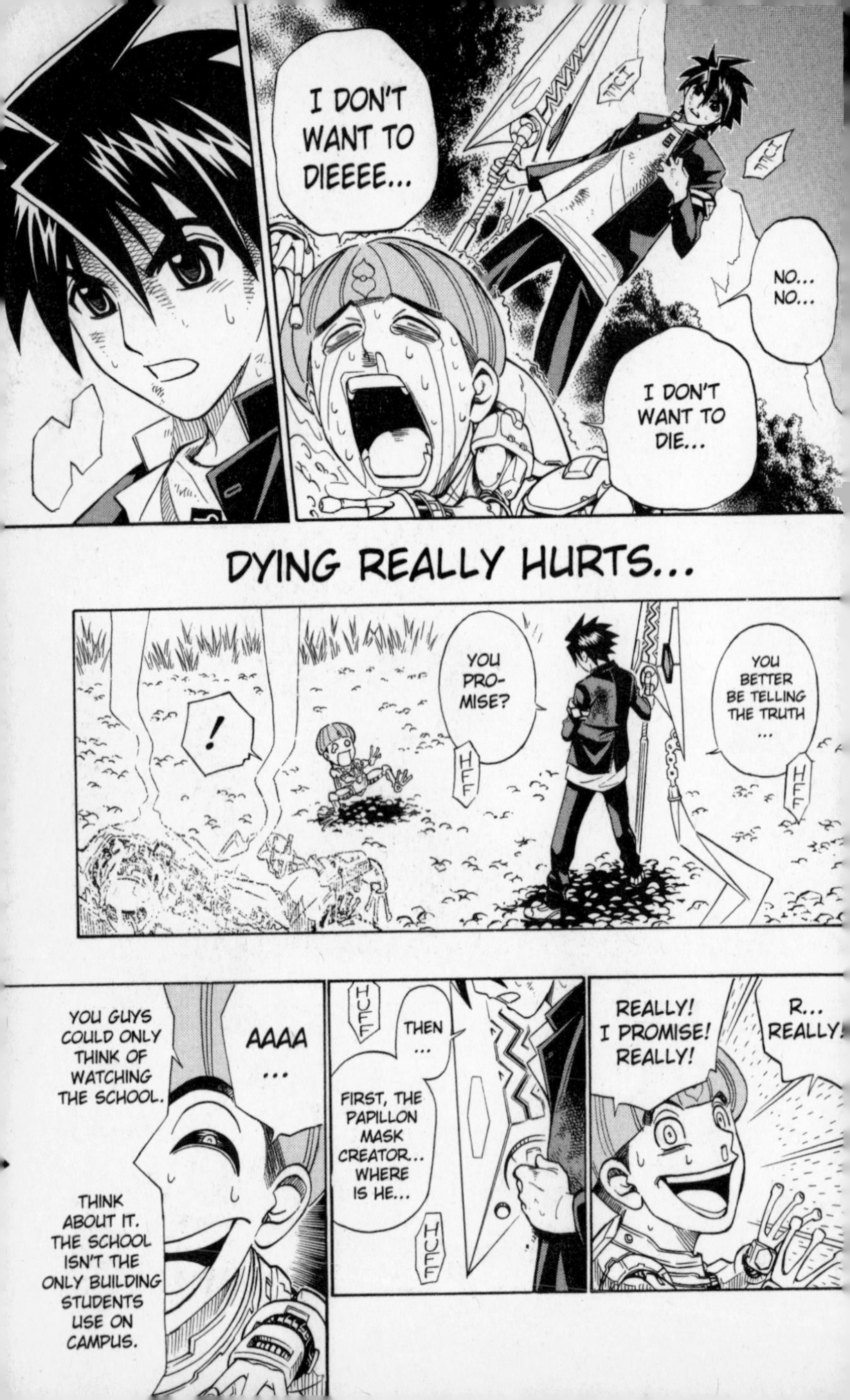
NO... NO...
I DON'T WANT TO DIE...
I DON'T WANT TO DIEEEE...
DYING REALLY HURTS...
YOU BETTER BE TELLING THE TRUTH...
HFF
YOU PROMISE?
HFF
!
R... REALLY!
REALLY! I PROMISE! REALLY!
HUFF
THEN...
FIRST, THE PAPILLON MASK CREATOR... WHERE IS HE...
HUFF
AAAA...
YOU GUYS COULD ONLY THINK OF WATCHING THE SCHOOL.
THINK ABOUT IT. THE SCHOOL ISN'T THE ONLY BUILDING STUDENTS USE ON CAMPUS.

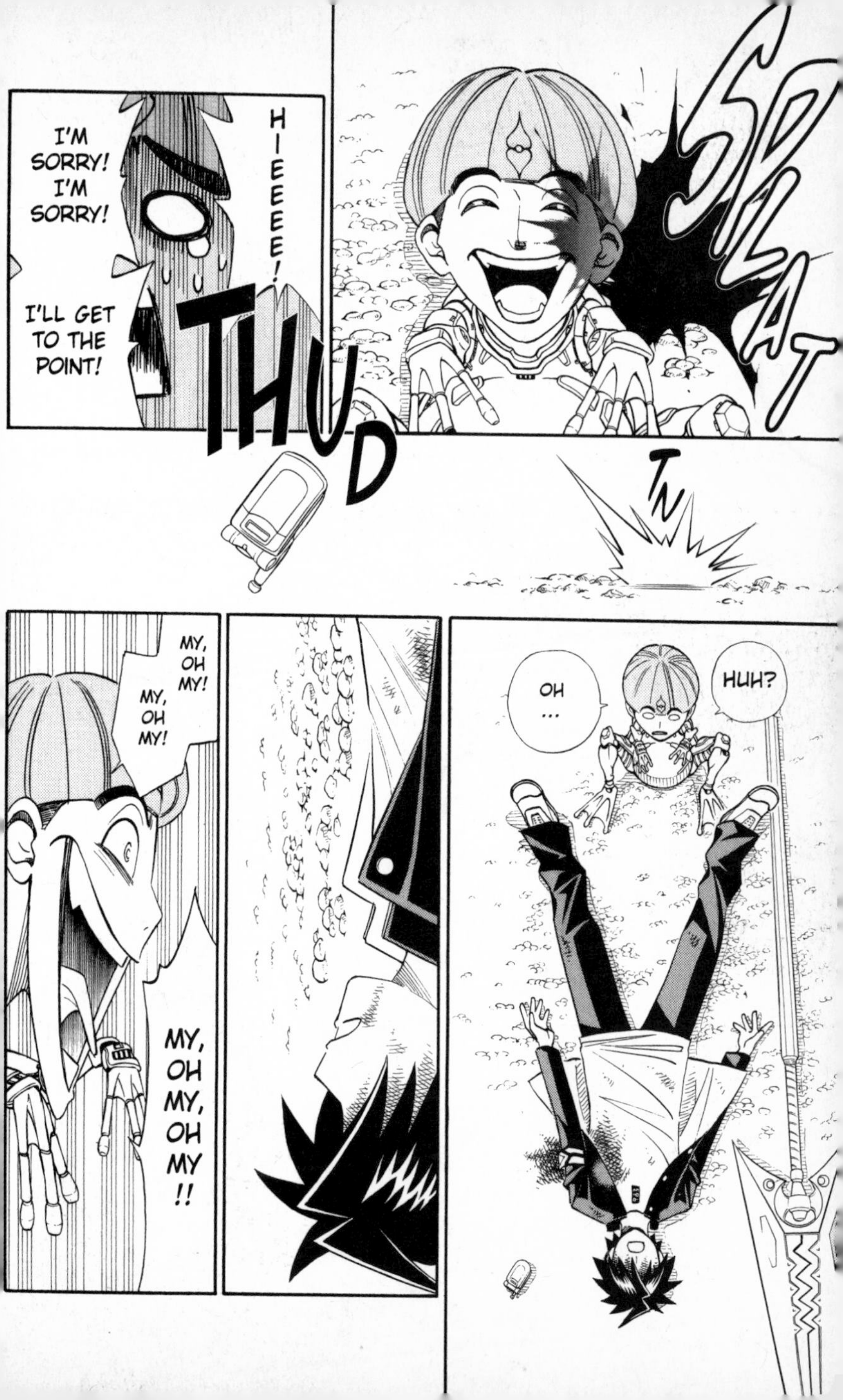
SPLAT
HIEEEE!
I'M SORRY! I'M SORRY!
I'LL GET TO THE POINT!
THUD
TN
HUH?
OH ...
MY, OH MY!
MY, OH MY!
MY, OH MY, OH MY!!

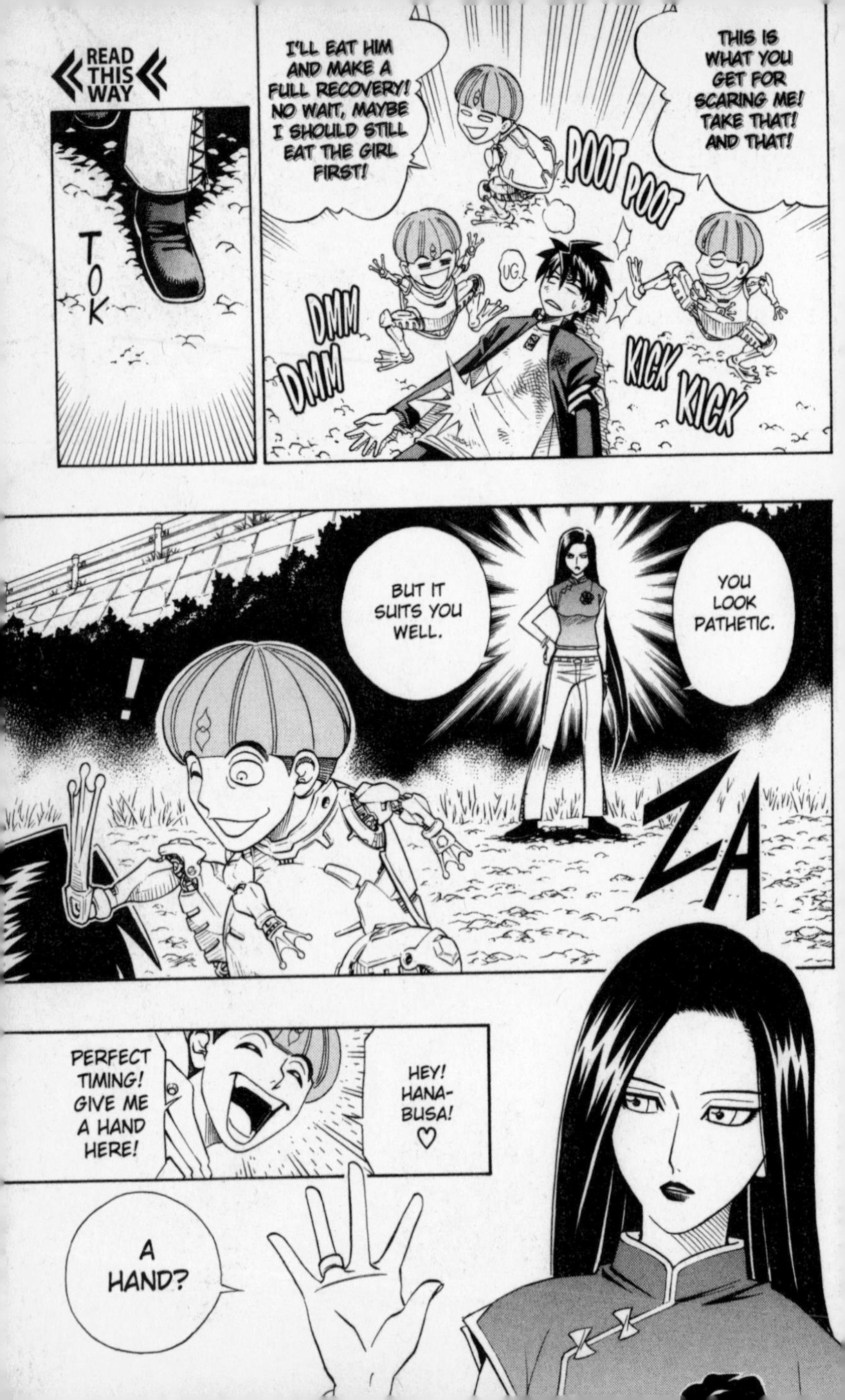
READ THIS WAY
THIS IS WHAT YOU GET FOR SCARING ME! TAKE THAT! AND THAT!
POOT POOT
I'LL EAT HIM AND MAKE A FULL RECOVERY! NO WAIT, MAYBE I SHOULD STILL EAT THE GIRL FIRST!
UG.
KICK KICK
DMM DMM
TOK
YOU LOOK PATHETIC.
BUT IT SUITS YOU WELL.
ZA
!
HEY! HANA-BUSA! ♡
PERFECT TIMING! GIVE ME A HAND HERE!
A HAND?

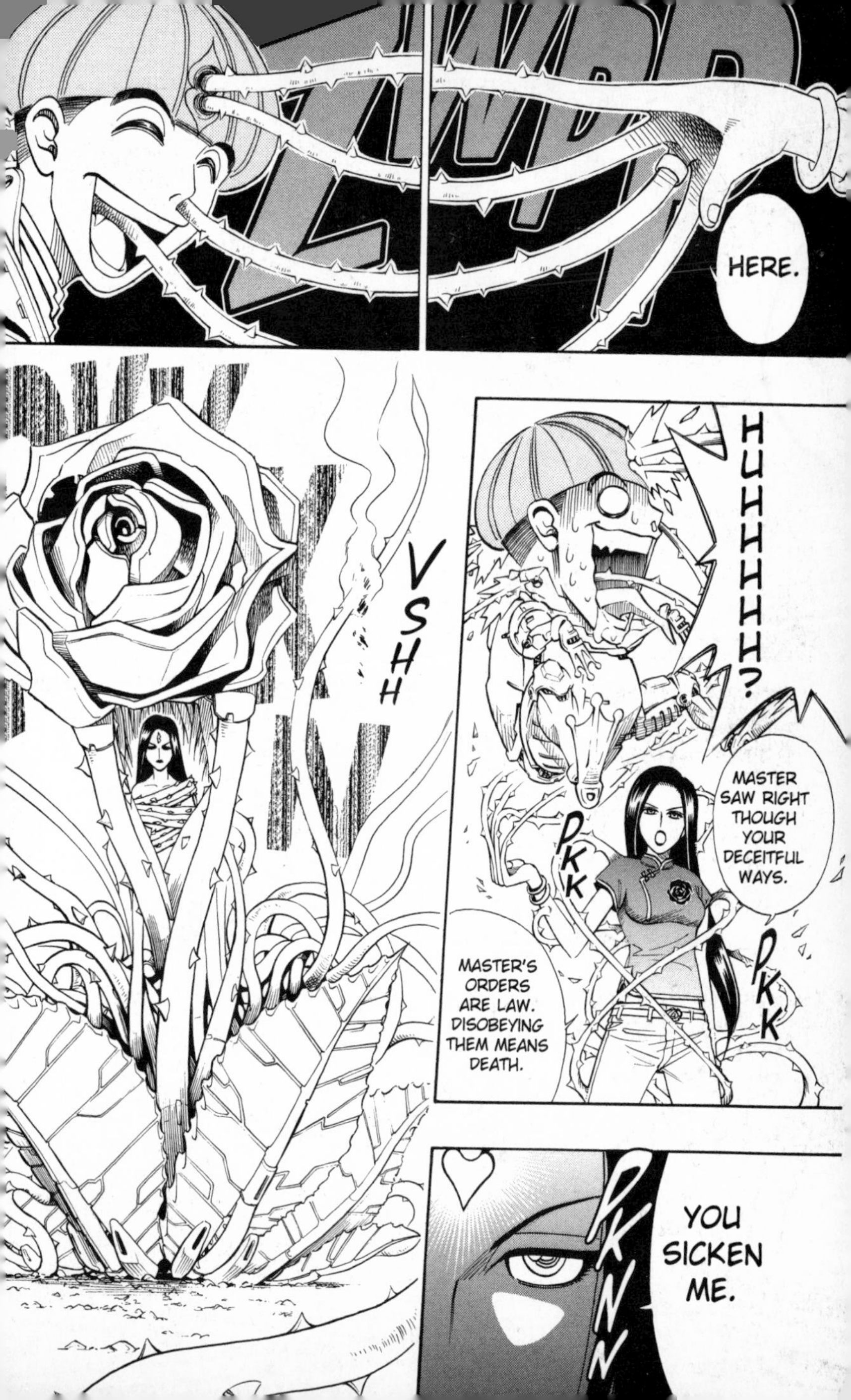
HERE.
HUHHHHHH?
MASTER SAW RIGHT THOUGH YOUR DECEITFUL WAYS.
PKK
PKK
MASTER'S ORDERS ARE LAW. DISOBEYING THEM MEANS DEATH.
PKNN
YOU SICKEN ME.
VSHH

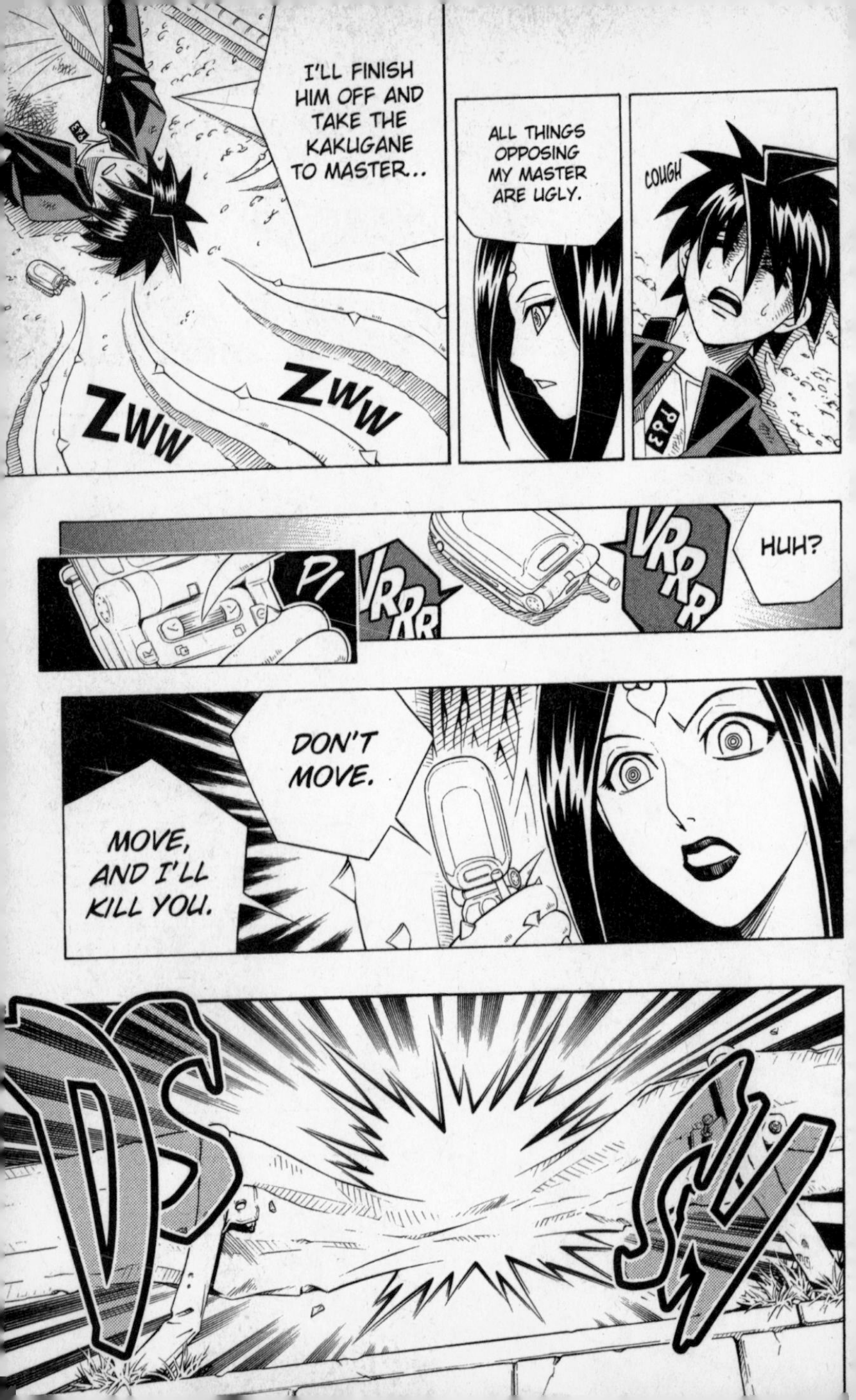
COUGH
ALL THINGS OPPOSING MY MASTER ARE UGLY.
I'LL FINISH HIM OFF AND TAKE THE KAKUGANE TO MASTER...
ZWW
ZWW
HUH?
VRRR
VRRR
PI
DON'T MOVE.
MOVE, AND I'LL KILL YOU.
DS

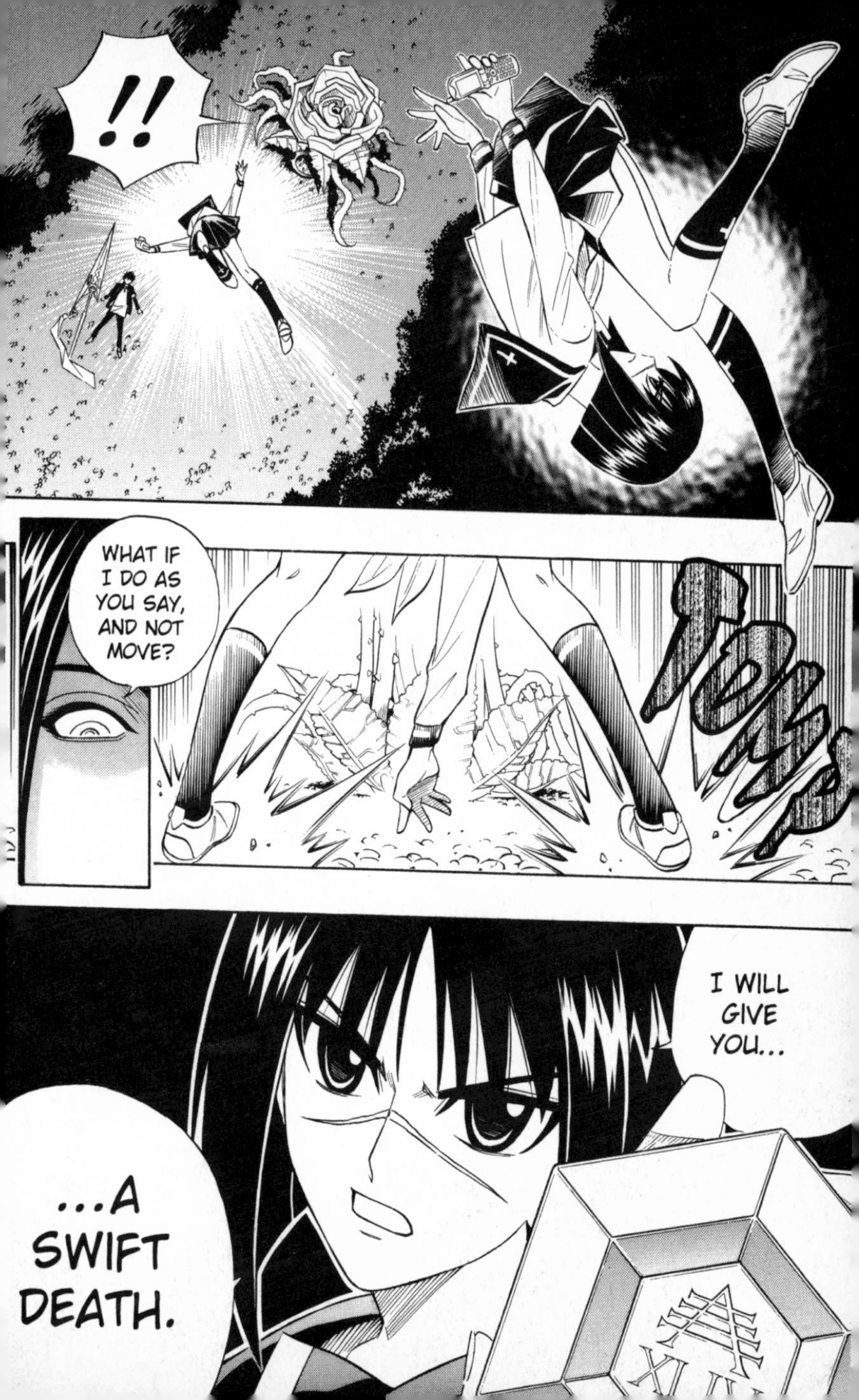
!!
TOMP
WHAT IF I DO AS YOU SAY, AND NOT MOVE?
I WILL GIVE YOU...
...A SWIFT DEATH.

READ THIS WAY

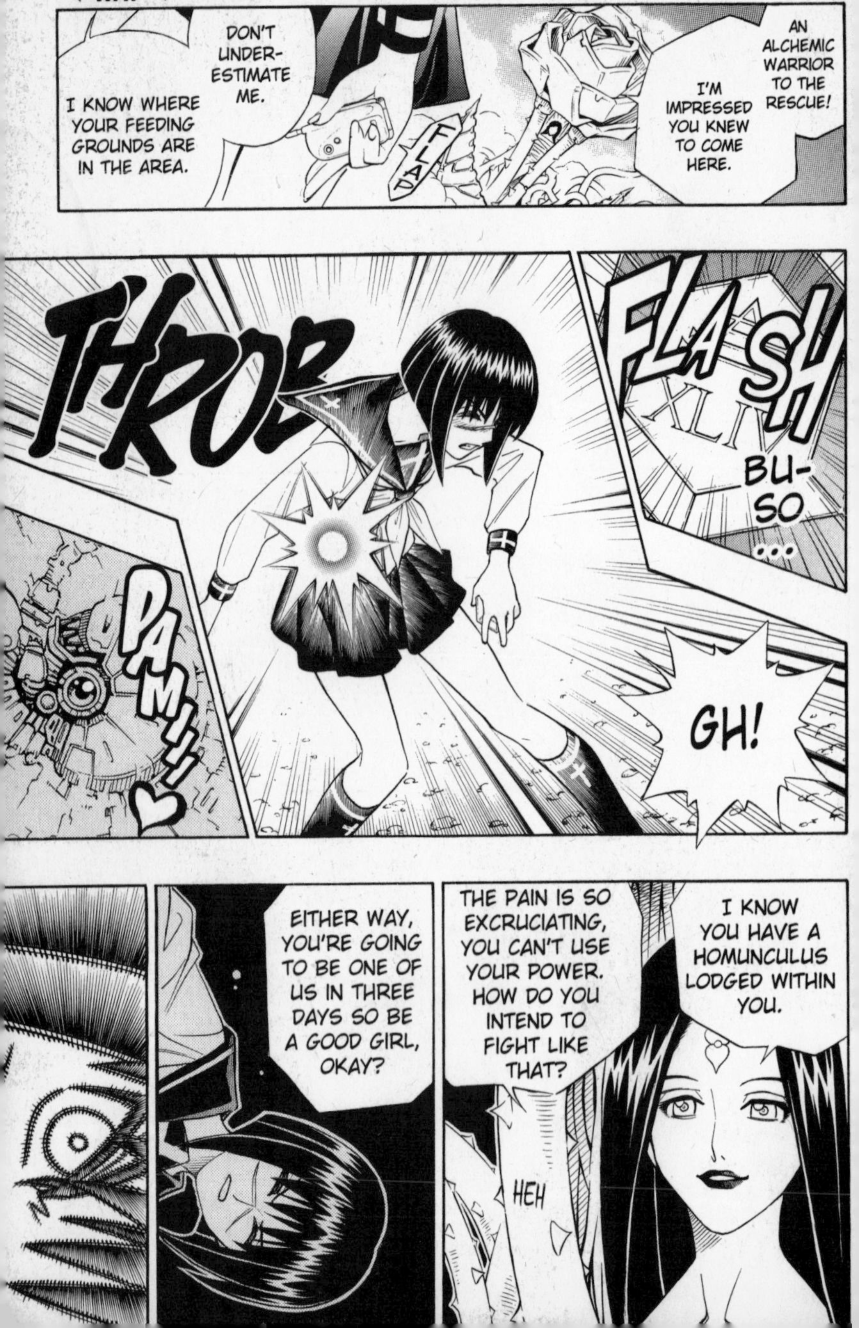
AN ALCHEMIC WARRIOR TO THE RESCUE!
I'M IMPRESSED YOU KNEW TO COME HERE.
FLAP
DON'T UNDER-ESTIMATE ME.
I KNOW WHERE YOUR FEEDING GROUNDS ARE IN THE AREA.
FLASH
XLIV
BU-SO...
THROB
GH!
PAM!!!
I KNOW YOU HAVE A HOMUNCULUS LODGED WITHIN YOU.
THE PAIN IS SO EXCRUCIATING, YOU CAN'T USE YOUR POWER. HOW DO YOU INTEND TO FIGHT LIKE THAT?
HEH
EITHER WAY, YOU'RE GOING TO BE ONE OF US IN THREE DAYS SO BE A GOOD GIRL, OKAY?

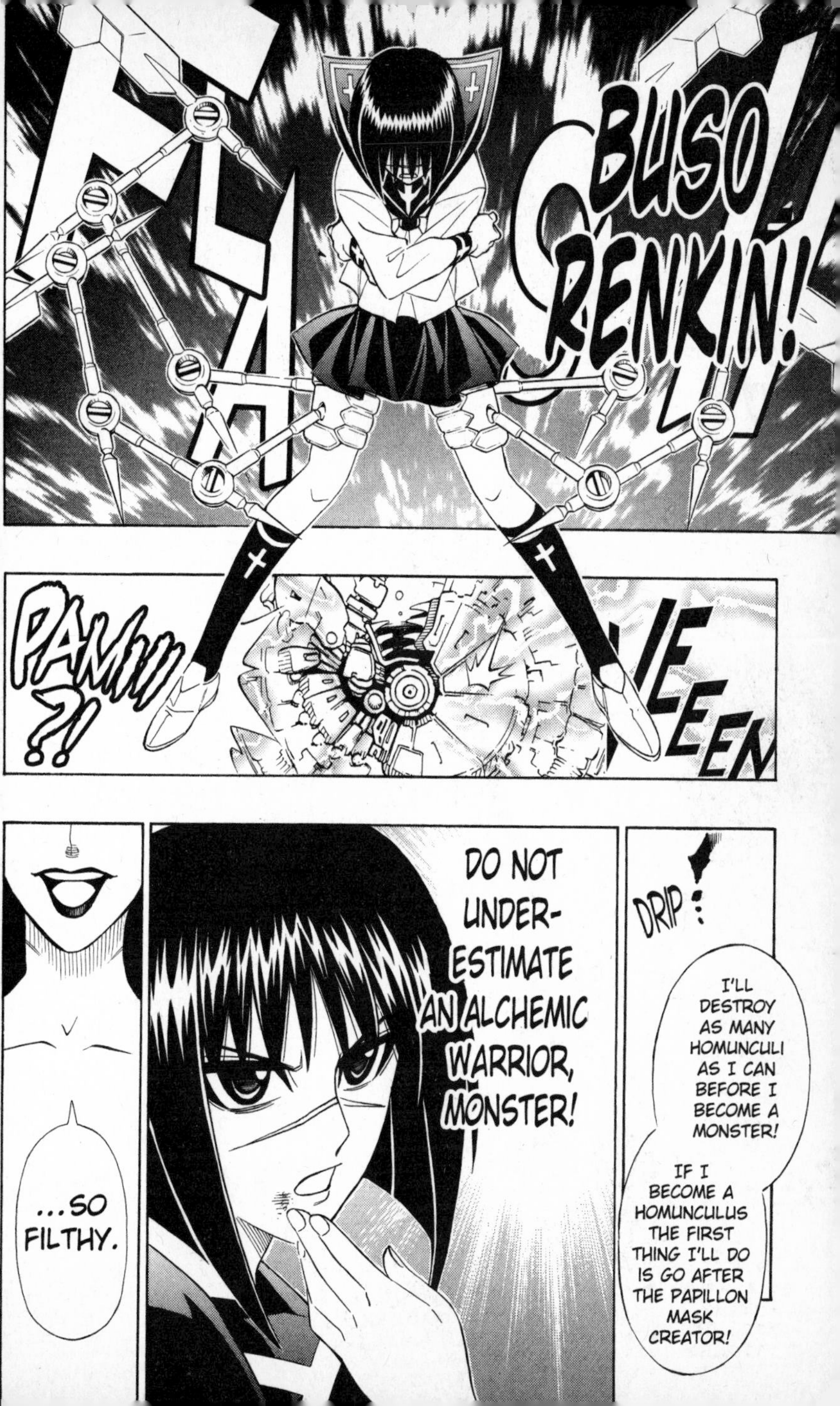
BUSO RENKIN!
PAM!!!
?!
DRIP
I'LL DESTROY AS MANY HOMUNCULI AS I CAN BEFORE I BECOME A MONSTER!
IF I BECOME A HOMUNCULUS THE FIRST THING I'LL DO IS GO AFTER THE PAPILLON MASK CREATOR!
DO NOT UNDER-ESTIMATE AN ALCHEMIC WARRIOR, MONSTER!
...SO FILTHY.

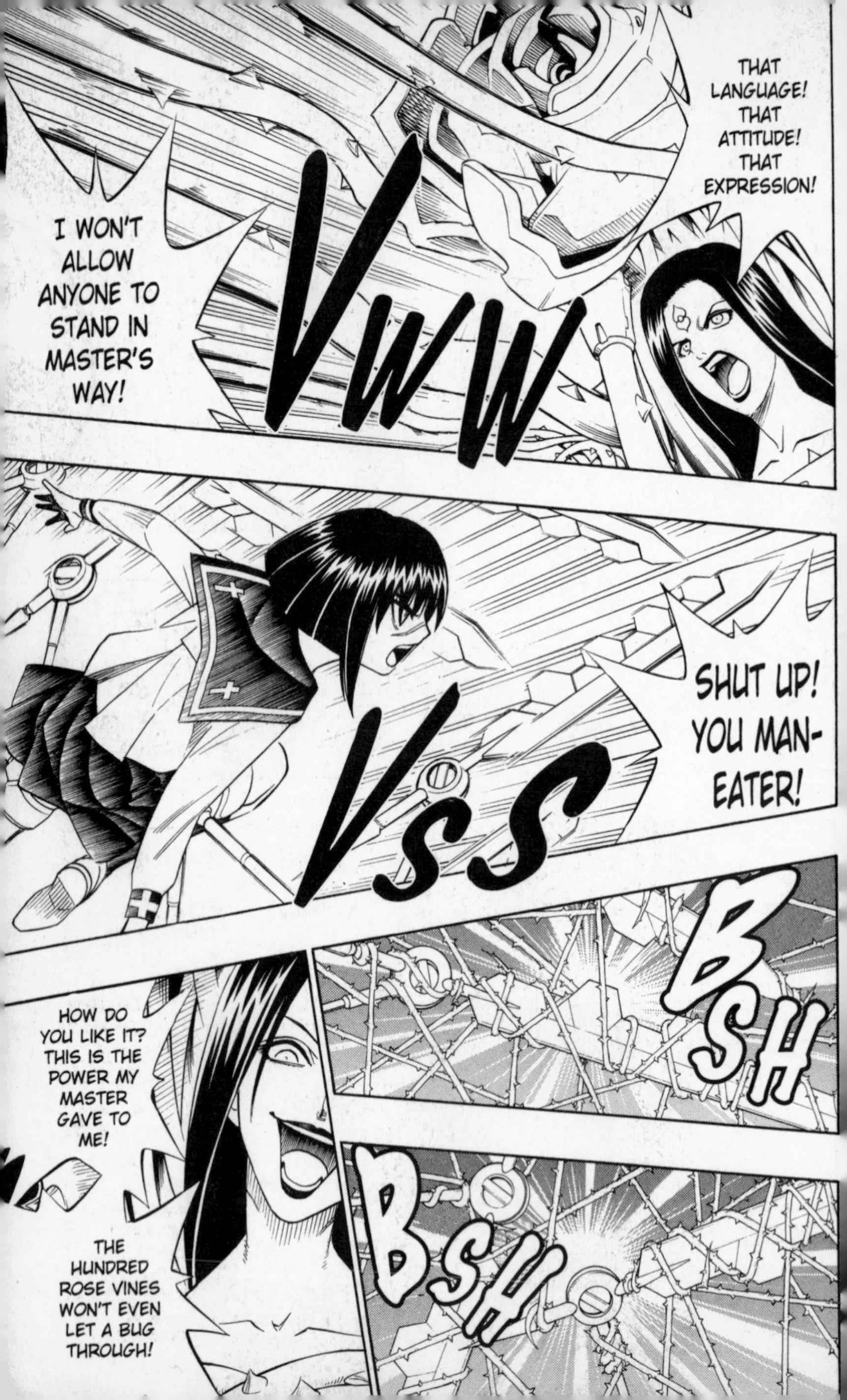
THAT LANGUAGE! THAT ATTITUDE! THAT EXPRESSION!
VWW
I WON'T ALLOW ANYONE TO STAND IN MASTER'S WAY!
SHUT UP! YOU MAN-EATER!
VSS
BSH
HOW DO YOU LIKE IT? THIS IS THE POWER MY MASTER GAVE TO ME!
BSH
THE HUNDRED ROSE VINES WON'T EVEN LET A BUG THROUGH!

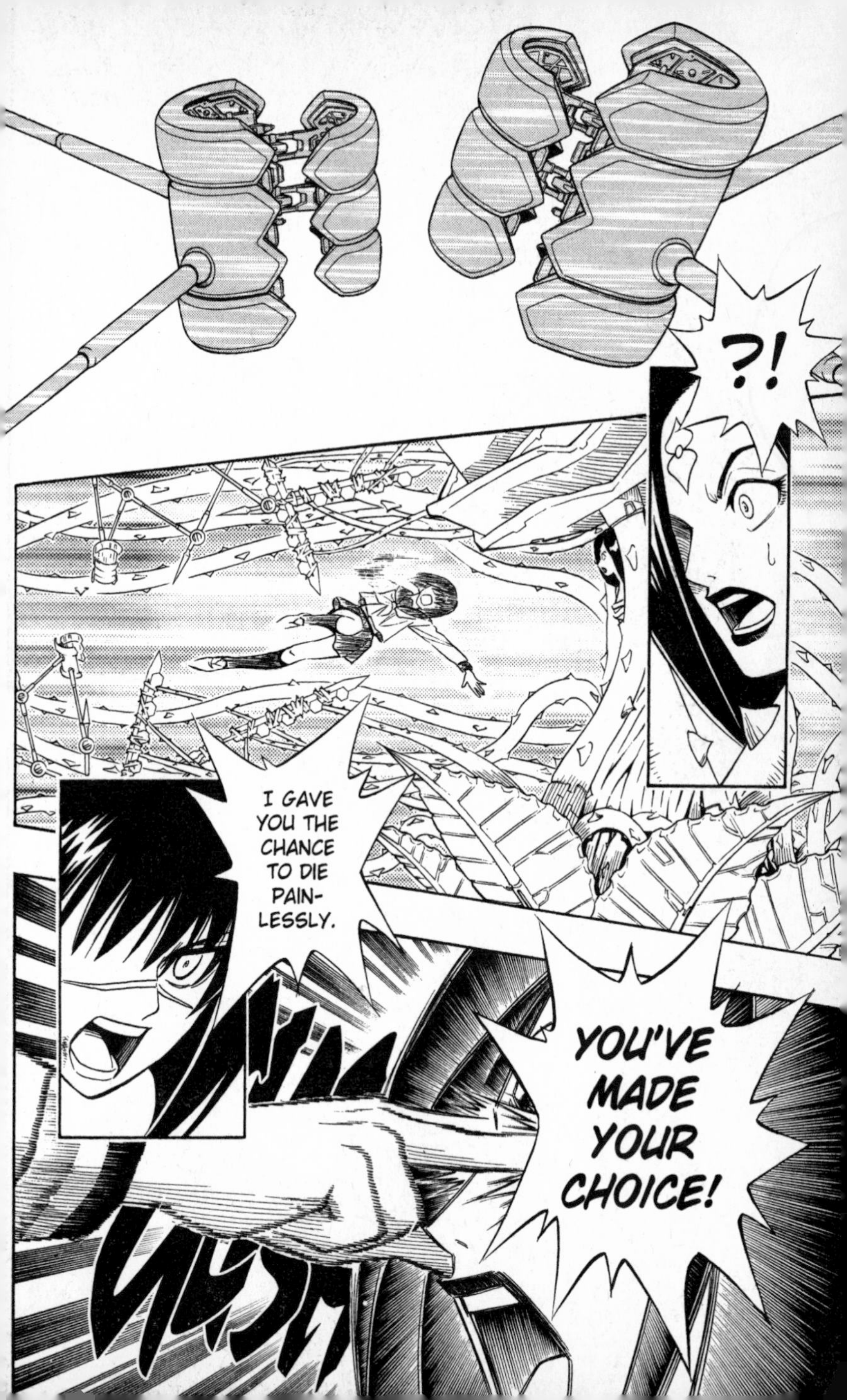
?!
I GAVE YOU THE CHANCE TO DIE PAIN-LESSLY.
YOU'VE MADE YOUR CHOICE!

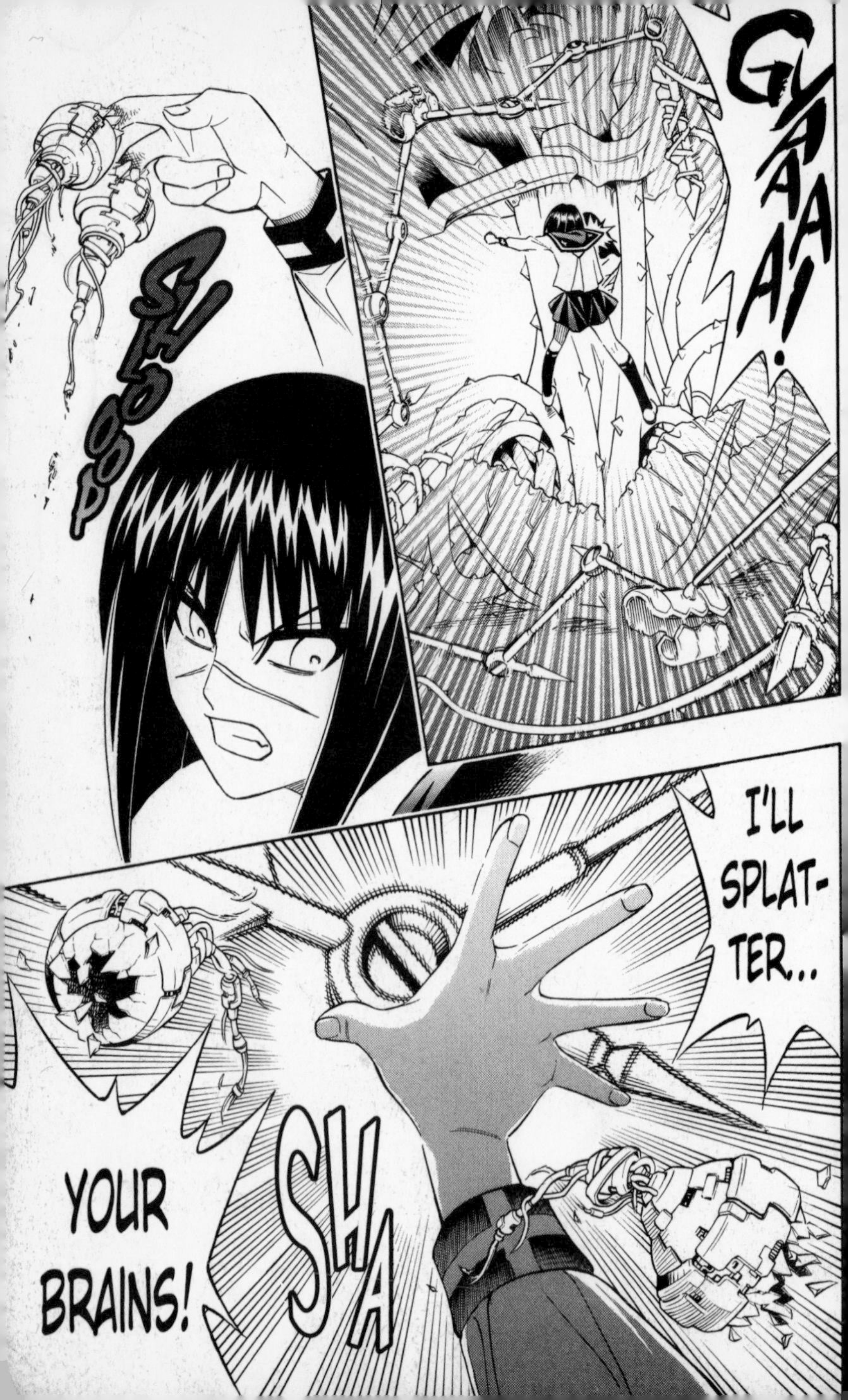
GYAAAA!
SHLOOOP
I'LL SPLATTER...
SHA
YOUR BRAINS!

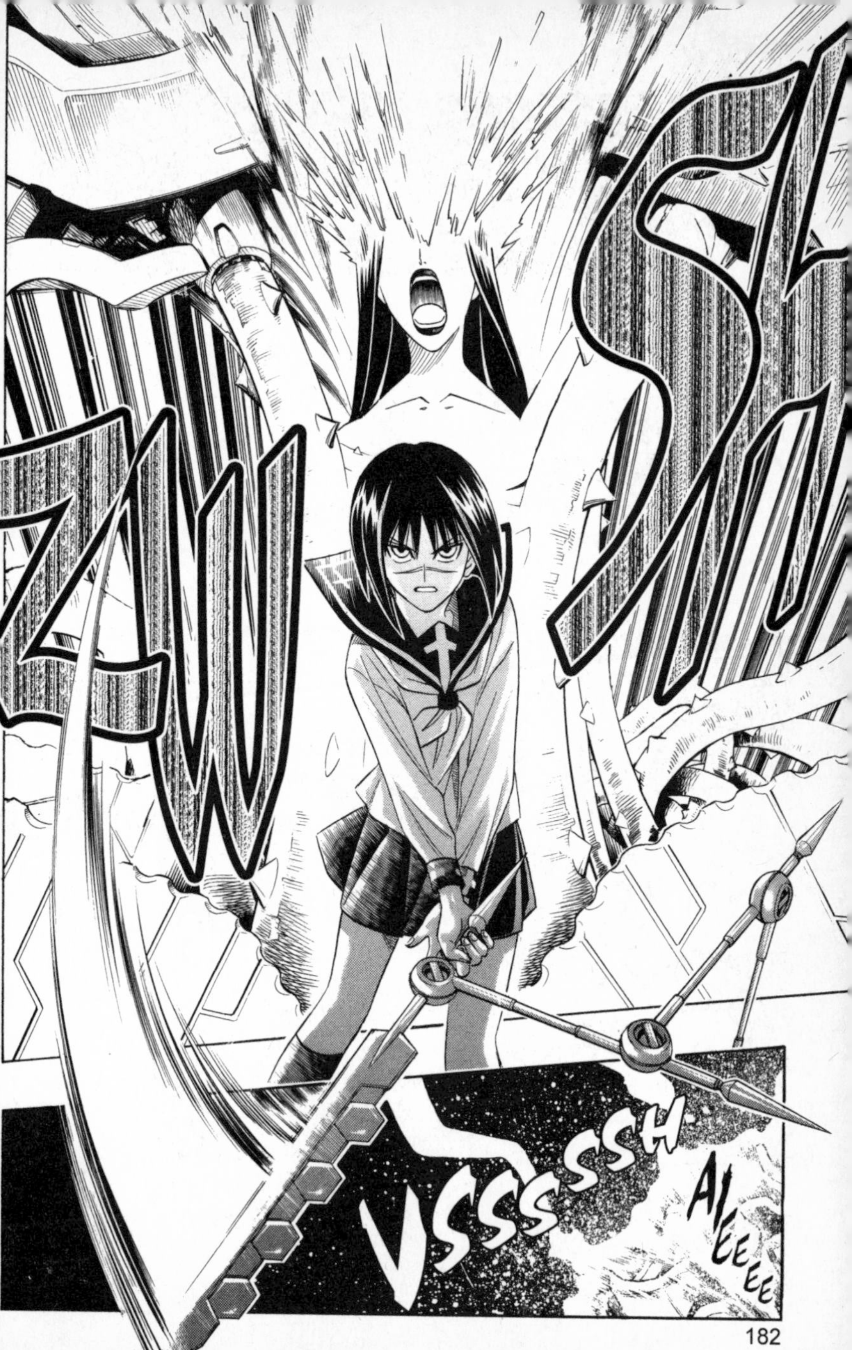
ZW
VSSSSSH
AIEEEEE

READ THIS WAY

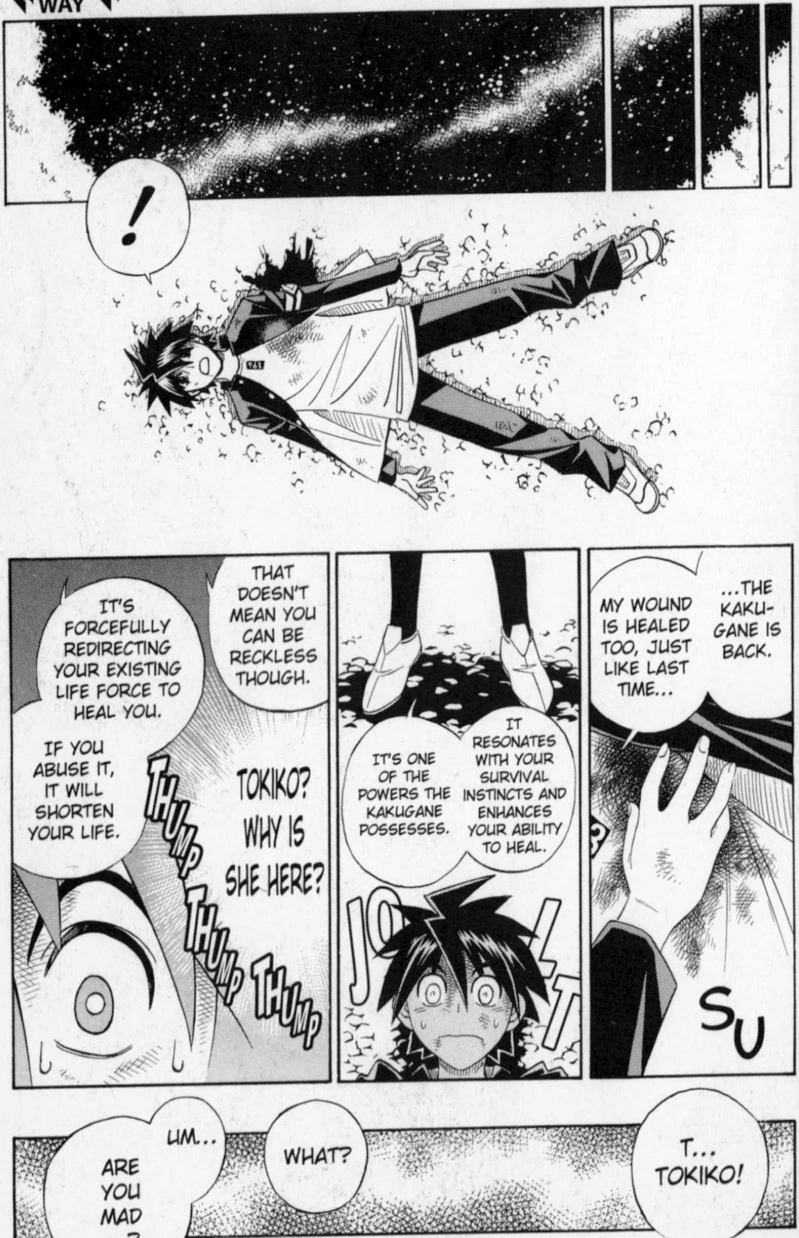
!
...THE KAKUGANE IS BACK.
MY WOUND IS HEALED TOO, JUST LIKE LAST TIME...
SU
IT RESONATES WITH YOUR SURVIVAL INSTINCTS AND ENHANCES YOUR ABILITY TO HEAL.
IT'S ONE OF THE POWERS THE KAKUGANE POSSESSES.
JOLT
THAT DOESN'T MEAN YOU CAN BE RECKLESS THOUGH.
IT'S FORCEFULLY REDIRECTING YOUR EXISTING LIFE FORCE TO HEAL YOU.
TOKIKO? WHY IS SHE HERE?
IF YOU ABUSE IT, IT WILL SHORTEN YOUR LIFE.
THUMP THUMP THUMP
T... TOKIKO!
WHAT?
UM... ARE YOU MAD...?

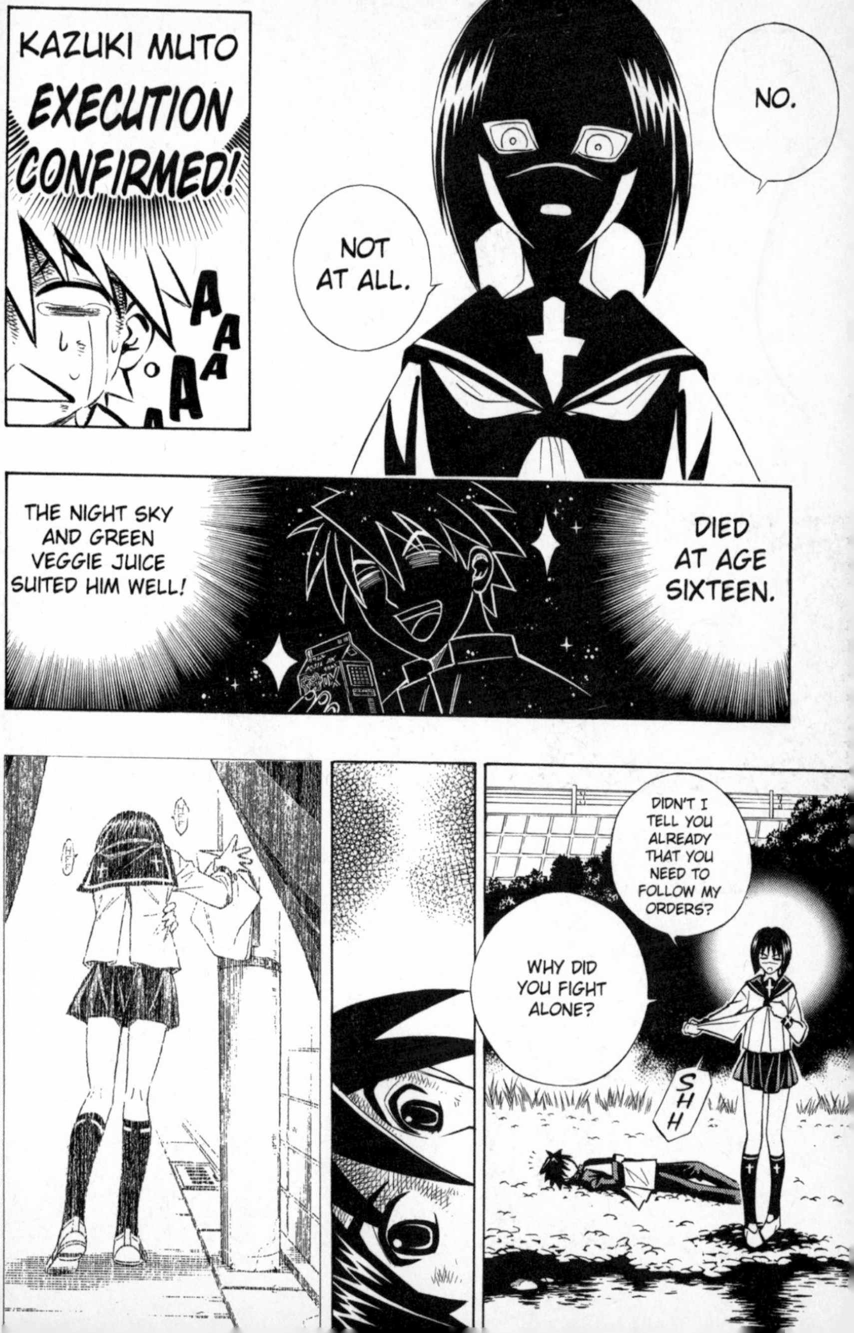
NO.
NOT AT ALL.
KAZUKI MUTO EXECUTION CONFIRMED!
AAAAA
DIED AT AGE SIXTEEN.
THE NIGHT SKY AND GREEN VEGGIE JUICE SUITED HIM WELL!
DIDN'T I TELL YOU ALREADY THAT YOU NEED TO FOLLOW MY ORDERS?
WHY DID YOU FIGHT ALONE?
SHH

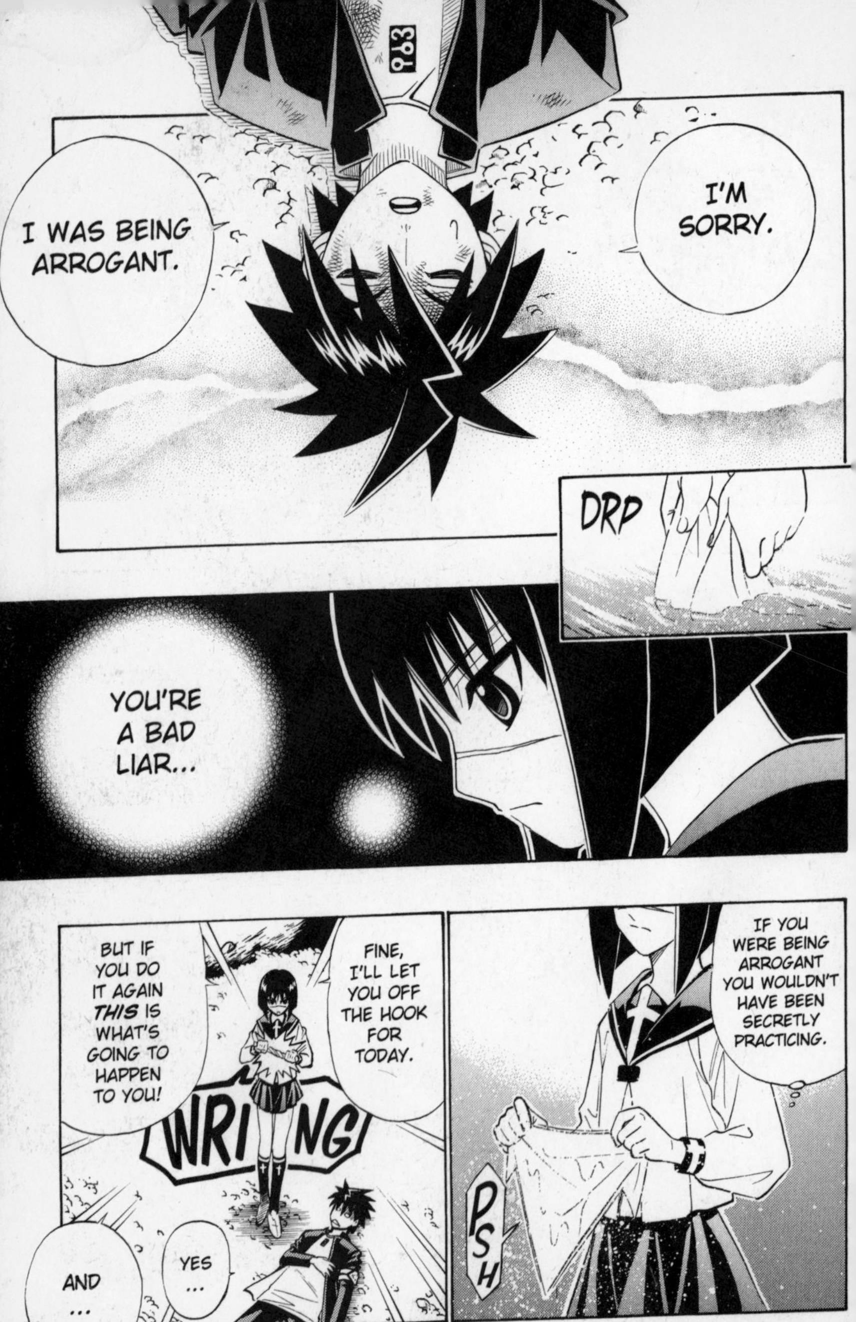
I'M SORRY.
I WAS BEING ARROGANT.
DRP
YOU'RE A BAD LIAR...
IF YOU WERE BEING ARROGANT YOU WOULDN'T HAVE BEEN SECRETLY PRACTICING.
PSH
FINE, I'LL LET YOU OFF THE HOOK FOR TODAY.
BUT IF YOU DO IT AGAIN *THIS* IS WHAT'S GOING TO HAPPEN TO YOU!
WRING
YES ...
AND ...

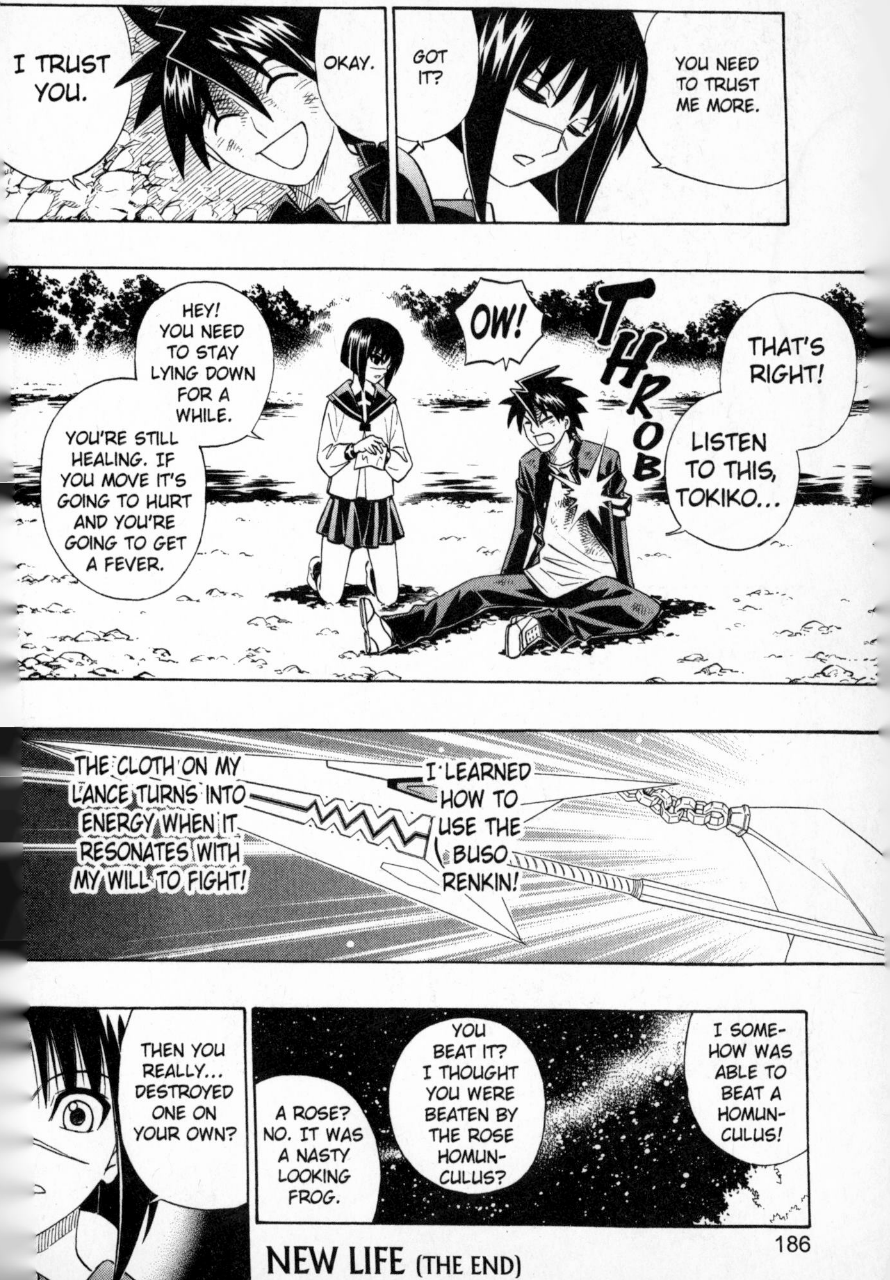
YOU NEED TO TRUST ME MORE.
GOT IT?
OKAY.
I TRUST YOU.
THAT'S RIGHT!
LISTEN TO THIS, TOKIKO...
THROB
OW!
HEY! YOU NEED TO STAY LYING DOWN FOR A WHILE.
YOU'RE STILL HEALING. IF YOU MOVE IT'S GOING TO HURT AND YOU'RE GOING TO GET A FEVER.
I LEARNED HOW TO USE THE BUSO RENKIN!
THE CLOTH ON MY LANCE TURNS INTO ENERGY WHEN IT RESONATES WITH MY WILL TO FIGHT!
I SOME-HOW WAS ABLE TO BEAT A HOMUN-CULUS!
YOU BEAT IT? I THOUGHT YOU WERE BEATEN BY THE ROSE HOMUN-CULUS?
A ROSE? NO. IT WAS A NASTY LOOKING FROG.
THEN YOU REALLY... DESTROYED ONE ON YOUR OWN?

NEW LIFE (THE END)

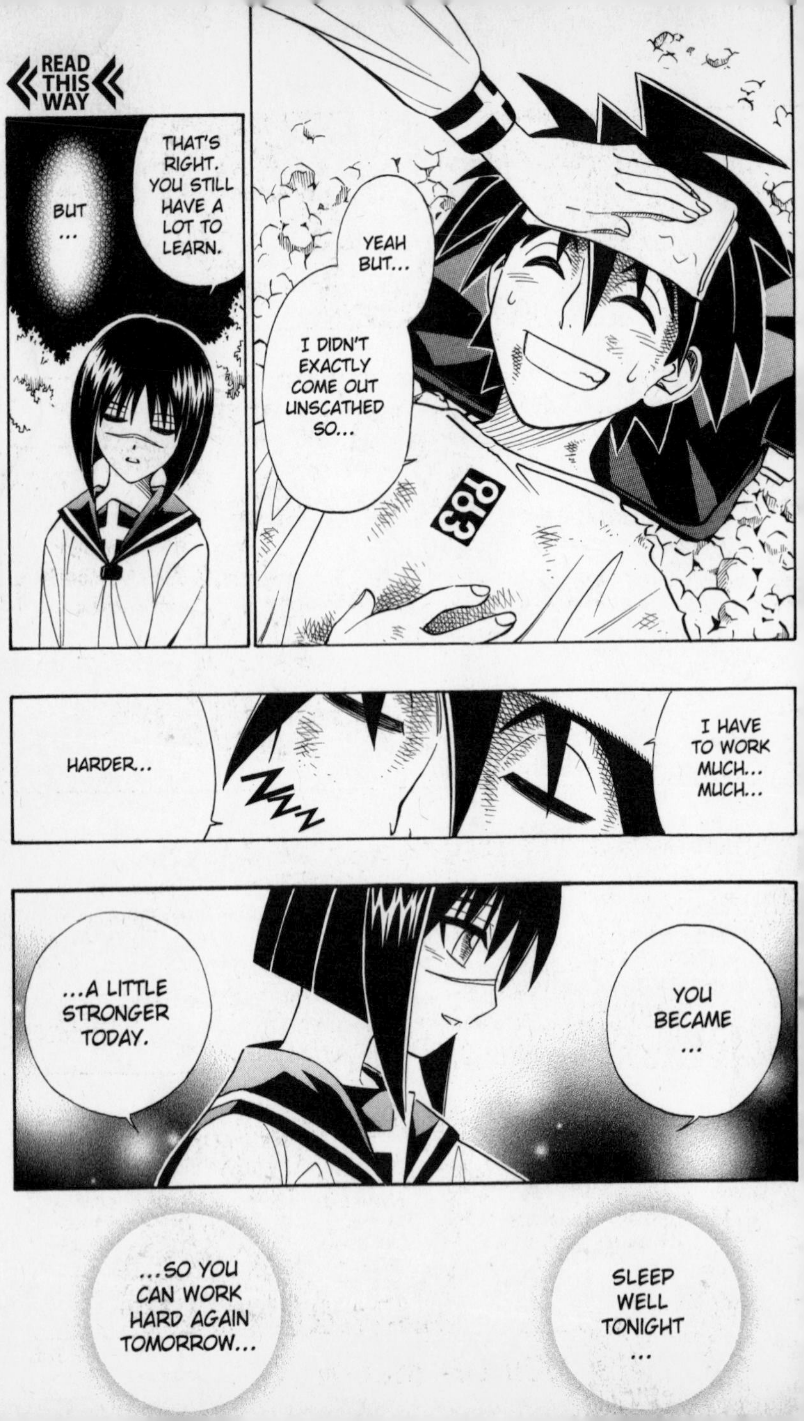
READ THIS WAY
YEAH BUT...
I DIDN'T EXACTLY COME OUT UNSCATHED SO...
THAT'S RIGHT. YOU STILL HAVE A LOT TO LEARN.
BUT ...
I HAVE TO WORK MUCH... MUCH...
HARDER...
YOU BECAME ...
...A LITTLE STRONGER TODAY.
SLEEP WELL TONIGHT ...
...SO YOU CAN WORK HARD AGAIN TOMORROW...

Chapter 5: VS. Kawazui (Part 1)

· The theme to this chapter was for Kazuki to fight on his own. It took an entire chapter to make him stern, as he's been so happy-go-lucky. It made me worry a little about what's yet to come.

· Personally I liked the uniform and phys-ed clothes joke. I liked it so much I brought it up again later.

· Kawazui's overalls got both positive & negative reviews as per its creepiness.

Chapter 6: VS. Kawazui (Part 2)

· This chapter's theme is a continuation of Kazuki fighting alone. I started drawing without finalizing parts of the page flow. I was really stressing about how to make a normal boy's mindset shift into a life of battles. To be honest I'm still stressing out about it. I felt like I finally figured out the reason why fantasy manga that has both battles and normal everyday life themes are sweeping the Shonen Manga industry. But my last two manga were similar to that as well. I'll do better next time…

· I heard comments about how the battle scenes didn't feel like it was enough because it only lasted for one chapter. I didn't feel like I got everything out either. I'll do better next time…

· The comment in chapter 4, "You need to control your passions," was a comment I was also making to myself.

Chapter 7: You're a Little Stronger

· I had to follow a bunch of restrictions for this chapter. Some made me cry and some made me laugh.

· The Kawazui mini-frogs were originally just the head and the spine. I designed them with machine-like parts, but that idea got shot down as it resembled a head too much. I ended up adding the body, but for some reason it started to get an eerie look to it, and I was very satisfied with it at the end. It was pure dumb luck.

· I imagined Hanabusa to be a character that puts emphasis on "Beauty". I wanted her to make a comment towards Tokiko's scar and have Tokiko reply so the plot would focus on her scar a little. I received a critique how it would be insensitive to say the scar on her face was ugly as people actually do have scars and injuries on their face from accidents and illnesses so I opted not to. I was a little disappointed but I totally understood why I shouldn't.

· The idea to directly show Tokiko shoving her fingers in Hanabusa's eyes did not pass as some children might actually act on it. Instead we hid it using the word bubble. This attack is where I could clearly show Tokiko's ruthlessness and I had envisioned it before I started the series. When the idea did not go though I was rather disappointed.

· Shonen Manga have a lot of restrictions you have to follow, which is a pain, but by working within those restrictions you learn new ways to express something. I think this is a good way to learn. As long as I get to grow I'm totally fine.

Hence… →

To be continued.

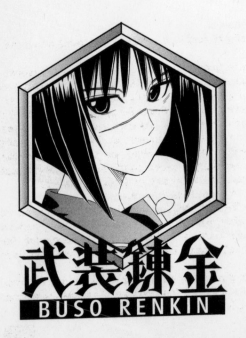

武装錬金
BUSO RENKIN

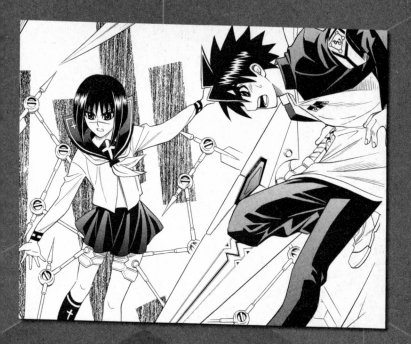

Coming Next Volume

Kazuki and Tokiko scramble to uncover the identity of the homunculus creator. Desperate to find the antidote to the homunculus that has attached itself to Tokiko, Kazuki suspects a sickly student at his school as the perpetrator. With time running out before the homunculus reaches Tokiko's brain and kills her, Tokiko hands her kakugane—an alchemical device that transforms into a buso renkin—to Kazuki. Let's just hope it's not too late...

Available in October 2006!

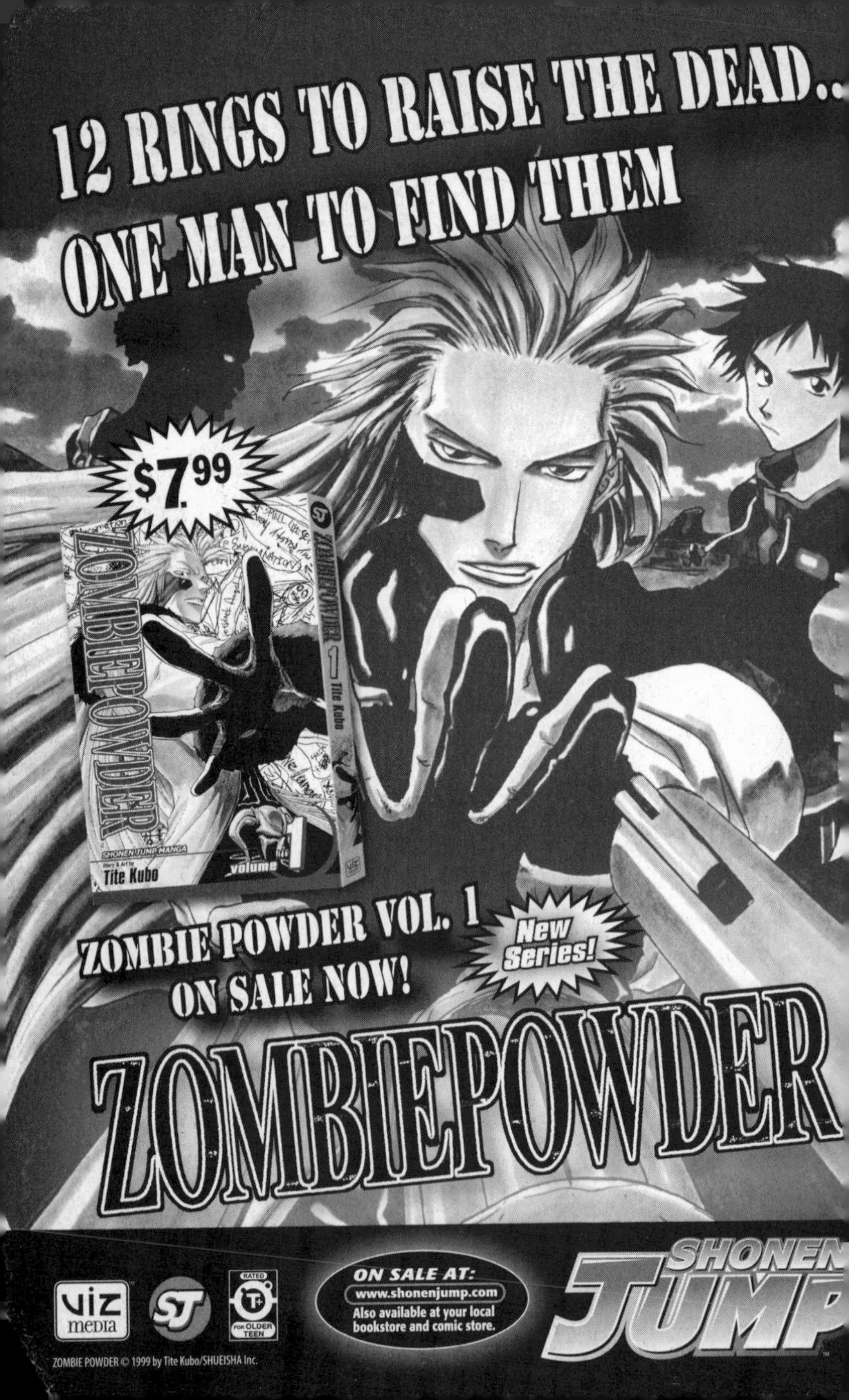

12 RINGS TO RAISE THE DEAD..
ONE MAN TO FIND THEM
$7.99
ZOMBIEPOWDER
1
Tite Kubo
SHONEN JUMP MANGA
Story & Art by
Tite Kubo
volume 1
ZOMBIE POWDER VOL. 1
ON SALE NOW!
New Series!
ZOMBIEPOWDER
viz media
SJ
RATED T+ FOR OLDER TEEN
ON SALE AT:
www.shonenjump.com
Also available at your local bookstore and comic store.
SHONEN JUMP
ZOMBIE POWDER © 1999 by Tite Kubo/SHUEISHA Inc.

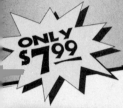
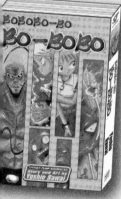
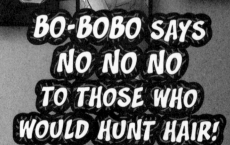
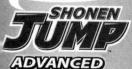

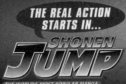

THE REAL ACTION STARTS IN... SHONEN JUMP
THE WORLD'S MOST POPULAR MANGA

www.shonenjump.com

FREE PREVIEW ISSUE! of SHONEN JUMP Magazine!

SHONEN JUMP Magazine: Contains Yu-Gi-Oh!, One Piece, Naruto, Shaman King, YuYu Hakusho and other HOT manga—STORIES NEVER SEEN IN THE ANIME!
Plus, get the latest on what's happening in trading cards, video games, toys and more!

Check out this ultra cool magazine for FREE! Then when you decide you must have SHON JUMP every month we will send you 11 more issues (12 in all) for only $29.95. A Price so low it's like getting 6 issues FREE!

But that's not all: You'll become a member of the 𝒮𝒥 Sub Club w your paid subscription!

𝒮𝒥 SUB CL Benefits!

- **Access to exclusive Sub Cl only areas of** www.SHONENJUMP.cc

- **Your Issues Delivered Firs**

- **Cool Gifts Inclu With Some Issu**

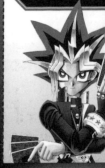

Get your FREE Preview Issue!

SHONEN JUMP Magazine — the blockbuster English-language version of Japan's #1 action comic book every month features 300+ pages of the hottest manga titles available in the U.S.! Plus the latest on what's happening in cards, video games, toys and more!

YES! Send me my FREE preview issue of **SHONEN JUMP** Magazine. If I like it I will enjoy 11 more issues (12 in all) for ONLY **$29.95** That's 50% OFF the cover price!

50% OFF the cover price!

NAME

ADDRESS

CITY   STATE   ZIP

E-MAIL ADDRESS

☐ MY CHECK IS ENCLOSED   ☐ BILL ME LATER

Make checks payable to: SHONEN JUMP. Canada add US $12. No foreign orders.
Credit card payments made SECURE & EASY at www.SHONENJUMP.com

Allow 6-8 weeks for delivery.

THE WORLD'S MOST POPULAR MANGA
www.shonenjump.com
SHONEN JUMP

YU-GI-OH! © 1996 by KAZUKI TAKAHASHI / SHUEISHA Inc.

P6SGN1

Check us out
on the web!

www.shonenjump.com

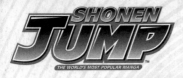

COMPLETE OUR SURVEY AND LET US KNOW WHAT YOU THINK!

☐ Please do NOT send me information about VIZ Media and SHONEN JUMP products, news and events, special offers, or other information.

☐ Please do NOT send me information from VIZ Media's trusted business partners.

Name: _____

Address: _____

City: _____ **State:** _____ **Zip:** _____

E-mail: _____

☐ Male ☐ Female Date of Birth (mm/dd/yyyy): ___ / ___ / ___ (Under 13? Parental consent required.)

① Do you purchase SHONEN JUMP magazine?

☐ Yes ☐ No

If **YES**, do you subscribe?

☐ Yes ☐ No

If **NO**, how often do you purchase SHONEN JUMP magazine?

☐ 1-3 issues a year ☐ 4-6 issues a year ☐ more than 7 issues a year

② Which SHONEN JUMP Volume 1 manga did you purchase this time? _____

Will you purchase subsequent volumes?

☐ Yes ☐ No

③ How did you learn about this title? (check all that apply)

☐ Favorite title ☐ Advertisement ☐ Article

☐ Gift ☐ Recommendation ☐ Special offer

☐ Through TV animation ☐ Read excerpt in SHONEN JUMP magazine

☐ Website ☐ Other _____

④ Of the titles that are serialized in SHONEN JUMP magazine, have you purchased the paperback manga volumes?

☐ Yes ☐ No

If **YES**, which ones have you purchased? (check all that apply)

☐ Hikaru no Go ☐ Naruto ☐ One Piece ☐ Shaman King

☐ Yu-Gi-Oh!: Millennium World ☐ YuYu Hakusho

If **YES**, what were your reasons for purchasing? (please pick up to 3)

- A favorite title
- A favorit
- There are extras that aren't in the
- The quality of printing is better th
- ver again
- Recommendation
- Special offer
- Other

If **NO**, why did/would you not purchase it?

- I'm happy just reading it in the magazine
- It's not worth buying the manga volume
- All the manga pages are in black and white, unlike the magazine
- There are other manga volumes that I prefer
- There are too many to collect for each title
- It's too small
- Other ______

5 Of the titles NOT serialized in the magazine, which ones have you purchased?
(check all that apply)

- Beet the Vandel Buster
- Black Cat
- Bleach
- Bobobo-bo Bo-bobo
- Claymore
- D.Gray-man
- Death Note
- Dragon Ball
- Dragon Ball Z
- Dr. Slump
- Eyeshield 21
- Hunter x Hunter
- I"s
- JoJo's Bizarre Adventure
- Knights of the Zodiac
- Legendz
- The Prince of Tennis
- Rurouni Kenshin
- Ultimate Muscle
- Whistle!
- Yu-Gi-Oh!
- Yu-Gi-Oh!: Duelist
- None
- Other ______

If you did purchase any of the above, what were your reasons for purchasing?

- A favorite title
- A favorite creator/artist
- Read a preview in SHONEN JUMP magazine and wanted to read the rest of the story
- Recommendation
- Other

Will you purchase subsequent volumes if available?

- Yes
- No

6 Of the following, what manga-related books would you like to buy? (check all that apply)

- Art books
- Character profile books
- Novels/Novelizations
- None of these

7 What race/ethnicity do you consider yourself? (please check one)

- Asian/Pacific Islander
- Black/African American
- Hispanic/Latino
- Native American/Alaskan Native
- White/Caucasian
- Other

THANK YOU! Please send the completed form to:

VIZ Media Survey
42 Catharine St.
Poughkeepsie, NY 12601

All information provided will be used for internal purposes only. We promise not to sell or otherwise divulge your information.